BOB MARLEY

LYRICAL GENIUS

© Kwame Dawes, 2002
This edition © Bobcat Books 2007
(Part of the Music Sales Group)

Order No: BOB11616
ISBN-10: 0-8256-7352-6
ISBN-13: 978-0-8256-7352-8

Exclusive Distributors
Music Sales Limited,
14 - 15 Berners Street,
London W1T 3LJ, UK.

Music Sales Corporation,
257 Park Avenue South,
New York, NY 10010, USA.

Macmillan Distribution Services,
53 Park West Drive,
Derrimut, Vic 3030,
Australia.

To the Music Trade only:
Music Sales Limited,
14 - 15 Berners Street,
London W1T 3LJ, UK.

Printed and bound in the United States of America by Quebecor World
A catalog record for this book is available from the British Library.

Visit Omnibus Press on the web at www.omnibuspress.com

BOB MARLEY
LYRICAL GENIUS

KWAME DAWES

BOBCAT
BOOKS

Contents

Prologue 7

Acknowledgements 14

Introduction 16

1 Catch A Fire And Burnin' 39

2 Natty Dread And Rastaman Vibration 101

3 Exodus And Kaya 179

4 Survival, Uprising And Confrontation 243

Epilogue 346

Bibliography 348

Index 350

Prologue

Every night I sing to my children after prayers. I stand in the hallway with the two bedroom doors open; I strum my guitar and I sing Bob Marley songs. Sometimes I convince myself that I am passing on a legacy, giving them something meaningful to take with them to bed; sometimes I tell myself that I am reminding them of a part of them that is Jamaican. But as soon as I begin to sing, I realise that I am discovering the tender pleasures of his epiphanies. I am consumed by the moment, the universe that is Marley's songs. Sometimes my children ask me what the songs mean. I start to talk about the songs and find myself talking about a world that extends beyond mere lyrics. I find myself describing a landscape, retrieving the many historical narratives that feed the songs. I find myself searching for words to convey the genius of his imagination. And as I talk, I realise that I am trying to pass on a feeling – the warmth of recognition that is my encounter with the songs.

Recently, I have been singing song after song from *Kaya* and *Exodus*. I can remember exactly when I heard both records. I know the feelings I had. There is a house in Jamaica, in Kingston, on a street called Carlisle Avenue somewhere off Red Hills Road. That is my old neighbourhood. Carlisle Avenue was a complex of middle-class streets spread along an open plain some 16 kilometres from the Kingston Harbor that stretched through a series of sprawling complexes with names that I still chant: Whitehall, Havendale, Meadowbrook, Duhaney Park, all made up of bungalows with flat roofs and brightly painted low-lying walls crowned by hibiscus and croton hedges. These were lush avenues with houses thick with fruit trees: mangoes, almonds, plums, breadfruit, ackees, sweet sops. The backyards were cool places where enterprising families reared chickens or planted vegetable gardens to supplement meals during the lean times of the 1970s.

Carlisle Avenue had no distinctive markers – just a simple avenue with houses I knew by the temperament of the dogs that lived behind the cement fences: the ferocious German Shepherds in the home of the Chinese, a massive bungalow that sat far back in the yard; the toothless noise-making mongrel of our next-door neighbours; the silent Doberman two doors away that simply leaped over the wall as you passed and then pounced on your calf.

That was my Kingston. A maze of roads that I studied for dogs and fruit trees – the path I walked along the six kilometres from Shortwood Practicing School, my public primary school. From our house, we could see the Red Hills bejewelled with the homes of rich eccentrics who chose not to live in the *nouveau riche* Beverley Hills, but instead built houses of opulence behind thick and safe *lignum vitae* trees.

When I think of Carlisle Avenue, I think of the bus dropping us off on Red Hills Road. The thick black acrid exhaust of the silver and green government jolly buses used to sting my eyes as I danced my way across the road to a narrow path that was unceremoniously paved with the gravel leftover by the men who paved Red Hills Road. I would turn right onto a very small intersecting road, then right again after three houses into Carlisle. On the right I would always look into the tree-shaded dirt yard so worn down by soccer players that it was virtually harder than asphalt. Sometimes, if I was lucky, I would see some dreads sitting in the porch garage peeling oranges, smoking weed, laughing. And in their midst, sitting on a soccer ball, sweat gleaming on his body, would be a 'red Rasta', that breed of lighter-skinned Jamaica burnished to a mellow brownness by the naked sun – Bob Marley. Not the reggae superstar, not the rock icon, not the touring giant – just a dread, sitting on a ball, chilling out. And I would smile at the casualness of Jamaica, and not even start to understand the weight of the moment.

Bob did not live on my avenue, but his friend Alan 'Skill' Cole, the soccer god of Jamaica, lived in a simple house on the corner where he held Rasta *groun'ations*. And in such simple and casual ways as those moments of watching men grunting and shouting and laughing around a worn soccer ball, reggae came to me as a way of breathing.

The sound filled our lives. It was never approved of in the 1970s. It was never the mark of high culture but it was ubiquitous, it was the sound of the people, it was the pulse of the streets, the smell of the food, the smell of the wood-fires that burned on the hillside, the sound of people talking through their daily lives, the manner of their walk, the texture of a woman's laughter and the roundness of her movement, it was a flame of anger and the cool balm of friendship – reggae was Jamaica in an uncanny way; an unofficial way that made it like breathing. Reggae defined our language and our sense of self like Rastafarianism did.

Sometimes we fought it – fought the image of the weed-smoking idle human being that was the construction of conservative middle-class Jamaica. But Rastas' sense of independence, self-reliance, racial pride and the almost quixotic sense that they could take on the world, permeated our socialist politics, our anti-colonial sensibilities, our non-aligned status in the world that shaped the political climate of the time.

At 13 I was arguing world politics. This was not at all an act of precociousness; it was, quite simply, the way the world came at us all through reggae at that time.

At number four Carlisle Avenue we lived in a yard of fruit trees, the occasional chicken-rearing experiment and the worn-out lawn where we played elaborate pick-up games of cricket. The house was a large one and different from the others on the street because it had a variegated complex of sky blue prefabricated roofing that made it highly visible even from a distance.

We were renting it from a wealthy light-skinned Jamaican family who had panicked at the whiff of socialism in the early 1970s and pulled up roots to settle in Miami. They rarely came back to see how their property was faring. We treated it as if we owned it, letting the expensive front lawn grass grow bush dry and crabby because watering lawns was not a socialist activity.

In 1980, after the elections that booted out the socialist experiment and replaced it with the Reaganite optimism of American Basin politics, my father lost his job and so we also lost the house. Our landlords returned as Miami-based entrepreneurs and chucked us out of it. Then they turned the house into a series of apartments.

I went back there a year ago. The walk up the lane was hauntingly familiar yet the moment of rooting I expected on seeing the old house did not happen. The house was not the same. The building has been spliced and divided into tiny apartments. The front lawn is crowded with expansion – more rooms, I suppose. The white and rusty iron gate has been replaced by a hefty piece of security that rises six feet in the air. It was not the same at all. The symbol that housed my childhood is now kept in that static place of memory in my mind. I associate that home with reggae. I associate it with my awakening to faith, politics, sex and fear. In that house I heard the songs of Marley for the first time.

Kojo, my older brother, was a music buff. He would set up elaborate home-made speaker systems in his room, gaudily decorated with gallons of coloured marker ink. His sound system was a shrine that remained his domain and his alone. During the summers of my 14th and 15th years, he had the misfortune of having to work full-time during the days. This left the shrine unguarded, and I would raid the room and desecrate it by taking up residence there for the entire day.

At about five in the afternoon, I would attempt to put back every record, every piece of paper, every wrinkle and ruffle of his bed sheets exactly as he had left them. But it was during one of those summers that I found the album cover with a massive, almost too realistically drawn (the bright greens of the leaf and the sharp white and off-white of the Rizla paper browning where the fire glowed) ganja spliff smouldering, and the word 'Kaya' emblazoned across the jacket.

It was Marley's latest album since his exile. I played the tracks again and again – the sinuously sly 'Sun in Shining', the melancholic and reflective 'Running Away,' the painfully ironic and deeply sorrowful, 'She's Gone' and the quietly threatening prophecy of 'Time Will Tell'.

I was sucked in by the complexity of the multiple guitar lines, the sheer mystery and density of the lyrics, the clearly coded narrative of confession and questioning that made the songs unique, and the fat dub reliability of the bass lines. I wanted to decipher, to find meaning in each lyric, each metaphor, each enigmatic proverb, even as I basked in the sweetness of the melodies. No other writer or artist had so drawn me into a view of the world around me as Bob Marley did with *Kaya*.

A year later, in 1978, my Kojo (who had somehow found out about my secret raids, and who had began to grudgingly accept that my motives were noble and healthy), came home late one night and ordered me into his room. He dragged a brown paper bag from his black shoulder bag, dropping the latter on the floor. Then, as if enacting a religious rite, he pulled an album from the paper bag. It was a jacket of deep gold, no pictures on it, just a stretch of gold with the word 'Exodus' scrawled across in a archaic script.

He pulled the black vinyl from the gold sleeve and placed it on the turntable. *Exodus* jumped at me like a revelation with its haunting propulsion – a regal energy that assured me that I was listening to a man who had become a larger-than-life figure.

And those horns, that one-chord complexity of 'Exodus' and 'The Heathen' – hinting of roots band Burning Spear, but travelling somewhere else, somewhere where the chant and rhyme seemed more adventurous – always flirting with the formal order of the pop song. The voice was so world-weary, so much older than all the voices I had heard from Marley before.

This was not the man who used to kick ball in the yard down the road from us. Something grander was filling the room. And yet it is the tiny acts of grace that I remember.

My brother played 'Jamming' again and again, telling me to listen only to the percussion, to Scully's percussions. Like staring at a trick painting, I kept trying to make out what he was hearing. Slowly, I heard it. The pattern – an even repetition of five different percussive sounds. They each seemed to find the spaces left behind by the music. That is the genius, my brother assured. That is the greatness of the man. Care for detail. The capacity to layer.

And yes, indeed, I could see layer upon layer going further and further back.

This man could transport me from the hot streets of Kingston, over the mountains and across valleys into the lush green and wood-fire smell of rural St Ann, where people made sense of the simple patterns of their lives feeding off the earth, nurturing it, planting seed and sweat into the soil; and further, to the ghettoes of Kingston where gunshots signalled the coming of night and people made beauty out of squalor; beyond that to Hope River curling through the purple Blue Mountains, a river full of large slabs of white rocks where a Rastaman could lay his head and contemplate the meaning of life in the sky.

But even beyond that, his layers of faith found me remembering my childhood in Ghana, the savannah, the yoyi trees, the taste of kenke, the smell of an Africa that was more than myth.

Marley could laugh and cry at the same time; he could flame me with the righteous anger of a political soul and balm me with the taste of a woman's skin all at the same time. Layers of meaning. Layers that even then I knew I would not understand until much later, until I had my own permanent woman, until I had children, until I had seen more of the world, until I knew what was in the heart of man, until I knew how people could kill other people.

I understood then that these songs would walk with me for years to come. And all this before I even began to hear the lyrics, before I came to understand what these songs meant.

And so here I am, 25 years later, in a three-bedroom house designed in what is called the colonial/ranch style, in the sprawling suburbs of northeast Columbia, South Carolina. Where a private golf course, won, it is rumoured, in a gambling game by Dave Thomas the late owner of the Wendy's fast-food franchise, winds its 18 holes of *nouveau riche* privilege through these stock houses, some with red brick walls, others in light pastel blue and tan vinyl walls, all with their neat, well watered lawns, their American flags and the orderliness of middle-class American Dream America. Here in this house that I own, in this house so far from the world I was raised in, I carry my guitar to my children's room and after we have prayed, I sing them songs – the songs I listened to when I was in another world, and another country in Jamaica.

They want to know about what it was like living in Jamaica. They want to know when I first heard the songs. They want to know about my older brother, their Uncle Kojo, and I tell them about it all, trying, I suspect, to expand their sense of home.

I tell my children about hearing these reggae songs and I try to share the meaning of the songs with them. Each sharing becomes a reflection – a reflection on a time. This music is the soundtrack of my living. It defines me. I give to them more than the songs and the grandeur of their poetry, I also give to them the making of me.

I tell them about how I had to learn to speak the patois that Marley sang with. How as a Ghanaian boy in Jamaica, I had to learn to speak patois by listening to the song lyrics and by trying to understand what they meant.

As I tell them about the songs I find myself telling them about my father, who came home one day and introduced us to Marley's 'Natty Dread' announcing that we should pay attention to that rude, unruly haired man because what he was doing and saying was important.

I tell them about the nights I would dress as a rude boy and dance to 'Natty Dread', with a thick rag sticking out of my back pocket, one leg of my pants rolled up to my knee, one side of my shirt tails sticking out and the other tucked in, my head covered with a too large tam that dangled as if weighted by locks down my back, my eyes darkened by mafia shades; and dance the skank to 'Natty Dread' for my father and his friends.

My children laugh at the thought, and ask me to dress that way again for them. They will think of their father as a boy whenever they hear these songs. And perhaps that is what I want. It is the burden and the hope of the immigrant.

In many ways as I write about these songs, as I try to give a sense of what is happening in the art of these songs, I am writing about what it means for me to be a poet, to be a man who wants to use words to leave something beautiful and meaningful with the world. These reflections represent a dialogue with art.

I know that as I write about these songs and as people read what I write, they will go and listen again to the songs. They will meet the songs in different ways, but they will meet the songs with the same freshness of insight that I felt when I heard them for the first time.

Acknowledgements

It was Stephen Foehr who told me to get in touch with Sanctuary Publishing – he said that they might be interested in my project. He had looked at my proposal, expressed the kind of interest in it that is encouraging and energizing and he gave me good advice as to how to improve it. His suggestion led me to a team of supportive and reggae-conscious people at Sanctuary including Iain MacGregor, Claire Musters, Yvonne Worth and so many others. Rick Black read the same proposal and gave some good ideas. The list of people who have to be thanked is a long one. Justine Henzell is a stalwart of assistance, good advise and incredible connections. She made the path to Chris Blackwell, Bunny Wailer, Neville Garrick, Garth White, Rita Marley and Esther Anderson possible. Not all gave me interviews, but all talked to me and showed kindness. They also linked me to the Marley world in remarkable ways. Talks with Clive Walker, Dermot Hussey, Jeremy Poynting and Mikey Bennett were important to the shaping of this book and the ideas that were generated in it. My good friend, Colin Channer, is the king of reggae trivia and a true reggae fan and musician. He is also a man who knows a little about this writing business. He allowed me to go through all his CDs to find obscure Marley tunes, and he gave me space in his home to work. His support as well as the generous support of his family, Brigette and the children, will someday be rewarded.

I thank the English Department at the University of South Carolina for allowing me the space to do this book. Much of what is written here comes from my reading everything I could find on Bob Marley's life and work. There are many books that help us to understand Marley, and I can't explain how invaluable many of these works have been to me. I am especially indebted to Ian Macann for collating so many important quotes from Marley in his book *Bob Marley: In His Own Words*. Most of the quotations I have used in this book have come from that source (all others are indicated next to the quotes themselves). I am also grateful to Ennis Edmonds whose writing about the history of Rastafarianism is reflected in this book. There is also a series of fascinating films, each with its own slant and truth, that has been helpful.

Most importantly, I have to thank my wife Lorna and our children Sena, Kekeli and Akua who are such supporters and the reason why this book has happened at all. It is quite typical for writers to say this, but I mean this completely. This book is a gift, it is also a piece of the legacy of who I am that I want my children to have. It has been a project that has allowed Lorna to show her love and faith in me in ways that are hard to explain. And I have written the book knowing that she will read it. I come from a family that gives meaning to the business of writing. My brother Kojo introduced me to Bob Marley's *Kaya* and *Exodus*, which triggered the whole desire of writing this book. My father played *Natty Dread* again and again at home and reminded the teenage boy that I was that this rude bwai from Trench Town was very, very important. My sisters keep me honest and remind me that I must stay true to who I am. My mother is my bulwark – the one whose confidence in me is always encouraging and sustaining. My younger brother Kojoui, is the voice and spirit of Bob Marley in the house and his heart is caught in this book.

Introduction

In 20 years Bob Marley produced a remarkably large body of work. Any attempt to examine his work must take into consideration the history of his development as a recording artist. While there are several discrete periods of growth in Marley's life as a songwriter, it is fair to argue that two major periods stand out as easy markers in his career. When, in 1972, Island Records released *Catch A Fire* in the UK, Marley was embarked on a new career that would generate the material that most of the world knows him for. This event would stand in the middle of these two defining periods in Marley's career and, importantly, his evolution as a songwriter.

The ten years before that were years of great productivity and, some have argued, the most innovative and creative of the two periods. I do not share this view, but I am acutely aware of the significance of this dividing line in Marley's development as an artist. Consequently, I have chosen to focus closely on only one of these periods – the period that I have crudely called the 'Island Years'. Nonetheless, I have had to explore many of the songs that were produced in the years before this because Marley reprised many of them and also because it is difficult to speak of his development without referring constantly to recordings that were done in the years before the Island recordings. There is a very fascinating book to be written about Marley's songwriting during the earlier period. Such a study would be looking at the work of a collaborative team of gifted visionaries, each with very strong ideas about what they wanted to say, and yet each with a clear commitment to the collective vision of the whole.

The Marley we meet in the Island Years is virtually on his own and seeking to forge his own artistic vision. This book chooses to explore the later Bob Marley and to treat his songwriting during that period as an outworking of the early years of experimentation and growth that took him through many mentors and associates. Marley learned all he needed to know about the recording business and formed his legendary work ethic from working in the studios of Coxsone Dodd, Leslie Kong, Lee 'Scratch' Perry and so many others. He also began to collect ideas, images, proverbs, scriptural references and folk sayings that would gradually find new life in his later recordings. But, most importantly, Marley would develop a greater sense of his political identity and mission by writing songs that seemed to be searching for a path. He would imitate the work of other artists, learning from them in the process.

Despite what is clearly a remarkably productive career, in which Marley's output revealed a consistency of themes, techniques and musical focus, there has been an unwillingness by many to recognize the seriousness with which Marley approached songwriting. Part of the reason for this may be because Marley did not 'write' songs in the conventional sense of putting pen to paper to generate his work. One of the curiosities that drove the writing of this book was to try and get a sense of just how Marley worked as a songwriter. There was, for years, an absurd rumour in Jamaica, that Marley did not write his own songs. It was a middle-class rumour, a condescending rumour based on the conviction that someone without an education could not have possibly written the kind of lyrics that Marley produced. But the rumour also came from somewhere else. It came from what seemed to be a clear disconnection between the songs Marley wrote and the way he spoke in interviews. Marley talked to the press a lot. He saw this as an important part of what he was doing as a speaker for his people and as a teacher of the ideas of Rastafarianism. In many ways, this openness to answer even the most absurd questions from an often bewildered and condescending press allowed Marley to develop a strong critical following among music writers. According to Island Records founder, Chris Blackwell, the press 'never gave Bob a bad review'. Nonetheless, Marley was much more comfortable presenting his ideas in song than in interviews.

Bob Marley's interviews are a study of proverbial play, trickery, Rasta mysticism and word play, and not a little irony and sarcasm. Sometimes Marley would toy with the interviewers because their questions were so absurd that they demanded either humour or anger. He rarely turned to anger. But Marley tended not to explain his songs, nor did he feel he had to. He worked hard on the songs and felt that they spoke for themselves – they spoke clearly and lucidly exactly what he wanted them to say. Marley also spoke in a deeper dialect than he ever used in song. His lyrics employed a Jamaican English that was, for the most part, quite accessible to non-Jamaicans. In interviews, Marley did not speak in anything but the most basic of Jamaican Nation Language. Consequently, people felt comfortable spreading the rumour that he did not write the songs. They believed some genius was writing these songs and giving them to Marley. It was felt that at some point, this person was going to emerge from the woodwork and blow the case out of the water. Marley would be exposed and the rumour makers vindicated.

It is this insult that Marley attacks when he asks with mocking irony, 'Can anything good come out of Trench Town?'. Anyone who has lived in Jamaica and has spent time reasoning with Rasta elders will understand quite quickly that a poetic intelligence rests at the centre of Jamaican folk wisdom. During Marley's early years as a musician, and before he embraced Rastafarianism completely, he sought out father figures from whom he gained a tremendous amount of knowledge and wisdom. Marley would replace these figures with Haile Selassie when he fully accepted the teachings of Rastafari and, from that point on, he sought counsel and mentorship in the teachings of Jah. If Marley's technical ability as a songwriter is what puzzled people, they can rest assured that Marley studied popular music with the diligence of a devotee. If Marley's capacity to create lines of stunning poetry is what shocks people, they ought to realise that Marley studied the Bible with the intensity of a novice priest. If Marley's ability to parlay his understanding of the world into song made doubters stop and wonder, they ought to know that Marley read newspapers, followed the news, listened to some of the most articulate scholars and historians in Jamaican society and studied the words of Marcus Garvey, Malcolm X, Walter Rodney, Martin Luther King Jr and

Haile Selassie, while listening to all the Black Power music emanating from the United States and the United Kingdom as he wrote his songs. If Marley's visionary power and his shamanistic persona confounded those who did not expect it of a man from his background, they ought to know that Marley was obviously a gifted man – his talent is as inexplicable as the talent of any of the great artists of all time. It is pointless trying to explain it.

As with most artists, we often take Marley and make use of him when we find him useful and politely allow him to be whatever else he wants to be especially when we don't understand or agree with this other aspect of him. Marley the revolutionary artist is easily co-opted by liberal action groups searching for a figure of resistance and hope. Marley the lover is easily appropriated – his words come to use when we need them, and we all need and enjoy these insights into passion and love. Somehow, the religious Marley is a puzzle for many. We accept his religion in our own image – that is, we apply the notions of his God to our notion of God and somehow allow our sense of uncertainty about much of what he believed as a Rastafarian to slide into the mystery of the man.

The problem, of course, is Rastafarianism. On the surface it strikes us as a rather fanciful belief system that is almost absurd in its assertion that Haile Selassie, the emperor of Ethiopia who was alive during most of Marley's life and during his period of devotion and praise to him, is God – the returned Messiah. Our instinct is to ask how a man, normally accused of being a brutish dictator who oppressed his own people and played a big role in the movement towards famine and deep poverty that was experienced by Ethiopia in the late 1970s, and the wars that would continue well into the 1990s, could be deemed a god. More importantly, how could a group of poor black Jamaicans select a man whom they had only heard about in news stories and in magazines, as a god – the true Messiah, the object of deep veneration and worship? Marley was wholly committed to this faith, and it is this faith that would drive much of what he wrote during the most productive period of his writing life.

And even when the news reports arrived that declared that Selassie was in fact dead, Marley and his Rasta breddren continued to hold to the idea that he was either still living or had gone to continue the fulfilment of his role on this earth elsewhere. This religion was flexible, capable of adapting to new crisis; the religion was thoroughly founded on faith – a belief system that was gleefully counter-rationale. Marley would release the song 'Jah Live' to remind the world that his faith in Selassie was not diminished by the rumours of his death. Marley would die a Rastaman, fully committed to Haile Selassie and to his faith.

As absurd as this belief system may seem to some, a brief review of the history of the religion helps us to appreciate that it is a faith rooted in a long tradition of resistance and hope that shaped the culture of Jamaica and the African diaspora. Rastafarianism did not suddenly materialize in Kingston in the 1930s out of nowhere. Hardly. It was a culmination of a series of traditions and strongly held Afrocentric beliefs that had sustained Africans in the diaspora for centuries. More importantly, Rastafarianism has to be understood in the same way that early Christianity was understood. While the comparison of Rasta's faith in Selassie with the Christ mythos may seem sacrilegious, it is clear that the parallels are, at the very least, interesting.

Early Christianity was a fledgling cult based on the charisma and claims of Jesus Christ, a carpenter who travelled through the relatively small geographical area of Israel preaching truths and professing a connection with the living God. Christ's followers would respond to his death and resurrection with a complex of faith and a passion for spreading that faith that would lead to a religion that has come to be one of the most influential belief systems in the history of the world. A poor people's religion, from a very small place. Of course, the teachings of Christ entered a world of suffering and oppression for the Israelites who were living under a pervasive Roman colonial authority, and belief in Christ was inextricably linked to a political resistance to Roman control and an embrace of Judaism redefined. Christ targeted the poor and the downtrodden, the dregs of society. He came for them. He came to bring dignity to their lives. His presence was founded on remarkable myths that would be solidified in a series of gospels that outlined the coincidence of the tragic arc of his life. Christ resisted the authorities, the upper-class and well kept Jews that he claimed had betrayed the interest of the poor Jewish people. He spoke for the poor. It is not surprising that much has been written about the political force of Christ's teachings and his confrontations with the Jewish and Roman élite.

When the disciples gathered after Christ's death and departure, they were not sure what was going to happen. The narrative was in flux. They were waiting for some guidance. The Day of Pentecost is the moment when the belief in Christ became a religion – a distinctive religion that would be spread around the world. The claims about Christ would have seemed decidedly absurd to those living during that time, and yet the attraction to the ideas offered by Christ's teachings rested in the way that he challenged the colonial authorities and sought to speak on behalf of the poor. His promises were clear: the poor would inherit the earth, the wicked rich will face the apocalyptic end with a guarantee that they would suffer; the sick would be healed and the outcast would have a place at the table. Christ's teaching was populist and attractive for these very reasons.

Rastafarianism emerged out of similar circumstances. Of course, while Christ assumed the role of charismatic leader and teacher, Selassie never expected to be the God of the Jamaican Rastafarians. The prophets of Rasta were themselves not necessarily aware that they were predicting the emergence of this religion. Rastafarianism drew upon a long history of Afrocentric belief systems that flourished in Jamaica and the rest of the diaspora for more than three hundred years before the advent of the religion. For all the efforts to indoctrinate African slaves to hate their homeland, there remained a strong sense of home in Africa that was rooted in a truly diasporal belief system. The song of the exile looking back to the homeland with nostalgia and desire was always part of the culture of slave societies throughout the New World. Indeed, even when blacks embraced Christianity, they emphasized those facets that found resonance in African belief systems. They embraced the connections between the poor and the select, between the oppressed and the select and between the enslaved and the select. They found solace in the apocalyptic vision of the end times that would bring about a cataclysmic end to the wicked. They enjoyed the promise of another land, a temporal land of return that would become the culmination of their journeying. The metaphor of diaspora journey that is so central to the Old and New

Testament teachings resonated with them. They also searched through scripture to find references to themselves, to their African heritage. In the Book of Psalms there is the promise that Ethiopia would stretch forth her hands – Ethiopia would be a place of power and hope in the context of Biblical prophecy. This connection between Ethiopia and Africa had long been an accepted one among European scholars. Shakespeare would refer to Africa, the land mass, as Ethiopia and to dark-skinned people as Ethiopes.

Rastafarians would find in Ethiopia a rich tradition that connected the people of Africa with the narrative of the Children of Israel. The *Kebra Negast*, a holy book with a complex history and a constantly controversial authorship, has long been a part of the folk and oral tradition of Ethiopia; but it has also been a part of the historical narrative of Ethiopia for over a thousand years. Marley would have heard the beautiful story of the *Kebra Negast*, the powerful telling of how the Ark of the Covenant came to be in Ethiopia after leaving Israel. The pride found in the Ethiopian Orthodox church and the strength of its traditions that dated back so many centuries would make Ethiopia a vindication for all the lies that colonialism had spoken to the black man, telling him that he had no history, no tradition and no connection to the glorious narratives of world civilization.

Marley, a boy living in a world that sought to demean the black person, would have found a disturbing but seductive way to look at the world in the histories, related by the well read and wise Rastafarians that he met in the ghetto. Marley admitted that he feared the Rastas. He was no different from so many Jamaicans who would have felt that this radical thinking – this suggestion that the black man is the true carrier of the seed of David and the power of prophecy – was the kind of heresy that could send you to hell. Marley would have wondered if these men were insane. Yet he was a fatherless boy, a boy in search of a place to settle his ideas of manhood and his sense of the value of his life. He found nothing to help him arrive at this point in the colonialist views of the Western church, and he found no power, no dignity, no youthful energy in the middle-class aspirations of the church. Rasta spoke to him and he embraced it.

Rastafarians proposed the most compelling of arguments. They simply asked why one should accept the narrative given to the world by King James and the church elders of some centuries before – people who clearly had no respect or love for Africans – and reject other narratives that were in existence at the time when these decisions were being made about the authoritative texts of the Bible. Rastas asked why the Apocrypha should not be read, and why the many other books that had sought to be included in the larger biblical narrative should not be examined. They asked why anyone should trust the judgement of white men who were as human as everyone else and who were intent on creating their faith in their own image. If they could do it, then why should the black man not examine these historical narratives and find himself in those stories? In Ethiopia a narrative had lasted for centuries – a narrative that celebrated the presence of Africans in the spiritual prophecies of the world. Rastafarianism, then, amounted to a restoration of what was lost. It was rooted in faith. It was a rough belief system, one that was finding its own truth gradually. It was one that found its own meaning and value for black people. Selassie's claim to the lineage of King Solomon was not a totally absurd one and if it could be embraced in faith, then a radical and affirming belief system would come to give meaning and dignity to a people living in the most abject of conditions.

The story of the Ark of the Covenant as told by the *Kebra Negast* and as repeated by Rastafarians to each other would move Marley to become the psalmist for this religion:

And the people came to the sea of Eritrea, the Red Sea, and when the holy Zion crossed over, the sea received them, and its waves were as whitecapped mountains which were split asunder, and the sea roared as the loudest lions and made a noise like the winter thunder of Damascus. And the sea worshipped Zion. But while its billows grew into mountains, the wagons of Ethiopia were raised above the waves, and the sound of the breaking sea mingled with the sounds of the people's horns and drums. And whales and fishes came forth and worshipped Zion. And birds flapped through the forth, and there was joy in the sea of Eritrea.

And they arrived opposite Mount Sinai and remained there while the angels sang. The children of the earth raised their voices in song and psalm and their tambourines made joyful noise. Then they loaded the wagons and rose up and journeyed until they came to the country of Ethiopia. And as they traveled, Zion sent forth a light like that of the sun and it penetrated the darkness.

The ideas that would give rise to Rastafarianism reach back, then, many centuries and can be said to have emerged out of the same energy and spirit of resistance that allowed blacks to sing negro spirituals in the Southern states of the US, and Haitians to formulate Vodoun in their efforts to resist the demeaning force of slavery. In Cuba, Brazil, Surinam and all over the African diaspora, Black people would find spiritual and philosophical vehicles with which to resist the oppressive tenets of slave culture.

According to scholar Ennis Edmonds, by the time that, in the early 19th century, African-American Black Baptist George Liele arrived in Jamaica to start a grassroots Baptist movement that emphasized baptism, healing and the charismatic gifts, the language of Africa as a promised land was already quite common among black intellectuals throughout the US and Europe. Liele would form a series of 'Native Baptist' churches that were fully occupied by blacks. He would refer to the members of his group as Ethiopians. He would have heard of the Ethiopian players in the US who were travelling around the country staging black plays, and he would have heard of those close to Washington who were advocating the establishment of an African colony made up of freed blacks from America. Repatriation was basic to the African diasporal experience in the 19th century, a feature that would culminate in the work of Marcus Garvey and the pan-Africanist in the 20th century.

Those men who would be largely responsible for the formation of Rastafarianism in the 1930s were not creating something entirely new, but were building on an old tradition that emerged from various threads of connectedness with Africa. Even outside the Judaeo-Christian trend of groups like the Native Baptists there had been, for years, a strong African element in an underground belief system that was almost always tied to resistance and rebellion among blacks against the systems of slavery. Some of the most dramatic and memorable acts of rebellion and resistance carried out in Jamaica were in fact fuelled and led by religious figures who were part of these Afro-Caribbean religious groups. In 1760 a rebellion led by Tacky, an adherent of Mayal, a religious system that specialized in countering the hex of evil people (namely the white oppressors), effectively destroyed large tracts of plantation land and ended with the murder of many whites. Tacky was caught and executed, but his rebellion remains one of the most successful in the history of Caribbean slavery. It is said that the slaves involved in the rebellion were convinced that they were immune to the bullets of the whites because of the power of their Mayal beliefs.

In 1832, Sam Sharpe, also known as 'Daddy' Sharp, a deacon in a 'Native Baptist' church as well as a known adherent to revivalist African religious practices, led a rebellion that also ended in defeat. But it played a significant role in pushing the British to eventually end slavery six years later. Sharpe, like many of the adherents to strongly African belief systems, understood that resistance to the white oppression was part and parcel of his belief system and there was no real contradiction between the force of arms and the act of spiritual worship. The apocalyptic vision of redemption from temporal oppression fed the rationale for this kind of radical action.

In 1860, over 20 years after the abolition of slavery, another church leader, Paul Bogle, would lead a rebellion in Morant Bay that would ultimately be crushed brutally by the then Governor Eyre. Bogle was also a deacon in one of the Native Baptist churches and he too saw the need for radical action against the unfairness of the post slavery society that was normal and acceptable. Marcus Garvey would continue this trend along more secular lines. But his call for repatriation to Africa was always couched in religious language, the language of the apocalypse. He called for the blacks to return to Africa, to the land where they could worship the God of Africa. He called for a movement away from the oppression of the West and an embrace of the culture of Africa. It was Garvey who pointed a finger to Ethiopia and to Selassie as an answer to the system of oppression faced by blacks. It was Garvey who arrived at the conclusion that a homeland for Africans was the answer to their problems in the New World. Garvey's vision was rooted in the same kind of diasporal hope of millions of Jews around the world. The belief was simply that there was a place of belonging for blacks and it was a place that had to be embraced with force.

Given the centuries of poverty and hardship that faced Africa after the advent of colonialism, it is understandable that Garvey would draw attention to the rich and complex history of the African continent during ancient times. He would join the many Africans of the time to celebrate the power of Egyptian civilization and the strong Christian history of Ethiopia as a centre of learning in ancient times. The link between Ethiopia and the lineage of King Solomon was a critical part of this paradigm. Ethiopia was one of the few countries that was waging a successful war against colonial oppression in 1930. Ethiopia was one of the few distinctive nations with a monarch who had managed to unify a landmass against the encroaching Italians. Politically, Ethiopia was the poster child of anti-colonialism and it made sense that people like Garvey and his followers would point to this fact as they celebrated the power and potential of Africans.

It follows, then, that most of the men who would be largely responsible for the emergence of Rastafarianism were in fact ex-Garveyites who understood the long tradition of celebrating Africa that had existed in the New World. They understood that their views were clearly going against the norm in Caribbean colonial society. In that society, Africa was seen as a place of backwardness and the things related to Africa – like blackness, rhythm and the language – were all seen as negative elements of the New World black's identity. Whiteness was celebrated as good and positive and this inculcation permeated most of society. Garvey was not looked upon with favour in the Caribbean and in Jamaica he was victimized and eventually forced to leave the island because his views seemed so radically different from the heavily Eurocentric beliefs that dominated the society at all levels.

Marley himself met many Rastas in Trench Town. He would admit later that at first he found the drumming and the strong African energy frightening and unsettling, but he would eventually come to embrace the wisdom of what the Rastas were saying largely because he could see a gentleness of spirit and a consistency about what they believed in many of the Rastafarians with whom he came into contact. Joe Higgs, a man that Marley would later call a 'big music man', was a Rastafarian and it was Higgs who taught the young Wailers much of what they would eventually know about harmony. He also taught them a tough work ethic, and the basic truths about Rastafarianism. Marley found in Higgs a man of integrity.

However, while Rastafarianism helps us to understand Marley's work, we must also appreciate that Marley was a product of Jamaica – of rural Jamaica that was, and still is, a place steeped in mysticism and a sensitivity to spiritual matters that is wholly African. Marley was decidedly respectful of the supernatural long before he became a Rasta. Even after turning to Rasta Marley would talk about the things that people could do to the individual through dark spiritual practices. Marley often insisted that his marriage to Rita was orchestrated by a series of rather dark magical schemes. Of course, Marley's sense of irony and his ability to create myth around things that he wanted to seem mysterious is part of his manner, but this story was one that he liked to tell. It was his way of defending his aversion to marriage.

It is understandable, though, that Marley would be so steeped in matters of the supernatural and the mystical. His mother, a country woman, believed that his birth was shrouded in mystery. Indeed, Marley was ill quite soon after his birth and his grandfather, Omeriah, declared him to be troubled by evil spirits and proceeded to heal him with herbs and charms. Omeriah, according to Cedella Booker, Bob's mother, was 'renowned through the district as a bush doctor and herbalist'. Marley's Rastafarian faith would lead him to reject the doings of spiritualists as things of the devil, but he enjoyed exploring the rich world of spiritual mysteries that were a part of the Jamaican culture.

When listening to songs like 'Mr Brown' and 'Duppy Conqueror', we need an understanding of the spiritual subtext of Jamaican life to truly appreciate that, as much as Marley was writing metaphorically about the forces of political life, he was also speaking in a language rooted in spiritualism.

Lee 'Scratch' Perry was, for a time, a most influential presence in Marley's life and he himself was a figure of profound mystery and mysticism. Bunny Wailer was regarded as the one Wailer who had access to deep supernatural wisdom and power, but he himself found Perry to be strange and not entirely trustworthy. Perry's antics – his burying of records, his rituals with candles and mystical incantations in his studio, and his statements about the grand genie that he had locked up in a room where Marley stayed, all pointed to his thorough immersion in mysticism. Marley lived with Perry for a long time and so he would have been exposed to the manic complexity that made up Perry's own spiritual sensibility.

Marley's world, then, was rich with the mysterious things of life and, as a Jamaican, belief in the power of Obeah, of Mayal and of other African-based spiritual practices was always a truth of the society. Marley was not exempt from any of this and so his work reflects a complete belief in the workings of 'spiritual wickedness in high and low places'. In other words, Marley's treatment of spiritual matters as elemental to everyday life – as part of reality – emerged out of the culture in which he lived. The divide between the secular and the spiritual was a Western preoccupation that had not permeated working-class Jamaican society.

Marley's Rastafarianism, then, was marked by mysticism and a belief in the supernatural. These elements would surface in all his work. It is true that his doctrinal beliefs would become increasingly orthodox in his later work. He relied more and more on the Bible for his spiritual references and maintained a fairly consistent commitment to teaching about the end times. But the legacy of his childhood and early life in Kingston was his absolute conviction that even as he sang about faith, about the supernatural and about the power of prophecy, he was, to his mind, singing about reality. Marley resisted attempts to call his beliefs religion. He insisted that Rasta was, for him, life. Asked when he turned to Rasta, Marley answered, 'ever since' – meaning, forever. His point is that he was always called to Rasta but he only understood it fully in his early 20s. His point is that his entire life was shaped by Jah to arrive at faith in Rasta. His point, ultimately, comes from his reading of the Book of Psalms when David declares:

For you created my inmost being;
you knit me together in my mother's womb…
My frame was not hidden from you
when I was made in the secret place.
When I was woven together in the depths of the earth,
your eyes saw my unformed body.
All the days ordained for me
were written in your book
before one of them came to be.

A trio of spiritual forces in Jamaican society helped to shape the songwriter Bob Marley. The first was the conventional church – a church shaped by a strong 'native African' tradition that grew out of the need to find dignity and hope in a world that was so heavily oppressive to blacks. It was not the church of the established élite, but the church of his mother Cedella, which was a church led by black people, a church where people worshipped with energy and a strong sense of the 'spirit' and a church whose doors looked out onto the hills where spiritualists carried out their work. It was the church in which people quietly prayed to God while calling on the herbalist and 'bush-doctors' to aid in times of crisis. Marley learned hymns, choruses and gospel songs in that church, and in many of his early compositions we hear a morality that would have grown out of the teachings of such a church. Given the fact that Jamaica holds the world record for churches per square mile, it makes sense that Marley, along with all his fellow reggae artists, grew up in church. But they also grew up in the rural world where they would have heard of the supernatural outworking of African belief systems. These formed the second force that would shape Marley. The third would have been the Rastafarian religion, rich with the teachings of Marcus Garvey and with a earnest and compelling relevance to the young male of the ghetto. Christianity was the religion of the mothers. Rastafarianism was the religion of the sons. Where the church failed to see the uneasiness and disquiet that the young men were experiencing in urban Jamaica in the late 1950s and early 1960s, Rasta saw it, understood it and gave it voice. Marley was one of those who would embrace this new and dynamic, male-driven youth force.

It is important, then, to recognize that there is a vast historical and cultural context for Marley's work and for Marley's character; and there was a living man behind these songs – a man who carried his pain with the tender disquiet of the best artists. He chose to devote himself to his art and worked hard to perfect it. Marley's genius was not immediately obvious to himself or to anyone else. It is doubtful whether he ever saw himself as a genius. He just knew that he had something to say and he wanted to say it in a way that would be most powerful. When Marley spoke of his art, he spoke of it as one would expect a poet to speak of his art. Music was a vocation for him.

> Understand, see musicians get mad because of music. Living my place in Jamaica a man might have a guitar and it drop on brick and the man get mad because he never get another guitar again for a long while. A musician he must search to find a certain phrase and him just can't find it, it trip him out in the head, y'know. Music is a delicate thing in the sense that it tek so much inspiration, you have to be there at all times. Same thing happen to me.
>
> (August 1980)

While preparing for this book, I began to ask people close to him what Marley's writing process was like. What most of those who knew him said was that he worked for a long time on his songs. Bunny Wailer made it a point to remind me that the lyrics that were produced by the Wailers came out of an intensity of human experience and feeling, but they also came through constant rehearsal and hard work. 'Dem never come jus' soh,' he said. Bunny Wailer knows that there is still a perception by many that the Wailers simply plucked ideas out of the air and did a quick thing in the studio to record the work. The perception is of course absurd. Bunny Wailer reminded me that much of their songwriting was done in an environment of intense creativity and innovation and in a world that demanded the highest standards from musicians and artists. They studied the music that was coming out of the US, but they also grew up listening to jazz and worked with some of the best jazz musicians Jamaica has ever produced. Songwriting was taken quite seriously in those days and the Wailers understood that they would have to work hard to compete with the other artists that were working at the time.

Here is how Marley describes the earliest years of his apprenticeship. Any musician or lover of music will understand at once that Marley's devotion to music and his study of popular music was thorough.

Yah see, my people was always amongst bars. You have to have jukebox and you always have music going on. I remember we used to have plenty-plenty music. And one time me saw a show down here [Kingston] with Brooks Benton and Dinah Washington. Like they all show up: Nat King Cole, Billy Eckstine, y'know. Even Frank Sinatra and Sammy Davis in a certain period when I was living on Oxford Street. But when I was living in Barry Street I used to hear things like 'Jim Dandy To The Rescue', 'Bony Maronie', 'What Am I living For', 'Don't Break your Promise To Me'. Heavy music. Then we go to Regent Street now, and me hear Brook Benton and some work with a guy named Danny Ray. But Fats Domino and Ricky Nelson and Elvis Presley and whole heap of lickle other music come on strong. Then we go to Second Street and start listening to jazz. Except me couldn't understand it. After a while me get to understand it and me meet Joe Higgs and Seeco Patterson who schooled me. After a while I smoked some ganja, some herb, and then I understood jazz. I tried to get into the mood where the moon is blue and understand the feelings expressed.

(1975)

Marley would also speak of The Skatelites, naming Don Drummond, the remarkable composer of over a hundred jazz/ska numbers for the highly innovative ska unit that did most of their work in the ghetto. Among that circle of artists were people like Roland Alphonso, the saxophonist who defined reggae horn-playing, and Ernest Ranglin, who is perhaps the most influential reggae guitarist ever. Marley met these men, worked with these men and learned a great deal from them. These were serious musicians, many of them classically trained and all of them trained in jazz music. They combined their strong pan-Africanist sensibility with their empathy for the people in the ghetto that produced them, to make music that was fresh, distinctive and wholly Jamaican. Given this environment, and given Marley's desire to learn by watching and imitating, it is not hard to see how he would emerge as a talented and ambitious artist fully conscious of his identity and his responsibility to his community. The music scene he was surrounded by was lively but taxing. Everybody, including Marley, wanted to find a path out of poverty through music.

In much the same way as happened in the emerging popular music industry in the States, aspiring Jamaican singers and songwriters auditioned in hastily arranged, impromptu meetings with producers who made their decisions quickly and ruthlessly. Songwriting, then, was inextricably connected with performance. This may seem like the most obvious idea, but it is an important one to appreciate especially when it comes to Bob Marley. He would audition for many a producer who was not simply listening to Marley's voice to test his potential as a singer, but was also listening to see if Marley's songwriting abilities could be used to supply other singers with good material. Everyone, in those days, wanted a hit. The singer did, the producer did and the world outside did. This pressure always shaped Marley's early songwriting. But Jamaican music had not yet arrived at the place where hits were a regular occurrence. There was still an interest in the new thing – the new sound. This gave shape to the songwriting of the Wailers.

Gradually it became clear to me that Marley rarely put lyrics to paper. There is some evidence that several of Marley's songs were written by hand, and no doubt he kept notes in all kinds of places to help him remember an idea or a turn of phrase. There is, for instance, a sliver of paper photographed in the jacket notes for the four disk set 'Bob Marley; Songs of Freedom' on which we see in what is called 'Bob's handwriting' the lyrics of a song that was never completed but that would have been written when he was working on songs like 'Guiltiness' and 'Running Away'. The caption suggests that Marley wrote these lyrics just after fleeing Jamaica for Nassau, because of the assassination attempt, where he recovered from his wounds. From there he would fly to England, where he would work on more than two albums' worth of material and where he would record some of his best work.

The lyrics in question are a curiosity largely because they seem to suggest that Marley, at least at this stage of his writing career, tended to compose in a wide open style, tossing his ideas on the page with what was clearly the intention of honing them into song lyrics when he went into the studio. But the sliver of lyrics shows Marley giving shape on the page to a lyric that reflects the fluid chatting style that would shape his work during this reflective period. The phrases emerge in compact units.

It is conceivable that these lyrics were the early stages of the song 'Ambush In The Night', which treats of the same subject matter, but the tantalizing taunt 'Good bye' and the attendant sentiment is no longer there in the finished song. According to Rita Marley and Cindy Breakspeare, Marley was deeply hurt by the attempted assassinations, less because of the great affront of this act, but because he felt betrayed by a people who he thought he could trust. He was hurt because it was clear that those who did it allowed themselves to be convinced by his enemies to go out and shoot Bob Marley. It is clear that something in him was convinced that the people were always on his side and they would not allow anyone to convince them to go out and take action against Marley for anything. They had betrayed him, and this shattered a sense of security and truly shattered his confidence in the poor people he lived among. So there is a taunt in the lyric – a taunt that says that Jah's protection is whole and complete and has come against their actions. But the lyric is a message to them and the message is decided: 'Good bye'. Marley was turning his back on Jamaica.

In this song, however, Marley does not assume the tough rude bwai. He is humbled by the experience and turns to Jah for his security and assurance. But he echoes the hope of 'Judge Not' in the appeal to divine retribution that was so central to his philosophy. The elements of 'Guiltiness' emerge in the lyric, at least in the final phrase: 'The innocent blood will be on you conscience'. In 'Guiltiness' he orders guiltiness to 'rest on their conscience'.

This example helps us to see that Marley would work on a composition until he felt he had enough to record. He would then record the songs in a two-track machine sometimes with just his guitar and at other times with the accompaniment of anyone who was around and part of the vibe. Marley would keep revising the piece until he was satisfied with the work. At that point, the full band would work on the tune. Apparently, there were times when he would ask others to write down the lyrics he was creating. Stephen Davis quotes Diane Dobson, Marley's long-time friend and lawyer's account of one such occasion.

> One night it was raining at Hope Road, and we were sitting down on the front step. And Bob siddung with his guitar and made a beautiful song. And then we never heard anything more about it. That particular one, I remember him making a remark, he said, 'Ah right now, you see me a-sing, you should be writing down the words what I'm doing.' I said, 'True, Bob.' I picked up the phone directory and turned to the back page and wrote the words of the song on it. He just did a verse and stopped. Two years later I picked up the phone book and was marveling at the lyric. It was so beautiful.'
>
> – *Bob Marley: Conquering Lion Of Reggae*

That Marley approached his song as an exercise in 'orature', a process that involved shaping the music and lyric together, tells us a great deal about how Marley achieved the organic merging of lyric and sound in his songs. You would never find him working hard to cram a lyric into a line. Instead he allowed the lyric space to find its own sound connection. His rhymes would not follow a rigid syllabic or line length, but would seem most natural in the way the song found its unity of melody and meaning. The richness of assonance, the play on language and the shaping of one idea out of the next suggest a spontaneity that must have been part of his creative process.

Marley always sounds as if he is in direct dialogue with the listener. There is no sense that he is about to render a 'piece'. He opens his songs with a declaration that suggests the beginning of a dialogue. And in some songs you almost feel as if you can hear him thinking through the logic of a lyric. There is a noticeable hiccup, a slight pause between the words 'they take a...' and 'yard' in his song 'Real Situation'. Of course, he was searching for the logical progression of the proverb and it may have slipped him for an instant while recording. But he chose to leave it there – an unusual act for someone who was notorious for his meticulous care at the way a song is voiced. He would record many takes on some songs until he was happy with them. It may easily be that the rest of the take was just too strong to bother about the hiccup. But here he let it ride and the effect is to make the song sound like a live moment, full of the energy of thought – present thought.

According to people who were close to Marley, his writing process led to him having a great deal of material on tape that he planned to return to. It seems like Marley would carry ideas and images in his head for a long time until he had a chance to work. In at least four or five instances, we know Marley worked manically and intensely in putting together a slate of 30 or so ideas. The earliest period of this kind of intense work would have to have been when the Wailers started to work exclusively for Coxsone Dodd in the mid-1960s. In two or three years they produced 30 songs, some of which were released as singles and others that simply remained as ideas. They covered material by a wide range of artists, altering sounds, and in the process found their own distinctive Jamaican sounds. Marley wrote a great deal at the time in a heady and clearly energetic collaboration with the other Wailers.

This burst of creativity happened again when he worked with Lee 'Scratch' Perry in the early 1970s. The work done during those years was often released immediately by Perry or by Marley himself on his own label. But in the space of a few months, Marley would put together quite a significant number of songs – songs that he would return to again and again throughout his career. He wrote with similar intensity when he was being paid by Danny Simms to write for Johnny Nash. Much of the work was material that others used, and some of it was recast material from his early work with Perry and the Wailers team, but it revealed that once given a space to work and the equipment to put down tracks that he could experiment with and return to again and again on a daily basis, that is what Marley did. Few use the word obsessive about Marley, but it is clear that when he was writing, his daily routine was driven by the need to make songs. In interviews he would mention that he was working on a song not long ago. He was always working.

By the time Marley had the security of a solid contractual arrangement with Island Records, his pattern had become consistent. He would enter the studio and work on new songs intensively for a few months. The work would then be honed with the band before he would take the songs to be mixed, overdubbed and generally engineered in studios in the US or in the UK. Stories abound of Marley plotting out songs while sitting in his hotel room or while riding on a bus. He would usually work with another musician who would play percussions or keyboards. The *Exodus/Kaya* recordings grew out of an intense four-month period of first writing work each day and then finally recording the tracks. The same is true of the *Survival* recordings. The 'drafts' of these songs are on two-track recordings and rough studio cuts.

It makes sense, then, that Marley's work would develop an organic interplay between music and lyric. They seem to have been built together. His lyrics took shape around an idea, but he clearly allowed himself to jam on a song, chant a range of ideas, whether by quoting scripture or toying with some catchy phrase, until he felt that he had something to keep. Working in studios that were often teeming with hangers-on and other musicians, Marley would pull ideas from those around him – the jokes, the encouragement, the wisdom of those who spoke with the natural poetic authority that many Rastafarians were known for. Marley's art, therefore, took shape, not in quiet isolation, but in teeming energy and community. Yet it is clear that most of his songs are intensely personal and emerge out of Marley's inimitable ability to withdraw himself from a crowd even when sitting right in that crowd.

In this book, I have tried to guide us through all the songs that appeared on the Island Records label, ending with the record *Confrontation*. Since then, Island has managed to release a large body of Marley's earlier work as part of an effort to put his art into perspective. I have borrowed much from this approach by contextualizing the Island material within the larger body of Marley's work. A reader, then, can find close readings of most of Marley's major songs produced and released during his lifetime. I follow Marley's art while placing it in the context of his life. What drives this book, however, is not Marley's biography so much as Marley's songs. While a purist might say that one should not consider an artist's biography when examining his work, I have to say that Marley sought to draw attention to his life as he created his songs. His songs represented a dialogue with his community and that dialogue often involved painful confessions and the sharing of the elation of living.

It is worth stating that the use of a simple chronology of song releases to chart the development of an artist can be misleading. The date of the release of a record is not necessarily the same as the date of a song's creation. Sometimes songs remain in gestation for years, and then finally appear on a record as if they just emerged. The things that may have helped shape a song may have occurred decades before the release of that song. This may seem obvious, but it is worth remembering, especially when looking at Marley's work. Marley songs grew over extended periods. He generated various versions of some songs. Often a single line or verse from an old song would reappear in a new song that seemed to want to return to the old theme and recast it. These progressions are not easy to chart, but wherever I think they are relevant to an understanding of Marley's craft, I have drawn attention to them. Despite all of this, however, I also feel strongly that Marley timed his releases to reflect his mood, his sense of what was important and to add to the body of work that he had already produced. Consequently, there is some value in examining Marley's life alongside the chronology of his record releases. Marley's albums were whole statements. They often came out of a larger body of work. The selection was guided by many factors, but one can sense that one of these factors was the artistic and political statement that he hoped to make.

My own personal hope is that the reader will leave this book with a greater appreciation of the genius of Bob Marley. As Bunny Wailer assured me, what I have written is my reading of the songs – a reading shaped by the peculiar details of my own life and my own relationship with Bob Marley and Jamaica. This is what Marley would have encouraged. The work was put out there for people to react to and feel. Yet this clearly subjective bias does not remove from me the responsibility to be faithful to the intelligence of Marley's vision as an artist and to try and at least come to as close a sense as I can of much of what Marley meant to communicate in his songs.

It should become clear to the reader that this analysis will in no way be able to capture the power and emotional breadth of Marley's songs because these songs come to us as perfomances. Marley's vocalization, his tone and his arrangements all come to shape the work we hear. This book is, therefore, best read with Marley music playing or with all transcribed lyrics at your fingertips. If the book sends you back to Marley's art then it would have accomplished a great deal.

1 Catch A Fire And Burnin'
Revolutionary Fire

'If you come from Trench Town, you don't stand a chance. Dat's a fact.'

– Bob Marley

CATCH A FIRE (APRIL 1973)
Concrete Jungle / Slave Driver / 400 Years / Stop That Train / Rock It Baby (Baby We Got A Date) / Stir It Up / Kinky Reggae / No More Trouble / Midnight Ravers

BURNIN' (NOVEMBER 1973)
Get Up, Stand Up / Hallelujah Time / I Shot The Sheriff / Burnin' And Lootin' / Put It On / Small Axe / Pass It On / Duppy Conqueror / One Foundation / Rastaman Chant

The Marley we meet in *Catch A Fire* is part of a reggae band – a crew of three men with varied personalities who are charging forward with a musical style that is distinctive and strange to an international market. We encounter these men in song. The packaging is unique, as the album cover is designed as a novelty to look like a Zippo lighter. Those who did not know the Wailers were being introduced not just to a group of men, but also to a way of life, to a philosophy about life, to a whole new culture, to a whole new landscape and to a radical way of thinking about popular song. With only two love songs on the album, it stands out as a deeply political selection that is balanced by two lyrically challenging tunes that seem at once whimsical and yet deeply complex: 'Kinky Reggae' and 'Midnight Ravers'. But the rest of the material presents the basic blueprint for the Wailer's political sensibility. This is an album that marches decidedly into the radical world of political advocacy and sophisticated readings of history.

However the album, in retrospect, was less politically and spiritually charged than Marley's later efforts, even when we take into consideration the often dismissed *Kaya*. While Marley wrote most of the songs on the album, the contributions by Peter Tosh offer an interesting counterpoint to Marley's work. Marley's largely political songs on the album are 'Concrete Jungle', 'Slave Driver' and 'No More Trouble'. 'Midnight Ravers' is peculiar for its strong spiritual allusions and the manner in which it comments on the society Marley lived in. 'Midnight Ravers' belongs to that group of peculiar social commentary songs that included much of the work Marley and the Wailers did with Lee 'Scratch' Perry. This included songs like 'Mr Brown', 'Kaya', 'Mr Chatterbox' and 'Kinky Reggae'. The last of these, however, is far more whimsical and intentionally surrealistic and strange. As a class of songs, this album would be the last one that would feature such tunes. On *Burnin'*, Marley would move on to include songs with a much clearer political intent as well as more overt Rastafarian songs. The progression of Marley's writing between these two albums was towards the kind of work that would shape the rest of his career.

'Stir It Up' and 'Rock It Baby' would be the last conventional love songs that Marley would release on an album until *Exodus* appeared several years later. People who encounter Marley's work only through the Island albums would get the impression that he did not think much of the love song. Anyone who followed his output for the ten years prior to *Catch A Fire* would know that he was more likely to write a love song than political songs. But Marley was maturing and he was growing in his sense of responsibility to the society in which he lived. His Rastafarian faith was pushing him towards the business of teaching what he thought to be true. In a political climate that was alive with discussion about revolution, change and the freedom of the poor, perhaps love songs seemed trite to him. Yet he would have to defend the re-emergence of his love songs when *Exodus* appeared.

Catch A Fire, though, set the tone for Marley's career and the reception that his work received. With songs like 'Concrete Jungle' and 'Slave

Driver' on this first album, followed by 'I Shot the Sheriff', 'Burnin And Lootin' and 'Get Up, Stand Up' on *Burnin'*, Marley established himself as a songwriter of radical political thought. He was dangerous. The decision to include the lyrics of the songs on the liner notes was brilliant. Apart from linking Marley with the rock music scene, it also underlined the idea that he was a serious songwriter and gave the listeners a chance to come in full contact with the tough political spirit that permeated his work. Without them, many would probably have had difficulty grasping the meaning of the lyrics.

Opening *Catch A Fire* with 'Concrete Jungle' is a statement in itself. In this moving song, Marley offers, in the most concise and moving way, his biography – his position as a ghetto man, as a sufferah.

'Concrete Jungle' is a musical introduction to the world that Perry Henzell reconstructed in his film *The Harder They Come*. The film had a soundtrack of striking power, and an number of the songs served as a useful backdrop to the story of Ivan. Desmond Dekker's 'Shanty Town', Jimmy Cliff's 'The Harder They Come' and The Slickers' 'Johnny Too Bad' all gave striking descriptions of the rough world of Kingston. But none of these would have the poetic immediacy of 'Concrete Jungle'. Apart from Cliff's 'The Harder They Come', which always seemed like a fictional song written specifically for the film's narrative, the songs were all outward-looking narratives about how rough the streets of the ghetto are. In 'Concrete Jungle' Marley wrote about this same world from the inside out. It is a moving lyric of such emotional weightiness and poetic artistry that a close textual reading of it will offer us some insight into what makes Marley a singular artist.

The rugged world of the rude bwai's Kingston is evocatively captured in the harsh images of Henzell's film. But even then, there is a romantic quality that the narrative allows that does not force us to see the stark realities of a Kingston ghetto – the smells, the despondency, the mad man strolling along the street oblivious to all around, the acrid dust, the blazing sun sucking all energy from the people who live in these streets. And yet, such abject cliché does not really capture the combination of despair and hope, the very normal manner of making ends meet with dignity that marks the ghetto. The life is at once normal – for everything is normal for all of us, normality is defined by the limits of what we know, what we are familiar with. I have watched documentaries that show the Kingston we are talking about, and the shanty towns look shabby. But I also know whose eyes are gazing at this world. For some odd reason, I feel distant from these images – the shaky shot of five children standing half naked and gazing at the camera, barefoot, looking everything like the poverty-stricken people they are supposed to be. But at least three of these children understand the difference between school uniform, home clothes and church clothes. The convenience of their garments makes sense to them. They run around as they do because that is their normal world.

I have walked those streets, too, and eaten meals in those yards, and while there I have not had the feeling of entering a place ripe for the Red Cross. It is not that the poverty is not real, not that there is no abjection there, but the camera misses the human beings that live in these places. The camera misses the television that is in the hovel. It also misses the rich array of family and extended family that helps to shape the imagination and sense of belonging of these children. They may die as victims of bullets, but their humanity is profound and not defined by the image that we see on the screen. The ghetto that Bob Marley lived in was a place that Bunny Wailer could nostalgically recall as 'magical' – as something like Hollywood. You can hear him talking about the roughness of the ghetto as a memory, something understood in retrospect. But he speaks of the ghetto – Trench Town – as a place of possibility, where people lived complex lives and dreamed rich and complex dreams.

When Marley dubbed these streets 'Concrete Jungle' it is clear that he also saw this place as a world in which the most profound of philosophical articulations could emerge. Marley was not surprised that something good could come out of Trench Town. The media was shocked – the media likes to tell the story of a great beauty emerging from abjection. But for Marley, Bunny Wailer and Peter Tosh, this beauty was always there. It made sense to them that it would come from that landscape. It is important that we understand that if we are to understand that great art can emerge from any source. The artist is the thing – as is their capacity to dream.

Many, of course, expected Marley to romanticize the ghetto and still somehow stay in the ghetto. That this was what he regarded as a sign of his continued connection with his roots, with his earthiness. But Marley's view was somewhat different. The ghetto Marley describes in his songs is not a place fit for human existence. It is a harsh place and not the kind of place that he hoped poor people would have to endure. Marley had no intentions of staying in the ghetto. He was in the ghetto, he understood, because he had to be in the ghetto. What he wanted for those he cared about and for his people in general was that they would not have to live in the ghetto. His distaste for the poverty of the ghetto did not extend to the poor. The people of the ghetto were not the ghetto as far as Marley was concerned. They were human beings full of promise and beauty. That they had to live in the ghetto was a tragedy of Babylon's system, and Marley would repeatedly point this out:

When I lived in the ghetto, every day I had to jump fences, police trying to hold me, you dig? So my job all the while was to try to find one place where the police wouldn't run me down too much. So I don't want to stay in contact with the ghetto. In contact with the ghetto means in contact with a prison, not people. (1979)

A year earlier he had to respond to the same question about his connection with the ghetto. This time his response was briefer and less patient:

Me always live in... in the ghetto. Me don't feel like the ghetto should be my future like we should always love live [living] inna shit. (March 1978)

Music critic Garth White, commenting about the Marley that he had met in the mid-1960s, said that Marley always seemed to have the belief, even more than Tosh or Wailer, that he could be a star. And not just a local star, but an international star – the kind of star that could walk around with a sense of entitlement. And indeed, despite his poverty, which was total during those years, Marley understood his difference in Jamaican society where skin complexion was sometimes as defining about one's place in society as anything else might be. Marley was 'red'. There was no other way to say it in Jamaica. It meant that he was of a mixed racial background and was light enough to be distinguished from most Jamaicans. Rita Marley would remark that she did not anticipate wanting to fall for a guy like Bob. She did not think she would like a fair-skinned guy. She went for the 'tall, dark and handsome' type, she said. But in that simple comment is contained something that is not spoken of much when one looks at Marley. His light skin was a distinction. The fact that his father was a white man was a distinction. Many people in the community would privilege Bob for his complexion, expecting better things from him, and he would no doubt have internalized this.

The colour politics of Jamaican society complicated Marley's position as a ghetto youth. It is not that he was the only light-skinned boy in the ghetto – he wasn't – and it is not that he was a strange phenomenon in Kingston, because there were many such mixtures around. But in 1960s' Jamaica, no bank would hire a full black person. All bank tellers and workers had to be light skinned. It was an understanding. I muse about this because I am sure that in many ways Marley's decision to assert his blackness – his Africanness – was simply that: a clear decision based on his strong sense of identification with Rastafarianism and Africa. But it also would have grown out of what would have to have been a far more pained sense of his difference from the white family that rejected him. If blacks like Tosh and Bunny Wailer understood the racist culture of Jamaica as a given, and if they expected to be looked down upon because of their skin colour and, finally, if they did not feel a personal connection with white society in Jamaica, Marley's position had to have been different. His white family was his family and they, for all intents and purposes, rejected him. Consequently, he lived with a more acute and immediate sense of his blackness and his identification with his blackness.

It is why the song 'Blackman Redemption' is such an important confession and anthem. The album *Survival* according to Neville Garrick (in his introduction to *Stir it Up,* a book about reggae album art) was initially titled *Black Survival.* One can see why the change was made. I have no doubt that the systematic pattern of trying to market Marley as an international voice of peace and goodwill had a great deal to do with the 'softening' or universalizing of the title of the album. But Marley's own statement on that album represents a total identification with the political realities of post-Selassie Africa – the Africa of Zimbabwe and 'Africa Unite'. Garrick refers to *Survival* as Marley's most political album. This might be a stretch if we are talking about pure politics but, in terms of a self-identification with Africa and a self-identification with a political movement, *Survival* may well be the most politicized album. The Africanness of Marley, anyway, is not something to be taken lightly or seen as a minor development. Marley was a black man because he chose to self-identify as such. He could have been a 'white Jamaican' – he had all the credentials to do so – but he opted to take the position of black African-Jamaican.

The truth is that he may have had no choice. He was from Trench Town and that defined him. In many ways, then, a part of Marley rejected him. He embraced the identity of his mother and her family. He never wavered from this even when he would try to be diplomatic in interviews – suggesting that race was not important to him. But Marley self-identified as black because the narrative of the African in the New World was Marley's narrative. He was poor, he was underprivileged and he was one of the lesser people in the society. He would carry that sense, always.

Despite this, it is also clear that Marley grew up with a sense of his difference and, one may speculate, a sense of entitlement. But there are conflicting qualities here that need to be looked at. Rita Marley admits that her first reaction to Bob was 'pity' – he seemed to warrant pity – a sense that he needed to be cared for and understood. She said that it began with pity and then turned into something else. His charm seduced her and won her over. In 1968–9 when Marley approached Lee 'Scratch' Perry, the maverick producer would talk about being drawn to Marley's seriousness and his intense sadness, his vulnerability. Marley sang a lamentable tune that touched Perry, it was Marley's willingness to speak of his pain in love that drew Perry. It was also Marley's honesty in his love songs that assured Perry that he was dealing with a man intent on articulating deep emotions. But one can't help but feel that Perry was seeing in all of these love songs by Marley an intense metaphor of his loneliness and his need to be appreciated and understood. Marley's love songs are always about pursuing or working hard to be accepted, to be loved. And in each song he would manage to articulate some sentiment and emotion that extended beyond his immediate problem with a woman; some larger sense of isolation and need would emerge – a quality that would shape much of his songwriting, even in his most political songs.

'Concrete Jungle' is a political song, just as it is a love song of sorts. It is an anthem to his environment, and in this single lyric Marley manages to create a love song, a political song, a lyrical confession and a song rooted in the larger history of a people. Marley's 'I' is himself and, at the same time, his people – his community. Finally, the song is a lament. Without the final verse, this would be a deeply depressing song. But there is a quality of defiant hope that arises from the tragic tones of the song – from the lament. It is a quality that Marley would show in all the songs from the Perry years and the early Island years. Indeed, the songwriter who returned from the States in 1968 to rejoin the Wailers largely under the influence of Perry was a writer torn between his realisation that the world of the ghetto was a tough one and a desperate one, and a strong sense of hope – a defiance in the face of hardship.

'Concrete Jungle' has one of the best instrumental introductions to a Marley tune. The version that the Wailers sent to Chris Blackwell was starker, and without the wonderful interplay of organ and lead guitar that marks the version we now know as 'Concrete Jungle'. But that sense of searching, that wandering feel of a lament is there in the organ lines and in the tentative way in which the guitar begins to insinuate itself on the ear. Once the laconic lead guitar is added, the feel is rock-centred, but not overwhelmingly so. The kick is on the one, it seems, but once the snare rattles in, we realise that the entire rhythm of the song is hardly rock.

Marley walks into this well made bed with a pained voice – a voice that seems to come from a long way off. But it is an assured voice that is constantly being comforted by the interplay with the backing vocals, which are as complex and central to the meaning of the song as any other part of the tune. Marley is dialoguing with the Wailers. They are not making Marley beautiful or enhancing Marley, as Tosh would say, but are actually communicating with him in a fascinating call and response discourse that achieves both the effect of refrain and counterpoint. So while Marley is declaring, 'Life must be somewhere to be found' the Wailers are adding, 'Out there somewhere for me...'

The lyric is a tightly shaped one, thick with metaphor and personification – a deeply poetic lyric that offers a sense of despair that is unrelenting:

The singer's world is devoid of playful sunlight and everything that is frivolous and hopeful. In this world which darkness dominates, the singer is left wondering where love is. Yet he is hopeful and adamant that there is love somewhere. herein lies Marley's optimism. In this city bereft of light, love, he argues, is lurking somewhere. Marley employs nature's imagery in a song that is about the physical place called the ghetto or the concrete jungle.

In the first lines the voice is that of the lover searching for meaning in a midst of some kind of rejection. But the love is greater than that. The love expands to something more complex – the love that sustains the poor, the love that suggests that the poor can be cared for and can have dignity. The biblical allusions of the second and third lines are not accidental. This is a moment of apocalypse, the moon has disappeared, the curse of day turning to night is upon the singer. Marley would return to this trope in a later tune. In 'Who The Cap Fit' he talks about those 'friends' who abandon you 'if your night should turn to day'. This darkness is at once depression, but it is also a metaphor for the sense of hopelessness that the singer faces. But the fact that he asks 'where is that love to be found?' begins to help us understand that the singer is in search of something. The hopelessness is not total. And to arrive at an answer, he appeals to his listeners and, in typical Marley fashion, he also draws them in to share his bewilderment and pity. How many times does he appeal, 'Won't you help me sing?' ('Redemption Song'), 'Ah wanna know, wanna know, wanna know now?' ('Is This Love?'). And in 'Who The Cap Fit'.

What would appear, therefore, to have been a love song becomes a lament about the ghetto. But these are not in opposition. Marley has understood that the greatest love lyrics are those that are rooted in the realities of his life and the greatest political songs are truly love songs. This Trench Town that has been his home is a place of hard living, hunger, suffering, oppression, persecution – all of these things. And yet, Marley is asserting that there is love somewhere in all of that. That there must be love out there for him and, by extension, for the people on whose behalf he is singing.

But here is what is supremely radical about the song. Marley is not merely lamenting his own life. He is speaking on behalf of others. He knows that the song will connect with some people in a direct way. He understands this like all the other reggae artists of his time. These songs are not just quaint metaphors for the artist, they are also the expression of a griot – a kind of spokesman for the community. By offering the lyric as he does he is not embarking on an anthropological study, but he is offering a way for him to see hope in the midst of abjection and, by extension, a way for his community to see the same hope. Marley expands the application brilliantly in the second verse.

In the second stanza, Marley turns to the language of slavery. He acknowledges that there is no actual slavery now – no chains on his feet. Yet there seems to be a larger enslavement, the enslavement to despair which is offered as a puzzling paradox: no slavery but no happiness; no chains but no freedom. In this condition the comforts of life's happiness and sweet caresses are not available, leaving him to laugh manically and absurdly at his circumstances.

Marley's rhyme scheme is part of the grace of this song. Because of the way the song unfolds rhythmically, his use of internal rhyme becomes part of the wonderful shaping of a line that is filled with a musicality even when spoken. Marley employs the echoing of sounds through assonance and through a play with symmetry and asymmetry of sound. In the first line of the song, the rhyme of the cleverly punned 'on my day today' is typical of a Marley construction. There is an implied comma after 'day' but, even without it, the phrase makes sense and suggests that the absence of sun is not just for today, but for his 'day to day' life.

Later we see the instinctive pattern of pulling assonance into a line to give it strength and a unity of shape that makes it clear that Marley was very interested in offering spoken phrases over a sweet rhythm, but was also much involved in the total fascination with sounds as they played against each other:

A quick technical look at just the first two lines of the verse will tell us a great deal about what Marley is doing as a craftsman. The first part of the first two lines reads an iambic line that collapses quickly into the rest of the phrase, therefore not calling undue attention to the 'around/bound' rhyme. But the shadow of them is partly what makes the lines compact and memorable phrases. As a songwriter, Marley would use half-rhymes and a great deal of alliteration and assonance to establish a musicality in the lines themselves. His rhyming is enhanced by the phrasing that breaks up any inclination towards doggerel.

Marley's sense of history – the shift from slavery to freedom – is emerging in this song. But he sees it as quite ironic. Freedom is a nebulous thing. Despite the absence of the chains of slavery, chains that were discarded over a century before, Marley is aware that he remains a slave in Jamaican society – one of the downtrodden. Yet the metaphor is a classical love song device, the notion of being captivated by love. Then in the third and fourth line, Marley captures a rhyme that is simply sublime. 'Happiness is'/'sweet caress is', then he returns to the wholeness of the 'ground'/'found' construction that nicely unifies the entire song as it returns to the 'around'/'bound' sound of the second verse. There is care in the construction of the song – a concern for formal structure and symmetry. Yet order is broken by the phrasing, for instance, the way his breath works on the last two lines of the verse. The natural breaks are a series of varied markers – from the fluid turn 'Won't someone help me, cause I', which ignores the natural break that is suggested by the syntax – 'won't someone help me / 'Cause I've got to…' etc – and instead goes for a series of stammering phrasings that capture the sense of desperation and need: 'won't someone help me cause I / I've got to pick myself / from off the ground.' And so rather than count syllables, Marley is interested in the melody – its flow, its improvisational nature, its fluid movement and, where necessary, its staccato pulsing.

In the next verse Marley expands the meaning and application of the song. It is his efficiency that is striking here. This Concrete Jungle is a place that evokes the memory of slavery and the history of the slave society. Marley wants to shake that memory, but throughout the song he is acutely aware of its hold on him and those around him. It is in these lyrics that Marley makes his own self-identification with the black race and with the race that was enslaved.

Of course his history means that he would have understood the nature and meaning of the slave society. His mother's relationship and marriage to his father, and the white customs of their district, were typical of the colonial arrangement that seemed unwilling to give up the patterns of slave society despite a hundred years of freedom. For as much as Marley's mother had a love affair with the elder Marley, the societal norms ensured that this affair could not be lived as a normal relationship. The white Marley clan was not going to accept this very black country girl as an in-law. And the elder Marley's arrangement with Cedella's father was a peculiar one that smacked of compromise. She was barely an adult and the man was old enough to be her father. She was an uneducated country girl far outside his status in society. As a companion, she was little more than someone who could cook and clean for him, provide a lively sex life and offer him the kind of care that he deserved as a white man in the district. Self-respect and dignity caused him to do right by her and marry her when she got pregnant, but this was no true marriage. It was an exercise in colonial power – the Jamaican woman as a field of exploit for the white colonial English man. Marley is a product, then, of the complex of colonial society and slave society. He understands this in very acute ways. He knows that, while he carries white blood in him, it is white blood that has somehow come through exploitation and an unbalanced relationship between the poor blacks and the wealthier, albeit pathetic, whites. He therefore has no ground upon which to willingly and honestly self-identity with his white family. They have, quite simply, rejected him.

The rejection leads him to the Concrete Jungle, a place where he experiences the complex ambivalence of being at home and being away. Marley may have been in conflict about Trench Town. He lived there out of necessity, but he would move out of Trench Town whenever he could. For some years, he and Rita would live in a small farmer's shack in St Ann, where Marley would till the land and try to replicate his notion of the true roots existence. He would also spend a year or so away from Trench Town in the US, where his mother had moved to. Eventually, he would, in the early 1970s, leave Trench Town for good, to set up his own community in the uptown area in a fairly sizeable home on Hope Road. Marley would always talk about Trench Town as his place of definition – his home. In the haunting posthumously released lyric 'Trench Town', he wryly and ironically comments: 'They say, "can anything good come out of Trench Town?"' In the song he declares that he is paying tribute to Trench Town, where his music emerges. Yet, tellingly, this revelation about the power of Trench Town comes to him while is out of Trench Town, far enough away to be able to reflect. The wonderful introduction to that song is one of the few clear articulations of landscape that we see in Marley's oeuvre, and it is a powerful one.

He paints a picture of himself lying on one of the massive rocks around which flow the Cane River where Marley used to escape from Trench Town. On these rocks he finds rest and is able to find spiritual sublimation there; seeing visions of the oppression of his people and further, coming to the conviction that their lives should not be a prison. As quoted earlier, Marley regarded the ghetto as a prison – a place of enslavement. Up in the hills by the Cane River he has the freedom to imagine freedom. Reflection, in true lyrical fashion, comes from a place of rest.

What is significant here is the way in which Marley draws Trench Town as something of a prison – a place of suffering that his people must find ways to resist. As with 'Concrete Jungle' the litany of evils of 'Trench Town' are laid out with candour and clear pain. The ghetto is a desolate place where he must struggle to find the bread of life. The weight of the reflection of Trench Town forces Marley to consider the source of this oppression and the silencing that poverty and the abuse of society on the poor can cause.

And then in the final stretch of lyrics and reflections the song returns to what 'they' say. They say that the people from Trench Town are 'the underprivileged people' and in so doing they manage to 'keep [them] in chains'. Marley may have written this song late in the 1970s, long after he had left Trench Town. But it is clear that he really had not left. He understands that he has come from there – this is clear – but he also speaks of himself as being there, as being part of the people from there. His own story of being able to speak, to articulate the truth of the world he grew up in, undermines the notion that these people cannot speak. But Marley, in this same song, manages to offer his own formula for the liberation of his people. It is a formula that is deeply personal and ultimately becomes the central rationale for Marley's political sensibility. In song after song and in interview after interview, Marley makes it clear that music is his hope of healing. He describes himself as a revolutionary who uses music as his weapon. In an interview Rita Marley would describe Marley as a dangerous man who used his guitar as his M16. In 'Trench Town' Marley is explicit, he sings, 'We free the people with music.' He is clearly emphatic, trying, it seems to both declare this truth and bolster his faith in this truth for, earlier in the song, what becomes the assertion quoted above, is in fact couched as a question: 'Can we free the people with music?' In such moments of clear honesty and deep questioning, we begin to understand that Bob Marley's art was devoted to speaking truth as best as he knew it and understood it. Here he asks the question and then later on he declares that it is so – music will free the people.

Marley's uncertainty is understandable. The Trench Town he grew up in would have been much worse by the late 1970s, and yet all the attendant problems of patronage, political exploitation and neglect were still extant. Marley believed that the people could find freedom with music even if the events of the last four years of his life caused him to wonder about what his music was doing.

In an interview, Marley declared, with a force and a sincerity that is striking, that if he was doing nothing for the people – for his people – then his life was also worth nothing. He said, 'den I don't want this life.' Many could have been sceptical about this statement and many perhaps were when they saw the interview. But it is clear to me that Marley was being totally sincere – not just sincere, but was actually speaking out of a heart that had long recognized that his riches, his success and his fame meant little in the face of his sense of mission. He was on a mission. He meant it. His lyrics would testify to that and so would his choice of themes and ideas in his songs. Marley, then, wanted to free the people with music.

Music, he believed, was the cure. In 'Burnin' And Lootin'' Marley plays with the idea of ghetto music as a counter to the evils of drug use.

And in that phrase he introduces the notion that there is a spiritual sensibility that is 'called' the music of the ghetto – a reality that suggests hope and not destruction.

He asks for food so he can grow, food that would allow the Rootsman, the Rasterman, to grow. The food is both literal and metaphorical. The food is bread and wisdom. He then warns the drugs will slow down his people, and in the fourth line of the verse he seems to suggest that drug use is not what he calls ghetto music.

The fourth line is however sweetly multi-faceted. On one level he is suggesting that it is drugs (not marijuana, of course, which was never a drug for Marley) that will slow down those who are seeking to take action, not, as some would like to think, the music of the ghetto. But there is another level at which this line works. Here the idea is that taking drugs and stunting action represents a way of existence that runs counter to the spirit of ghetto music. So such actions are not 'the music of the ghetto'. No, the music of the ghetto is revolutionary but, more importantly, it is a source of salvation and liberation.

In 'Trench Town' and 'Concrete Jungle', Marley is singing about that very power in the music. But he is also seeing Trench Town as more than just a place that has produced these great sounds. He is seeing it as a place where the love of a people can give strength and guarantee that 'they' will have to repay. In Trench Town good things happen – art finds its voice despite the suffering. Marley's sense of the jungle that shaped him is deeply complex because he does not romanticize that world, nor does he want to grant to the world its own limited understanding of what a ghetto is. A ghetto is not merely a news byte – the place of the underprivileged. It is more than that. It is the home of a people who can find a way to speak through art and through their own resilience. 'Concrete Jungle' is an assertion of this truth – this confession of hope in the midst of suffering.

In a more obscure song, 'Music Lesson', which, though produced in the late 1960s, was not actually released until 1985 with significant redubbing and reversioning, Marley and the Wailers sing about the importance of music as being a source of information for history. The lyrics are therefore rooted in the notion of the reggae artist as a teacher.

Burning Spear's declaration, 'we build this city... on reggae music' ('We Build this City'), or Marley singing 'Music, oh, music a de key / Talk to who? / Please talk to me', ('Chant Down Babylon'), all speak about this same powerful role of music. The lyrics, as is typical of so much of the Wailers' work, echoes themes that recur in many other tracks. Here we hear lines that will later be echoed in Peter Tosh's 'Yuh Cyaan Blame The Youth'.

The implication is clear – the music that these artists are producing is the counter-voice, working against the miseducation shaped by the colonial system. The question, of course, is clear: why not teach them about great Africans – great people who look like the people themselves. For Burning Spear the lesson is always to teach the youth about Marcus Garvey and all great men: 'Let's recall great men / Who been fighting for our rights...' ('Great Men'). Marley sees the music as being the path towards such learning – music is the key, and this music emerges out of Trench Town.

It is this same complexity that we see in 'Concrete Jungle'. He actually confronts the jungle and begins a dialogue with the place – a dialogue that is assertive and combative. In many ways he wants something from the place – he virtually taunts the place, trying to answer the series of questions that shape this song. He asks the jungle, 'What you got for me now?' and then later he asks, 'Why won't you let me be, now?'

Like a man who has suffered at the hands of a demanding lover, Marley is now desperate to know whether this Concrete Jungle will offer him anything, any kind of solace for his life. But the question is rhetorical in the sense that he is asking a question for which he already seems to have an answer. The place is not giving. This is why he then demands of the place, 'why won't you let me be, now?' At once we understand how consuming the jungle is – it has a hold on him and it dominates his existence. At the same time, he wants to be done with the place, he wants to be freed from it. Trench Town is the task master, the slave driver. For Marley, there was no difference between the world that he lived in and the world of the slave. The politics of slave society were as real to Marley as anything else. He sang about slavery, the oppression of the slave system, in the present tense. For him, this was not mere history, but a present reality.

In 'Concrete Jungle' he wants to be freed. He makes this plea for his freedom after he has made it clear that his only path to healing is by picking himself up off the ground. He knows he must do this in order to survive and to thrive. It is the antidote to the cynicism that seems to creep into the lyric when he declares that he will be 'always laughing like a clown'. For Marley, this jungle is a place that will drive a person to distraction and turn such a soul into a fool, or worse, an insane person. The laughter is used to block the tears. It is a neurotic act of deception – a way to survive. But Marley also knows that only a clown (ie a fool) would laugh in the face of this suffering.

'Concrete Jungle' introduced a larger audience to the powerful marriage of the personal and the political that was the standard of the Marley song. Marley is vulnerable here and is openly self-identifying with the oppressed. But beyond that Marley was making art out of material that had barely been touched in Caribbean writing. Anthropologists and sociologists had entered that world and sought to give it voice. They failed. Marley gave it voice because it was his own voice. When the audience heard 'Concrete Jungle' they knew they were encountering the real thing – a man who understood the ghetto, who was known for his ghetto credentials, who sometimes glorified the ghetto and used his ghetto power to get his way, but a man who, ultimately, understood that the ghetto was a prison – a place that would continue to trap the poor and the oppressed. Marley's conflicted voice is what makes the song such a powerful one. But there is so much more to the song that takes it out of the specifics of the ghetto and the politics of poverty in Jamaica. This wider truth is found in the self-assertion that is the point of hope for the song. It is not Jah who will release him from the bondage of Trench Town; it is his own strength, his willingness to pick himself up from the ground, that will bring any possibility of hope. This is not a reactionary statement about pulling oneself up by one's own bootstrap, but a song rooted in the tough guy idiom – the guy who will take a licking and bounce right back.

The song is followed by 'Slave Driver', which is really the title track for the album as the title is derived from the second line of this song. In 'Slave Driver' Marley continues the remarkable business of making historical matters as relevant to the current time as they can be. Here, he speaks with the same incendiary intensity that he will show in an even greater way in the *Burnin'* and *Natty Dread* albums. By the time *Catch A Fire* comes out, these wailers are quite clear about their religious and political beliefs. In 'Slave Driver' Marley reveals the lessons that he has learned about the history of slavery and explores how this history shapes the life of a ghetto youth in Jamaica. The Rastafarian teachings are now central to the world view of Marley and the Wailers and their education at the feet of men like Mortimer Planno has been thorough.

In a society that for years had avoided teaching anything but European and British history in school, and had found sophisticated ways to make euphemisms of the period of slavery, Marley and the Wailers were convinced of their mission to educate through music. They were part of a fraternity of singers who had been influenced by the Civil Rights Movement in the US, the Black Panther Movement and the work of Marcus Garvey. In Jamaica they would have felt the reverberations of the work of Walter Rodney, a young Guyanese intellectual who, while teaching in Jamaica, would spend a great deal of time reasoning with the poor and the Rastas in the slums of Kingston about the issues of history and the position of blacks in that history. It was Rodney who would write the critical book *How Europe Underdeveloped Africa*, and it was his expulsion from Jamaica in the late 1960s that led to an explosive street riot in Kingston, which resulted in several deaths and a great deal of collateral damage. The Wailers would have been part of the culture of consciousness raising that became characteristic of that period, and the ideas that were swirling around in the US and the UK would have found their way into these ghetto streets through the music.

The Wailers had covered, with 'the Upsetter' Lee 'Scratch' Perry, songs by Civil Rights activist singers like Richie Havens, Curtis Mayfield and James Brown. In the last two years of the 1960s, the Wailers recorded 'Black Progress', in which they sampled James Brown's chant, 'Say it loud, I'm black and I'm proud'. And there were other trends in Jamaica that pointed to a gradual shift in the way that race and identity was being viewed by the people.

Haile Selassie's visit to Jamaica marked a tacit acknowledgement by the government authorities that black identity and a sense of African connectedness was shaping the mindset of the Jamaican people. The University of the West Indies had carried out at least one important study in 1961, conducted by two of its most promising young scholars, Rex Nettleford and J.A.G. Smith, of the Rastafarian community in Kingston. The government had already been forced to deal with a series of petitions from the Rasta community that demanded that Rastas be repatriated to Ethiopia. The government had not agreed to this, but the leaders did make a point of requesting that Selassie comment on this matter during his visit. Selassie said he would welcome hardworking Jamaicans interested in coming to build the nation. While a number of Rastas did travel to Africa and settle there – what was important about these developments was that there was a growing consciousness of the idea of Africa as the ancestral home for most Jamaicans. In a society that had systematically denied or sought to downplay the connection, this acknowledgement was a critical one and spoke volumes about the way people were thinking in Jamaica during the late 1960s.

By the time Michael Manley rose to prominence in the early 1970s and rode on his popularity to win a hard-fought election in 1972, he had long understood that employing a populist platform that openly celebrated the African reality of Jamaican society would be a crucial political strategy for success. He used, with poetic and rhetorical force, the language of liberation and a sophisticated anti-colonialist discourse that essentially declared that it was the time for the black man now. So effective was Manley's performance that the fact that he was a white Jamaican with clear connections to the élite seemed to be subsumed by his ability to speak the language of the people. Manley's great act of political genius was to use a wooden staff as his multi-purpose personal symbol. It was his rod of correction, which would whip the opposition and keep them in line. It was his staff to guide the wayward sheep – the people. It was his sceptre of authority and symbol of his right to coronation. It was an anointed staff of miracles and blessing that would achieve the parting of the Red Sea and the miracles of healing and transformation associated with the Moses narrative. It was his phallus of power – a part of the sexual dynamic that shaped his appeal. Finally, and most importantly, this was no ordinary staff. This was a staff, he claimed, that had been given to him by Haile Selassie himself when Manley had visited him in Ethiopia to convince him to come to Jamaica for a state visit. Manley would wield this staff, which he dubbed 'the Rod of Correction', throughout the 1972 elections.

Manley was also careful to do a number of other things that reveal a great deal about the state of the nation at the time. He, already three times married and divorced, began to have a fairly open affair with a black, afro-haired woman, Beverly Anderson, who was a popular radio host with an unassailable connection to the reggae world. She had worked hard to promote the music of the Wailers on the radio and was the person who managed to open doors into the street culture of Jamaica for Manley. She played a major role in forming the reggae tour that followed Manley around the country during his campaign in 1972. Artists like Jimmy Cliff, Toots and the Maytals and the Wailers joined this tour and essentially served as the warm-up acts for Manley. On the radio, popular song stylist Delroy Wilson's 'Better Must Come' became the official song of the People's National Party and the theme of the campaign. Manley learned to quote it during his notoriously charismatic turns on the stump. Beverly Anderson, who would later become Manley's wife and the First Lady of the island, had also worked with Perry Henzel on the making of the film *The Harder They Come* and had a small part in that film. Her links with the reggae world and the working-class world gave Manley the kind of legitimacy that he needed. More importantly, it was clear that there was a growing awareness, especially through reggae, of the politics of race and its place in the Jamaican society. The assumption that blackness was not something to be celebrated was now being usurped by a strong black sensibility.

Marley and the Wailers understood themselves to be a part of this struggle. They also realised that by turning to Rastafarianism, they were in fact placing themselves outside the main stream of Jamaican society and in many ways were asserting their true rude boy credentials. But in their embrace of Rastafarianism they were also offering a way to challenge not only the religious mores of the society, which were rooted in the idea of Eurocentric privilege, but also the language and art of the society by introducing a world view that emerged out of the working people. They were aware of what they were doing and its significance. They had arrived at this place after much growth and change. Their music would reflect this and would come to lead much of what was happening in the music scene in Jamaica.

They had good leaders for this. The Skatalites of the 1960s had led the way by creating compositions whose titles showed that the sense of Africa and Africanness was becoming central to the psyche of the people. The Skatelites had been working with such Rasta philosophers as Count Ossie and Mortimer Planno who became the spiritual gurus of the young musicians working in Kingston's ghettos at the time.

So, the strong political statement that opens *Catch A Fire* is hardly a new development for the Wailers. It is part of a process of maturation that had led them to this place. One senses that after trying so hard to break into the US market with the JAD record outfit by trying to write R&B love songs and tunes that were seeking to imitate the American style of arrangement, the Wailers, when faced with the chance given by Chris Blackwell to simply record an album, decided to do what was most important to them. The cuts they sent Blackwell included two other tracks that he eventually eliminated. One was a song of brotherly unity and one of those intimate looks at Marley's take on motherhood and the way that the relationship of family becomes a metaphor for a wide range of love relationships. 'High Tide Or Low Tide' is not, strictly speaking, a love song but it offers a rich expression of love between friends that is quite remarkable. The other song 'All Day All Night' is a straight ahead love song full of Marley's penchant for sexual innuendo. A lively and danceable track, it may have been omitted by Blackwell because its themes, even if not its tone, were similar to 'Stir It Up'. And where 'Stir It Up' offered a more conventional songwriting style, with metaphor-driven images and a verse/chorus pattern, 'All Day All Night' is largely repetitious lyrically, even if it is far more musically sophisticated than 'Stir It Up'.

'Stir It Up' is built around a metaphor that is so firmly grounded in the Jamaican world that it makes the song a truly Jamaican love song.

When writing this song, Marley was at the height of his love-song writing ability and, by then, he had put together a quite remarkable body of love songs that remain wonderful studies in the imagination of a young lover. Marley would return to the love song some years later when he recorded *Kaya* and *Exodus*. But the Marley in those later songs was a different man – a more mature man and a man whose engagement with the world and women was now seasoned and marked by a stronger devotion to his faith. Marley's persona in his early love songs was almost always that of a man who was trying to win the affection of a woman who was decidedly hard to win. If this was not the scenario used, it would almost always be the other standard scenario: Marley reproaching a woman for having abandoned him for someone else. The third category of Marley love song was the decidedly sexual song – the song of seduction that relished the idea of sex and found joy in telling stories about the sweetness of sex. However, Marley's love songs were being written at a time when word play and euphemism were important ways to construct tunes of seduction. There were songwriters of that period who wrote songs of overt sexual content, but Marley seemed to prefer songs that allowed sexual innuendo to guide the seduction process. Marley's lover was always alone, always desperate, always in earnest and always trying to show the woman that she is the only one, the special one. His songs would unfold as stories – couples with a history, a man who has been trying for years to win the affection of a woman, a man who has just been told by his woman that she is leaving him.

The women in his songs were never distinct individuals. They were almost always generic figures. After all, the songs were not really about them. A case can be made for saying that Marley's love songs revealed a consistent view that he had of women: they were lovely, they were objects of adoration and sexual attraction and they were creatures who could hurt him. More than that, Marley's love songs revealed his own sense of vulnerability and his sense of being a man alone in a hostile world. Marley's standard approach to winning a woman's attention was to plead for some 'sympathy'. In song after song, this word would arise. The woman's failure to respond amounted to an act of cruelty that would cause the singer to complain and, best of all, weep.

However, Marley was not incapable of retribution in the area of love. In 'It Hurts To Be Alone', Marley seems to relish the pain that the woman who has hurt him will face with the man she has gone to.

If he is not gloating in the promise that her need over will break her heart and cause tears that will teach her how it 'hurts to be alone'. This is the hurt he has felt at her hands. In "Cry To Me", the promise is the same: she will go through the heartache and pain, and she will shed tears because of her cheating. Then in "Stand Alone", there is an edge of anger and impatience. Marleys women tend to abandon true love for false love and in the process come to suffer pain and regret. Marley's persona relishes the opportunity to say "I told you so", but it does not seem to assuage the hurt. He is haunted by memories of the hours and days he has committed to these relationships. They are wasted days, he sings. Like a man who has developed his standard, tried and proven pick-up lines over the course of many years, Marley developed his own favourite entry into a love song. In song after song he would tell the woman that he has been waiting for her, waiting to say something to her, waiting for a chance to speak to her, simply just waiting and watching. In 'Nice Time' he reminds the woman, 'Long time we nuh have no nice time / Do you, do you, do you, think about that?' In 'Touch Me' he sings of a woman who he sees walking past his way again – she has been doing this for a while and he is now appealing to her to touch him. In 'I'm Still Waiting' he complains about his feet hurting from waiting at her door. In a fairly obscure duet with Marcia Griffith recorded at Studio One, Marley pleads, 'Oh my darling, I was so lonely / Searching for you and for you only', and in 'Lonesome Feeling' the lover tries to flee but must return: 'Tried to run away / But the road leads back to you / Tried to forget you / But the memories linger on…'. He would return to this theme of waiting in the love songs on *Exodus* and *Kaya* – it is, quite simply, a Marley trope. He uses it to full effect in 'Stir It Up'. But he also engages in yet another Marley theme, that of the pleasures of sex.

Many of Marley's love songs are thick with such sexual longing. This is particularly true of the songs produced with Perry during the Upsetter days. In 'Guava Jelly' he asks the woman to 'rub on [his belly] like guava jelly', which is as sweet and textured an image as one could want. In

'Rock My Boat' he asks his woman to 'keep it stiff' and to let him rock her. In 'Lick Samba', the dance tune creates the mood of a rub-a-dub dance as he goads the woman to move her body in the appropriate manner: 'Bring it up a licky one time. Right here! / I'll set a little flame/... morning time, noon or night.' In 'Do It Twice' there is no mistaking what he wants to do twice, 'Baby you so nice, / I like to do the same thing twice'; while in 'No Water' Marley declares, prefiguring Gregory Isaacs now classic 'Night Nurse', 'No water can quench this thirst / I'm in bed send me a nurse ...'

The third feature of Marley's love songs is his appeal to nature and everyday detail of Jamaican life. The moon features in a number of songs. It appears as one of Marley's standard mood setting images. The moon is often pale, as in 'How Many' when he sees her 'walking through the pale moonlight', a line that is repeated almost exactly in 'Baby We've Got A Date'. In a later song, 'Turn Your Lights Down Low' he encourages his lover to open her curtains so 'Jah moon' can come shining in. In 'Mellow Mood' he equates his love to the quiet night that creeps into his lover's room. In other songs he treats a rural landscape as a fitting place for love. This is especially true in 'Do It Twice' in which he pleads that he needs some company in the woods where he lives alone.

These three elements come together in wonderful fusion in 'Stir It Up'. Marley begins with his trademark narrative: of a man who has been waiting to get the attention of a woman who has long been on his mind. Now that he has her with him, he then proceeds to seduce.

The chorus employs the image of cooking to capture the circular motion of love making. But there is also the element of seduction. Marley wants to stir up trouble and a great deal else with the lover. The image is earthy and grounded in everyday experience. This becomes even clearer in the second verse which makes use of a wickedly naughty pun that would easily be lost to a non-Jamaican audience.

The metaphor of cooking is fully exploited here. The image is of a couple cooking a meal in a pot in the yard. This is not a well equipped kitchen with a gas stove. Instead it is a humble outdoor kitchen where a fire is glowing beneath a single pot that is cooking a meal for the man and his lover. The man's role is to keep the fire alive, and the woman's role is to make sure that the food is properly cooked. This alone would make the sexual dimensions quite appetising, but Marley also introduces a Jamaicanism that makes the song quite explicit to a Jamaican audience. In Jamaica, the penis is often referred to as the 'hood' or, alternatively, as the 'wood'. When he offers to push the wood his intentions are not entirely culinary. Marley then returns to an old plea – one of the oldest in popular love songs – thirst. Her love will quench his desire and help cool his ardour.

Marley stays consistent with the extended metaphor all the way to the end. He achieves this in a manner that makes it almost impossible to accuse him of using sexually explicit language without admitting your own inappropriate thoughts. He does something similar with the metaphor of dancing in 'Baby We've Got A Date'. In this song, the sexual beckoning comes in the repetitive rocking of the music itself, matching in intensity the chant of the Wailers as they sing the chorus. The singer remains somewhat vulnerable. He is not sure if the woman will show up. His song, like 'Stir It Up', is really an appeal. It is important that this appeal remains masked by the promise of a good time at a party. It is a date and he will meet her at a proper time. He then prepares her for what they will be doing on their date. Dancing is the functioning metaphor. It is one that Marley makes rich use of in many earlier songs. In 'Mellow Mood' he promises to play her 'favourite song' so that they can 'rock it all night long'; in 'Lick Samba' he calls his woman to dance the new dance as a sexual act. In 'Rocking Steady' he muses, 'When first I heard rock steady / Thrill me to the bone / When I talk bout rocking steady / You need a baby for your own', later warning his woman that 'she better be ready'. Here he promises her that they will 'rock it' all night. But Marley also includes a more romantic element to the song. It arrives in a bridge in half time – the equivalent of full strings in the reggae song.

These two songs, 'Stir It Up', and 'Rock It Baby', would represent Marley's farewell to the love song for a long time. It is significant that this constituted a major change in his output. The change, of course, coincided with his stronger embrace of Rastafarianism. But we also know that the shift was not caused by a reduced interest in women on Marley's part. Indeed, his prolific collecting of women would pick up in intensity during the 1970s. Perhaps it was this fact that may have led to Marley no longer needing to write songs about hurt and loss. By looking at the love songs of Marley's teens and early 20s, it would appear that he fell in love again and again and found himself constantly trying to convince women of his love for them. The same energy, almost hunger, that marked these love songs would seem to parallel Marley's desire to make it in the music business, and his manic expressions of desire and the need to be loved reflected his basic hunger for success.

Catch A Fire was slow to win an audience. The album itself was quite a remarkable one because it was really the first of its kind. By the time it was released in the UK in 1972, Lee Perry had orchestrated something of a coup by releasing a Wailers LP called *African Herbsman* at the same time. The latter was more successful in winning the attention of the roots reggae crowd in the UK. *Catch A Fire* was seen by some as a watering down of the Wailers' sound. But this may not have been why *African Herbsman* held greater appeal. The answer may lie in the fact that the Upsetter production had far more tracks, and these tracks reflected the spirit of innovation and daring that permeated the recording sessions with Perry. There were far more love songs on that album, and those songs, cleverly witty and full of Marley's vulnerable and longing human side, would have given listeners a better sense of his range and personality than the more deliberate selections on *Catch A Fire*. As a production, Perry's album was more cohesive in style. If the selections were eclectic, that eclecticism became its distinction and, ultimately, its identity. Marley did not dominate that album – Perry's producing did.

Catch A Fire, however, gave Marley a chance to begin to formulate the style and themes that he would pursue in his later work. In that regard, one of the more important songs to emerge from *Catch A Fire* is 'Slave Driver', which grows out of the history of Jamaican society and out of the streets of Kingston in 1972. The song leaps out at you with the wailing announcement that the tables have been turned on the slave driver and his descendants, and that a rebel spirit has emerged to burn down the domination of the 'slave driver'.

The spirit of the early 1970s and the old pattern of seeing the black person as less than the white or the brown is announced in the song.

There is a bold declaration of war here – a statement that the inevitable transformation of the cultural landscape has taken place. What Marley does by addressing the slave driver is to suggest that there is a direct lineage between the slave system that ended officially in Jamaica in 1838 and the system of patronage and oppression that still operated in Jamaica in 1972, which was more than a century later. More importantly, the song declares a radical shift that places the oppressor at the mercy of the oppressed. The burning of cane fields was one of the signal actions carried out by slaves during their many rebellions in Jamaica. Here the fate of the slave driver is not a good one. By shifting the race of God, by declaring Ethiopia to be the promised land and by creating an art that made use of the Jamaican language, a turning of the cultural tables has taken place and this is the crux of what Marley is declaring in the song.

Marley shows the depths of his songwriting skills when he enters the verse of the song. In his inimitable manner of contracting a tremendous amount of history into a compact and emotionally resonant few lines, he also displays the force of his lyric writing. In this verse, he declares that remembering slavery is an important act that chills his blood towards cold-blooded anger and to fear or inertia. The source of his anger is the memory of the middle passage.

The true impact of slavery is, for Marley, less a physical one, than a spiritual one. The brutalizing of the soul is the deepest tragedy of slavery, and it is a pain that the singer experiences viscerally at the trigger of the sound of a whip. The cold blood is at once a fearful reaction and a stoning of the emotions to take action. The radical action suggested in the opening declaration is part of the political aggression that had come to characterize these Wailers songs. But while the song appears to be a recollection of the hardships of slavery, Marley brings the theme of oppression to bear on contemporary Jamaica. As in 'Concrete Jungle' he challenges the general notion that slavery ended in 1838. The new slavery is poverty, illiteracy and the economic juggernaught working to exploit the poor.

The 'history' that suggests that slavery has ended is essentially a failure of education. The term 'illiteracy' is directly synonymous with a lack of education in Jamaican society at a time when an intense literacy campaign was being undertaken on the island. Marley is calling into question the educational system that fails to recognize that the legacy of slavery is still with the descendants of the slave system. The new slavery, of course, is poverty and this poverty is shaped by a social contract that privileges the inanimate object – the machine – over the human being. Marley is, of course, punning on the idea of the money machine that drives the world that has oppressed the poor. There are echoes of this pattern of connecting the history of slavery with the current realities of the oppressed in so many classic Marley songs including, 'I Shot The Sheriff', 'Babylon System', 'Crazy Baldheads' and, most famously, 'Redemption Song'. For the Wailers there seems to be a strange time warp that contracts the 150 years between the end of slavery and the 1970s. But for Marley the interim is packed full of examples that reveal that the slave system never actually ended. In his songs he would acknowledge the struggle of important figures like Paul Bogle in the 1860s and Marcus Garvey in the 1930s as being part of a long line of sufferahs who have struggled through the 'slave system' that is at the heart of each of these songs.

On *Catch A Fire* the other two clearly political songs belong to Peter Tosh. While these are fascinating examples of Tosh's songwriting in their own right, I will only briefly comment on them here as part of the environmental and social influences that helped to shape Marley's own work. Marley's collaboration with Peter Tosh and Bunny Wailer was decidedly symbiotic; the three fed off of each other's individual ideas and moods. Tosh tended to have a fairly sardonic approach to the love song, while his political songs were rich in the politics of slavery and black history. Tosh sought to teach others through his music and, from as early as I can tell, he also positioned himself as a student of black history.

There was in Tosh something of the tough guy whose boasts and daring and combative stance would never leave him. Where Marley enjoyed writing love songs and felt that love songs would be important in 'breaking' the group, Tosh remained devoted to the political song. Bunny Wailer's songwriting often involved a strong gospel quality, making well shaped hymns that followed a fairly melodic musical style. This is not to suggest that Tosh and Wailer did not write love songs. They did, but there is no question that Marley was the most prolific love song writer. Both Peter Tosh and Bunny Wailer embraced Rastafarianism before Marley did, and it is clear that they were quite influential in shaping Marley's own spiritual life.

'400 Years' picks up on the exploration of slavery and argues that the system of colonialism and its attendant machinery of subjugation has been targeted at the black man. '400 Years' is a youth anthem and is part of a series of songs by Tosh that advocate the rights of the youth. The 'same philosophy' is still operating after 400 years. For Tosh, the people as a whole have somehow come to accept this philosophy and so are themselves unwitting victims of a system of oppression. But Tosh will not simply acknowledge the problem. He embarks on a rallying cry to the listener to join him in fighting the battle against the 400 years of oppression.

'Stop That Train' is, perhaps, one of the most revealing songs on the album because of its open vulnerability and the quietly stated plea for aid. It borrows heavily from the blues lyrics of the Deep South and Chicago. The train is a vehicle of escape – of flight in America, but hardly so in Jamaica. Yet so many blues songs explore the idea of the train as a means of escape from the Jim Crow South so that Tosh, who was clearly heavily influenced by gospel and soul, felt it was quite natural to draw on that metaphor. Of course the train is more than just a vehicle of temporal escape. In songs like 'This Train' – a latter-day negro spiritual, the train represents the vehicle that will take the saved to a land of milk and honey.

During their ska/rock steady days, the Wailers would cover this spiritual, perhaps basing theirs on the rendering of it that was done by Richie Havens. In 'Stop That Train' there is a sense that the persona – the speaker – is trying to leave, to escape to another place. These all seem like the perfect elements of a love song, and there is a sense in which Tosh employs a love song tone and melody in the piece. The plea, the sense of despair and the acknowledgement of loneliness all point to the conventional themes of a love song. But it is clear that Tosh is offering something much more complex than that. His loneliness – his position as a man who has felt abandoned and alone – is a powerful idea that he develops within the song. He is lonely, however, because people have failed to understand what he has tried to teach them. There is a sense of mission contained in the persona – a mission to help his people, to teach them the truth. But they somehow abandon him and the song is about the desire to escape from the burden of trying to teach them all over again. Yet the despair is also tempered by an edgy hint of a larger apocalypse that will come, 'said it won't be too long, whether I'm right or wrong.'

But where Marley always finds a point of hope in his songs, Tosh, at least in 'Stop That Train', offers a blues posture – a song of seeming despair that becomes a statement of hope by its mere existence. And for us to understand the possibility of hope in Tosh, we must understand the function of the blues as a vehicle for expiation and a channel for the expression of pain and hardship through the formation of song, which in itself becomes a radical act. Tosh expresses the hardships in both '400 Years' and 'Stop That Train'. But in the latter he does not offer hope, does not offer action – he merely states the truth about the situation. And he does it through lamentation, which is contradicted by the danceability of the song. But the lamentation and quality of despair is unmistakable. 'Stop That Train' ends with an observation of the hardship faced by the poor – their desperation and the fact that there seems to be no easing of the pain. People are scattered, misdirected, many are living successfully, but most, he observes, are struggling and starving. It is a tragic hopelessness that dominates.

'400 Years', however, is action-driven and pushes for a communal response to the hardships of slavery and poverty, assuming the role of a leader who will not accept the position of saviour but who will happily wear the mantle of prophet and guide. Tosh calls the people to 'make a move'. While he can't save the youth, (being a mere mortal), he can point them to hope and possibility.

The promised land, the 'land of liberty', is the hope and Tosh is commanding the people to turn from a life of pain and suffering and enter a land of hope and possibility. But the call is not purely for a metaphorical promised land, but an actual land. Always behind the lyrics of Marley and the Wailers was the hope of repatriation to Africa.

In 'No More Trouble', Marley penned another of his classic anthems based on the uncanny use of repetition. The verse sections of the song are quite tightly written with slight repetitions and echoes that ensure that the chant that wails through the song remains locked in the imagination. This is a song of peace and it offers the idea that 'what we need is love' – the pragmatism of this statement is clear throughout the song. Marley manages in short sparks to shape what become proverbial rhymes of tightly wrought bites of wisdom.

Emerging out of a culture where violent action was quite commonplace, the call for peace is very much rooted in the tradition of anti-rudie songs that Marley would produce in the 1960s. Where 'Simmer Down' offered a whimsical warning mixed with a rude boy threat, 'No More Trouble' seems to extend beyond the confines of the ghetto to establish a philosophy of geo-politics that allows the song to be perfectly suited as a performance companion for the later song 'War' in his live recordings. In it the singer declares that love will 'guide to protect'. Love will allow those in power to be merciful and those who are strong to be kind to the weak.

Marley's call for love is one that he would repeat in many songs after this one. His call for love would become increasingly rooted in the idea of Jah's love, rather than the more generic love of 'No More Trouble'. Yet in this song, as with the politically charged songs of *Catch A Fire*, the construction of Babylon was far less defined than it would become in *Natty Dread*, *Rastaman Vibration* and especially in *Survival*. Marley would work on giving definition to Babylon with each album.

Marley's own vision is quite clear in similar political songs, but it is obvious that his lyrical intentions had been altered greatly by the work of Lee 'Scratch' Perry. Two songs on the album, 'Midnight Ravers' and 'Kinky Reggae', have that whimsical quality of mystery and strangeness that was central to the spirit of the Upsetter period. 'Midnight Ravers' is a surreal walk into the nightmare of the last days – as if the singer has walked into a world of debauchery and strange ways. He is disturbed by what he sees and yet he becomes a part of that world. Yet the apocalyptic vision dominating the second part of the song points to the Rastafarian mysticism that was driving much of what Perry and Marley were concocting in the studio during those years. The song begins with a vision of the world of the late 1960s where all the 'normal' assumptions about life, the things that bring security, have been transformed into a weird place where gender seems to have become non-existent. As a statement about Babylon, this image reflects what Rastafarians would call an absolute abomination.

The world described is seen as a pollution of what should be normal. Apart from the gender-bending dress (and the attendant role confusion implied in this), these people are confused and though they have problems, they seem to have no solutions to these problems. This is a Rasta attack on the 'soul-man' patterns of the late 1960s and early 1970s that would explode into the eccentric fashions that would dominate the rest of the 1970s. Marley calls these people 'midnight ravers' – they are party people and they live a life of drugs and psychedelic reverie.

Yet if the singer seems to be assured in his self-righteousness in the opening verse, it becomes obvious to us in the chorus that he is anxious about what this world of sin can do to him. He pleads that he not be 'let down'. He does not want to be sucked into this world. Like a panicked pilgrim staring into the abyss, he pleads to be saved from this madness. It is out of this fear that the next verse emerges. Here the vision of the end times arrives like a warning.

The vision of the ten thousand riders recalls the arrival of the angels of God come to do battle against Babylon. No doubt the language is influenced by the *Book of Revelation*, but it becomes a means of mastery to create the apocalyptic in the contemporary moment. But this reading is not sustained by the rest of the verse. The chariot riders suggests a host of bike riders arriving at the grand rave. In the late 1960s, the vehicle of preference was the cheap and sturdy S90 motorbike. Armies of gunmen would stream to dance on these bikes – horsemen on chariots and not horses. That their faces are covered speaks of the clandestine nature of their intentions. The party is becoming increasingly attractive to the singer, who sees these riders as part of a 'musical stampede'. Marley is drawing freely on a range of images to create this dreamlike picture. It is spoken like the biblical revelation by John and one is tempted to interpret these with the same care for detail as good believers do when reading the Book of Revelations. The midnight ravers are a nightmarish troop that carry the values of a world going further and further into sin. They are 'swingers' and cross-dressers – all abominations to the Rastafarian. It is therefore fascinating when, in the final verse, we note that the singer has somehow become drawn into this world. He is now a victim of the horrors of this culture and his woman has fallen prey to their ways. In typical Wailers fashion, the woman becomes the first to fall into this sinful life. The verse singles out the woman whose mind is 'confused with confusion'. But in this verse, as if led astray by his woman, he becomes a 'night-life raver', as well.

Once he, too, becomes a 'night-life raver' he has fallen into the new life. He has enough energy to appeal to the world to rescue him from this world. The problems that he has faced in the world have no solution. With his woman gone, he is trapped by the world that he knows is a place of debauchery and sin. The curious thing about this song is that Marley never resolves the dilemma of the singer. There is no appeal to Jah to bring salvation or judgment on the 'ravers'. Instead, the song ends like a cry from the depths of hell – a man caught in the party spirit crying to be brought out of the hell that he has described.

As puzzling as this tune is, there is something appealing about Marley's willingness to experiment with the symbols in the song, and more importantly, his unwillingness to force an easy ending to the song. The surrealism of the images would return in some of the songs he wrote in the late 1970s. If 'Midnight Ravers' seems to present an ambivalent take on the world of Babylon, 'Kinky Reggae' seems to more gladly relish the odd world of reggae. 'Kinky Reggae' is set, at least in part, in London. One imagines that it is the London setting that allows us to read the song as a gleeful satirical commentary on the strangeness of 'foreign'. Yet in both songs, the singer is not comfortable with the world he is encountering and feels a strong need to take flight. In 'Kinky Reggae' he determines that he won't join the fun because he is not planning to stay in this 'kinky part of town'. In the song we meet an intriguing cast of characters, from Miss Brown with her 'brown sugar' to Marcus with his 'candy tar'. As in 'Midnight Ravers', the singer is trying to get away from a great temptation.

The word 'kinky' when used in Jamaican does not immediately evoke ideas of sexual oddness and experimentation. A 'kinky' person is someone who is insane, strange, different. The sexual dimension is only secondary and not immediately implied. 'Kinky Reggae', then, is reggae that is slightly off-kilter and strange. In that sense the song is actually a celebration of the off-the-wall elements that can emerge in reggae. Some critics of 'Kinky Reggae' have simply accepted that the song is about a man trying to buy ganja in the middle of London. Because there has always existed a coded language for weed trading, it is quite possible that the song is indeed about efforts to buy weed in a place hostile to such sales. Nonetheless, there is a sexual element to the song that is suggested by the lyrics. Miss Brown, one imagines, is at the very least a woman with a sweet sexual lure. The brown sugar on her 'boogu-woogu' suggests that her sexual abilities are significant; significant enough, in fact, to tempt the singer to think about sticking around to 'join the fun'. But Miss Brown is likely to be a prostitute or a woman whose sexual talents are not entirely on the up and up. A young man, heeding the Proverbs of Solomon, recognizes that he must flee the woman who appeals to him from the streets. The narrative then continues when he heads to Piccadilly Circus where the encounter with Marcus suggests something sexual and yet hints at drug use. It is hard not to read phallic connotations into the the 'chocolate bar' and in the cry of 'nice one'. Yet the 'candy tar' seems to be referring to some sexual aid – perhaps a topical ointment that will increase sexual performance. Beyond that some have read the lines as referring to drugs. Regardless of what is the accurate reading, it is clear that the lure is significant, and that the singer realises that he must flee from these temptations. As he flees, however, we can hear Marcus and his chorus saying, 'nice one, nice one', but the singer will not pay for any of it – he must run from this 'kinky' part of town.

Of course, the singer's ability to flee is not entirely triumphant. The line 'But I had to hit and run' is filled with ambiguities. On one hand there is the suggestion that he had to leave immediately after his arrival (hitting), while we are almost tempted to see him at least tasting the delicacies offered by Miss Brown and Marcus – the word 'hit' having clear sexual and drug connotations – before determining that this cannot be a habit. The playfulness of the song is part of what Rita Marley said Lee 'Stretch' Perry brought into Marley's life. Marley's playfulness would continue, not so much in adventures into morally ambivalent songs, but in the application of Perry's inimitable ability to use word play to produce sharp commentary on the ways of his enemies. No doubt, many will continue to debate what exactly the candy tar all over Marcus's chocolate bar might be. Some have suggested that in both 'Midnight Ravers' and 'Kinky Reggae' Marley makes his only statements about homosexuality, which Rastafarians see as abhorrent. There is, however, not enough evidence to make that a definitive reading.

What is definitive is that Marley's vision of Babylon included everything that seemed to go against what he saw as the natural order of things. 'Kinky Reggae' and 'Midnight Ravers' paint a picture of a fallen world, but an alluring world, and the singer who stands in the middle of this world is vulnerable, capable of being tempted. He flees the sin, but he only barely gets away. Marley would never allow himself to seem so seduced by sin in any of his other songs. The Marley in *Catch A Fire* is the artist as a young man who is working his way through the complexities of his sexuality and his religious beliefs, before arriving at what would become his assured voice.

In the year following the release of *Catch A Fire*, the Wailers found security in the knowledge that they had a solid international record deal and that they had someone who would work with them for the next few albums until something significant happened with their music. While the record sales for *Catch A Fire* were modest at first, the band was well received as they toured the UK.

Bunny Wailer stopped being a touring member of the band after the UK tour and the Wailers would tour the US in 1973 without him. Joe Higgs, the Wailers' mentor from the Trench Town days, filled in for Bunny. The tour was gruelling and critical because it represented the first time a reggae band was touring the US. By this time, Bob Marley was in full command of the band and deeply connected with Chris Blackwell and a close circle of friends.

While in Jamaica, Marley was working hard in the studio, developing a lasting friendship with Alan 'Skill' Cole whose influence on Marley's Rastafarian sensibilities would be significant. Marley was no longer living in Trench Town, but was spending time in Blackwell's house on Hope

Road, in Bull Bay, a seaside village a few miles east of Kingston, and in Nine Miles, St Ann, where his family lived. Marley could now afford to write songs and to work in his usual manner, building songs with his guitar in the company of his closest friends. Marley was also becoming more engaged in Rastafarianism, finally allowing his hair to grow into locks once and for all. At the same time, Marley's drive and ambition were now at their most intense.

There was good critical reception for the new album and a buzz was developing around the lead singer. *Catch A Fire* forced the rock world to take reggae seriously for the first time. It was not novelty music but music that had something to say, even if much of what it was saying was not easily understood at first. But Marley's performances were compelling and gradually writers wanted to know more about him, about the Wailers and about the mystery surrounding their ideas.

Burnin' was released in 1973, which was just a year after *Catch A Fire*. It included songs by Bunny and Peter, but it was totally dominated by Bob Marley's vision and ideas. As on *Catch A Fire*, the Wailers combined old songs with some new tunes and the contrast was stark. Marley's new songs, 'Get Up Stand Up', 'Burnin' And Lootin'', 'I Shot The Sheriff' and 'Rastaman Chant' represented the new direction of the Wailers. The older songs were gems from an earlier time – 'Small Axe', 'Duppy Conqueror' and 'Put It On' – but they were not as confrontational and aggressive as the new material was. Their reach was rooted in the Jamaican landscape and in the internal affairs of artists working in Kingston. The material supplied by Bunny Wailer and Peter Tosh was decidedly more subdued and devoted to themes of unity and love – themes that were not especially interesting to Bob Marley at that time. The differences between these songs would make *Burnin'* a mixed bag of an album, and offered clear evidence that the band was definitely beginning to move apart.

There are many who still regard the work that the Wailers did together as the best of Bob Marley's material. It is the kind of debate that tends to surround every artist. Bob Dylan, The Beatles, Paul Simon, Sting and Elvis Presley, among so many others, all have fans who have divided their loyalties between the early years and the later years. In some instances, there is truth to the claim that some of the early work was the best they ever did. In other instances, however, it is clear that these artists continued to develop and grow in their artistic skill and in their ways of viewing the world. I earnestly believe that Bob Marley is one artist that falls into the latter category.

The period with the original Wailers that culminated in *Burnin'* was a distinct period in Marley's own development, in which he took on musical challenges that reflected his growth as a man in Jamaica. With the help of the other original Wailers, he found a way out of those challenges. As he matured, he was again faced with new personal and musical challenges. His work would expand with these – and this made him into an artist that had a willingness to grow, to experiment and to dig deeply into experience to create art that would never change for the rest of his life.

Although *Burnin'* ends with 'Rastaman Chant', in many ways this is the defining note of the album. There are far more famous songs on the album, songs that would establish Marley as an artist devoted to social change and to singing against oppression in society. Yet it is in 'Rastaman Chant' that the Wailer's offer the world a clear sense of their faith – a faith that would ultimately guide everything each would do from that point on. 'Rastaman Chant' establishes, in the simplest of ways, the world view of the Wailers, and it helps us to understand the psychic and intellectual foundation of all their work. There are two chants performed in this recording – 'Fly Away Home' and 'Babylon You Throne Gone Down'. These two statements present us with the Rastafarian view of the temporal world and the spiritual world and the individual's relationship to those worlds; and then reveal the second most important feature of Rastafarian teaching – the position of Babylon. Babylon's role as the enemy of the Rastafarian is the galvanizing and defining force in that religion. The song is not a reggae song. It is performed as a Rasta chant, which means that its musical basis is entirely that of the Rastafarian drumming, a distinctive entity. Even though Rasta drumming would later enter reggae music a great deal, rhythmically, it is sacred music, and its rhythm is almost always employed as part of worshipful meditation.

The Rasta worship ceremony usually takes place in a yard somewhat isolated from the hustle of the world. The Rastas sit in a circle, some with drums, some with percussion instruments and others with just their voices. The three drums of the Rasta drum circle are the bass drum, a middle level drum called the funde and a high-sounding drum called the 'keke' or 'repeater'. Each drum plays a different rhythm. The bass carries the foundational heartbeat boom, the funde echoes the bass but adds small embellishments that do not vary much from a repeated pattern. The 'repeater' is the voice that speaks over this foundation creating syncopations, rapid explosions and a range of complex patterns that create the sense of movement and energy that is part of this music. Occasionally, these circles also include other instruments – horns, keyboards and a bass guitar. However, these instruments are always peripheral to the lead taken by the drums.

Marley would have discovered the drum circle through his association with senior Rastafarian elders like Mortimer Planno, Count Ossie and Ras Michael. The last two were quite famous for their respective drum teams that produced many recordings over the years and played a significant part in giving a roots quality to the music of the Skatelites and the reggae music that emerged in the late 1960s.

So, by including 'Rastaman Chant', the Wailers, at this point more than anywhere else, were making a clear statement about their spiritual affiliation. This is quite separate from the lyrical statement that they were making. The song is not a dance number and it was not recorded to be played for revellers in the dance clubs and parties. It is a sacred song and it is therefore presented as such. Marley's voice is that of the leader – the chant director. In the pattern of the call and response, Marley assumes this role of the leader. The authority of that position was important in establishing Marley's leadership of the band too. It was a leadership that was musical but, more importantly, it was also a spiritual leadership.

There is something quite ancient and African about the song that would captivate the interest of those in America who had come to enjoy the roots and folk patterns of the Folkways recordings done by the Lomax brothers of black and poor white communities in the hinterlands of America. Those recordings fascinated rock musicians and led many to attach themselves to the blues singers of the south for inspiration, affirmation and ideas; they pointed to the importance of folk tradition in shaping popular music. The Wailers were positioning themselves as a roots band – a band deeply rooted in the folk tradition. The truth, however, is that this is who the Wailers were and the recording was a genuine worshipful act, not a musical excursion into exotica. The voice of Marley that cries out across the drumming is the quintessential Marley wailing from as deep in his soul as he can. His voice has the weariness of a man who has journeyed far. He is singing of a voice that he has heard, but it is his voice. He is the 'I-ya Man', he is the 'higher man' and he is connected to the most superior 'Higher One', Jah, Rastafari. The voice cries out from the wilderness that Babylon's hegemony is going down.

Language is the force that brings about change and the ability to transform society and the world through the use of the word is the core message of the song. Here the Rastaman carries power in his words as he 'chants down' Babylon. The curse to the larger system of Babylon would resonate with the Jamaican society who heard in it a cursing of the police and all forms of repressive authority.

The reference is to the Book of Revelations in which John sees a vision of the destruction of the throne of the Whore of Babylon. The Rastas sing the song as a confirmation of this prophecy. The battle is already won and the Rastaman only needs to claim that victory. The millenarian eschatology that we see here is the foundation of much of the reggae music that would find its voice in the 1970s. This view is fundamentally shaped by John's prophecy and the song simply reiterates the vision of the arrival of the angel who announces the fall of Babylon. It was John who saw the 'angel with the seven seals'. The angel declares that Babylon has been defeated.

The authority of the Bible is the foundation of the Rastafarian faith and the word, then, having been made flesh, and having come to dwell among us (1 John 1) in the form of Haile Selassie, is the word that arises in the song – the word that breaks the chain. In another such Rastafarian chant recorded by the Wailers, the same weight of the word of the 'Conquering Lion Of Judah' is celebrated. Again, this is an adaptation of a gospel hymn that was sung in the Baptist and Pentecostal churches of Kingston.

For the Lion of Judah
Shall break every chain
For the Lion of Judah
Shall break every chain
The Lion of Judah
Shall break every chain
And give us the victory
Again and again.

The second part of the song then presents the second tenet of the Rastafarian faith – the desire to be repatriated to the promised land. The Wailers take an old spiritual sung by slaves and transform it into a song, not about the flight to a promised land after death, but the flight to a promised land in this life. The song itself is rich in allusions. In one of the earliest Wailers recordings, 'Wings Of A Dove' they would express their desire to 'fly away and be at rest'. That song, however, ends with the realisation that they did not have any wings. Instead they would sing. For them, the song became the means of flight and escape.

The pragmatism of that earlier song reveals that the Wailers had not quite embraced the teachings of Rasta that promised escape not merely from the hardships of daily life in the ghetto, but also an arrival in Ethiopia where a true sense of belonging would be restored. 'Rastaman Chant' is not a death song in the manner of 'Oh Freedom' in which the singer declared 'And before I be a slave / I'll be buried in my grave / And go home to my Lord and be free.' In 'Get Up, Stand Up' the Wailers made it clear that such 'pie in the sky' notions are a lie, just to keep the poor in poverty, arguing that the savvy will not look for hope in the after life but will demand their's while on earth.

Where the old spirituals promised that the believer would fly away home to 'glory', the Wailers sought to be taken to Zion. Zion was in Ethiopia. This homecoming would take place at the end of all the labours within this world, on that 'bright morning' of repatriation.

Marley, however, would gradually extricate himself from songs that seemed to maintain strong vestiges of the Christian ethic as he matured in his Rastafarian belief. 'I'll Fly Away' is a song that remains fully rooted in the songs of slavery and the songs that held to the fatalistic idea that the lot of the black man was simply too hard here on earth and that the only hope of solace and peace would come with death and the flight back to the homeland. The affirmation of the connection to Africa contained in many of these songs is something that was not lost on the Rastas when they adopted these songs for their rituals of worship. They embraced the strong sentiment that the world, in which they lived as slaves to the Babylon system, was an alien world, a place of captivity, a place in which they were chained to the daily grunge of labour. Hope came from dreaming of a land of the ancestral memory – a land from which they were taken. In so many folk tales from the African diaspora, stories of slaves taking flight and leaving the slave fields abounded. Flight was a theme of spiritual escape for many of these groups and the Rastas embraced the idea of the return to Africa as part of their own doctrine of repatriation. The Wailers would sing this song as men caught in the rugged world of the ghetto – the prison of the ghetto. They wanted to escape it. They wanted to do so now. But they also sought an escape that would come through music, through consciousness and through a defiance of the system of Babylon.

I introduce the album with this examination of 'Rastaman Chant' because, in many ways, the song is the foundation for everything else that appears on the album. More importantly, it was a defining song for it established quite clearly, and to an international market, that Bob Marley and the Wailers were not merely pop singers or singers of revolutionary songs – rebellious mavericks of the rock 'n' roll ilk – but that they were in fact men deeply inscribed in a set of religious beliefs that presented them with a distinctive world view – a way to see the world that would be radically different from anything that had hit the international music scene. Unabashed, wholly committed and assertive, these songs were laying the foundation for Marley's unique career as a solo artist.

'I Shot The Sheriff' is a carefully wrought narrative ballad that begins with an enigmatic assertion that, in the course of the narrative, is explained, commented upon and expanded. The battle is a mythic one filled with the archetypes of literary legend: the sheriff, the person who shot the sheriff, the great showdown and the denouement. This is a cowboy movie in all its dramatic force and weight. The outlaw figure is being celebrated, but this outlaw is not asserting his guilt from a posture of sheer 'badness' and deviance, but from a position of assumed righteousness. He is asserting that he is a victim of a system that seeks to destroy him. His act of rebellion, then, is a stance against injustice. Sheriff John Brown, the quintessential symbol of oppression is the brown instrument of colonial authority, he is bestrade in Derek Walcott's *Dream On Manley Mountain*, he is the classic figure that is bent on destroying the sufferer, the destroyer of the sufferer's seed.

The shift in the first verse, from the singular noun – 'Kill it before it grows' – to the plural, expands the metaphor, or, at least, draws attention to the metaphorical intent of the image. The seed is not merely the 'seed' he farms, but all seeds of potential and possibility that the singer is nurturing. The destruction of the 'seed' is a destruction of not just his potential but the potential of everything that he produces. Marley manages to give us these two different but related meanings by his ability to shift from the personal to the collective effortlessly. It is something that he achieves with subtle variations of person and number in several of his songs.

In 'I Shot The Sheriff', then, Marley is creating a parabolic narrative that is uncannily locked into the violence and sense of oppression that characterizes the ghetto world. The 'freedom' that meets this figure who is both sharecropper and slave is one that undermines the authority of the sheriff, who is clearly not simply the law but the larger social structure that works against the persona of the piece. The persona admits to shooting the sheriff in self-defence, but he denies having taken on the deputy. The implication is both comic and loaded with the bravado of the rhygin figure. The suggestion that the persona may have shot the deputy, the secondary figure in the power structure, amounts to an insult. Here, the singer is determined to make it clear that he has taken on the 'head-honcho' – the 'bull bucker', 'the boss'. Marley's amusing comment on the meaning of the song while he was on tour a few years after the song was out was that he really wanted to sing, 'I shot the police', but he couldn't because, he said, the Government would get very upset. So Marley avoids direct problems with the authorities by making use of a parable. But it is a parable that he knew the community would understand. Marley understood, also, that by allowing the song to work as a seemingly fictional tale, he was making it accessible to a wider audience.

Commenting on Eric Clapton's recording of the song, Marley speculated on why Clapton may have chosen to record it. In doing so, Marley reveals, in his own indirect way, that he knew he was drawing on an American myth when he wrote the song.

> Clapton asked me about the song because when Clapton finished the song he didn't know the meaning of the song. Him like the kind of music and him like the melody and then him make, 'I Shot The Sheriff'. I don't know if [he did it] because Elton John say 'Don't Shoot Me, I'm Only The Piano Man', Bob Dylan say 'Take the badge off me, I can't shoot them anymore' and this one man say 'I Shot The Sheriff'. That song never fit no-one else but Eric Clapton, right beside Elton John and Bob Dylan. (July 1975)

The connection with Dylan's song is especially significant and informative because it shows how much Marley appreciated Dylan's use of popular American forms, such as the Hollywood Western, to make some very pointed statements about the society he was living in. Marley's reference to Elton John's song is even more interesting because, while there is no obvious connection between the narrative structure of both songs, it is interesting the way in which he saw John's image of the piano player being threatened as a backward version of the 'I Shot The Sheriff' parable. The implied meaning of John's line is that the piano player is NOT just a piano player, but is in fact dangerous, and that music is dangerous. Marley's message in 'I Shot The Sheriff' was directed at those people he saw as his enemies, and he was warning them that at some point he would have to explode and do something. In an interview with Dermot Hussey in 1975, Marley would admit that he wrote songs like 'I Shot The Sheriff' about people who annoyed him and whom he regarded as his enemies.

It is possible that the British-bred blues-inscribed Clapton was drawn to the aggression of the lyric, mingled with what is essentially a wailing cry for justice. Indeed the song, as rendered by Marley, is achieving what he described as defining about reggae music – 'a happy rhythm with a sad sound with a good vibration'. Here the contrasting sensibilities are created in the music itself, which is easy-paced and tinged with plaintive and almost tragic guitar lines, yet this is also riding a danceable rhythm.

Clapton's rendition was extremely successful for it seemed as if the song had tapped into the American consciousness. Marley himself was generous about Clapton's rendition in interviews, at one point suggesting that Clapton's version may have been an improvement on the original. But played by Marley, it is clear that 'I Shot The Sheriff' is a monumental song that borrows and transforms an American narrative to make it elementally Jamaican. The transformation occurs because of Marley's use of the Jamaican language, and because the lyric is so rooted in the urban Jamaican experience. Above all, the complex arrangement in this composition – the dialogue between the wailing Wailers and the lead singer, the call and response and the sheer 'dubness' of the version done by Marley is dread and dangerous in a way that Clapton's version is not.

Marley does not hesitate on this album to make full use of the Jamaican dialect. His use, for instance, of the proverb that ends the song, is one of the ways in which Marley can be said to have given Jamaica's language a chance to explore complicated themes and ideas. Marley's contribution to his culture really lay in his unwillingness to accept the idea that the language of the people was only capable of being used for comic purposes or as peculiar examples of 'native' culture. Marley, drawing on the way that Rastafarians had chosen to take over the English language and bend it to suit their own ends, allowed himself to use proverbs and his rendering of scriptures to explore profoundly philosophical and political ideas. Before the songs by Marley and so many other reggae artists, the Jamaican dialect appeared in popular culture as a vehicle for humour. Only characters in plays and novels spoke in dialect. The omniscient and thinking narrators always spoke in standard English because that was the language of authority. Marley' songs would, however, change this and introduce a new way of looking at the language. But it was new only to those who were locked into the colonial values that made all things European appear more valuable than things Jamaican. In 'I Shot The Sheriff', Marley takes a common English proverb and tells it in the Jamaican dialect. 'Every day a bucket go a well' he states, 'one day de bottom a-go drop out'. Marley uses the dialect that was spoken to him when he heard this proverb, probably as a child.

The message of this song, like most of the songs on *Burnin'*, is quite radical. There is the message of some impending danger. In song after song, there is a catalogue of violent insurrection that cuts through in no uncertain terms: whether he is commanding people to stand up for their rights and not give up the fight, to burn and loot, to bomb a church or to chop down the symbolic big trees, Marley is leading a brigade of warriors into action. Marley's action-driven lyrics would change gradually over the years. Soon he would be more likely to prophesy doom to evildoers than to order action against the evildoers. In 'I Shot The Sheriff' Marley warns those who are attacking the poor that at some point the poor will not take it any more and will react or explode, as Langston Hughes warned in his poem 'Harlem'.

If 'I Shot The Sheriff' warns about the possibility of an explosion, 'Burnin' And Lootin'' makes clear that a cataclysmic explosion is about to happen. The song was a precursor to the pointed revolutionary lyrics of 'Natty Dread'. The song grows out of a deep anger and an intense sense of injustice. Marley always called the ghetto a prison or the place were slaves toiled. He basically could not see how the economy and social arrangement of slavery had changed much since slavery had been abolished. The poor lived under the fear of the whip and were subjected to all kinds of abuses by the henchman of the landed class – the policemen. That Jamaican police were called Babylon by Rastafarians spoke of the disgust that Rastas felt for them. This dislike of the police would become, by the mid-1970s, something of a national condition that was fed by reggae music. As political violence increased, and the crime rate rose after each election, the police themselves became embroiled in the kind of politically driven interaction with the poor that could never be positive. But Rastafarians were especially subjected to the wrath of the police. The police were clean-shaven and wore the uniform of the system, while the Rastas would not allow a razor to touch their heads. It would not be an exaggeration to say that in many ways there was a war between the police and the Rastafarians. While the police could use brutality and harassment as their weapons, the Rastas relied on language and reggae music to fight their battles. The police took great pains to harass the Rastafarians who defiantly smoked ganja in public places, often in front of the police. As the Rastas grew in popularity because of reggae, they became the peaceful heroes who were being harassed by the less than peaceful police. In Henzell's *The Harder They Come* the Rastaman is shown to be a man of peace, a man who just wants to care for his son, a man who would do nothing to betray his brother and a man who could be brutalized by the police on a whim.

But there was another dimension to the Rastaman that Marley reflected in his songs. The Rastaman understood how to prophecy and throw curses at Babylon. Phrases like 'fire burn', and 'blood and fire to all heathen' were phrases I learned in the streets listening to Rastas taunting policemen from a safe distance. Soon the language of confrontation that would appear in song after song would become a part of the street parlance and the instinctively lawless character of Jamaicans latched onto the often justifiable Rastafarian distaste for the police, and prompted a palpable anti-police feeling in the country. As a result, Marley's songs were quite dangerous because they fed into a growing anger that people were feeling in the larger society, whether they were Rastafarians or not. The police, called upon to maintain law and order, were the ones who would face the anger of the people. Many knew the stories of police brutality and would have found Marley's song a tale with which they could identify.

According to Rita Marley 'Burnin' And Lootin'' is based on a true incident. Apparently, during their early years together in Trench Town, a late-night police raid startled the family. The police came with guns pointed in a typical raid in the area. Eventually they were convinced that the Marleys were decent people and left them alone. Marley, of course, could not forget the indignity of the raid and the easy assumption of the police that anyone living in Trench Town was fair game for their raids. As with many of Marley's songs, the incident that triggered the song would soon take a back seat to a larger statement about the conditions of the poor in Jamaican society and about the larger narrative of the cosmic battle between good and evil. For Marley, the incident spoke to his own sense of history and his sense of the journey of the black man. The song becomes a lament that turns into something aggressive and quite dynamic. Marley first tells the story in tightly rhymed lines that include an image that is so brilliant for its efficiency and appropriateness.

The picture Marley paints is vivid and marked by careful detail. It is early morning and a curfew is in effect in his area. Marley makes the story immediate by declaring that the incident happened 'this morning'. We are in the perpetual timelessness of art. He is reading a moment in time that has been transformed by his art in to something beyond time. The conditions of suffering persist for Marley and he captures this by the very powerful use of the phrase 'this morning'. The lines that follow continue to paint the picture. Marley says he was a prisoner which suggests that he was arrested or held in custody. However, as we have shown, for Marley, the ghetto was a prison and all suffers were, as Bunny Wailer would sing in his powerful prison lament, 'battering down sentence' – or fighting the imprisonment of poverty. Marley cannot recognise those who are confronting him, but he knows that the attire suggests that they are members of the police force, storm-troopers of Babylon.

The figures who are standing over him are strangers in his home. Both their visage and their uniformed acts of repression are caught in the fourth line that describes them as wearing 'uniforms of brutality'. It is enough for Marley to identify them as uniformed people. In that single image he makes it clear that they are policemen. Their uniform – their conformity to the dictates of the government in terms of their dress – is what distinguishes them from Bob Marley and his Rastafarian brethren.

In the face of this act of violation, Marley asks a question that will build into a series of questions which will climax in the inevitable chorus. The question is full of allusions that are worth noting here. Marley borrows an image from Jimmy Cliff, who spoke in his song about the daily struggle of a man in an alien and hostile world.

Cliff's image of the crossing of rivers is taken from the stories of the negro spirituals that embraced the crossing of rivers as a symbol of freedom. They borrowed the image from the story of the children of Israel crossing the Red Sea. The river in black diasporal culture represents a place of rebirth – a place of baptism that will result in resurrection into a new life. The many crossings of rivers constitute the many journeys to try and retrace the path across that large river of divide, The Middle Passage, which separates the black man from his homeland. Marley is drawing on this rich history of images when he asks how many rivers will he have to cross to meet the boss. What Marley does that is quite important is to use an image of everyday Jamaican life to ground this larger image.

The 'boss' – to whom Marley wants to talk to – is, in Jamaican parlance is the man who can give someone a job. He is the person who is in charge of an area. The boss is the big person in the area. The boss is the slave master in the plantation economy. But there is a bigger boss who is God himself. But this God is associated with the boss of the plantation and so he is not the same figure as Selassie. Marley wants to talk to the boss because, in the power scheme of things, the boss is the one who needs to be dealt with if things are to improve. At the same time, speaking to the boss would mean that the poor man who has been crossing so many rivers will finally have arrived at some place of equality.

In a barely discernible shift of person, Marley takes us from the first person singular to the first person plural and in doing that he expands the symbolic meaning of the song. It is deft writing. The grand loss that now haunts him is nicely associated with the boss by the convenience of rhyme. The things that have been lost extend beyond the loss of dignity that the raid represented. Marley is pointing his listeners to something broader, something historical. When he says, 'we must have really paid the cost' he is alluding to the New Testament gospel scripture that asks us to count the cost before taking up the burden of the struggle that Christ is offering. Marley says that the poor have paid a high price by the things they have lost. In 'Natty Dread' Marley would command, 'children get your culture' – this is what has been lost. What has been lost is the memory of Africa; what has been lost are the languages of African; what has been lost is the culture of Africa – all of these were stolen away.

It therefore makes absolute sense when Marley arrives at a simple conclusion: 'That's why we gonna be burnin' and a lootin' tonight!' Marley has not forgotten the time sense he has established. The act of repression takes place early in the morning – the act of rebellion will take place the following night. There is nothing subtle about burning and looting. These are the acts of rioters. Marley does not try to finesse his call by declaring a holy war or a symbolic war. Instead he suggests that in the face of the abuse that has been suffered, the only recourse left to the black man is to burn and loot. Jamaicans in Kingston knew quite well what burning and looting was. In the six years before this song appeared, Jamaica had seen several major riots led by youth – riots that brought the country to a standstill and led to a number of deaths and a great deal of destruction.

Marley, however, does not leave the song in that place. It is a basic truth about Marley that he almost always introduced to each song of rebellion, a song of reproach and correction for his people. But even this begins with yet another set of demands.

First he asks that the poor be given food to eat. Marley's call here, too, is not merely symbolic. Hunger was a real part of his life and the life of those who suffered in the ghetto with him. The next demand is a strange one. The roots man is no doubt the Rastaman, but it would seem as if Marley is asking that he takes a beating or some sort of knock. At the same time, one has the impression that the phrase 'take a blow' is referring to something positive; that the 'roots man' should be given a chance. In the next lines, Marley points to the role of music as a transformative force in his life and in the life of the poor. He uses music of the ghetto as a metaphor for that which is good. The music of the ghetto is the language of the ghetto and the way of the ghetto. The drugs, Marley is saying, will slow down the people and that (the taking of drugs) runs counter to the principles of reggae music. Marley, needless to say, is not referring to ganja in this statement. Part of the stricter Rastafarian teachings often advocated that the drugs that were being dispensed by doctors were in fact designed to poison and brainwash the poor. These involved conspiracy theories, which had already crept into the lyrics of the Wailers on earlier albums. Often they came in the form of radical deconstruction of the educational system and the things that were being thrown at the poor in songs like 'You Can't Blame The Youths' by Peter Tosh and 'Brainwashing' – a funny exposé of the foolishness of nursery rhymes ('It's just the poor's brain washin' / And I don't need it no longer, I don't want it no longer.') For Marley the music of the ghetto, which is reggae music, is a positive music and a music that uplifts. But with the hunger and suffering that the poor have to face, Marley's second chorus oscillates between a threat and a lament.

He promises weeping and wailing tonight, and interjects a series of statements that suggest that those who will be weeping and wailing are the poor: 'we've been suffering these long years'. The final rhymed interjection is full of Marley's sharp wit and edge. When he asks 'will you say cheer?' he is asking if his people could be so insensitive as to gloat over the pained sorrow of the poor. The question is rhetorical. Of course they will and when they do, the burning and looting will begin in earnest.

Marley always sought to create a lyric that could function at various levels. He often grounded the song in a narrative that had immediate implications and then he would allow space for the song to gain symbolic meaning. In interviews, Marley would choose which reading to emphasise depending on what seemed politic. About 'Burnin' And Lootin'', Marley would explain that the song was not a literal call for rioting and destruction, but a call for the symbolic destruction of Babylon: 'dat song about burnin' and a-lootin' illusions. The illusions of the capitalists and dem people with the big bank accounts.' Marley was not being disingenuous at all. Such a reading is wholly consistent with the idea of the boss and the deprivations faced by the poor. The third chorus does ask for the burning of illusions and pollution – the images of Babylon's decadence. And Marley is careful enough to place that particular chorus at the end of the song in order to grant it an interpretive authority.

'Small Axe' is another of those songs in which Marley allows various levels of reading. It is often cited as the perfect example of how Marley coded his messages in songs that spoke in revolutionary tones. That a clever pun is at the heart of this bit of poetic trickery lends it a certain notoriety. The truth is that most listeners, including those in Jamaica at the time, would not have been able to work out that 'Small Axe' represented a warrior-like rude bwai attack on the three major record labels that were dominating the recording industry in Jamaica. On the surface, the song is a full-blown attack on the evil ones who seek to bring down the chosen ones of God. Marley relies heavily on scripture for this song and even allows himself to use the archaisms of the King James version of the Bible to grant weight to the pronouncements. 'Small Axe' is one of those odd Marley songs that could have been quite comfortable on the *Survival* album, which was devoted to outlining the wicked ways of Babylon. The song helps us to see that there were a number of biblical passages that Marley would draw on again and again throughout his life. The most important and defining one was based on the Book of Ecclesiastes, which outlined the vanity of the world – the vanity of riches, the vanity of lust, the vanity of man's wisdom, the vanity of idolatry. The others came from the Psalms, in which David encouraged himself with promises that God's justice would prevail over the work of the wicked. The divine order of retribution ('no weak heart shall prosper') is one that Marley would hold onto even during the most difficult periods in his life. We will see in the examination of *Uprising* that there were moments when he sometimes appeared to waver in his faith to belief that this divine order was assured. But these were human moments of doubt that would eventually be rescued by another song of hope. 'Small Axe' is a song of rebellious action and faith in the workings of Jah. But, as with almost all of Marley's early political songs, this one also demands some sort of action – it offers that while God will be on the side of the warrior, the warrior must still fight. In later songs, Marley would just sit back and allow Jah to do all the dirty work.

The 'evil men' are the prototype of Babylon and the habit is to boast, to seek material gain and to build their lives on the unreliable vanities of the world. Theirs is an existence based on duplicity and sham. They pretend to be smart and are convinced of their intelligence. This is the worldly figure that Paul spends a great deal of time excoriating in the first Book of Corinthians, speaking highly of the unattainable wisdom of God that seems like 'foolishness' to those who are wise in their vain imaginations. The language is rich with the bombast and force of the King James version and Marley relishes it.

First he grounds the song in biblical authority by using the archaism 'boasteth'. The question is rhetorical, why are evil men boasting and 'playing smart' when their foolishness is so obvious to those who are watching. The works of iniquity (another Elizabethen phrase) are central to this identity of these evil doers, and the stand in direct antithesis to the 'goodness of Jah-Jah' which Marley declares, again using the archaic form 'mixed with Rastafarian coinage, 'Edureth for-Iver'. The very phrase 'achieve vanity' is a clever oxymoron that presents the absolute absurdity of the efforts of the 'evil men'. Marley then informs them of their fate.

The battle between the underdog David and the clumsy and boastful Goliath is the basis of these lyrics. The song is only enriched by the knowledge that the 'big tree' is a natural Jamaican pun on the phrase 'big threes' that, when rendered in Jamaican dialect becomes 'big t'ree'. That the song, then, became a sound-system boast – a statement from one studio to the other – only enhances the layered meaning of the tune and grants it a street-level power that the Wailers were always looking for.

This Perry/Upsetters song, first released in 1969, was written in direct response to the competition that Perry's outfit was facing from the dominant record companies – Federal Records, Dynamic Sounds and Studio One. Perry complained about the big 't'rees', Tosh coined the hook for the chorus and the song was born. It was a popular song, like many of the Wailers songs produced at the time. Given this coded reading of the song, the second verse can be seen to be rich with a layering of meanings that marry the rituals and doctrines of the church of musical recording and the rituals and doctrine of Rastafari.

The master – to whom these words (the prophecy) are credited – is, of course, Jah, but the master is also the mix-master and the studio master Lee Perry, who was guiding the work of the Wailers at the time. The Rastafarian term 'weak heart' referred to those who were heathens, those who did not follow the teachings of Jah. They were cowards and they were the same as baldheads. All of this language emanated easily from the Psalms of David. By calling the competition 'weak hearted' the Wailers were actually accusing the sounds of these studios of being weak in power and, more importantly, weak in soul. Perry was especially proud of the soul in his productions.

'Duppy Conqueror' emerged a few months before 'Small Axe' and was a massive hit in Jamaica. Along with the love songs 'Lonesome Feeling', 'Rock My Boat' and 'Run For Cover', it established the Wailers in the late 1960s as having a daring and radical sound that brought fire to their Rastafarian rhetoric. This is where the character of the Wailers – the one that Marley would ride on for the next few years after the band broke up – was being defined. To understand the street-level popularity of the Wailers at that time, one would have to look at the way the modern day dancehall scene operates. The Wailers were essentially the Cobras, Bounty Killas and Elephant Mans of their time. They were young and locked into the street discourse of the ghetto. Their songs were full of brash bravado and were never reticent about expressing anger and threatening violence. In 'Duppy Conqueror' the identification with those who were coming out of prison was not a fanciful notion. The Wailers had recently welcomed Bunny Wailer, who had done hard time in prison.

When I spoke to Bunny Wailer about the work that emerged after that time, he was quite clear about it. He described his song, 'Battering Down Sentence', as a 'prison yard song' a tune that grew out of hardship. He then used that song to point out that the songs that the Wailers were creating were not vain imaginings, but songs that grew out of experience, that grew out a lived encounter with the tough things of the world. 'Duppy Conqueror', however, is not simply about coming out of jail. There is a toughness to it that would even lead to a version of the song being pulled from air play because of its harsh lyrics. The version that we hear on *Burnin'* is a sanitized version. An entire verse is eliminated from the song.

Opening with the typical Marley narrative of personal experience, the song then employs a rural image of spiritual warfare that draws greatly on Perry's notorious mysticism. The 'duppy' is, in the simplest of translations, a ghost. But duppies are never innocuous. They are in fact the spirits of the restless dead that are said to haunt the living. A duppy can be placed on a person by a master of the darker crafts and duppies tend to have quite distinct personalities, all of them seeming to be viciously impetuous and quite devious. The Wailers had already introduced their audiences to a rich diet of duppy talk in songs like 'Mr Brown' ('Mr Brown is a clown who rides through town in a coffin / In a coffin where there's three crows on top and two is laughing / what a confusion!' – a brilliant song of surreal and impressionistic absurdity; and 'Screw Face' ('Duppy know a who fe frighten / duppy cyan frighten duppy') is a song in which the tough guy confronts those who are trying to scare him by warning that he too is a screwface and a duppy. These songs give us a clue of the way we must understand who the Duppy Conqueror is. Of course, the most obvious understanding of the duppy conqueror is as one who manages to defeat the duppies of the world. Duppy conquerors were therefore people gifted with the power to handle the spirits of the dead and to defy them. As a term adopted by the toughest of gunmen in the ghetto, it would make sense that the duppy conqueror was one who defied death and who also did not fear death. But the duppy's physical attributes tend to compound the issue. The duppy was often depicted as a white-faced monstrosity – a figure often associated with white people with their blanched faces. In Jamaica it is not unusual for someone to say of a white person or a really light-skinned person that 'dem look like duppy'. Thus in the implied battle between the systems of Babylon and the righteous black man, the duppy was almost always the ghost of the colonial authority that would not go away. Given the circumstances of the song, it becomes clear that the system that put the man in jail, the system of policemen, judges, prison guards and politicians, constituted the forces arrayed against the Rasta. These forces are collected in the image of the duppy. The story, then, functions on several levels, creating one of Marley's more complex songs. Though they are big trees, the singer and all the people he represents, all the suffers, the poor, the Rastaman – will be the small axe that will bring down these monoliths of oppression.

The dehumanizing world of prison represents a weapon of the duppy system and the singer enacts the ritual of the welcoming of prisoners back to the community that was enacted first by the burru drummers – who gave the Rastafarians both their tough reputation and their drumming style. The Wailers are enacting a ritual that would have been quite common in the ghetto in which people were often arrested and jailed for minor infractions or for no really good reason. Marley understood the imprisonment of people as a means to destroy them, to break their spirits and their souls. But this could not be done to the singer. However, his mood is not one of giddy celebration, but one of serious affirmation. He gives Jah credit for keeping him around and for forcing them to 'turn him loose'. The image of that last line is a powerful one as it suggests the freeing of a wild animal. But the allusion is biblical and in that sense it is a reference to the promise that the prisoner's chains shall be loosed as Isaiah prophesied. Yet the turning loose of the duppy conqueror is an ominous moment and so even as the singer seems to be grateful to Jah for orchestrating his release, he is quite clearly not arriving in the world a broken or tamed individual. Indeed, in the bridge that follows, the singer decides to take on those who are seeking to prevent him from arriving at his place of spiritual strength and full liberation.

The Mount Zion that he sings about is the promised land and it is a land in Ethiopia. It is a physical place – the destination of those who will be repatriated. But Mount Zion is also the place of inner peace and a place of security with Jah. The bridge that is referred to is the transitional place – it is the crossing point that will take the prisoner out of jail, that will take the believer to the land of hope and allow the oppressed to go free. To 'cold up' is to kill the fire in a person, to treat them in a cool and demeaning way. To 'cold up' is also to handle roughly, to effectively bully into submission. The acts of Babylon, then, are aimed at 'colding up' the fervour of the Rastafarian and trying to bully him so that he cannot arrive at his destination. Marley does not turn to Jah for assistance at that point. Instead the dread resorts to the tough language of the street fighter: 'If you a bull-bucka...' The 'bull-bucka' is literally a bull that bucks anything that comes in his way. But in Jamaican folk mythology, the 'bull-bucka' is a type of disembodied spirit not unlike the 'rolling calf' (a cow that travels around rural parts with an assortment of bells and whistles – the creature is an apparition that will petrify anyone that looks at it, and all manner of spirits). Marley identifies himself as the 'duppy conqueror' who clearly trumps any duppy or spirit.

As Marley matured in his Rastafarian faith and, some would argue, as he created distance between himself and Lee Perry, his use of the language and ideas of folk spiritualism diminished significantly and was replaced by a closer application of the Bible. But the shamanic function that we see being enacted in these songs is one that never left him. It continued to shape his willingness to speak curses on the enemies of himself and his people and his willingness to be the 'duppy conqueror' against all forces of darkness.

One of the unfortunate things about the version of the song that appeared in *Catch A Fire* is the absence of a final verse that the Wailers recorded in at least one Perry release. One is never certain why these cuts are made, but apart from shortening the length of the song only slightly, a rather inflammatory set of lines was excised. I suspect, though, that lyrically the Wailers preferred to allow the song to function on the spiritual plain of Rastafari that ends the version on *Burnin'*. In the alternate version, the song returns to the streets and the singer would seem to have lost none of his aggression and willingness to take action against his enemy. Consequently, instead of pointing us to the spiritual and larger political interpretation that the *Burnin'* version does, this takes us back to the sentiments of Peter Tosh's 'Stepping Razor' ('If you wanna live / Treat me good / I'm like a stepping razor don't you watch my size, I'm dangerous'). In this additional verse he warns those who are watching him not to show off by encouraging their friends to laugh. He calmly threatens that he will 'cut them' up and in so doing reserve the 'last laugh' for himself. Yet, in a quite contradictory moment the singer ends the verse with the lament 'I'm crying'. On one level it is a cue up for the chorus which is a cry from the poor, but it is, indeed, a genuine expression of the blues.

Retribution, then, will come from the knife. But there is something about the direct confrontation in these lines – the sense that there is a world of people who are mocking the one who has been imprisoned – that is quite compelling. This is the kind of bullying that generates the fiery anger that remains so much a part of the Jamaican culture. Yet the last line, while a cue for the chorus, is also quite loaded in itself. It is here that the song then assumes the status of a lament and a quality of vulnerability emerges that is nowhere near as clear anywhere else in the song.

'Duppy Conqueror', seen in this light, becomes more than a mere boast – a tough guy's threatening. It becomes a kind of blues song, a lament that is rescued from hopelessness by faith. But there is something terribly human and vulnerable about the lyric. It is a vulnerability that would become clearer and clearer as Marley matured as a writer. In this song, though, we are being trained by Marley and the Wailers to expect multiple layers of meaning, emotion and symbolism in a single song.

That it is quite likely that an actual story of a man's release from jail – a specific man with specific friends and associates – tells us that what the Wailers had understood quite quickly is the value of transforming the details of everyday experience into a larger political, religious and social statement. Once they could get us to identify with and experience the raw emotion at the most personal narrative level while all this is going on, they had achieved a great deal in popular songwriting. There is little doubt that, as early as 1969, the Wailers and Marley were mastering the art of the popular song.

The non-Marley songs on the album, Tosh's 'One Foundation' and Bunny Wailer's 'Pass It On', reveal something of the contrasting personalities that made up the Wailers. Bunny Wailer's song is typical of his carefully constructed hymning style and the assured manner of his offering of truth. In moments, his lyrics have the poetic sophistication of American songwriters like Richie Havens – language almost self-conscious in its use of poetic form. Wailer's lyrics were almost always quite literary when placed beside the seemingly spontaneous and impressionistic approach of Marley. Ther lyric is filled with personification and a careful literary style.

Such balanced lyrics would become the hallmark of Bunny Wailer's art in the years that followed. In 'Hallelujah Time' we see the same literariness – the same care for image and for a syntax that is reaching for note-perfect standard English. While Marley spoke and sang in clear Jamaican dialect, Wailer was almost always careful about his elocution and his desire to offer his lyrics in the official language of the Queen. Both Tosh and Bunny Wailer tended to work in that idiom, in contrast to Marley who, with Perry, explored more and more the

Jamaican language. Bunny Wailer's 'Hallelujah Time' unfolds with clarity and grace. This is as far from a Marley lyric as one can get. Yet what both artists shared was a seriousness of purpose in the writing of songs, one that was matched by Tosh's work.

Tosh's 'One Foundation' seems to present a side of Peter Tosh that his later work would seem to eclipse. But Tosh, who was always seen as the more radical one of the group, sings a song about love and unity that is striking for its lack of irony, lack of wit and its uncritical embrace of the notion of world peace and unity. The 'one foundation' is an allusion to the New Testament teaching that Christ is the foundation of the church. Tosh calls on the world to come together to love. In the face of the other songs on the album, the lyrics at times seem quite absurdly trite. The sentiments are hard to argue with – no denominations, no segregation no organizations or there will be no love. Yet one is aware that this was not the best work by Tosh. Its inclusion, however, is not diabolical. The sentiments were an important balance to the harsher rhetoric of Marley in some of the songs on the album. Also, Tosh's performance is rich with his baritone and his assured mastering of rhythm.

While it has often been suggested that the reason for the break-up of the Wailers was because Bunny Wailer did not want to travel and Peter Tosh was difficult to work with, it is clear that something else was going on in the artistic realm. These were three distinct songwriters with quite different ideas about how language is to be used and how a songs lyric is to be constructed. For the albums to have some coherence, one songwriter would have had to dominate. The Tosh and Bunny Wailer songs on these two albums show us that, while it is likely that the three collaborated on songs, they generated songs quite independently of each other in terms of theme and style. Were their visions not so strongly defined, it would be conceivable to see them working together as a team for many years to come, but Tosh, a songwriter in his own right, produced songs that needed the space to carry his brand of intelligence and his character. The same was true of Bunny Wailer and, of course, the same has to be said for Marley. There is no clearer confirmation of this than in the three albums that they produced when they split up. They could never have produced these albums together. The power of their voices, the range and depth of their respective musical skills and the consistency of their lyrics in forming a statement that reflected their personality in 'Black Heart Man' (Wailer), 'Legalize It' (Tosh) and 'Natty Dread' (Marley), confirms that these were artists who had to work on their own. Nothing that Marley could have written would have added to the brilliance of 'Black Heart Man' or 'Legalize It' and nothing that Tosh and Bunny Wailer had on their albums would have found a comfortable artistic space on Marley's *Natty Dread*. This is not to say that they did not influence each other or that the songs they wrote together were in any way less than those they did on their own. On the contrary. They would all continue to perform songs that had been created when they were working as a team. However, I am saying that that both *Catch A Fire* and *Burnin'* gave us hints that artistically these men were ready to separate and to embark on songwriting careers that would give voice to their often contrasting talents.

It is in songs like 'Put It On' that we see how they managed to find artistic common ground and create songs of subtlety and force. Yet the songs that managed to show the trio at their best were those that emerged from a sense of the collective. 'Put It On', a prayer that sometimes turns into a rude bwai anthem, is a song that was generated by the collective energy of the early Wailers. 'Put It On' is essentially a song that comes out of the gospel tradition. First recorded as a ska tune for Coxsone Dodd, the song went through several versions before arriving at this prayerful version on *Burnin'*. The trio sings through the entire song in tight harmony with Marley improvising a side commentary throughout.

Superficially this is a pious spiritual song that gives thanks for the blessing of God. The singer speaks of putting on the garments of God. Here there is an allusion to the robes of glory – the garments sanctioned by God, the clothes of righteousness and holiness. The singer receives these robes which mark his commitment to the faith with gratitude.

Lord I thank you
Lord I thank you.

At the same time, the singer is seeking God's mercy and grace to allow him to wear this garment of praise, thanksgiving and holiness despite the hardships he's going through. So in a refrain he pleads, 'Do lord help me'.

The craft in this simple lyric is actually quite deft. The song begins with a clear invocation of the 'spirit'. It is at once a revival song – a song that would make sense in Jamaica where the strongly Pentecostal revival cults operated in tandem with the African-derived spiritual cults like Pocomania, dinky-mini and Mayal. 'Feeling the spirit' is elemental to these practices because it revealed a connection between the celebrant and the divinity that gave blessing and healing to the celebrant. The song progresses through a series of refrains – 'feel them spirit', 'feel alright', 'no more crying' etc – before arriving at the anthem refrain, 'I'm gonna put it on'. The spiritual ritual is seeking to evoke a sense of hope and possibility that is credited to the good lord. And here, Marley is not quite evoking the Rastafarian God but the Judaeo-Christian God.

On this superficial level, which is sincerely articulated, the song functions as a powerful spiritual. However there are hints that there are other levels of meaning at work in the song. Although the verse 'I'm not boasting / I'm not boasting / Feel like toasting' could be read as a statement of humility or a use of the metaphor of chanting lyrics to articulate the desire of the singer to use his voice to praise the Lord. As Garth White, (reggae journalist) pointed out to me in an interview, we are also being goaded in another direction and this direction is the rude bwai idiom. Once we enter that space, it becomes clear that the song is actually a defiant boast with an edge of violence that is made clear when we understand that part of the parlance of that period on the streets was the use of the term 'put it on' as a gesture of violence. When a man used a ratchet knife to cut another man, he would be said to be 'putting it on' the other fellow. Thus, the spiritual song of piousness becomes something more ominous and disarming.

But the layers go deeper. The same term also has a strong sexual connotation in street parlance. And this is typical in Jamaican language, where the language of sexual activity is often rooted in the language of violence. So that while the word 'slap' connotes a physical act of 'slapping someone in the face', is also a term used in reference to having sex. DJs have for decades exploited the richness of this use of language to create amusing and often harrowing images that walk an uneasy line between sex and violence. Jamaican language, of course, is not the only language that manages these connections. The English language and the offshoots of that language that can be found all over the world are replete with similar uses of violent terms as euphemisms for sexual activity.

But given all of that, 'Put It On' assumes a sexual dimension – a sensual dimension – not unlike the way in which the soul songs of the 1960s employed gospel and spiritual tropes to create deeply sexual songs. Indeed, it is often said that part of the genius of the Motown sound was its ability to invoke the sound of gospel in all its compositions. Since most of the Motown artists started in the church, and since many of them were constantly flirting with the contradictions of the spirituality and their sensuality, it makes sense that their music would reflect this wonderful tension. Some of the most overt articulations of this could be seen in the songs of Otis Redding and Sam Cook, but most blatantly in Marvin Gaye's hit 'Let's Get It On'.

What becomes clear in the reggae song, and what makes it depart from the US pattern, is the fact that Jamaican artists did not see themselves as exploring a contradiction. Marley's genius lies in the fact that for him all these things are related. The appeal to God in each instance is telling because even when the song is an act of banter and bravado by a rude bwai, he is still compelled to look to the good Lord for help. Hence the song remains a prayer even as it seduces, threatens and offers up praises.

Burnin' was the final statement of the original Wailers. The album announced the end of the collaboration in a clear way. Marley was moving in a direction that would yield a body of work that would place him apart from the rest of the Wailers. Yet *Burnin'* helps us to understand the extent to which the later Marley was shaped by the work that he did with Bunny Wailer and Peter Tosh in the early days. By the time *Natty Dread* was released, Marley had already began to embrace his role as prophet and as a person speaking for the poor people of his society. This was not significantly different from how he viewed himself during the earlier days, but what had changed was that he was now the leading reggae artist in the country and was gradually becoming the best-known Jamaican in the world. Marley's years of experimentation were essentially over. Now his developments were those of a mature artist stretching his art form so as to offer his message in as effective a manner as possible. With greater control, Marley would become the spiritual presence in each album. *Natty Dread* would introduce a new era in reggae music. At the same time, Jamaica would enter a most trying period in its history. When it entered the Cold War as an antagonist to the US, Jamaica's international presence became more pronounced. So, as Marley grew in his international status, so did Jamaica. The combination of the two would generate some of the most revolutionary music to be produced by anyone in the 20th century.

2 Natty Dread And Rastaman Vibration
The Prophet Has Come

'It easy to write an ordinary love song, y'know: 'Hey baby I love you but you don't treat me good'. But that don't interest me anymore, it don't live long. If you sing the right words it can live. It can live through the world and when the next world comes you don't need that anymore, there you need new words.'

— Bob Marley, 1976

NATTY DREAD (JANUARY 1975)
Lively Up Yourself / No Woman No Cry / Them Belly Full (But We Hungry) / Rebel Music (3 O'Clock Road Block) / So Jah Seh / Natty Dread / Bend Down Low / Talkin' Blues / Revolution

RASTAMAN VIBRATION (APRIL 1976)
Positive Vibrations / Roots, Rock, Reggae / Johnny Was / Cry To Me / Want More / Crazy Baldheads / Who The Cap Fit / Night Shift / War/ Rat Race

In 1971 I lived at the bottom of a narrow sloping street called West King's House Drive when Marley moved into the mansion in 56 Hope Road. I say this now not because the event was of any importance to me, but because I like to think of how close to Marley I lived for two years. To get to the Marley home on 56 Hope Road from my flat-roofed bungalow, I had to walk the up the treeless hill to King's House Drive, which continued through an avenue of high green hedges until it opened out on the busy Hope Road that, during those days, was not a dual carriageway, but a simple street. I would then turn right and head up towards the hills, passing the cream façade of the St Andrew's Memorial Hospital on the right, the outer gates of the private school, Priory, which was then reserved for the élite and the children of foreign diplomats who could not abide by the use of uniforms that applied to all other schools in the country. I would walk past the wide open lawns of the Prime Minister's Office in Jamaica House, which was a three-storied modern building positioned far back from the road. Crossing Lady Musgrave Road, a major intersection, the pavement would disappear and be replaced by a stretch of gravelled paths that would continue all the way to Liguanea – the next major intersection. But I would not be going that far at all. Just above Lady Musgrave Road, the outer walls of the Marley home would begin. This eight-foot wall, I am sure, was there in the early 1970s, but it is hard to recall now. I do know that the yard was full of trees and it was always hard to see the house from the road. But I knew that was where Marley lived and I also knew that the gate was always open and the driveway was always filled with cars and very comfortable looking people – dreads all, hanging out, eating orange, eating cane and basically just taking up space as Jamaicans can do.

Most books about Marley speak of his arrival in that house as a major affront to the neighbours. My suspicion is that the writers were talking to the neighbours, or perhaps for them the story of Marley's move from a bunking with Lee 'Scratch' Perry in his less ostentatious digs a lot further down Hope Road than 56, and from very humble settings to a fairly large home on Hope Road was too rich with the rags to riches possibilities to let pass. Marley's 'new' home was not really in the most prestigious part of town, in fact.

He did not have a home in Russell Heights, Jacks Hill, Stony Hill, Cherry Gardens, Beverley Hills or in the lofty environs of the Blue Mountains where only the really wealthy and established lived. He did not have a place in the plantation homes in the country where the truly wealthy white Jamaicans hid away, sending their children abroad to school and really separating themselves from the rest of the population. The house on Hope Road was a nice house, an expensive house, but this was not like Marley moving to an area infested with wealth. They were not hidden away. Hope Road is a main road – a main thoroughfare that buses ply and a street that people from all walks of life would walk along if they were heading for the hills or from areas like Papine, Stand Pipe, Liguanea or Hermitage towards the downtown.

To get from Hope Road to downtown Kingston was fairly simple by bus. You took a bus from the bus stop just in front of 56, down to Half Way Tree, a busy business area that was five minutes away from 56, and then continue down town to Marcus Garvey Drive or Spanish Town Road. This was not a gated community – it was accessible, and Marley clearly liked it that way.

I say all this to remind us that Marley's wealth was not that conspicuous even by Jamaican standards. Those who made much of it were those who saw his movement from a ghetto rebel to a man living what was essentially a middle-class life as something of an affront. He, after all, they implied, did not achieve his wealth through hard work. He just 'smoked his ganja, made silly music and now look at him'.

For Marley, the move would have been significant. Trench Town, like Tivoli Gardens, Denham Town, Jones Town and all the other notorious areas of West Kingston where the poor lived in large numbers, was, like most small villages and communities in the country, isolated and closed. People would spend most of their life in the small confines of these communities, rarely venturing out to places where they felt they did not belong. Schoolchildren would sometimes go elsewhere to school and, occasionally, some of the citizens would need to go up town to work as domestics or gardeners. But the city of Kingston was effectively divided and it was not typical for people to venture out of their territory. This would become even more acute during the election period when it was quite dangerous to find oneself in the wrong place at the wrong time. So Marley was leaving a closed world and entering a whole new space. But he liked the comfort of the space. He liked the trees in the yard and liked the sense of being in the country. Those things he liked. He also liked the fact that he had an area where he could play football with his friends, who could find their way to his gates because the place was fairly accessible from downtown.

The beauty of being a superstar in Jamaica was that Jamaicans had not yet learned how to treat their own as superstars. The mobbing of singers, the harassment on the streets, the need for protection and the need to be hidden away was not as intense in Jamaica as it would have been for others living elsewhere. As his fame grew, Marley probably felt that he had less and less privacy, but it is clear from stories that many tell that he felt free to move around Kingston and the rest of the country without worrying about being harassed. He drove his own car, when he eventually got one, and was in constant dialogue with the world around him. He was also known to spend a great deal of time down in Trench Town after he moved out. The story is that he never had to lock his car because everyone knew it was his car and so they would know better than to try and do damage to the car or steal from it. He would go down there and reason with his friends, play football and also do 'music business'.

Marley was not isolated from Kingston and from the world he sang about. The world was alive around him – the smells, the dust, the acrid exhaust smoke, the scent of good food cooking in yards, the teeming of humanity, the street-sellers' calls, the madmen and women who walked around the city as a part of its colour, the stories of murders and acts of brutality enacted by the police and the constant sense that they were Rastas and thus subject to harassment by the authorities. This was Marley's world and he would write about that world in his songs.

By the time Marley came to compile the songs for *Natty Dread* a great deal had happened in Jamaica. This was an oddly optimistic time for Jamaica – optimistic for some, anyway. There was an air of change wafting through the society, rooted in a strongly and charismatically articulated vision of self-assertion that was being propagated by the then Prime Minister, Michael Manley. His new government was full of youthful, inexperienced visionaries who were convinced that they were going to change the country and lead Jamaica into a new era of success. They all belonged to a generation that shared a lot in common with the Wailers. They had lived through the period of adult suffrage in Jamaica, which culminated in 1944 with universal adult suffrage that allowed Jamaicans to vote in a limited government. They were part of the formation of the first major political parties in Jamaica, and they had been a part of the post-war generation that was convinced that independence from England was not simply a good idea but an absolute necessity. They were older than the Wailers – but only by a decade or so. They were an élite group of well educated people, many of whom received their tertiary education among the first set of university graduates completely educated in Jamaica at the still new University College. Most of them, however, had also travelled abroad to be educated in the UK and the US. There they honed their ideas about their Caribbean culture and their nationalist sensibilities. From England they were determined to return to their homes to make a difference. Some stayed on in America and the UK while others formed links with other developing nations. With the arrival of the progressive People's National Party in power, many were wooed back to Jamaica to contribute to this new nation. Africa was part of their imagination. They shared the socialist ideals of seeking for the empowerment of the people and, in many ways, they could understand the passion of the Wailers. They, too, saw in reggae something of home – something indigenous and something to be proud of. They too had learned the rhetoric of freedom and black consciousness. They saw the struggles in South Africa, the American South, Vietnam, Rhodesia, Nigeria and Kenya as their own struggles and there seemed to be a global sensibility that shaped their thinking.

But, despite these connections, it is clear that the leaders were also quite different from the Wailers. The Wailers had, quite early in their careers, made a clear decision about what they believed in. They had determined that they would find their affinity with the rude boys in the street – the tough guys, the radical poor youths who felt somehow that the world was passing them by. The Wailers, as we have seen, were committed to defending these people – defending their actions and suggesting that until the youth was dealt with fairly by the politicians and the élite they would not remain quiet.

The Wailers also knew that their racial difference was a crucial factor in determining what happened to them in Jamaican society. The politicians and new leaders were almost always progressive brown-skinned individuals. They belonged to the old mulatto class and, while they seemed to find a great deal of connection with the poor, they were clearly different and, as would eventually become clear, were more interested in power and the uses of power than anything else. But there was a point of connection – a point where it seemed as if the youth – the rebel youth represented by the Wailers – were gaining some strength and influence. The politicians were relying on them more for their empowerment; they were finding in the power of reggae music a way to connect with the people and influence the people. With the Wailers growing in international fame, it was clear to these politicians that they were people to pay attention to. But even in 1974, when *Natty Dread* appeared, the Wailers were relatively poor people. They were still shunned by the larger Jamaican population as a useless set of vagabonds. They were Rastas and their heresy was heavily frowned upon. The politicians themselves had children who were turning to Rastafarianism and this was not always seen as a good thing.

But given the confluence of these two groups, it makes sense that Marley would have to find a way to articulate his views about the relationship between temporal power and religious devotion. Jamaica was, in the early 1970s, a place where ideological discussions were central to everyday life. Politics in Jamaica have always been a focal point of much that has happened. Basically, the party structure of Jamaican politics replaced the patronage structure of the plantation – at least in terms of the dynamic relationship between the leader and the people. The 1950s began a pattern by which the minister for a constituency became a godfather figure who was depended upon to ensure that the community was well looked after. As the politicians spoke of the new ideologies that would shape the new nation in the early 1970s, it was clear that the people were developing their own loyalties with those leaders that they felt would be most likely to help them in their everyday life. The pattern has not changed much.

Two years ago, my novelist friend Colin Channer and I were travelling on a London bus when a short explosion of a man bounced on board. Right away we knew he was a Yardie – he had that bounce, that screwface, that look of complete ownership and authority. His arms were scarred with long lines of colloid marks and there was a thick dark line running down the side of his neck. He smiled broadly when Channer said, 'Yes, my Lord,' and it took nothing to get him to open up, once Channer asked him what sound system he followed. Channer is a sound-system aficionado so he was able to talk about the DJs that moved with the sound system and all the popular venues where the system operated. This was inside information and so the man opened up. He told us that he was in London on a furlough – his word. The heat was too much in Jamaica and his 'boss' had arranged for him to take a trip. I kept nodding and staring into his eyes – they were easy eyes that never stayed locked – he always looked around. I also realised how young he was. He suddenly began to celebrate his 'boss' and it became clear that he was talking about Edward Seaga, the leader of the opposition at the time and the man who has controlled Tivoli Gardens (where this man was from) for years. It was clear that no one could say anything wrong about 'his boss'. He admitted, without prompting, that some things that had been done by the boss were harsh, and that things were corrupt in Jamaica, but one thing would not be changed – he was devoted to his boss, 'One boss til deat" he declared.

This devotion, this almost religious commitment, is part of what has made Jamaica such a volatile place when it comes to politics. But for every act of devotion shown by a youth like this one, comes a forceful weight of authority that was exercised by many of these politicians. Patronage is founded on the exploitation of the young and generally idle man who has found himself incapable or unwilling to find work outside the system of patronage. Political patronage allows the young man to feel as if he is truly free to exercise his power and strength and gives him the capacity to be defiant while eating well. He is, however, inextricably tied to the politician and once the elections have passed, he is left armed and with no war to fight. Marley would have seen this pattern played out again and again in the ghettoes of Kingston. He may himself have been drawn into some of this by his involvement in the work of the People's National Party during the election campaign of 1972. Simply put, if Marley was to be associated with any political party, it would have to have been the People's National Party because that was the party of Trench Town, and Michael Manley was one of the central leaders for that area. Yet Marley would know also that all this patronage was predicated on a system of dependence and that indeed little was done to truly improve the situation of the poor. But no progressive could have been condemned for being drawn into the energy and passion that exuded from Manley during those early years of the 1970s.

They wanted to change the conditions of the poor and they wanted to celebrate the fact that Jamaica could sustain itself despite the legacy of colonialism. Michael Manley's wife Beverly was a black woman and Manley himself would start to speak of Jamaica as a black country. This black consciousness did not go down well with all Jamaicans but it is clear that Manley and others had been listening closely to the music and were aware that Rastafarianism had transformed the psyche of Jamaicans, making them far more conscious of issues of race and identity. Africa was a positive place now and Jamaicans were dialoguing with Africans for the first time in a long time. Leaders from Africa were visiting and Manley would meet each one as a fellow African leader. Cultural troupes were visiting from African countries to perform and the government had recently appointed the first black Jamaican, fresh from 15 years in Ghana, as the Assistant Director of the Institute of Jamaica. Shortly thereafter, the Institute had established the African Caribbean Institute of Jamaica to explore connections between Africa and the Caribbean. The work entailed an exploration of folk retentions and a more open engagement with Rastafarian thinkers and leaders and musicians. Cedric IM Brooks and the Light of Saba Band, Ras Michael and the Sons of Negus, Count Ossie and his drumming troupe among others – all Rasta drumming groups – were now very much a part of the cultural expression of Jamaican society and their work was being studied carefully by scholars, musicologists and historians.

My father was the new Assistant Director of the Institute of Jamaica, and it was clear that he believed that Rastafarianism was an important force in Jamaican society, and that reggae was a seriously transforming force in society. If I had any doubts about that, they were erased when one day, while were living somewhere off Red Hills Road, he arrived home with a small package with a 45' record in its jacket. He put the record on the turntable and played the song. We listened. He played it again. We listened. Then he played it again. Afterwards, he announced that this was very important music and we should pay attention to it.

The song was the single 'Natty Dread'. My father loved the song. I could not understand why then. I liked the song, of course, but my father was a jazz man and I was not sure what was making him so hip to the most contemporary music around. It makes sense now, of course. He was seeing in Marley the kind of artist that was writing the world of Jamaica in ways that few other artists had done in the past. He was hearing in Marley a visionary with the capacity to lend a poetic integrity to his telling of the Jamaican story.

Quite quickly the record became one of the most played records in the house. My father must have seen us playing a concert game one afternoon, with me dressed as a rude bwai, one side of my shirt tails out and the other tucked neatly into a pair of trousers, one of its legs rolled up. I had on a large woollen tam stuffed with kerchiefs to simulate locks, and I had a thick wash towel dangling from one of my back pockets. I was performing the cripple skank to Marley's 'Natty Dread' – a dance that involved spastic actions of the shoulder and trembling of the hands to suggest someone who was physically challenged but rhythmically gifted. He was clearly impressed – so impressed, in fact, that several days later, when he had guests at the house for a drink, he called me out to perform the dance. I did. And as I did, I imagined myself walking through Trench Town declaring to the world that Africans should have a sense of their history and place in the world.

It is hard to explain how significant my father's interest in the song was to me. He was not just listening to the song, but actually singing lines from the song. He would always begin to sing at the lines: 'Children get your culture / And don't stand there and gesture / for the battle will be hotter / and you won't get no supper.'

When he listened to jazz, we listened with him, but we understood quite clearly that we did not hear what he was hearing in these jazz pieces. He would play Thelonious Monk again and again, nodding and smiling to himself at particular moments while sipping his gin and smoking his Rothman King Size cigarettes. Marley was our music, not his. But we were of course wrong. Marley was for him the fulfilment of everything that a Pan African, post-colonial socialist hoped for in his country. Marley was a poor man who had found voice and was creating the kind of art that was forcing the rest of the world to see the beauty and power of the art of the folk. That is probably how he would have put it. We liked the music and we listened to him when he said that this was very important music and that we should pay attention to it.

The album on which the single 'Natty Dread' appeared, and which was Marley's first without the Wailers, is in many ways a kind of farewell to Trench Town. It is true that in terms of solidarity and spiritual connection, he never really left Trench Town, but there is a sense in which he was now speaking of the place in the past tense. He was not rejecting it – hardly, he was embracing the memory of it and finding a way to enshrine it in the imagination of the people in the same way that Paul Simon would write of New York, Jimmy Buffet would write of Key West, John Denver of Colorado and the western US, Bruce Springstein would inscribe New Jersey in our imaginations and Bob Dylan would name American places in his songs in ways that would make them part of the larger ownership of the land by Americans. Marley would name Kingston and draw pictures of that space in his songs on *Natty Dread*. He would sing about what he knew and would sing of it in ways that would remind us that this place is worthy of poetic articulation. Marley was determined to sing about his people and in *Natty Dread* there is a clear sense in which he is speaking about his people – crying for help for them, trying to express their pain and granting them hope. In these songs, Marley is talking to his people and offering them a path. In these songs, too, Marley's religious fervour is most pronounced. Rasta is the answer. Political action is important, but it must be rooted in the teachings of Rasta. Marley's authority as a songwriter is most pronounced here. This should not have surprised anyone. His apprenticeship had been a long one. For 14 years he had collaborated with gifted artists and had learned a great deal about himself from them. Now he was working on his songs with an assurance that would mark the rest of his career.

It is telling, though, that apart from the prophetic 'So Jah Seh' and the affirmation of 'Natty Dread', which calls on the Rastafarian to 'ride', the album is remarkably 'secular' if that word can be used. It is a political album, and one that is filled with songs that make scant reference to Rastafarianism and Marley's own devotion to the faith. This highly political quality is something that would evolve in later albums that sought to marry the highly political with the spiritual. There is little doubt that Marley was intent on speaking of the Jamaican situation. There is also little doubt that Marley had not yet assumed the position of prophetic voice – the leader of a Rasta movement. In many ways he still spoke as a radical revolutionary whose devotion to Rasta was part of the rude boy defiance. There is, of course, enough evidence in some of the songs that he wrote during his time with Perry, and even before that, that Marley was working through his own faith and commitment to Rastafarianism. In *Burnin'* and *Catch A Fire*, there are clear references to his faith and devotion to Selassie, but Marley would come to write stronger songs about that faith much later on in his career. In these early albums he is working through the ideas of a political radical. The 'natty' does not connote a Rastafarian so much as it does a rude boy, a ghetto dweller whose cosmology is now marked by the co-option of the clearly culturally unpopular Rasta belief system. In 'Natty Dread', Marley moves from the broader history lessons of *Burnin'* and *Catch A Fire* to the editorial commentary of the happenings in the island. He would get into trouble for this. But this is not all that the album is about. The album is also about his relationship with Trench Town, his relationship with Jamaica and his relationship to the people of Jamaica. In both *Natty Dread* and *Rastaman Vibration*, Marley tackles current affairs head on.

Of course, looking at the writing credits for both albums would lead anyone to believe that Marley had actually stopped writing altogether or had embarked on a new era of collaboration. It is clear, in light of some of the legal cases embarked on after Marley's death, that he was busy employing his own street-smarts to get out of contractual arrangements that he had made with the J.A.D. production team that he had signed with when he was working with Johnny Nash. This is generally how the songwriting credits on the album are explained. But there is much more to these credits, it seems. Those songs that were credited to people other than himself were clearly tracks that Marley had written more recently or tracks he may have written a few years back but had not released in any way or published. There was clearly no dispute about 'Lively Up Yourself' which was recorded in the late

1960s on the Wail N' Souls label with Lee Perry. The same is true of 'Bend Down Low', which was the first title he produced on the flip side of 'Mellow Mood' after his return from Delaware. 'Revolution', a new track, was credited to B Marley – an unusual label for Bob Marley. Other tracks like 'No Woman, No Cry' (Vincent 'Tartar' Ford), 'Them Belly Full' (L Cogill and Carlton Barrett) and 'Rebel Music' (Aston Barrett and H Peart) were credited to people close to Marley whom he knew would not make any legal problems for him. But in at least one instance, the process of giving credit was an act of homage to a good friend. It has been said that Vincent 'Tartar' Ford was one of the people who fed Marley and gave him a place to sleep during his harder days in Trench Town. According to Timothy White, Ford would continue to receive royalties for 'No Woman, No Cry' while Bob was alive. The song that is credited to him is an anthem about those tough days in Trench Town and there is a sense in which Marley was acknowledging the input of his community, those close to him, in the writing of these songs.

'Lively Up Yourself' is a clear articulation of the pleasure that Marley found in reggae music. A strongly religious man at this point, Marley understood quite clearly that reggae was a music about dance and about the sensuality of this art. Marley employs a funk line from James Brown and makes much of it in the line: 'Reggae is another bag'. Here we see Marley's tendency towards the hip and deeply American energy of very black-conscious funk music. In this statement, however, he is speaking to an audience outside of Jamaica. He is declaring to them that reggae is another form of art quite different from the music they are used to. At the same time, however, it is a music that they are expected to understand and be drawn to. It is, in other words, part of that push for a new thing, a new style and a new musical experimentation that was part and parcel of that international pop world. Marley continues to vamp on that metaphor at the end of the song in a scat improvisation that is witty and playful. He laughs through the song and shows his sheer passion and joy in the celebration of the music, declaring at the end with an indulgent laugh, 'I don't believe you!'.

In the tradition of the dance craze, Marley introduces his audience to this reggae music and creates a song that instructs movement that simulates the sexual act because of its back and forth motion. Thus, while the song is a call to dance – the call of a musician to his audience to get up and dance, it is, at the same time, a deeply sexual song of seduction.

The American language that dominates this song is part of the curiosity of the song. In phrase after phrase, Marley is basically 'twanging', which is a Jamaicanism for speaking in an American accent. If there is any doubt that Marley, at least at the time when he wrote the song, was deeply intrigued by the need to capture an American audience, this song proves it quite clearly. But the 'twanging' is decidedly Jamaican in the sense that the lexicon oscillates between American slang and Jamaican patois to create a hybrid that is actually distinctly Jamaican. In so many ways it typifies the fluid nature of Marley's interests and his writing. The dualism of language here is clear in the way that Marley uses the phrase, 'don't be no drag', which is a decidedly American phrase and hardly one that would be spoken in normal conversations in Jamaica. Later on he uses words and phrases like 'you'all' (a southern black construction); 'gonna' (a most American phrase that becomes standard in Marley songs – the Jamaican version would be 'gwine'); and 'big daddy'. But he keeps switching back and forth.

The phrase 'lively up yourself', for instance, is a fully Jamaican construction not unlike the phrase 'small up yourself' that you would hear on an overpacked bus in Kingston. This roots the song in the Jamaican world. But then the choric, 'Yuh rock soh' makes use of the word 'so' that suggests the standard English 'in this way' and, at the same time, it is a very Jamaican construction. Sometimes the confluence of the two languages creates puns that Marley indulges in with some glee. The sexual play of the chorus is rounded off nicely by the call 'You come soh, you come so,' creating the suggestion of a call to dance and celebrate as well as a call to have sex. The rocking, the dipping, the skanking and the coming are all quite clearly intended to be read as both sexual and dance related. The phrase 'come soh' in Jamaican means, 'you behave in this manner' and it can be used to refer to any activity. But Marley enjoys the pun here. And if there is any doubt about the sexual intentions, he declares himself 'big daddy', a fully African Americanism that suggest the pimp and lover of the Blaxsploitation films of the 1970s.

Marley, of course, makes use of a clever device of distancing the voice of the singer from the commands that are made in the song. At times he implies that there is a third party that is ordering certain actions – 'big daddy,' and 'the man' – but these are third-person renderings of the singer that grant him a certain authority. At the same time, there is a lively sense of dialogue going on – an active conversation that is rendered in a half-talking, half-singing manner. The song is addressed to men, encouraging them to satisfy their women so that the term 'lively up' no longer means just come alive, but also to arouse, excite, seduce, please and excite.

It is no surprise that Marley almost always opened his concerts with this song. The bass line is one of those constant circular repetitions that Family Man reserved for the truly danceable Marley tunes. The introduction is a set piece that in earlier renderings was marked by bursts of horns followed by the sharp snare roll and then the voice of Marley crying into the ears. It is typical of a trait that Marley would employ in many of his compositions – opening up with one of the highest vocal notes in the song. Filled out with full-blown harmonies, there is something compelling about this kind of opening line.

After the call to dance of 'Lively up Yourself', Marley takes us gradually into the world he lives in. It is a carefully arranged selection of songs because the movement towards the harshly political songs is gradual and almost seamless.

'No Woman, No Cry', the second song on the album, is easily one of Marley's most famous songs. It is, at the same time, one of his most important because of what it achieves lyrically. The version on this album is the fast-paced, totally reggae version, which would later be replaced by the soulful ballad that eventually became a number one hit in England after the release of the live album in 1975. The swelling organs and the slow, sensual lead guitar solo of that live version is quite different from the tightly organized version on *Natty Dread*. Marley's voice is distinctly higher and more youthful, so that the chant, 'Everything's gonna be alright' seems immensely perky and hopeful. Yet the deep reflection of the lyric is still the guiding force in this version.

This is one of a series of clearly autobiographical songs by Marley that differ from songs like 'Talkin' Blues' and 'Burnin' And Lootin''.

Those, though cast as personal narratives and clearly rooted in a specific set of experiences, remain largely symbolic and metaphorical songs. The narrative in them tends to serve the same kind of purpose as the clearly fictional or symbolic narrative in 'I Shot The Sheriff'. In 'No Woman, No Cry' there is an immediate sense that he is talking about a specific set of experiences and that he is locating the song in a specific place and time from the opening lines. This deeply lyrical quality, with all its specificity, is not a common thing in reggae music. It certainly wasn't at the time. It would be nice to say that Marley was breaking new ground here, but it is clear that he was simply expanding on something he had begun years ago during his apprenticeship days. His love songs always seemed to suggest that desire to go beyond the cliché of catchphrases and easy renderings. Marley sought to employ a certain amount of specificity, a certain biographical guise that would give greater passion to his songs. This tendency also ensured that his love songs were more than simple thoughts on love. They tended to drag in the details of everyday life, the hardships, the context in all its complexity and all its rootedness in the Jamaican landscape and culture. Marley's best love songs have managed to achieve this quality and 'No Woman, No Cry' is a classic in that regard.

It is a love song, but quite clearly there is nothing conventional about it. Marley's progression as a singer of love songs was something he was conscious of. He understood that he was trying to bring to the love song an honesty of language and experience that ensured the longevity of the lyric. Marley clearly cared about songs that lasted – he indicated in an interview that 'if you sing the right words it can live' beyond this world into the next world.

And one has the impression that when Marley would step into that song while on tour around the world, the Jamaicans in the audience did not embrace it as a love song in the old manner, but entered a space of memory – a kind of nostalgic journey into 'home'. That is the true power of the song. On the one hand it offers the quite generic and tried and true hope that everything will be all right, while also placing that home in the rich series of images that are about a specific time and place in Jamaica. The elements are not ones that all Jamaicans could identify with. They did not all live in Trench Town, but most Jamaicans would nevertheless understand the humble comfort of cornmeal porridge. Not all Jamaicans could say that 'their feet is their only carriage', but all could appreciate the communal sense of life in an island where the business of one person is the business of all. But in the very act of naming people, of locating the song in detail, Marley is giving the song such truth and integrity that all audiences, regardless of background, would connect with it. 'Georgie' is the only person outside of historic or heroic figures that Marley has named in any of the songs that have appeared on his major recordings.

'No Woman, No Cry' is, by any standard, a deftly crafted lyric – a piece of fine poetry that would lead Nobel Laureate Derek Walcott to admit on the BBC that it remains an enviable work that manages, in simple ways, to capture an emotion and a place cleanly and efficiently. Apart from the rich imagery, there is also a framing of this lyric that gives it its beauty and balance. Marley's use of rhyme is careful here, never overbearing, but always placed to anchor the song.

Note how the 'hypocrites' softens 'sit', which is a rather jarring end sound that almost begs for a really daft easy rhyme. Then Marley further softens the rhyme with 'meet', which creates an interesting echo, but one that also does exactly what it needs to do, ensuring that none of the song seems to flitter away into nothingness. The word 'Town' is never rhymed, but it is actually a refrain. The second verse echoes the first literally. Marley is thus establishing a formal device of locating the place where the song is set and, perhaps more importantly, he is emphasizing that the song is about memory, about the nature of memory between this man and this woman.

The second and third rhymes in the first verse are handled in different ways. The 'lost/past' rhyme maintains Marley's inclination to go for the half-rhyme, the more subtle rhyme that never quite announces itself, but yet makes the song achieve its unity of sound. While the 'way/say' rhyme seems quite patently loud and harsh, a quick listen to the actual rendering of the song will make it clear that the sounds are quite different. 'Way' is offered as a long sound that is echoed in a sweet and full harmony by the backing singers, the I-Three (in the live version), while 'say' is short and sharp.

And there is much more to this first verse that is worthy of note. Marley makes use of repetition that allows him to explore the dualism that is central to the entire song. The heart of the song is that while there is pain, there is a great need to hope. A series of contradictory impulses shape the first stanza. The song rocks back and forth between the positive and negative energies that are part of the ghetto world. The variation of sound in the rhyme scheme is part of that back and forth movement. The dualisms are worth noting: the hypocrites mingling with the good people; the good friends that are had and lost and, finally, the wonderful paradox of the future and past in the line: 'In this great future you can't forget your past.' The great future that Marley is looking at is really his. It is the future that he sees for himself when he looks back at where he has come from. But, in seeing the future, he recognizes right away that he cannot lose sight of his past, not simply because it is not decent to do so, but because he can't help but recall the sweetness of that past despite its pain. Marley is clearly saying that he can't avoid the past and the past for him is the ghetto – it is Trench Town. But he defines what he will hold onto about the past. Marley is not singing the thug song that declares that he will always be a thug *à la* Tupac Shakur. Nor is he trying to bully the woman or his listeners to return to the abject conditions of the past. Hardly. He is, instead, making it clear that the slums that produced him also placed inside of him something that was positive – a rich sense of community, a wisdom about how to deal with people and a capacity to hope for that great future.

One imagines that the song is being sung to someone – his woman, his mother, his friend – who is looking at the struggles of this 'great future' and lamenting the pain of that. Marley is encouraging her by pointing to memory, pointing to a past that ultimately led to survival. There is a sense of shared hardship and joy in the song, the kind of thing that makes us tempted to assume that the song was written for Rita Marley – she really did suffer with Bob Marley during those harsher years in the ghetto when they really could not afford much and when they truly struggled to make ends meet.

The rocking quality of the song – its movement in ideas through a series of wonderful dualisms – continues in the second verse. Marley achieves wonderful rhymes in this verse as well using the principle of the subtle turn. Again, note the way he negotiates the 'it' sound in the first line around the 'light' and 'night' sounds in the third and fourth lines. Again, 'Town' is left alone, which draws more attention to 'Trench Town.' This is his intention – Marley is declaring on this album where he is from, what his place in the world is. Trench Town is central to that understanding. Marley then offers a swirl of assonance – those deep 'oo' sounds in 'wood', 'would' and 'through' in the third and fourth lines, before the 'porridge/carriage' rhyme, which is a moment of sheer genius. These two phrases are so inextricably connected because they define the poverty that he speaks of. Cornmeal porridge is a staple for poor people but a meal of sublime sweetness when made with nutmeg and condensed milk. It is a healthy and filling meal, and one that would be served to infants and adults alike. Marley has stamped his life – the life of a man who eats cornmeal porridge and shares it with his woman. The moment is rich with the romantic and yet this romance is not one of escape and fantasy, but is rooted in harsh realities.

The richness of the description should not be lost on us. Marley visualizes the moment – Georgie making a fire and the smell of logwood burning is a distinctive one, just as the smell of cornmeal bubbling on an outdoor pot is also distinctive. These people are not out camping. What Marley makes clear is that they live in a government yard, a tenement in which all cooking was done outdoors in the yard on wood fires because other fuel was too expensive. Life was lived communally – people lived in small spaces and shared everything. Marley helps us to understand this by capturing the moment with vivid detail. The decidedly clever line, of course, is, 'My feet is my only carriage' which is rich with meaning. Marley has found a perfect rhyme for porridge, but more than that, he has employed a word that is loaded with allusions. He is a pedestrian, and that is all he has. That is poverty. Yet in the language of dualism, he is comparing his poverty with the symbol of wealth – not the car, not the motorbike, but the carriage, which is the vehicle of the aristocracy. But Marley is actually making literal use of the word 'carriage' for he does mean that it is the only thing that carries him around. His feet are, quite literally, his carriage.

Note again how the verse makes use of the dualism – almost the call response construction that is captured in the very melody of the song. There is a lift to his voice when he sings, 'Then we will cook cornmeal porridge', and then a kind of closure, a blues closure that completes the circle of the construction in the phrase, 'Half [of] which I share with you'. He does the same thing with the lines, 'Then Georgie would make the fire light / As it was logwood burning through the night'. The basic structure of the song owes much in this kind of construction to the patterns of the psalms and proverbs in the Bible: 'thou preparest a table before / in the presence of mine enemies / Thou annointeth my head with oil / My cup runneth over.' The structure of the lines is formed around this dualism. Sometimes these dualisms are contradictory and thrive on the contrasts while, in other moments, the second clause places emphasis on the first – offers a sharper variation, as it were. At times the second clause has a causal relationship to the first – it is the answer, whether it be a narrative conclusion to one action or the rationalization of an action or thought by the second one. Marley is so thoroughly imbued in the language of the King James Bible that it makes sense that he would reflect these patterns in his songwriting.

If, then, the statement is that poverty was real for Marley and his lover, there is a parallel statement or a balancing statement that drives the energy of the song, and it is that all will be well. There is such an aggressive desire to declare hope in this song that we must take it at face value. Marley pleads with the woman not to shed a tear, not to weep, because everything will be alright. Many non-Jamaicans have often misread the title of the song to mean that women don't cry – a statement of fact and not what it is, an appeal, a plea, an effort to convince a woman not to cry. The proper pronunciation of the title and the refrain would make this clear to a Jamaican speaker. While consistently written as 'No Woman, No Cry', a more accurate rendering would be 'No, woman, nuh cry'. The 'nuh cry', which makes use of a shorter vowel sound for the 'no', is the equivalent of the contraction 'don't'. For example, in the phrase, 'nuh wan yuh fe galang soh', which is a deep patois phrase meaning 'I don't want you to act in this way', 'nuh' means 'don't' as well. So the title and refrain here amount to an appeal to the woman that she stops crying.

This is a love song that never uses the word love. It is a love song that does not rely on the discourse or patterns of the American pop song for its source of language and its construction. It is also a love song that speaks in the Jamaican language. It elevates the love of two ghetto people to a place of nobility and quiet grace. This is, then, a Jamaican love song that emerged at a time when the love song belonged to the soul singers and the American pop singers. After all, Marley and the Wailers spent a great deal of their time imitating and covering those same love songs, while they sought to write their own. What Marley achieves here, though, is something that he has hinted at in other love songs. In 'Do It Twice' Marley departs slightly from the underlying sexual play of the phrase, 'Baby you so nice, I like to do the same thing twice', to offer a tightly wrought narrative that creates a tropical landscape for the telling of his love story. He is smoking weed, he lives alone in the woods, he speaks in patois and all these elements form a love song that was written in the mid-1960s. In 'Stir It Up' Marley introduces a metaphor that is totally locked in the urban Jamaican landscape – the pot boiling out in the yard and he puns on the word 'wood', which has absolute Jamaican resonance. There are others that show him trying to create a Jamaican love song, one that speaks from the heart and that manages to avoid the trappings of the American accent. In 'No Woman, No Cry' Marley somehow manages to bring all the elements together to create a song of deeply expressed sentiment that never seems imported, and that could never be imported.

It makes sense then (as ironies tend to) that decades later the Fugees, an American/Haitian rap group, would cover this song and alter it to fit into a Black American landscape. The specificity of the song never undermines its appeal to a wide cross-section of listeners. Wyclef Jean, the Fugees lead singer, does pen a few changes in the lyric to capture the sense of a New York landscape. But the bulk of the song remains the same and proves decidedly relevant to all experience. I have talked so much about the lyrical content of the song, without giving any attention to the music. Of course, anyone listening to the song in the quicker *Natty Dread* version, or the full-blown torch song quality of the live version, will see that Marley managed to marry a wonderful lyric with a great melody that captured the dualism of the lyric. Marley's live versions always seemed to hint at a more conventional love anthem with the full-blown organs and the sweeping harmonies of the I-Three. But in almost every version of this song, there is always that hint of the slightly off-beat reggae sound and Marley's vocalization was always shaping the beat around a reggae pattern in which he always toyed with the phrasing. Marley would never start a line where you would expect it, and he would truncate phrases to create the syncopation of the reggae rhythm.

Were I to try and marry songs with the circumstances of Marley's life, it would be tempting to imagine it as a lyric that Marley wrote for Rita about his need to leave Jamaica for Delaware just a few weeks after their wedding. But Marley intentionally leaves the subject of the song as 'lickle darling' and, in so doing, wrote an anthem for all Jamaican women – all women with men who have to go out and struggle and hustle to make ends meet. It is a decidedly male song, a song of masculine care for the female, a song that positions the male as a responsible figure who understands his role to be one of caring for and protecting his woman. And in so doing, he manages to offer an insight into his own sense of proprietorship for those he cared about and those who would come to depend on him. Few ever complained that Marley did not seek to support all his children including the many born outside of his marriage. Marley's sense of the role of the Rastaman as the king of his home and as the one responsible for his queen is key to the assumptions that underlie this song. In it, Marley is establishing his belief that the songs that come out of his little country are songs that will resonate around the world.

By the time he arrives at the third song on the album, 'Them Belly Full', he is ready for a sharper observation of the ghetto. 'No Woman, No Cry' is hopeful, and smacks at times of the nostalgic. It hints at departure – a sense that the ghetto is the past. But 'Them Belly Full' drags us back to a stark reality. Marley will establish here that his affinity is with the poor. Here, the 'we/them' praxis is clearly laid out. Marley will use the same dualism in this song that we see in 'No Woman, No Cry', but here the call/response is far more assertive. This is a call to arms. Marley makes use not just of the Hebraic dualism, but also of the call and response of Jamaican folk songs. The song is clearly written in a more decided dialect and Marley sings it in that manner. One is almost assured that when he entered that kind of dialect, he was directing his song to a Jamaican audience. The song is full of proverbs that he piles one on top of the other. He not only takes existing proverbs and appropriates them for the song, but he uses the structure of these proverbs to create his own proverbial lines. Here we see him continuing the agenda of drawing on the Jamaican language and culture to create his songs. He does this without apology, but he does it carefully with a quality of innovation and care for craft that is remarkable.

The song opens with an almost childlike taunt. The melody that opens the song will be repeated again and again forming a chant, a taunt, a tease of the lyric. The scat that the I-Three sing lends the song a playful quality that belies the tragic seriousness of the lyric. Marley begins with a world-weary tone. The line is sharp in its summation of truth and it lays out the battlelines. This is a song about the 'we' and the 'them'. Here Marley is acutely aware of the conditions of the poor in the ghettoes of Kingston. Despite the promise made by the Manley government in 1972 of 'better must come', it is clear, at least to Marley, that better has not come yet. But what is clearer is that Marley is convinced that better has come for some. There are those who are moving around with full bellies and those who must be content with hungry bellies.

It is telling that Marley manages to couch the message of the terrible conditions of Jamaica's economic situation in what would seem to be a dance song – a song that declares: 'Forget your troubles and dance / Forget your weakness and dance.' Is this a call to escape, to take flight from the realities of life and become consumed by the false securities of partying and dancing? The song appears to rest on a fundamental contradiction: on the one hand the conditions of the poor are clearly laid out for all to see, and on the other hand the call to action is, seemingly, a call to inaction – a call to something useless like dancing. For those who had seen the Wailers and their Rastafarianism as an affirmation of the idleness of poor youth, this song confirmed everything they had been saying. All such people did was not work, smoke ganja and spend their days and nights terrorising people. Marley knew of this opinion and played on it. The song is only fully comprehended when we understand the point of the dance in the context of reggae music and also in the context of Rastafarianism.

Marley grew up in rural Jamaica where he saw the value of the church and the communal acts of worship, which helped to sustain the community. He would have seen in the country, as well as in Kingston, the cult groups that held ceremonies of worship, healing and community affirmation in prayer circles, dance circles and song circles. He would have seen and heard the chanting, drumming, tambourine beating and the flat antiphonal singing of the revivalists and he would have understood that dance for them was not merely an act of escape into fanciful movements, but was, in fact, central to the ritual of connecting with a spiritual centre. It was part of the act of community and part of the act of transformation in the movement towards healing. In Jamaica, many Afro-religious cults are defined by their dance and little else. Pocomania is defined by the dance Kumina, which is a complex of movements and ritual action that culminates in possession and healing. And there are others: dinki mini, Mayal, brukkins and more. Each of these are clearly defined dances that Marley would have seen, for in all of these instances the spectator was as much a part of the ritual as were the participants. In Kingston, Marley would have seen the Burru men beating their drums and doing the welcome dance for those of their number who were returning from prison. The Burru men were part of a cult that had strong West African elements, but they belonged to a decidedly disenfranchised and ostracized group – the lowest of the low. They were cultists and they were notorious as criminals. The Rastafarians fled the rural areas where they were attacked and threatened by the ever-weary authorities – who were convinced by claims by Rastafarian leaders like Howell that they were planning to take over the government of Jamaica. They therefore attacked their encampment in the hills, scattering them throughout Kingston. In Kingston, the Rastafarians settled in areas like the Dungle, where they met up with the Burru men. Rastafarians would later borrow their drumming style from the Burru men. Marley would have seen these men and seen the importance of dance in their communities. He would also have seen the swirling dancers of the Niyahbinghi dance, which was associated with a radical and warrior sub-cult of the Rastafarian movement. It has been noted that Marley's distinctive spins and drunken swirls, his high-kneed struts and swaying torso movements on stage all emerged from the Niyahbinghi dance. In this context, dance is not escape, dance is as declarative as prophecy – an enacting of the dancer's position. In such a case, dance is defiance.

Finally, Marley was a central part of the dance craze that took hold of Jamaica in the 1960s. According to singer Derrick Morgan, who was one of the first people to encourage Marley to perform, Marley's biggest problem was that he loved to dance more than he loved to sing. He would go on stage and expend so much energy dancing that he had little breath to sing properly. Marley was a dancing man, and he understood that the music of the 1960s – the ska, especially – was a music for dancers, a music to help ritualize the pseudo-spiritual world of the dancehall.

The dancehall was a place where one expressed a sense of self, a sense of belonging and a sense of difference. The dancehall was a place where songs with deep sexual and romantic content were sung, and yet a place, as well, where political songs were presented along with religious and cautionary songs. It makes sense that anyone who visited the dancehall appreciated the fact that dancing was not simply a fanciful flight from reality. Dancing is part of the ritual of multi-levelled communication. The dance is an act of defiance, an act of communal celebration and, most significantly, an act of individual affirmation of self. So when Marley sings, 'forget your sickness and dance' it is as close to a call to spiritual healing as one can get in a secular pop context. This is not an exhortation to forget things in the sense of a dumb obliteration of memory. On the contrary, it is an exhortation to dance despite all these things – dance rather than become entrapped and petrified by these hardships. It is only in the light of this reading of the term 'dance' that we can see the revolutionary and incendiary quality of this song. In that regard the statement 'a hungry mob is an angry mob' becomes deeply ominous. But make no mistake about it, Marley is being clever about the articulation of his political views. In many ways, he cannot be accused of inciting rebellion. He is merely asking people to party and have a good time. But Jamaicans knew better. The power of the song lies in the clear way that Marley comments on the conditions that exist in the island. He is a voice speaking what he liked to call 'the news'. This was his role in the society, and he offered the country a way to understand the realities around it that was succinct and disturbing in its accuracy. Marley dragged his language from the streets, from the newspapers, from the speeches of politicians and economists as well as from the rural folk whose words of wisdom ground this song. Here Marley is not trying to reach for the American voice. The language is now increasingly Jamaican.

The proverbial equations employed in the song make use of a riddle structure. Each proverbial phrase is an expansion of the one before, and all come together to describe the condition of the world in which the artist lives. The statements are simple truisms: 'a hungry mob is an angry mob'; others are witty turns of phrase: 'A rain a-fall but the dutty tuff.' This last statement relies on a Jamaican proverb. Despite the rain that is falling, the ground remains hard and unresponsive to the labours of the workers. Marley relies here on a farming metaphor, as he will in so many of his later songs. The image of the pot on the stove suggests the communal pot of the ghetto. The message is clear – things are bad, they are actually quite difficult, but there is a promise, a hint of hope that is constantly being undermined by the reality. Again, Marley makes use of the dualisms that help to draw attention to the contrasting experiences of the wealthy and the poor. So each line begins with a positive observation: 'Dem belly full', 'Rain a-fall' and 'Pot a cook', and then closes with a negative and stark observation of the reality. The hope that was promised during the 1972 elections won by the socialist People's National Party is in fact not being realized at all. Marley is aware that there are those who are suggesting that things have improved, and he is arguing that what may seem like an improvement is in fact a façade concealing the true abjection faced by the poor.

From this outlining of the hardship of the ghetto life, Marley then commands the audience to respond with dance. The order seems absurd at some level, but we have come to see that the command to dance is not a trite one. In many ways, the very construction of the phrase helps us to understand that he does not see dance as a secular act, but as a deeply spiritual one. The dance is to 'Jah music', which makes it clear that the dancer is acknowledging the music of Jah. The dancer is worshipping

Jah as he or she faces the hardships of life in the ghetto. In this regard, the act of forgetting troubles, sorrows, weakness and sickness is not one of escape but one that points to the work of Jah in solving these problems. Worship, then, redirects the pain and the anger – it points them to the source of solace and hope.

The second verse makes it clear that Marley sees this moment as an apocalyptic one. Establishing this idea is central to the success of the song as an act of defiance and resistance and not as a mere lament of pain and hardship. The song is about facing the hardship and coming to the conclusion that Jah will somehow right the wrongs of society that have caused the poor to suffer as they have. The language of economics is used here, but Marley is also delving into the true meaning of the phrase. The cost to live is high. The loss of life to police bullets, to starvation and to the acts of terrorism enacted by ghetto criminals are all part of the cost of living. But Marley is writing about 1970s Jamaica, where the cry of poverty was increasingly extending to both the poor and the rich. By 1975, the exodus of middle-class brown Jamaicans was in full swing. The rich were distressed by what they felt was Manley's courting of the likes of Fidel Castro and alienating himself from the US. Manley was no longer just talking about nationalizing major industries, but was actually doing it. On the streets, the hints of major shortages of food and other basic goods that would become the norm in the mid- to late 1970s was already clear. Marley could see that something of a 'tribulation' was at hand. He was writing these songs at a time when other reggae artists were employing this concept of the apocalypse, convinced that something quite serious was going to happen – something cataclysmic and explosive.

By the time Marley comes to repeat the first verse, he has shifted to the more intensely Jamaican language that encodes the lyrics in Rasta-speak: 'A pot a yook but the yood nuh nuff,' is the Rasta rendering of 'a pot a cook, but the food nuh nuff'. The use of the 'y' to replace the hard consonant, along with the ubiquitous use of the 'I' to replace other consonants and by so doing to somehow grant a holiness to the word, become devices that Marley will employ as he enters the language of his faith. This transformative act creates distance between him and his non-

Jamaican audience, but it is something that Marley would employ again and again as both an act of rebellion and a clear affirmation of his commitment to using the best language for a given song. This sense of truth-speaking is central to the Marley mode of writing and performance.

In the face of tribulation, the angry mob makes complete sense, and the call to 'chuck' makes even more sense. For the listener who continues to think that the call to dance is the call to party or the call to somehow deflate anger and tension, an understanding of the word 'chuck' will show how absurd such a notion is. Marley is relying on the true revolutionaries to understand that when he says 'we gonna chuck' he means that he is invoking the spirit of the rude boy/warrior who is ready to 'chuck badness' against the oppressive system that is causing all the problems in Jamaica. The word 'chuck' has various connotations in Jamaican language. To chuck may be to throw, to push or to walk or dance in a posture of defiance and aggression. The act of pushing someone in the chest as a declaration of one's intention to fight is to chuck. So, when Marley calls the people to chuck to the music, he is in fact encouraging aggression. This is a posture that is not about dancing away troubles through the obliviating of awareness, but one that is about enacting resistance to the oppression.

This is radical stuff. It is politically disturbing stuff and, in many ways, it would cause some concern among the ruling party at the time. It is true that Marley was a friend of Manley, but it is also true that in this song, and in the entire album, Marley is creating some distance between himself and Manley. The normal practice would have been for Marley, a Trench Town man and, by normal logic, a PNP man, to have now simply celebrated the revolutionary ideas that the PNP was espousing and not make much of the continued oppression of the poor. Marley does not merely attack the historical system of oppression, as would have been safe, but suggests in the very contemporary line, 'cost of living get so high', that he is not speaking of the past but about the present, about what has happened in the last few weeks. And while there is a passive suggestion that the cost of living has just happened to get high on its own, everyone is aware that Marley is pointing a finger at the people responsible for these economic matters – those who speak in the language of economics – the government. He is using their language to attack them. It is a sharp piece of protest songwriting, the kind of 'cussing' writing that he had honed while working for the sound-system men Coxsone Dodd and Lee Perry. Now Marley had changed the enemy from a rival dancehall to the larger political system. It is in this act that we begin to see how Marley saw his role as spokesman against those who seek to oppress the poor.

For Marley, the method of rebellion and resistance was always the song. It is not clear whether he expected people to rise up and burn down the city or act in truly rebellious ways, but what is clear is that he saw the music not simply as a vehicle of resistance, but also as an act of resistance. On one hand the song was a way to educate and inform and, as such, was defying the entrapment of ignorance that was holding back the people. At the same time, the music was a music that was seen by the élite as something bad, something uncouth and something that went against everything that is good and decent in the community. But chanting his song, by playing reggae, by ensuring that it got air play, Marley was actually enacting resistance – his own kind of resistance. The making of songs about poor people, the writing of the story of the people of Trench Town into history and time, was an act of defiance and resistance. Prior to this, no one had written their stories, and so they were likely to vanish from the history of the society. Marley will say again and again that he was single-handedly fighting a war with his music. There is a sense in which he saw the making of the song as the sum of resistance, even more than what he felt it would cause people to do. One has the distinct sense that he regarded the education of the people as central to their capacity to survive in the ghetto. He also saw his songs as a way to speak to those who oppressed the poor and to let them know that the poor had a sophisticated understanding of what oppression was about – that they were not living in ignorance.

The element of escape, however, is part of Marley's view of the value of music. In his way of thinking, the poor need a means to escape, to enjoy life in the midst of pain. This is part of their survival. Marley's praise of ganja was not always based on what he saw as its sacramental value. He would say that 'all people need to get high'. He explains in interviews that the quest for a high is natural to all human beings. He just did not approve of the use of alcohol and harder narcotics that were damaging to the body. For him, the peace and flight afforded by marijuana is a good thing. In *Kaya* he sings about the desire to escape, to touch the sky, to get above the falling rain. For him, this is not counter-revolutionary, this is merely a condition of the human. More doctrinaire Marxist revolutionaries would look at any mechanism that seemed to dull the senses of the poor and helped them to escape their reality as somewhat suspect – a kind of opiate. Tellingly, the poor have always understood that their need to escape is part of their revolutionary act. In Haiti, Trinidad, Brazil and New Orleans the carnival is that place of flight and escape. Its political value lies in what it does to sustain the body and soul of the poor. Edwidge Danticatt, the brilliant Haitian novelist, writing about carnival in Haiti quoted a Haitian director of the Jacmel carnival and a philosopher of the spirit of carnival. He offers this most poetic explanation of the value of escape and pleasure in the act of revolution:

> Carnival has always been a break from life… This is a country where people are poor in money perhaps, but rich in culture. Carnival is our chance to show our kind of wealth. If people were only concerned about bread, would you ever have any artistic expression at all? Would people paint, write, make music? It's like the proverb says, 'After the dance, the drum is heavy.' But during the dance, you're not thinking about the weight of the drum. You forget your troubles and have a good time. (*After The Dance*)

As with the blues artist, the reggae artist finds a radical hope in the ability to create, to allow the making of music to serve as a declaration of his or her humanity. It is this that Marley is pleading for when he says dance. Dancing is not an empty and useless escape. It is a long-held tradition of hope that has sustained so many oppressed people over the years. But there is an understanding that humanity has always been celebrated and affirmed when someone is creating, making something out of nothing. Reggae, like carnival, is evidence of that remarkable alchemy. Therefore Marley says, 'Forget you troubles and dance / Forget your weakness and dance...' This is hope, not mere escape for its own sake. It is definitely not a lowering of arms.

The formal qualities of this song are worth noting here. In this lyric, Marley shows his inclination to create a unity of sound and phrasing to ensure that the song feels compact and well formed. The use of the 'a' to open the second, third and fourth lines is part of this pattern of coining phrases to create the opening line rhyme. By the time Marley gets to the end of the song, virtually every line of the opening verse begins with the 'a' sound, which, while suggesting a present continuous in what is happening, is really a sound device that reminds me of some of the forced rhymes that Jamaican DJs would use to ensure the harmonics of their own lines. This is a call-and-response song and because of the strong use of repetition, Marley avoids having to use a stricter rhyme scheme. That would be too much here. Instead, he allows the slow repetition to grow naturally into a mantra. There is no narrative here, just a series of observations that cut right through to the reality of the situation. The song is at once prophetic, didactic and purely an act of observation. While the song could be read as a call to arms, it can also be justifiably read as a prophetic promise of something dangerous to come. Finally, Marley could have argued that he was merely lamenting the tough situation faced by the poor. The truth is that the song combines all these factors. Above all, it is a communal song that relies on the call-and-response technique to assure its popularity – its effectiveness as a song that is hard to forget.

In 'Rebel Music', however, Marley returns to the storytelling approach to songwriting that he had previously mastered. The story is personal and yet it is quite clearly a parable too. If the song is a blues of lamentation, the title indicates that Marley is doing far more than that – he is singing a song of rebellion. The song was formerly titled 'Road Block'. That title was changed. The reason is obvious. 'Road Block' is a blues lament; 'Rebel Music' is a reggae anthem of resistance. The song makes this clear from the first line. From the unsettling wail of Marley, whose voice cuts across all sound like the wail and shout of a warrior about to do battle, to the opening phrase 'Dis a rebel music', Marley is stating very clearly that this IS rebel music. It is rebel music because it is defiant and it is commenting on the brutality of the police force and the authorities who have made life difficult for the poor and black.

Jamaica in the early 1970s was developing a fairly disturbing police system that entailed the marriage of the army with the police constabulary to enforce everyday law and order. The 1972 elections had ensured that the same principles that operated in the dancehall during the 1950s and 1960s were now being employed in the political arena. Rude boys, whose job it was to attack rival sound systems and destroy their equipment and damage their prize DJs, were now being employed by politicians, who made it quite clear that the system of patronage was essential for their survival. A politician who lost an election and a seat in parliament was not going to be able to deliver jobs and opportunities for his community. The young men knew that without the patronage of the politicians they would have nothing. So they became supporters of the politicians – loyal unto death. Jamaican elections have increased in violence year after year. The violence has almost always been focused on the poor. Intense warfare between rival areas is simply a part of the Jamaican social fabric, particularly in Kingston.

Marley was very aware that the ruling government was made up of people who had been fighting for such power for generations. In many ways, their ability to harness the support of the working classes was a triumph in their quest for power. Independence meant that they had finally realized the aim of self-government, which was part of a larger sense of entitlement that they felt they had as Jamaicans. But the Jamaica that they ruled and sought to propagate was one that still maintained a status quo that gave privilege to the middle class and ensured that the working class always remained available to serve that middle class. If all of this sounds like the language of a Marxist reading of the situation, in many ways it is. But this reading was definitely one that was current in Jamaica at that time. Marley had heard Manley speak of this circumstance in his quest for power and he would have, for a while, believed that Manley would bring about the revolutionary change that was so desperately needed.

In 'Rebel Music' it is clear that Marley is not convinced that the change has come. According to Stephen Davis, 'Rebel Music' was written after Marley and some of his friends, including the legendary soccer star Alan 'Skill' Cole and lover and actress Esther Anderson, were stopped by police at a road block while they were returning from a break in St Elizabeth. While driving through rural Jamaica, they had been enjoying a smoke of herb. But they knew that were they to have been stopped with herb in the vehicle, they would face arrest and possibly worse. The irony is that this was a crew of Jamaican celebrities – popular people who the authorities would have known. Furthermore, they were brown people – Marley was half white and Alan 'Skill' Cole light-skinned. Esther Anderson's parents were Indian and European. So simply on the basis of their complexions, these people were privileged. What they were worried about was not the vigilance of the police force, but about the fact that they were Rastafarians with dreadlocks – men associated with the cult that was looked down upon by middle-class Jamaica. It is not clear what could have happened to these people, but Marley and his companions were concerned enough to try and make sure that no traces of weed were in the vehicle when the police approached. Marley's Trench Town connections would not help. He was a ghetto boy regardless of his growing popularity.

The song is an angry one. It is founded on a strong sense of affront by Marley who speaks of his island as an 'open country'. This is a hope. The hope is that he wants to be able to roam through Jamaica freely, he wants to be able to live here as if he owns the space and is free to live how he wants to live in this space. The song, then, is as much about the fear of the ruthless authorities as it is about marijuana and the freedom that Marley demands to smoke it in a free country. The illegality of smoking herb is not at issue here and was never an issue for Marley. The Babylon system of Jamaica declared ganja to be illegal and Marley saw that as a profoundly immoral and idiotic position. Tosh made it clear that he found the position hypocritical as all Jamaicans, including the very ones persecuting Rastas for possessing the herb, smoked or used the weed in some other way.

But Marley is able to make his song about more than just the problem with his freedom to smoke weed. He is declaring himself a part inheritor of the island. He asks why he can't roam a free country. He is challenging the very notion of freedom. For a Trench Town youth, this is not open country. For all Jamaicans, he is suggesting, this is a police state, a state with road blocks that prevent people from expressing their freedom. The metaphor will grow as the song expands its implication – when Marley speaks directly to the policeman telling him that he has no birth 'cerfiticate' on him.

This wonderful moment of humour in the song is also, perhaps, the most powerful statement in the song. Marley address the authorities sardonically. Mr Cop is demanding identification, and Marley addresses the absurdity of the question by letting the policeman know that he does not travel with a birth certificate. But he does more than that – he is pointing to the sense of imprisonment that the demand for identification implies. This request for identification from a man of the country, a free man in the country, smacks of the pass laws in South Africa – laws that Marley would have been aware of. Marley rejects the system of identification that has been developed by the state. He denies the source of his authority. His birth certificate would grant him authority because it would point out that he is the child of a European – a white man of some status in Jamaica. Marley has been rejected by that white man and his family. When Marley approached the family of his late father for some help to get started with farming in St Ann, they told him and Rita that he may be the child of Norval Marley, but Norval had left nothing for him and they would not be able to help. Marley was disappointed and angry, but he had given up on that connection long ago. The privilege of his birth certificate was not something he wanted to rely upon for, in turning to it, he would be doing the very thing that he saw the élite doing to the poor in the society. Marley therefore suggests another source of his sense of self and identity and his position in Jamaican society. He speaks to the policemen and, in so doing, he is speaking to the larger audience. This is how they will find his true credentials; by checking his soul and his life.

He is therefore ordering them to look into his soul, to look into his life if they want to find his place in the society, if they want a justification for his presence. The road block becomes a symbol of all the barriers placed before a man from the ghetto. This is not an open country, and it was increasingly police-controlled in the 1970s. His act of defiance is to deny the cops a chance to see the 'ticket' that they want him to show. Marley's rendering of certificate as 'cerfiticate' is entirely Jamaican. This 'mispronunciation' can be explained well by linguists, as they also explain why Jamaicans say 'flim' instead of 'film', and 'apprrr' instead of 'apple'. What is clear to me is that Marley would easily have altered this pronunciation of the word if he felt it was necessary. He clearly did not. For him the rendering positions him squarely as a sufferah. More importantly, the pronunciation becomes a mockery of the word – he is laughing at the rules of the authorities and what they value. He is defying the request for him to show his 'ticket'. Such a pun would not have been lost on him.

In this, as in many of the songs from this period, Marley is enjoying the dialogue that he has developed with the I-Threes, his newly formed backing singers. As the single lead voice for the group, Marley had to change the structure of the songs to exploit this new arrangement. This was no longer a trio or quartet – a band of voices that held solo positions at different points and that spoke in direct banter when vamping on an idea. In a song like 'Get Up Stand Up', Marley, Tosh and Wailer are sparring, offering different perspectives on a single theme, strong voices soloing. The call/response is there, but this is not the leader/chorus structure – it is dialogue; voices that find their strength in the rich clash of tones, textures and ideas. Once it was clear that the original Wailers were done, Marley decided to work with Rita and her two friends, Judy Mowatt and Marcia Griffith, on a more permanent basis. They worked together to complete Natty Dread and were the voices behind the entire album. This time, Marley was the lead voice and they were the choric voice. They made up a single voice, not a series of voices. They were supporting Marley, echoing his ideas, carrying his message and granting the audience a position in the dialogue between singer and community. Marley worked hard on their vocal parts, adding lines to songs that would lend them ironies, humour and strong echoes for emphasis. And where the original Wailers developed fairly complex backing vocals that allowed the three-part harmonies to shine, with the I-Threes Marley treated their voices as a single unit. They worked three-part harmonies together and Marley's high tenor rode around their full harmonies. The structure of their harmonies was never complex – not as complex as the stuff done by the early Wailers, which modelled the doo-wop styles of Motown. Here, Marley created a true choric group that allowed him to rest, to find other spaces for his phrasing while they reliably retained the basic structure of the songs.

So, in a song like this, the first verse arrives with the clear emphasis on key themes in the song carried by the I-Three. He asks why he can't roam this open country, and they repeat the words 'open country'. Then he asks why he can't be who he wants to be, declaring at the same time that he wants to be free. They echo and support him with 'want to be free'. This is the shape of the call-and-response. Indeed, in this song we hear Marley coaching the I-Threes, dragging them along to speak back at him. When he says, 'let me hear you down there' he is calling for the backing singers to enter the song and join in this lively taunt of the police. He says, 'I say hey', and they echo 'Hey!'. Immediately afterwards, he calls to the cops, 'hey, Mr Cop.' He has used the I-Threes to draw the audience into the taunting. Their function becomes quite clear – they are speaking for the audience.

One of the interesting things about the relationship between the I-Threes and Bob Marley is the way in which their language registers contrasted with each other. There is such care in the trio to enunciate carefully and 'properly', sometimes to a fault. This clean sound sometimes helped the non-Jamaican listener understand much of what Marley was saying, but something else was going on there. The I-Three were a decidedly female presence in the songs and they brought a finesse to contrast starkly with the raw energy of Marley. In an odd way they served to soften the music that went out as well as draw attention to its radical nature by the sheer contrast between the tough message and the sweet harmonies. They offered their songs in 'respectable' tones, yet the content of their songs was incendiary and deeply radical. This complex of tones was central to Marley's art. 'One good thing about music, when it hits, you feel no pain' (from 'Trench Town Rock'). The I-Threes helped to deaden the blows of the music – but the message was never compromised.

In 'So Jah Seh', Marley lays out clearly the negative side of his relationship with this 'home', where home is Jamaica, the land of captivity, which relates to Egypt in the symbology of the Jewish Diasporic tradition. 'So Jah Seh' is a stunning achievement of songwriting because in it we see Marley explore a more varied and complex melody structure, and his phrasing takes full advantage of the openness of the reggae song – a song that is about spaces and the use of those spaces to create rhythm. Marley is quoting scripture in this song, but here he is doing what he will do again and again – is to speak scripture in the language of Jamaicans. Marley is translating the Bible into Jamaican parlance and, in so doing, he forces the listener to appreciate that the Jamaican soil is a proper place for the working out of such epic and monumental matters as the dynamic relationship between God and his creation. So Jah's declaration, as quoted by Marley in the opening lines of the song, collapses the promises of the Bible with the world of the ghetto. His children (his sheep) will not be beggars of bread on the sidewalks of the city.

This is a bold statement to make since many of the sufferers of the ghetto are doing exactly that – sitting on the pavement and begging for bread. But this is a song of prophecy, not a statement of the current reality. Marley is the preacher who is looking at the Bible and discovering in it the promises that Jah has made with his 'sheep'. By positioning himself as a sheep of Jah he is defying any idea that he belongs to the unblessed and the downtrodden. The song then unfolds as a series of promises that are available to the chosen people. By declaring them, Marley is seeking to assure those who are listening that there are good promises awaiting them even as they try to survive in the ghettos of Babylon. He makes it clear that the ghetto is a place where suffering is inevitable. Thus the lyric seems to be disjointed: there is a conflict between what the promises are and what the reality is.

It is in a bridge that Marley shows this strange paradox. First he lays out the promises, and then the truth about reality. Finally, he offers the hope – a hope of faith, a holding on to the promise. And this hope becomes communal as well as individual. Marley turns to the quintessential Rasta phrase that speaks to the very heart of the Rastafarian philosophy of the relationship between the individual and the community. The phrase is, of course, 'I and I'. The clue to this phrase is a simple one. It means both one person – the person speaking the words – and the community to which the person belongs all at the same time. It can mean both or just the one. The thing is, the heart of Rastafarian thinking makes it impossible for a truly righteous person to mean one and not the other. Indeed, 'I' in Rasta parlance is a profoundly fascinating word as it functions as a pronoun. For instance, the word 'iya' can often be translated as 'higher' in standard English. But it can also be a substitute for the word 'man', as in 'Yes, iya,' or 'yuh cyaan do dat, iyah'. Then there is the phrase 'De I', which transliterates to be 'the I'. It actually means 'you', for the word 'I' does not automatically suggest the first person. Of course, there is a clear logic to the system: we are all 'Is' and so it makes sense that the same word should have such rich possibilities. 'I and I' therefore, means 'we', 'us', and 'me/I'. 'I-man' means 'me'. I will not attempt an in-depth linguistic study of the phrases here, but suffice it to say that when Marley employs the phrase 'I and I' to declare what he and his people will do, he is invoking the spirit of Rastafarianism and is also managing to counterbalance the seemingly tragic reality that he lays out in the song. He announces that he and his people will 'hang on in deh' and will not 'leggo' (let go). What they will not let go of is their faith in the promises that are clearly spoken in the verses that precede this chant.

This freedom to speak of his faith is one of the most striking things about Marley's writing. Marley could easily have assumed a rather secular and iconoclastic position in his movement into the heart of the rock world. But he does not embrace that kind of nihilism. Instead he allows the clarity of his own confession and the passionate truth of it to permeate his lyric. There is no irony in Marley's devotion to Jah. It is a plain-spoken faith and one that is never compromised in song after song. Marley always revealed a clear sense of the larger cosmology and metaphysical sensibility that shaped his way of viewing the world in all his songs, whether they were political songs, love songs or revolutionary songs. It is clear from many of the statements made by Marley that he never regarded his speaking about Jah as a particularly religious activity. For Marley, the easy dichotomies expressed in Western society between the secular and the spiritual make little sense and can find no relevance for him. When asked by reporters about his religious beliefs and their place in popular music, Marley answered that Rastafarianism was not a religion, not a culture but a way of living, a natural way of dealing with the world. For Marley, spiritual truth was relevant to all aspects of life. His songs would reveal this holistic vision of the world. Given his often stated view that when he wrote a song the words were given to him by Selassie, it makes sense that in 'So Jah Seh', Marley would ground his social commentary in a larger vision of redemption and hope.

The figure of Jah is presented here not as a figure of apocalyptic force, a deity bent on the destruction of the enemies of the elect. Instead, the figure is that of a benevolent and caring father – a reliable benefactor and someone who will never let his children down. For Marley, the Jah is a distinctly different figure from any father that he might have known. But his vision of Jah is all-encompassing. Speaking of the Jah whom he saw in visions, Marley would say: 'Man, it's so sweet, it's me brother, me father, me mother, me creator, everything.' In later songs, we hear the extent of his projection of trust and dependence in Jah – on Selassie – when he sings: 'If Jah didn't love I / Will I be around today / Will I be around to say?' ('Give Thanks And Praises'). For Marley, the grace of Selassie is elemental to the message he has to offer to the people. Selassie represented the prospect of redemption, especially for black people. In 1976, Marley would say: 'I have a duty to tell the truth as I have been told it. I will keep on doing it until I am satisfied the people have the message that Rastafari is the almighty and all we black people have redemption just like anyone else.'

What is clear is that Marley appreciates the fine differences between the Rastafarian insistence on a life lived fully in the here and now rather than holding onto the more Christian view of suffering in the here and now with the hope of redemption and peace in the hereafter. For Marley, the message of the negro spiritual that suggested a reliance – at least on the most superficial level – on the hope of peace and riches AFTER death, was something he did not want to adhere to. Death, for Marley, was contrary to Rastafarianism and so, while he would quote what is normally one of the most basic scriptures that speak of the afterlife and the promise of riches in glory, he was not satisfied with that alone. Marley makes this clear in a 1975 interview: 'The greatest thing them [the church] can say is about death – them say you die and go to heaven after all this sufferation. To go through all this sufferation for that! It's like after me sick me go to the doctor. No, the greatest thing is life.'

Marley's point is that the promise of a rich afterlife is essentially a panacea, a kind of stop gap to appease the person who is suffering. For Marley, doctors are not figures of healing, but evidence of sickness, evidence of frailty and evidence of death. The man who must go to the doctor is already sick. The man who must rely on an afterlife for joy has already accepted death. The promise of Jah in 'So Jah Seh', ('I go to prepare a place / And where I am, thou shall abide.') has to be temporal, so that when the singer declares that he will hang on in there and he won't let go, he is declaring that he will hold out for some respite from the suffering and the hardship.

For the Rasta, and for Marley, the place being prepared is not a mythical place in heaven, but a real place in the land of his forefathers. The place is Ethiopia. But, typically, Marley is seeking a world of unity and peace in the here and now. The proverbial interrogation that sits at the heart of the song establishes that. He asks, if 'puss and dog' can get along with each other why can't humans do the same? Love is, for him, the answer to the suffering of the poor because it is the absence of love that has caused the suffering in the first place.

The title song of the album fully articulates the heart of Marley's vision as a Rastaman. *Natty Dread* encapsulates the fundamental challenge of Rastafarianism because 'Natty Dread', the song, speaks directly to the ambivalence of the whole album about the meaning of home. The ambivalence is acute. In 'Rebel Music' Marley speaks of the open country that is his and he makes it clear that he does not think he should be treated as a lesser person in his own country. But he also knows that, according to his faith and to his evolving cosmology, Jamaica is Babylon – Jamaica is not home. Home is far away. Yet he knows too that home is the Trench Town of 'No Woman, No Cry' and home is the Trench Town that he enshrines in 'Natty Dread'. There is a strong sense of affinity to this home. Marley is thinking hard on these matters in 'Natty Dread'. He is articulating the painful truth of the Rastafarian philosophy, a truth that will return to him again and again in so many songs. This man is the same person who will sing, 'Smile Jamaica' as well as 'Babylon System'. He is singing about the same place, and yet he understands that his loyalty to these two places is in constant conflict.

Marley's 'Natty Dread' covers a vast sense of history and social commentary while proposing the new Rastafarian philosophy about the Rasta's relationship with the Babylon world in which he lives. Jamaica, as I have suggested earlier, is a site of some conflicted feelings for Marley. When asked about seeing Jamaica as home, he makes it clear that while he likes Jamaica, he sees it as a place that has been spoiled by the history of colonialism and slavery. There is a sense in which Marley sees no real hope in Jamaica. This, of course, complicates the politics of his message for if there is no hope of finding peace and security for the Rastaman in Jamaica, then what is the point of the political effort in his song to bring about a righteous order to things? It is a question that Marley answers when he suggests that what is happening in places like Jamaica is that a new order is being established, one in which the righteous will prevail and the wrongs of the past will be corrected. Marley sounds decidedly temporal when he tries to explain the heart of his song, 'Crazy Baldheads'.

The superstructure of faith and belief that shaped everything about Marley's art was predicated on one simple, but far-reaching idea – the concept of Babylon. Babylon is a biblically based term that owes its meaning to the story of the tower of Babel in Genesis, and the historical kingdom that was notorious for its attack on Jerusalem and for forcing the children of Israel into exile – an exile that would eventually become the prototype of a pattern of exile and repatriation that is part of the Jewish experience. The Christian of the New Testament would appropriate the idea of Babylon as a symbolic representation of the Roman Empire. Such vast empires are associated with evil, hubris, a rejection of God and a rich array of social and cultural debauchery that comes with the intoxication of power. Rastas have come to apply the term to the entire Western apparatus of power and exploitation, seeing it as an extension of the forces that have been working against the purposes of God. With such a colourful source, Rastafarians have effectively constructed a notion of Babylon that is perhaps one of the most unifying elements of a faith that has not yet developed a unified doctrine or series of teachings. Babylon, and all that it represents in the context of world politics, has now become so much a part of the way that Jamaicans view the world that it is now hard to see the concept as purely Rastafarian.

The success of Rastafarianism may, in fact, be credited to the clarity with which the concept of Babylon was expressed. Babylon is the symbolic description of everything that has conspired to bring about the downfall of the African. The system of slavery, the system of colonialism, the post-colonialist policies of Europe, the neo-colonialist policies of formerly colonized nations, the influence of America, the perpetuation of oppressive ideas by racist Christianity and any force, system, or philosophy that was seen as destroying the black man amounted to Babylon. This all-encompassing system was the object of Rasta resistance. While it is true that Rastafarianism is a religion and emerges out of the convictions normally associated with faith, what cannot be ignored is the fact that Rastafarianism was a conscious attempt to construct a belief system (or discover a belief system) that responded to the oppressive religious systems that prevailed in Jamaica and the rest of the diaspora during the early part of the 20th century. The leaders of Rastafarianism understood that there were, in Jamaica, many threads of resistance to those forces that they viewed as being destructive to blacks, and these threads were not being harnessed as a single entity. Apart from the political work of people like Marcus Garvey, there were the often illegal and clearly folk-centred cults of Mayal, Pocomania and other systems of divination; and then there were the long-standing Ethiopianists who employed messianic notions of some grand redemption in their belief systems; and finally there were those Afro-Christian sects that interpreted the Bible as a text that speaks directly to the black experience and that offered a millenarian view of the world – a view that promised an apocalyptic end to all oppression. Rastafarians saw in the coronation of Haile Selassie a perfect expression of the emergence of the African world, and found ways to bring all the elements of resistance to bear on a new belief system. With such a background in resistance, it makes complete sense that the Rastafarian beliefs that Marley would espouse could not, in any way, be divorced from a strong political consciousness. It is fair to say that

Rastafarianism, in its inception, did not radically alter the Judaeo-Christian concepts of good, evil, redemption and the promise of salvation. It did not challenge the notions of a fallen world in need of redemption. It certainly did not reject the Bible and turn to truly African religions like those practiced by the Yoruba, the Fanti and the Ewe people who, as it happens, were the true ancestors of these Jamaicans. Instead, Rastafarianism turned to the Bible for some clear authoritative validation of the black man's place in the larger prophecies of the world. In other words, Rastafarianism is a truly Caribbean religion because it is founded on resistance and, more crucially, founded on the radical reinterpretation of the oppressive systems that once kept the black people in bondage. At its core, then, is the very act of resistance and this, no doubt, explains why it was attractive to Marley because, as a youth, he was inclined towards rebellion and deeply sensitive to the political realities that faced the poor blacks of Jamaica – people like himself.

So when he opens 'Natty Dread', he does so with as overt a celebration of the Rastafarian as he could muster. The song begins with an address – that is, he seems to be addressing the Natty Dread, as he does throughout the song. At the same time, the opening line is a descriptive statement – an introductory announcement of what he is about to express. The introductory summary does several things. First it establishes the subject of the song and does so with boldness by drawing attention to the very thing that would normally cause offense – the dreadlocks. Secondly, he locates the Rastafarian within the world of Babylon, establishing, in the process, that this is a song about exile – a song about the need for the dreadlocked Rastaman to find his true home once more. Thirdly, Marley tosses out a few key words that are central to the theme of the song. If the song is about exile, then it is also about the recovery of roots, of a sense of history and of an understanding of home – the true home of the black man.

The terrain of Babylon just happens to be the same terrain as his beloved Trench Town. But Marley is never nostalgic about Trench Town. He has said again and again in song that Trench Town was a harsh place, a hard place where the living is hardest. Trench Town was a place that forced people to do things that were hard and tough. But the dreadlocks man begins to enact a walk through the ghetto. It is a specific walk that takes him from one end of the town to the other. Marley creates a chant based on a counting song – a device that he uses in songs like 'Misty Morning' (where he counts the days of the week) and 'Work' ('five days to go, working for a nex' day / Four days to go, working for a nex' day…'). In this instance, however, the numbers of the street are actually the street names of the roads in Trench Town. The small grid of streets that make up Trench Town move from First Street in the southernmost end near Marcus Garvey Drive, and then onto second, third and fourth streets in a northerly direction. Marley, therefore, appears to be enacting a visit to Trench Town in these lyrics, and the singer speaks of the streets with familiarity and some affection. The constant refrain throughout the song is 'Natty Dread' so that a call and response dialogue takes place between Marley and the I-Three.

The town is full of people that he knows – dreads he talks to and meets up with. This is home for him. And yet, having established this intimacy with the streets of Kingston, Marley quickly reminds us that this place is not quite home – that it is, in fact, 'a thousand miles away from home'.

But the stage by stage journey that the song enacts assumes a mystical quality that seems to be producing the progression of the Rastafarian through various levels of consciousness culminating in the magical 'seventh level'. This place of understanding is elemental to any hope for the black man. Marley speaks directly to the audience and he addresses them as 'children'. It is an important gesture that we will see Marley use whenever he is assuming the role of teacher and pastor. He calls on the 'children' to get their culture.

For Marley the embrace of culture is an act of radical consciousness. Culture, for him, is not something that you just happen to have. Instead it is something you can lose. The condition of the black man for him is one of loss and alienation. The black person has to take a hold of his or her sense of history and then apply that to present life. The consequences of not doing that are expressed through a series of lines that would sound familiar to a Marley fan. He resurrects the ominous threat of the rude boy in 'Simmer Down': 'Simmer down, cause the battle will be hotter /

Simmer down, and you won't get no supper'. In 'Natty Dread' however, the threat is far more significant. The stakes are much higher here because the issue that is being focused on is the very issue of identity and the meaning of existence and survival for the African within the diaspora.

For Marley, Trench Town, with its grid of streets, is essentially a metaphor for Babylon, and so in the lyrics he walks through the city enacting the journey of the Rastaman preaching in the streets of Babylon. But as abject as the conditions of Trench Town are, and as much as the poverty and the struggle of living in that place constitute the very heart of the alienation that Rastafarians feel in Babylon, the song 'Natty Dread' does not become a pathetic song of lament. There is something quite upbeat about it, and there is that final image of hope and possibility that drives the spirit of the whole song. After admonishing the 'children' to get their culture, Marley then begins to speak as a Rastafarian, as a man who is bent on defying all the norms of society in order to set out on his own path.

Here he is optimistic and defiant. Regardless of what the world might say, he cannot go astray. He cannot, that is, be wrong about what he believes or about the struggle in which he is involved. More than that, the Rasta will see things unfold in the way that he has prophesied – things will go his way. The image of a brilliant new day becomes another instance in which Marley embraces sunshine with hope and freedom. In all of this, Marley uses the communal phrase 'I and I', making his declaration at once a statement of personal defiance and a prophetic statement about Rastafarianism.

This statement of hope is rooted in a faith in the 'new world' that is to come. It is a new world that Marley sings of in his song 'I Know'. In this new world, the downtrodden will be the head. The stone that the builders refuse will be the head corner stone. And embedded in the song are the references to basic traits of the Rastafarian. They appear to be throwaway phrases, dropped into the lyric for sound effect more than anything else, but Marley is always more careful in his later compositions.

These descriptors for the Rastafarian are, therefore, quite important, for they explain quite succinctly what the radical core of the song is. They include, 'Roots Natty, Roots Natty,' and 'Dreadlocks binghi, Congo

I'. The former draws attention to the importance of roots and history. The latter is more complex for it draws attention to the headdress of the Rasta, a critical symbol of resistance for the Rastafarian ('grow your dread locks, / Don't be afraid of the wolf pack'). But the other two references are critical ones. First he refers to the 'binghi', which is a reference to the Niyahbinghi – a radical warrior sect of Rastafari whose commitment to the extermination of Babylon is sometimes quite dramatic. The 'Congo' points to Marley's attempt to associate Rastafarianism with Africa and the grand symbol of Africa that the Congo represents.

The song is locked into the apocalyptic vision that shaped much of what Marley would write during the middle of the decade. In 1975 he made it clear that that sense of apocalypse that was clearly flowing through Jamaica was something he could feel as well.

> It's the last days without a doubt. 1975. It's the last quarter before the year 2000 and righteousness – the positive way of thinking – must win. Good over evil. We're confident of victory.

Quoting Haile Selassie, Marley declared in that statement his conviction that things would work out triumphantly for the Rastafarian.

If 'Natty Dread' offers a preacher's perspective on the dilemma of the Rastafarian in Babylon – that is, if the song is public in its articulation 'Talkin' Blues' is deeply personal. Marley's own sense of the lyrical and the peculiar position of the singer as someone who is telling his own story and yet one who positions himself as a spokesman for the community, is well demonstrated in this song. But the most striking thing about 'Talkin' Blues' is that it reveals quite clearly the extent to which, lyrically, Marley recognized that reggae music, while rooted in other traditions like the blues, is a distinctive form that offers a view of the world that is radical and transformative.

Marley's rebel songs are characterized by a blues-like expression of suffering and pain, a certain vulnerability that emerges as a lamentation. The rude bwai must justify his suffering, his position in society that is dominated by a system of oppression. This rude bawi's sense of self becomes defined by a sense of being stymied by the 'Babylon System' –

the police force and other agents of the 'Society' (a term for the Jamaican social establishment) – and he seeks to break from that oppressive rule. So there is a quality of lamentation, a narrative of suffering that is akin to the blues. We see this pattern very clearly in many of Marley's compositions of the late 1960s and early 1960s, which was a time when he was not totally inscribed in the 'peace-loving' doctrines of the Rastafarian, but had embraced a revolutionary stance of righteous rebellion – an explosive quality that was tempered by values like vulnerability. It is the dance between these two elements of the rude bwai as understood by Marley that we begin to discover the complexity of Marley's lyric.

For while we sense in Marley a willingness to sustain the notion of the poet as griot, we also recognize a lyrical quality to Marley's work that will become a trademark structure: the movement from the persona, 'I', construction, to the communal assertion. It is the structure of the 'witness' or 'testimony' in the Jamaica working-class Church and the pattern of the Rastafarian articulation of self that becomes collapsed into the mystical and complex notion of 'I and I'.

In 'Talkin' Blues', Marley begins with the personal: 'Cold ground was my bed last night / And rock was my pillow too', but that will shift into the communal in which he begins to address the community: 'And who's gonna stay at home / When the freedom fighters are fighting?' In compositions like 'Talkin' Blues' we see a pattern that will repeat itself throughout Marley's oeuvre. Marley owns the narrative with a series of deeply evocative images and metaphors, and then expands the projection of his articulations through a series of proverbial declaration that are at once enigmatic and at the same time part of the code language of the Rastafarian and the folk community.

The rebel that emerges in Marley's work is an extremely angry and volatile individual whose desire for revolutionary and violent action is unmistakably clear. But what is distinctive about the Marley lyric is that the sincerity of the expression of anger and the call for violent action is underlined by a vulnerable confession, a kind of blues lamentation. These blues, however, are never enough – for in Marley's work it is not enough to simply express pain, but it becomes absolutely necessary to articulate the need for explosive action.

Marley, though, understood the blues as a musical form and, as we have seen, he listened to and enjoyed a lot of blues music. It makes sense, then, that 'Talkin' Blues' begins with a decidedly blues structure. The blues line is structured around the repetition of a single phrase followed by a rhyming third phrase that constitutes a kind of punch line.

The structure is predictable and, as with most forms, an affirmation of a culture's sense of order and predictability. The blues form, then, like all other forms, is comforting. The blues apprentice must understand both the ethos and structure of the form. The blues will introduce a dilemma and then find a way, if not to resolve it, to at least offer a perspective on that dilemma – a way to manage it. The act of making a blues song, then, is not merely an effort to simply express oneself, not simply to vent, but to – through the art of voicing – bring the pain under control. The blues song seeks to manage pain and to grant power to the person telling the story of the pain. This is why the blues song does not always evoke sadness but, in fact, despite its seemingly morose themes, often evokes laughter, acceptance and, less often, action.

Yet there is something passive about the blues song. It rarely calls for action, rarely serves as a way to express the collective pain of a community. The blues, then, in contrast to the negro spiritual, for instance, is a deeply individualistic musical form. It is focused not on the community, but on the individual. The blues song is not a choric song, it is a solo song. It is, then, quintessentially American. And this is why Marley seems to discover the limitation of the blues song.

Marley's lyrics flirt with the blues idea and, in many ways, it is the lyricism of the blues that distinguishes Marley's lyrics from those of many other reggae artists of his generation. Marley always seemed intent on exploring the lyrical, the personal, even as he struggled with the tension between the 'I' and the 'I and I'. As we have seen, then, Marley songs would assume a pattern that led him from the first to the second again and again.

In 'Talkin' Blues' we see how that path is reflective of Marley's own musical journey. The first few lines of 'Talkin' Blues' are blues lines in structure and mood. After repeating the line 'Cold ground was my bed last night and rock was my pillow, too', he introduces the punch line, which announces that people have said his 'feet are too big' for his shoes. The second blues verse begins with the predictable structure – mirroring the structure of the first verse. The singer states that he has been on the rock for so long that he has what he terms a 'permanent screw'. The rock is a hard place but it is also one of the Jamaicanisms for Jamaica. Jamaicans call their island, 'The Rock' or 'Jam Rock'. The image evokes both the solidity of home and the hard-scrabble existence associated with living at home. Marley is alluding to the latter image, but he is making it clear that his condition is of one who is 'down' on the rock.

In the first verse Marley draws on a standard blues phrase, 'cold ground was my bed and rock was my pillow'. It is witty, clever and grows out the hyperbole of pain that is central to the blues song. More than that, the metaphors are rooted in everyday things – grounded in an Earth-centred reality. In the second verse he turns to a Jamaican phrase, the 'permanent screw'. The 'screw' is a facial expression – a scowl that comes on the face of someone who is angry, feeling pain or is simply disgruntled. But the screw is also a mask of defiance and aggression. The 'screwface' is the bad man, the dangerous person who is not just angry but willing to do something about it. In Jamaican talk, to 'screw' does not always mean to have sex. To 'screw' can also mean to be angry, to be upset, to be ready to act aggressively over some injustice that is done. The 'permanent screw', therefore, is the condition of being a sufferer and being angry at the world. It is a mask that the person who is constantly hurt by society wears.

Our expectation is that these two lines will be followed by a third rhyming line that is marked by some twist of thought or satisfying observation about society. It is at this point that Marley decides that the blues mode is inadequate for his purposes. He abandons the blues and shifts the discourse into something aggressive and active. The lamentation is still there, but the defiance is radical and politically.

Marley attacks some key figures in this explosive assertion. He begins by declaring that he will face the rays of the sun in defiance. Yet he is also making it clear that he is going to rely on the blessing of Jah to help him in his act of resistance. He will not accept the cold ground and the rockstone (a wonderfully hyperbolic Jamaicanism that combines 'rock' and 'stone' to emphasise the hardness of the ground) forever. He plans to take 'one step more' and this step is to 'bomb the church', the symbol of religious oppression, because he has found out the 'preacher is lying'.

That Marley returns to the chorus – 'talkin' blues' after this incendiary articulation is evidence of his sense of irony, and his ability to shift modes to suggest that what is clearly a statement of political aggression is merely a lament. It is a ruse, of course. But it is a ruse that Marley has to employ in a culture that is so politically volatile.

This song fits so perfectly into the tone of *Natty Dread* because, while it appears to celebrate a revolution of Rasta ideology, the incendiary nature of the articulation is too easily linked with the politics of right and left in the 1970s. Many other songs by Marley could be read in this way for Marley, if nothing else, held to the idea that he represented the 'People', that his affiliations were with the working class and, in this, his thinking was at least attractive to socialist rhetoric.

Even though Rastafarianism was a largely conservative belief system, it represented a radical departure from the cultural norms of the largely colonialized Christian ethos of Jamaicans. So that when in 'Talkin' Blues' Marley attacks the church, it makes complete political sense for radical ideologues and for socialists. And the use of the term 'freedom fighter' is clearly part of the socialist language of revolution that was taking root in so many parts of the Third World in the early 1970s.

But Marley's quarrel with the church, as it happens, was not necessarily the same one that Karl Marx had. The lie of the Christian church of colonial society was that blacks were not a people of dignity, that there was not spiritual richness in African experience and that white culture and ideas were the source of all that is good and valuable. This was a lie that Rasta sought to expose and Marley sought to do the same in his songs. Yet, Rastafarianism's commitment to social justice and equality married too well with the ideas of socialism and thus created in Marley a revolutionary voice that would influence many around the world.

'Talkin' Blues', then, moves from the deeply personal and enters the realm of the larger political arena by essentially asserting a reggae ethos over and above a blues ethos. 'Talkin' Blues' is therefore not a blues song, but a song that employs the blues. It argues that the revolutionary instinct has to move from the lament of the blues into the action of reggae revolution. Here Marley shows the sophistication of his songwriting – showing that he was drawing on, and expanding, the popular song from various traditions and, in the process, creating something that was uniquely Jamaican.

The proverb that is echoed again and again in the song is filled with irony and the kind of sly defiance that Marley uses in 'I Shot The Sheriff' and 'Revolution'. The 'they' who keep saying that 'your feet is just too big for your shoes', are those who are trying to keep the individual down. In many ways, they are happy with the blues singer who is simply going to stay within the confines set by society and merely wear the face of defiance. Marley decides to break away from the these confines – to burst out of his shoes by shouting revolution and defiance – simply by not talking blues anymore. So that, when at the end he sings, 'talkin' blues / They say your feet is just too big for your shoes', he is in fact arguing that those who settle for 'talkin' blues' are accepting the proverb 'your feet is just too big for your shoes'. Marley is speaking to those who are telling him that he is treading on dangerous ground as he writes songs of revolution – he is telling them, with some irony, that all he is doing is 'talkin' blues'; just harmless, fatalistic blues.

'Revolution', the last song on the album, is likely to have been the one that would have brought Marley the most trouble. To appreciate the implications of the song, one must understand the intense nature of Jamaican politics. Political affiliations were often as self-defining as race, class or even gender. There are two major parties in Jamaica and have been for the past 50 years. The problem with overt political affiliation was that it placed a great deal of pressure on the individual to consistently display support of anything that that particular party did. One of the central tenets of Rastafarianism was that they eschewed such political affiliations as they saw themselves as above the political machinations of Babylon. While Marley had shown some support for the PNP during the period leading up to the 1972 elections, and though it is rumoured that Marley had developed a friendship with Michael Manley, there is little doubt in my mind that Marley would have denied any suggestion that he had a strong affiliation to any single party. 'Revolution' seemed to settle the question. The clear socialist language of the song and the use of the word 'revolution' would have been troubling to the conservative JLP (Jamaica Labour Party) followers because it was the kind of language that was being spoken by Michael Manley as he began to strengthen his ties to Cuba and other clearly revolutionary states in Africa and around the rest of the world. 'Revolution', then, could be misread as a manifesto for the socialist trends in the Jamaican government at the time. A closer examination of the song, particularly in the context of the larger Marley philosophy, and especially in the context of this particular album, would reveal, however, that Marley was not calling for a secular revolution – indeed, he was actually challenging the secular revolution of the PNP, and offering an apocalyptic revolution that would lead to the destruction of Babylon.

One of the most satisfying ways to read this song is to imagine it being addressed to 'my friend' who happens to be a politician. I have always imagined Marley singing this song for Jamaica's number one revolutionary of the time, Michael Manley. Quite suddenly, it becomes clear that Marley is commenting on the language and ideas of revolution that are being espoused in the country and their inherent contradiction and failure to address the real needs of the downtrodden and the poor. What I am suggesting is that, rather than declaring his loyalty to and support of the PNP and his 'friend' Michael Manley, Marley is working hard to disassociate himself from this group and to point to a higher order of revolution – the one that will bring about some hope for the Rastafarian. Marley begins by accepting the basic tenet of the revolutionaries. He agrees that it takes a revolution to make a solution. It is a devious opening line because it seduces the listener into thinking that this is a song celebrating and championing socialism. But the next two lines make it clear that what is going on in Jamaica is not a solution. The confusion and frustration that come next stem from the contradiction that is apparent between the idea of revolution and the practice of it in Jamaican society.

This then allows us to make sense of the next lines. After establishing something of a flux – a confusion – Marley then inserts himself into the narrative by stating that he does not want to live in the park but wants instead to be free. The idea of living in 'the park' grows out of the Jamaican dilemma of homelessness. In various 'parks' throughout Kingston, many homeless people find shelter for the night. Marley is looking at a revolution and yet is stating that his greatest fear is of living in the park where he is vulnerable and where the shadows of the dark are full of dangers. There is a quality of paranoia and mistrust that permeates these lines. The hint of betrayal is not hard to note. Tellingly, he addresses the 'friend' in the next line. It is possible that the 'friend' is merely a generic term, but in light of the developments going on in Jamaica at the time, it is likely that Marley is addressing a specific group of people. He is addressing the champions of revolution and telling them that as long as there are prisoners – political prisoners – in jails, then there is no real revolution. Marley is returning to his complaint in 'Three O'Clock Road Block' for he is wondering why he and these prisoners can't 'roam this open country'. The freedom of the prisoners is associated with nature, with the idea of liberty and a sense of ownership of the land. It is this that they are being denied.

The structure of this song is one that allows these layers of meaning to unfold. The clarification of each line takes place in the subsequent lines. Marley is being careful about the way he is using language and the way he is dealing with these troubling ideas. He is constructing a rhetorical structure and an ideological framework that will then allow him to make the most radical call at the end of the song. There is something of a verse shift after the line, 'The prisoners must be free, yeah.' The melody returns to that of the opening bars, and the new verse seems to come out of nowhere. Yet it contains one of the most astute observations made by Marley in all his songs – an observation that he tries to assume as a manifesto for his own political sense. He has left aside the 'friend' and has now turned to the larger community to make it clear that he is not deceived by the 'revolution' being espoused by the 'friend'. He warns his listeners never to allow a politician to grant them favours. They will, according to Marley, want to 'control you forever'.

Marley understands what he is doing in this song. He knows that many will assume that his song is about supporting the PNP's revolution, and he has played a trick on the listener by leading him/her along a path that would suggest that he is doing just that. Then he throws a spanner in the works by declaring that he is actually breaking any connections with politicians. As a dramatic monologue this song compares well with one of Marley's equally clever and playful monologue songs, 'Running Away'. The clue to these monologues lies in the way that Marley shifts from one kind of audience to another. Thus by teasing the audience he is hinting that if the politician had what he wanted, Marley's song would be about the secular revolution of the ruling party. Instead, Marley has now distanced himself from such things and is giving himself the room to speak of true revolution. From this point on, the song is violent and decided about the call for the destruction of the enemy. The phrase, 'If a fire mek it bun / if a blood mek it run' amounts to a resignation that for this revolution to work, sometimes the most violent means have to be employed. He is saying, in other words, 'if blood must run, then let it run, and if fire must burn, then let it burn.'

At once, he makes it quite clear who is fighting this war and who is the real revolutionary. It is the Rasta who is out on top. And this shift is a trickster move by Marley. The fact is, he says, 'you can't predict the plot'. The plot that we thought we understood at the beginning of the song has been cleverly undermined, and what he has managed to do is introduce a completely new plot – a plot that positions the Rasta as the one who will lead the charge towards change and hope. Once this has been established, Marley then begins to slash away, using his lyrical machete, at all those who are seen to be working against the vision of Rastafari.

There is in this lyrical bridge an impatience with what he calls 'weak heart confessions'. The 'weak heart' is someone who lacks the spiritual and moral fortitude to withstand the seduction of Babylon. The 'weak heart' is also the 'baldhead', and also the lack within Babylon. More than that, though, the 'weak heart' is Babylon because despite its temporal strength, say Rastas, Babylon is weak and already defeated in the face of His Majesty. The only acceptable fate of weak hearts is to be banished from all of creation. This judgement is extremely harsh. To 'vank' is to kill, to destroy, to put away. Marley is calling for the complete annihilation of the weak heart and, by extension, Babylon, in order to enact the true revolution. The very song, then, becomes a revolution in itself – the turning around of certain assumptions that the listener might have already been making about Marley and his political views.

By the time Marley came to put together *Rastaman Vibration*, he had developed enough of a following around the world to see himself as being an international star. Between *Natty Dread* and *Rastaman Vibration*, *Live* had been released and the single release of the brilliant live version of 'No Woman, No Cry' was riding high in the British charts. Many regard *Rastaman Vibration* as one of the purest roots albums ever to be put out by Marley. This may be a slight exaggeration but, coming out when it did, and because of the number of signature roots tunes that are on the album, a case might be made for suggesting that the album signalled Marley's maturation as a commentator on the daily politics of Jamaican society.

The term 'roots' may need some explanation here. 'Roots' reggae was the kind of reggae that dominated the recording industry during the early 1970s. It is was music that founded itself on themes related to black consciousness and a self-conscious effort among the singers and songwriters to examine the history of the African in Jamaica. Roots songs were ostensibly about serious matters and were almost always advocating some political position. The religious themes were invariably shaped and defined by Rastafarianism and the act of celebrating that religion became an expression of the concern for 'roots' and history. The non-roots songs were those that did not seem to be locked into the business of teaching about the relevance of the past to the present. Non-roots songs tended to be concerned with trivialities and the everyday details of life. The roots song was always a music that accepted the idea that the masses would need to be guided through the suffering they experienced each day at the hands of Babylon.

Eventually, a certain musical style became associated with roots, which then allowed even love songs to be roots songs. Roots would become associated with the kind of reggae music that was founded on the drum and bass and that rarely strayed from the foundations of dub stylings and committed lyrics. Marley was a roots artist; so were Dennis

Brown, Burning Spear, the Mighty Diamonds, Peter Tosh, Bunny Wailer and so many others.

Marley's constant growth as a songwriter is reflected in this album. A distinct quality in Marley's lyrics is the range of approaches he uses in a song. During his years as an apprentice musician in the studios of Coxsone Dodd, Lee 'Scratch' Perry, Leslie Kong and so many others, Marley would always assume the role of talent scout and studio supervisor. He may have done some engineering, but his tendency was to learn as much as he could about the music end of things, largely because in doing that he was training himself. Dodd would point out that eventually Marley became a close assistant whose judgment about various recordings he highly respected. Marley would soon learn virtually every song that came through Coxsone's studio, which was also a sound-system headquarters.

In those days, producers spent a great deal of their time trying to match international hit songs with the voices of the local artists. As Marley found a niche in various studios, he would learn enough to be able to carry out this task. Soon, the Wailers were covering a wide range of songs from abroad. Where bands in the US and the UK tended to do most of their experimentation in clubs and small dives, Jamaican bands did most of their work in the studio. Those who, like Marley, were fortunate enough to be trusted by the producers got to spend a great deal of time in the studio writing songs, covering songs, learning from session musicians and basically learning as much as possible about arrangements from the best musicians on the island. Marley most likely learned to compose his songs in the studio – pulling together lyrics and quickly trying them out while a tape was rolling. Many of these experiments were never intended to be complete songs, but offered Marley hints of what he would want to do in later compositions. By the time Marley had the record deal with Island, and by the time he had the assurance that whatever he did was to be released in a legitimate way and treated to the best studio engineering available in the pop and rock world, Marley began to capitalize on the work he had done over the years. He would frequently pull old tracks from the vaults, listen to them and then recast them with lyric changes and arrangement changes. At the same time, Marley would continue to treat the studio as his creative space. There are, apparently, still a few song ideas that Marley put on tape over the years that have not been released. No doubt, most of them are not salvageable as complete songs, but the elements contained there would probably offer even greater insight into the manner in which he wrote his songs.

All this experimentation and covering of songs gave Marley a remarkably wide repertoire of styles that he could then imitate and shape into his own ideas. *Rastaman Vibration* is an album that reveals Marley's range. Sometimes the songs would be directed at an enemy, a figure, a 'you' that is specific. At other times the third person mode of storytelling was employed. At other times, Marley assumes the position of teacher, while on other occasions it is clear that Marley was in a meditative mood and was somehow speaking directly to himself. Marley rarely assumed the voice of some fictional figure in his work, but there are some songs that do that – even if the line between his persona voice and that of his fictional figure is often blurred. 'I Shot The Sheriff' is one such song. The cowboy motif carries the song, but we are also aware that Marley has somehow become the cowboy. I say all this to point to the fact that Marley was an artist who found the mechanics of songwriting fascinating. He understood himself to be a songwriter and for a while, when he was working with Johnny Nash, that is all he was and he seemed to throw himself fully into this role. Many of the songs he wrote for Nash, while maintaining something of Marley's own personality, were written for another voice and another singer. When Marley would eventually cut his own versions of these songs, they would be quite different in phrasing, and even lyrically, from the versions done by other artists.

The sharp drum roll that kicks off 'Positive Vibration' signals a monumental moment in reggae music. Marley stands tall with a great deal of confidence here. He speaks to the audience directly and he is comfortable prophesying. In song after song, the sheer energy and positive drive of his songwriting leaps out at the listener. The songs locate their revolution in their very shape and presence and Marley connects the act of singing, the very idea of reggae, with the resistance that he is calling the people to. That the record hit the stores in the midst of one of the most ideologically divisive periods in Jamaica's history is an important point.

That many of these songs would be banned from airplay is also instructive. Marley is scathing in his attack on all political groups. He positions himself as 'the real revolutionary' and the sheer force of his anger against the system makes it clear that he is not convinced that the socialist government has really altered the order of oppression in Jamaica.

Marley's uncanny energy and exuberance is announced in the opening lines of the song. The stark sound of the drum and bass reminds us that this is militant and radical music. The ghostly wail that cuts through the speaker is defiant and yet full of the startling energy that Marley knew how to replicate and surpass on the stage. Then, as if he is crying out into the world, Marley establishes his position: he will live, he will dance, he will praise his God, but it is up to you to do the same if you want. The cry 'live if you wanna live' is a challenge. For Marley, at least, at this stage in his life there is enough of the youthful cockiness coursing through him that allows him to understand his Rastafarian beliefs as self-defining and not fatalistic. Marley declares that what he has to give are positive vibrations and a 'good vibe'. Suddenly, there is that pregnant gap in the music, and as the body shifts to fill the space, we realise that the one drop beat is insinuating itself into the pulse. Drum and bass dominate again as Marley, filled with the wisdom of his ways, starts to speak directly to the audience. This is the kind of song that Marley would perform on stage with his right thumb and index finger clutching his pick, and the cupped palm covering his right eye. His left hand pointed outwards, his hip moving with a subtle grind – the roots of reggae pulsing behind him. This is Marley at his most intense and his voice would emerge with an authority born out of the sheer conviction of his voice. The tone is conversational, the phrases unfolding with a natural syntax rendering the sentiments with the simplicity and clarity of a proverb. He offers that those who allow themselves to 'get down', to debase themselves and quarrel daily' are in fact supporting the agenda of Babylon; they are, that is, committing acts of profound idolatary by 'praying to the devil'. Marley's answer is love.

The message is a direct one, addressed to his people. Marley is arguing that the violence that characterized much of the life of the poor was self-destructive and service to the devil. The worship of devils is the counter path to the worship of Jah and the worship of Jah is manifest in the act of trying to 'help one another on the way', which Marley finds to be the easier path. That burden of love is, as Christ argues, 'light' and 'easy'.

Marley's voice then rises again into that quarrelsome admonition: 'you can't live in that negative way' and, just as he finds the solution to all of this, the music grows mellower and the danceable sounds of keyboards and guitars replace the dread sound of drum and bass ushering the 'new day', the 'new time' and the 'new feelin'' that Marley is promising. Marley's optimism abounds here. His vision of the world has not been darkened by what he sees around him and his faith in people and the world is still intact. For him it is completely counterrational to persist in what he calls the 'negative way'. The 'positive day' is the hope for the future because its promise is the news that he carries. Marley's voice is clear, forceful and wholly compelling. There is a familiarity to his tone, a suggestion that he is not talking to strangers but to people who have now come to expect truth and wisdom from him. It is confidence; it is authority; it is the maturation of Marley's artistry that we see here.

Marley would describe his music as 'news'. There is definitely that quality of a man carrying a new idea and a fresh revelation in his songs. What he is saying is that what he is singing is the true news, not what the newspapers and the television are announcing each day. The song has one clear verse – beyond that Marley embarks on a jam that is filled with his words of encouragement and guidance to the people listening. Music and the message of change are meshed into a single force. As the rhythm begins to chug along, the bass line repeating itself with relentless consistency, Marley encourages them to 'pick up'. His question is whether they are catching the energy of the song, but he is also asking if they are understanding what he is saying. And in the midst of this, he makes a benediction that is echoed by the I-Threes – the request for the protection of Jah's love.

The song establishes the tone of the album in that Marley, fully aware that the themes he will deal with here are troubling ones, makes it clear that at the end of the day and in his cosmology the truest order of things will be brought on by devotion to Jah. Jah's love is the healing force and the single hopeful power that speaks to the hardships of the world that

Marley will sing about. 'Positive Vibration' is a mantra of peace that ushers in the meditations on hardship and struggle that the album offers. If there is a vehicle for hope, Marley places it in music. In the two opening songs, music becomes the force of change. In the first he wants the people to 'pick up' – to catch – the contagion of peace and the positive vibrations that are bubbling through the speaker.

In 'Roots, Rock, Reggae' Marley offers his manifesto on his art. This is as clear an articulation of Marley's commitment to his work as there is. The three elements are essential to Marley's sense of his art. The roots point to his commitment to an examination of historical truth, a commitment to being rooted in reality and rooted in the details of everyday life and, finally, his deep association with Africa – the ultimate roots of the black man. The 'rock' alludes to Jamaica, known by Jamaicans as Jam Rock. At the same time, the rock suggests hardship and difficulty even as it points to the kind of music that helped Marley find his voice: rock steady, a sensual, sexual and feel-good music ('Rock to the rock / Sock it to the sock / Move and groove' ['Rock to the Rock']) that Marley and the Wailers mastered in the late 1960s. The rock in that style of music was not an allusion to rock music, but to the rocking motion associated with the swinging ease of the music. But Marley is also nodding at the rock music ethos that helped to grant him a clear vehicle upon which to reach the world's audience. By the time Marley was recording *Rastaman Vibration*, he knew that Chris Blackwell's formula of marketing Marley as a rock star was working. Marley would embrace the rock ethos, but he would also grant it his definitive stamp. This stamp, of course, was reggae, the third part of the manifesto of Marley's art. Reggae would become for Marley a sacred form of music that carried in its very shape, structure and purpose the message of his faith. Marley was devoted to reggae and grew increasingly convinced of its potential to bring about change as he matured. Indeed, the journey of Marley's maturation is a journey deeper into a belief in the power of music. Even as he became disillusioned by other forms of political action, he held on to his one source of power: 'All I ever had / Redemption songs'.

'Roots, Rock, Reggae' is distinct because it personifies reggae music. Marley creates a persona called Mr Music who embodies everything positive that can be found within music. The song kicks off with an appeal that echoes Shakespeare's 'If music be the food of love, play on'. Marley calls out to the world to play him and his people music. The backup vocals chant back 'Dis a [is] reggae music!'

The two verses that follow are compact reiterations, reminding us that Marley's songwriting here is driven by the idea of rhythm and the orchestration of party sounds. The radical voice is contained in the joyous celebration of reggae music. This is radical because the music was still not seen as the music of the educated, but as a music of the street. The prompt is to bring music to people so they can dance. And dancing is an expression of freedom and, therefore, an expression of radical action. This song belongs to Marley's arsenal of songs that celebrate dance as a means of liberation – songs like 'Lively Up Yourself' and 'Trench Town. The music is something of a drug to Marley. He speaks directly to music, personifying it in a similar way to what Burning Spear does in 'Mistress Music'. Marley confesses that he can't refuse reggae music, suggesting a certain fatalism to his addiction to music. The music makes him 'feel like dancing' as an expression of his freedom. Yet, Marley makes it clear that what he feels in response to the music is communal – he wants the world to dance with him.

But if we make the mistake of assuming that Marley's motivation for making music is entirely spiritual, we can see quickly in the second verse that Marley's drive for success was quite material. He does not hesitate to celebrate the fact that by 1975, his records were starting to make a mark on the US and UK charts. Marley saw this as a fulfilment of both his promise as an artist and the promise of reggae music – a music that he always felt could have an international appeal. Here he is celebrating his recent entry onto the R&B and Top 100 charts.

Marley would make the Top 100 charts many more times in his career, and his work would reach even further on those charts after his death. There is a sense of elation in these lyrics – an elation that spoke of Marley's optimism about his future and the future of his music. Despite this, Marley is actually making a blatant appeal to the US market to give attention to his work in this song. He is demanding that the radio stations that played R&B music and that catered primarily for an African-

American audience also play his music. Marley embraces the African-American community as 'his people'. Fully aware that the business of music has a great deal to do with what is played on the radio, Marley makes this demand, which becomes both an appeal and a plea by the time the song is over.

Marley never did see his star rise fully in the African-American market during his lifetime. Until Stevie Wonder openly embraced the music in the late 1970s, there was little hint that African Americans would allow reggae to enter their imaginations, which were fully occupied with a rich and dynamic range of R&B and funk music. Reggae was black music, but it did not seem to grow clearly out of the roots of Black American music – the blues, gospel and the negro spirituals. Of course, this was not true. Reggae owed as much to those expressions of black experience as did R&B and funk. What reggae had that was hard to embrace, however, was a rhythm that eschewed the reliable four-four time of the funk, and a mysticism that did not gel well with the fairly orthodox evangelical Christian cosmology that grounded African-American music. Reggae was foreign and strange. While it seemed to fit comfortably into the hippie image, it did not seem to share as much with the Afro world of black culture – despite Marley's work to try and bridge the gap. He never stopped trying. One of his last shows before his death was to open for the Commodores in Madison Square Gardens. The bill was ridiculous – the Wailers had just come off a European tour where they filled stadiums with over 100,000 people, yet in the US they were an opening act. That was the reality, and Marley just accepted it and continued to work to change things.

'Johnny Was' is credited to Rita Marley. In terms of style it is different from anything else that Bob Marley wrote. It is a ballad – a straightforward ballad complete with the use of repetitions and a narrative structure – that tells a story that many felt was based on actual incidents. While 'I Shot The Sheriff' told a story in much the same way, it was essentially a fictional narrative with an extended metaphorical conceit. 'Johnny Was' is a straight ballad that introduces a conundrum for the person who has watched so many tragedies in the ghetto. Marley does not resolve the tough question of why these tragedies happen. He leaves the matter open.

It is something that Marley would do again and again. Easy closure was something that Marley was not satisfied with as a writer. The song itself ends with a question: 'Can a woman's tender care / Cease towards the child she bears?' The question is rhetorical. The answer is no. But the implication is that nothing that anyone, including the passerby (the narrator) can say will ease her pain and suffering. Marley's tenderness here is riveting. He does not call for revolutionary action, he does not have a clear villain – the bullet was, after all 'stray' – all he has is a world of poverty that opens itself to these kinds of tragedies. That theme guides the songs on this album. The world of Jamaica is laid out in unflinching detail. At times he reminds us that this world is Babylon and that the realities of Babylon can be overwhelming for the poor. Often he calls for revolutionary action. But, always, he seeks solace in music and in the teachings of Selassie. The woman's conundrum, however, is not resolved even by faith. The singer asks how the woman can rationalize her belief that good people will be blessed with life by Jah when her good son has clearly not been blessed.

If, indeed, Johnny was a good man, then he should not have died in this way. Not if the world was a fair place. Marley wrestles with this tragedy, and all that he can offer is the communal eulogy: 'Johnny was a good man'. Yet there is something in the song that suggests that the persona's dilemma is more profound than meets the eye. If we understand that the person who is calling Johnny a good man is his mother, we begin to see that hers is a vain hope that she may be right. There are two stories that are told in the song about how Johnny dies. The first argues that Johnny dies from a 'stray bullet'. There is more than a hint of irony and cynicism in this explanation because it was the typical reason given to many families by the police when they shot one of their relatives for no apparent reason. Often the killing was a cold-blooded execution, but without any way of showing that the killing had taken place without any action from the dead, the police would describe the killing as an accident. They would often say that the person was killed accidentally in a shoot out. When the 'passerby' attempts to explain the death to the woman, she is left with a troubling question. Was Johnny killed because of something that he did? Was his death an outworking of Christ's teaching that 'the wages of sin is death and the gift of God is eternal life'? Her response is to cry that 'Johnny was a good man.' In the second pass on the song, Marley then introduces another explanation. This time 'the system' is blamed for the death of the man. Marley is not accusing anyone specific of having killed Johnny, but he is leaving it open. The mention of the system, though, is a coded wink at the idea that the 'stray bullet' excuse is a sham. The only person who is so vulnerable that she has to believe the theory about stray bullets is the mother. Marley puts himself beside the woman. He tries to comfort her, and then she begins to repeat that 'Johnny was a good man'. Marley's persona then intones, 'I know, I know, I know'. He joins her in the lamentation. Despite the implied questions about why Johnny may have been killed, Marley determines that Johnny is a victim. He is a victim of a system that is bigger than he is.

The grace in the song lies in Marley's determination to humanize the men who were being killed each day on the streets of Kingston. These were men with families, with mothers who had deep feelings for their sons. By forcing us to confront the extent of the tragedy of the death of someone who most outside of those communities would regard as unimportant, Marley becomes an articulator of the conscience and heart of the poor in ways that few had managed before. The effectiveness of this lies in its complexity. Marley could easily have written a simple lament blaming the police or the system, and positioning the mother as a completely heroic figure. Instead, he allows us to appreciate that regardless of why Johnny was killed, he was caught in a terrible circumstance, and that his humanity, above everything else, is most important. Yet, Marley's lament extends outside of the specifics of this tragedy to speak to the larger tragedy of his people. When he asks at the end of the song: 'Can a woman tender care / Cease towards the child she bear', he is quoting from the Book of Isaiah where it states: 'Can a woman forget her suckling child that she should not have compassion on the son of her womb? Yea, they may forget, yet I will not forget thee.' Isaiah is quoting God, who looks upon the children of Israel, the subject of his words, as a mother views her children. Marley therefore stands as a prophet looking at the hardships experienced by his people in Babylon, exemplified by this moment in which the system destroys a man, and prophecies that Jah will not forget. The allusion complicates the song, turning it into a remarkable expression of faith and hope in the midst of tragedy.

Marley follows this song with two songs that take us back to the Marley of the late 1960s, whose output of combative songs was quite significant. 'Cry To Me' is largely a warning to the cheating lover that his actions will somehow be punished by the wrath of Jah. The story is quite simple – the woman has cheated. In many songs that seem to be ostensibly about something else, a scriptural allusion reveals that Marley's intentions are for a more layered reading of the songs. Yet there are some songs that arrive with a simplicity of emotion and expression that we engage with immediately. 'Cry To Me' is an old-fashioned Marley love song. Lyrically it reminds us of the Marley love songs of the 1960s – songs in which he allowed himself to lament the things done to a man by his lover. 'Cry To Me' is about a woman who has played a 'cheating game' on her lover. He is hoping for retribution against her. Marley roots this desire for retribution in a biblical understanding of the way that God will avenge the righteous. 'Want More', like 'Cry To Me', establishes a specific figure and then proceeds to deride that figure. While 'Cry To Me' is clearly a love song, 'Want More' seems to be a song attacking a colleague. Yet both become more general commentaries on those who enjoy the system of Babylon.

In 'Cry To Me', Marley creates a scenario of retribution that takes the culprit back through the pain that she has caused him. Thus, the very heartache that he has felt and the pain that she has inflicted on him will be returned to her in full force because the order of the universe demands that such is the way that Jah works. The singer is now in a place of security and rest: 'Now I'm by the still water / You've got to cry to me, yeah.' The 'still water' is the place of peace that Jah takes the singer to. The allusion is to Psalm 23 in which David takes assurance in the thought that his shepherd will lead him by the still waters and 'restore' his soul. He has now escaped the heartaches and the pain and, while he stands by the relative security of the calmer waters, she must experience the turmoil of a tearful regret. The song's tone is not one of anger or vicious intent. There is, instead, a gleeful energy that is captured in the bouncing rhythm of the song and in the teasing refrain. Every time the I-Threes and Marley sing 'cry-cry-cry to me yeah', one imagines a playground with children teasing each other.

'Want More' is also a song of playful censure at first, but the playground is not childish. Instead it is the world of adult human relations – a world full of 'backbiters' and 'back-stabbers'. The song is a perfect partner to 'Who The Cap Fit', as both offer the kinds of social commentaries that Marley first sang about in his debut recording 'Judge Not' some 15 years before. Marley makes use of folk wisdom to ground his ideas. These proverbs grow out of his relationship with the country. His grandfather, Omeriah, was a farmer and a man who spoke in the language of proverbs and well seasoned wisdom. Omeriah's folk wisdom combined with Marley's mother Cedella's strong Christian beliefs to create in him a poet who could draw on these ideas whenever he needed to. In 'Want More' the chorus offers a combative question, 'now that you have gotten all you have wanted, do you still want more?'

Greed is elemental to the character of the 'you' that Marley is addressing. This figure is clearly a figure who will be seen by the larger society as something of a pariah. Greed, a propensity to betray and a smug sense of assurance are all traits that demand justice. The backbiters are unaware of their vulnerability, and so consequently they fail to recognize the signs of the times. Marley's voice is full of combative energy and a threatening quality when he suggests that those who think things are over are unaware of the fact that the battle has just begun. Then, with breathless energy, he pronounces a curse on the 'backbiter.' Marley's enemies share a number of traits that he will come to locate squarely in Babylon in later albums. The 'backbiter' in 'Want More' is sometimes indistinguishable, for instance, from the 'hypocrites' of the late 1960s song of the same name. Marley's assurance in the face of the enemy is the same one that he displays in the love song 'Cry To Me'. While they are stabbing the righteous, confident that he is not looking, he is being looked after by Jah. The allusion is to the Psalmic statement that God has them in 'derision', but, in true Rasta style, Marley transposes a meaning that makes more sense to his quoting of the scripture. Hence the place is a place of judgment – the valley is the region of decision where Jah metes out justice.

There is much that 'Want More' has in common with 'Who The Cap Fit'. They both base their arguments on folk wisdom and they are also street-level songs that would form proverbial sources for the Jamaican listener. While 'Want More' is, at least in terms of language, quite easily accessible to the non-Jamaican listener, the chorus of 'Who the Cap Fit' is based totally on a Jamaican proverb in the way that some of Marley's earliest songs were. By the time Marley was recording this album, he had clearly decided to stick to the decision he had made with *Catch A Fire* to keep the international audience in mind in his lyrics. Yet Marley enjoyed playing with Jamaicanism in many of his songs. Whether this was consciously done or not, it added mystery to his lyrics and allowed his audience to appreciate that they needed to come to his work on his terms. 'Who the Cap Fit' is not unlike the late 1960s–early 1970s song 'Screw Face' for its combative tone and its attempt to teach lessons to his enemy. The difference is that 'Screw Face' is so thoroughly inscribed in Jamaican language and idioms that a glossary of terms would be needed to help the non-Jamaican grasp the meaning of the song. The same is not true of 'Who The Cap Fit', but in the chorus Marley allows himself that one indulgence. He manages to do so because he has already given an explanation for the proverb in a more standard form. The proverb: 't'row mi corn / me nuh call no fowl' grants the song a quality of humour and playfulness that seems to go against the rest of the song. Marley is winking as he plays with this proverb. In fact it is this amusing chorus that rescues the song from being a series of seemingly strident aphorisms.

Of course, in light of what would happen to Marley in less than three years, the song seems to resonate with significance and meaning. Marley would return to these themes in later songs. It would seem that the trait Marley resented most in people, and the one that he attacked most viciously, was disingenuousness. He was always aware that he could be betrayed by those closest to him and he would sing about this concern again and again. For him, such duplicity was elemental to Babylon's way, but it was most painful because those who were caught out in these acts had to be the brothers – the best friends, the lovers. In this song, also, we begin to see Marley becoming aware of the way in which people can gravitate to you when you appear to have something. Marley assumes the posture of social commentator that he uses in 'Want More'.

Marley's mistrust of those close to him, a mistrust that sometimes degenerated into paranoia, is outlined with deliberate care here through a series of proverbial statements. The world he paints is one in which what seems to be is not what is. Enemies may be best friends and assumed best friends might well be enemies. Those closest to you – those, that is, who have access to your secrets – are the ones who will betray. The people with whom you commune and socialize are the ones who will gossip about you, 'sussing' with the kind of destructive gossip implied in that word. In such a world, Marley understands that he has to be able to discern the good people from the duplicitous. Slyly, he will not show his hand. Instead, he sagely pronounces that those who are betrayers know themselves. The posture echoes Christ's calm statement at the table when he declared generally that someone would betray him. Eventually, guilt destroys the betrayer, a guilt that is borne out of his putting on 'the cap' himself.

As with 'Want More' and 'Cry To Me', Marley argues for the protection of Jah for the righteous one in this battle. In the second verse Marley continues to warn that those who do not mean well are the ones who will only be there when things are going well. The tightly rhymed couplets used here are easily remembered because of their syntactic consistency and the use of full-bodied rhymes. But Marley is playful in the chorus. He is letting the listener know that he is not planning to name anyone. But the implication is that he is singing this song about some very specific people. He dispenses his wisdom with a riddle of a proverb. Literally the lines mean: 'I throw my corn, but I will not call the fowls to eat the corn.' The sardonic 'cok-cok-cok, cluck-cluck-cluck,' is a taunting attempt to simulate the calling of chickens. Marley is saying that while he is putting out these stories, he is not going to call the fowl out because the fowl who is going to be baited by the words will come out eventually. Thus, by simulating the call of the fowls, he is priming the pump, teasing out the culprit. The meaning is not unlike the phrase, 'who the cap fit, let them wear it', but the more Jamaican proverb is not as passive. There is a baiting going on here that is part of the combative spirit. More importantly, it points to Marley's confidence that he will not be tricked by these hypocrites. It is a confidence that is not as obvious in the rest of the song. Indeed, without the 't'row me corn' proverb, the trickery, and the confidence associated with that trickery, would be lost.

There is something of that trickery in 'Crazy Baldheads', but this one works in quite a different way. 'Crazy Baldheads' is the song that finally convinced me of the power of the album *Rastaman Vibration*. What struck me with both 'Rat Race' and 'Crazy Baldheads' was how contemporary they were and how daring Marley was in his confrontation of the political establishment in Jamaica. In both, Marley makes his most pointed attack on the political landscape of Jamaica since 'Revolution' on the *Natty Dread* album. Marley wrote this song out of a strong need to circumvent the assumptions that existed in Jamaican society at that time. The most critical was that everyone had to have some allegiance to a particular political party. For Marley, the assumption was that since he was from Trench Town, his allegiance would have to have been with the PNP. No one could have been blamed for making such an assumption given the intensity of political patronage that existed in the ghetto at the time. Yet, as we have seen in 'Revolution', Marley was busy trying to extricate himself from such easy reasoning. He tried to do this for a number of important reasons. The first had to do with his growing realisation that politicians were simply not people that could be trusted.

Marley understood the pragmatism of politics and the fact that politicians were likely to exploit friendships and relationships to achieve their own ends. Power was most important to politicians and the track record for Jamaican politicians was that they would do anything to gain power. Marley also understood that in the scheme of Jamaican society, the politicians largely belonged to an élite class of people. They were often brown-skinned, middle- to upper-class Jamaicans who cultivated a relationship with the poor only because it was necessary for them to do so to win elections. The two most important leaders of political parties in Jamaica happened to be light-skinned or brown Jamaicans of some independent wealth and status. Marley knew where he stood in this equation and did not want to feel like a lackey of any politician. Because Marley had in some ways helped usher in the leadership of Michael

Manley, he was aware that the hopes of great reprieve for the poor that may have prompted his involvement in the campaign of 1972 had not quite been realized by 1975. Marley understood that if he hoped to be able to speak to the evils of the system, he would have to have some distance from the political hierarchy. But, perhaps the most important reason for Marley's desire to extricate himself from any political affiliation would have to have been his now full embrace of Rastafarianism. Rastas, at the most basic level, simply could not subscribe to the rulership of any temporal government in Babylon. Rastas understood that Jamaica was Babylon and that their loyalty was first and foremost to Haile Selassie in Ethiopia. For Rastas to remain true prophets, they had to have no alliances with Babylon. Rastas taught that the brethren should do their best to find employment that did not make them reliant on any member of Babylon's authority. Rastas turned then to crafts, to fishing, to farming and to music because of what they promised in terms of independence from the snares of Babylon.

By 1975, Marley had established quite clearly that Selassie was his ruler – his king. In many of the songs that he recorded in Lee 'Scratch' Perry's Black Ark Studio, and in the studios of the Jamaica Broadcasting Corporation (where the Wailers' independent label, Wail N' Souls, recorded many of their songs), Marley confessed his embrace of Rastafarianism ('Selassie Is The Chapel', 'Put It On' and 'Satisfy My Soul Jah Jah'). The growth of his artistry paralleled his spiritual growth and the strengthening of his convictions about Rasta. In the late 1960s, the experimentations with music matched his own intense search into the teachings of Rasta and the honing of his philosophies about his faith. In as much as we can see the product of these complex experiments with music in the confident and assured songwriting and production in his later recordings, we can also see Marley's growing sense of assurance about his beliefs and his desire to share these with the rest of the world.

'Crazy Baldheads' is one of the many songs that reflected Marley's celebration of the hegemony of Rastafarianism even over the language of Black Power that seemed to be competing with his Rasta ideas during the late 1960s. It is not that Marley had jettisoned the Black Power ideas that he had experimented with, but now they were being defined and understood through the teaching of Rastafarianism. Marley's meditative manner, his comfort with the position of being an outsider and his scepticism about political groups suited the teachings and lifestyle of Rastafarianism that he encountered very well. Yet, in 'Crazy Baldheads', Marley shows that his warrior credentials were definitely still intact. The action that is demanded of the people is to chase the 'crazy baldheads out of town'.

The baldheads were, at the most basic level, those people who did not have locks. But many Rastafarians accepted that there were those who were Rastas at heart who did not grow locks. Toots Hibbert of Toots and the Maytals has always been a strong believer in Rastafari, but he never did allow his neatly trimmed head of hair to grow beyond a certain point. He was not the 'baldhead' Marley was referring to in the song. Marley in fact makes clear who the 'baldheads' are. The story he tells of colonialism, imperialism and the neo-colonialism of post-independence society is one of the most efficiently outlined arguments about the impact of so many years of history on the people of the Caribbean and other developing countries. Marley, by using a very personal tone, and by using the intentionally ambiguous pronoun of 'I and I', manages to present a narrative of epic and tragic dimensions that never gets lost in the impersonality of history. In Marley's art, history is present. It is important only when it is brought to bear on the present. Marley makes use of the farming metaphor that he used to great effect in 'I Shot The Sheriff' to discuss the exploitative economy of colonialism. He presents the economy of imperialism with a parable. He and his people built the cabin, planted the crop and slaved for the colonial state. In response, while the exploiters, the 'you' in the song, devoured all the corn grown by the people, they treated the poor farmer/worker/slave with scorn and utter disdain through discrimation, classism and racism. The answer to such treatment is simple: revolution.

The cabin is the symbolic site of the pioneering spirit. It is the first abode of those who went to settle in the New World. Marley makes it clear that as the builder of the cabin and the planter of the corn, the black man was the engine behind the economy of colonialism. This is the same sentiment that Langston Hughes wrote about so many decades before in his poem 'The Negro Speaks Of Rivers' in which he describes the labour of blacks that went into the building of pyramids. Marley then presents the most indicting statement, which is that none of what the African has done in the New World has been viewed with respect, instead, the very corn that the worker has produced is taken from him.

The answer that Marley presents is rebellion. But instead of the destruction of the land or the destruction of the farm that we see in 'Burnin' And Lootin'', the Rastafarian chooses to throw the oppressive element out of town. Anarchy is not the answer. Systematic revolution is. Jamaicans would have appreciated quickly the direction of this song from the chorus. In a society in which the term 'baldhead' was readily associated with anyone who was not a Rasta – a term that was not seen by the average Jamaican as entirely abhorrent since most Jamaicans did not want to be associated with the dreadlocked Rastafarians – people understood right away that Marley was associating the well known and universally maligned oppressors of the slavery era with all non-Rastafarians in contemporary society. If not radical and incendiary, it was certainly a piece of audacity on Marley's part, many would have thought. Also, in the same way that Marley seemed to be outlining the basic tenets of the socialist creed in the song 'Revolution' only to turn it on its head in mid-song, the song could have been read by those of the socialist ilk as an endorsement of their push to nationalize industry and, in the process, to chase the oppressive middle-class élite out of the country.

Though it was not spoken of a great deal then, Manley, for all his work to bring parity between the rich and the poor in Jamaica by policies that caused an genuine exodus of much of the upper middle class, never really touched the most élite families of Jamaica. This is a testament to the extent of their wealth and power and to Manley's own realisation that his power was limited. Nonetheless, Manley had managed to make it a popular thing to say to multi-national corporations and wealthy Jamaicans that if they don't like the changes, they could just get out of town.

But before Marley allows his listeners to get comfortable with such a reading, he undermines it with the next verse. In this verse he brings the narrative to contemporary times and creates a parallelism that is decidedly damning. The penitentiary and the schools, built by the labour of the poor blacks, are treated as related institutions. The insult comes because the baldheads are still in the business of forcing the black man to labour purely for the benefit of the oppressive force. More importantly, the cynical system makes the black person complicit in his own oppression. Marley was aware that the hallmark of colonialism was its ability to make Englishmen out of African people – Englishmen who willingly marched each Empire Day singing, 'Rule Britannia, Brittania rules the waves / Britons never, never ever shall be slaves'. The irony ought to have been apparent to the poor slaves who were assuring the British of this truth: it is certainly not lost on Marley who sees the education that emerges out of this system as a 'brainwash' education, which leads to an intense self-loathing among blacks. Marley argues that the complicity of the black man in his own demise grew out a desire to show love. The payment he gets for such acts of kindness is 'hatred' arising from the scorn and greed that the baldhead displays in the first verse. While Marley may not have been consciously alluding to Shakespeare's *The Tempest* in this song, it is understandable that Marley's critique of the colonial system reflected the sentiments of Caliban who complained of the betrayal he felt on showing kindness to Prospero and being rewarded with enslavement. Shakespeare's ambivalence about this matter does not make him a particularly useful model for Marley's song, but the model repeats itself throughout many Native American narratives – that of a feeling of betrayal on showing hospitality and being destroyed because of it. Marley does not suggest lamentation, however. He suggests that the baldheads be finally evicted from the town.

In a dub-driven bridge to the song, Marley settles the question of who he is referring to once and for all. He describes the 'con-man' in the language of the politician. If Jamaicans became politically astute in the 1970s, it was because one of the most important repercussions of a deeply ideological battle between the two parties was the preponderance of new plans – plans that were supposed to alter the course of all things. These plans required sacrifice from the people and an intense level of commitment. Michael Manley was adept at selling his plans and many of them were successful in creating a genuine sense of nationalism in the country. But Marley did not buy it all. To him these were 'con-plans' that targetted the most vulnerable in the society. They were nothing more than elaborate bribes. He understood quite clearly that political patronage was basically a complex form of bribery. For Marley, survival required that the Rastaman did not accept the bribes or embrace the con-plans of Babylon.

'Rat Race' clearly offers us a catalogue of all of these con-plans, in language that cuts deep into the fabric of Jamaican politics. He manages to achieve this intense directness by making use of humour. Yet the humour is not the kind of witticism that worked so well in calypsos – a wit rooted in puns and double-entendres. Marley's wit is wholly Jamaican – a direct, dry humour that can slip in and out of seriousness quite comfortably. The song opens with the kind of introduction normally associated with DJ music. Marley is consciously doing this to prepare us for the 'rudeness' of his song. He then goes on to point out the characteristics of the rat race. The rat race refers, of course, to the political race. The figures who are part of this rat race are presented in the opening phrases of the song. Marley alludes to issues that were quite current in the larger public at the time. Shortly after taking office, Michael Manley decided to do away with what he regarded as a passé and unfair system of depriving the children of unwed parents the rights and dignity of all Jamaicans. Prior to his arrival in office, 'bastard' was an official term, and children who were 'bastards' were not afforded the privileges that 'legitimate' children were. Manley understood that the vast majority of children born out of wedlock were in fact poor people. By abolishing the system of 'bastardry' Manley won a great deal of favour in the public's eye. One of his more popular campaign songs of 1976, intoned 'No bastard nuh de ya again / No bastard no de yah again!' Marley is not challenging this new law at all. Indeed, Marley would have had good reason to regard it as a fitting law. But he is suggesting that it takes all kinds to run in the rat race. He lists all the different kinds of people according to their potential legal status, to let us know that they are all part of the rat race. But there is a subtle dig at Michael Manley and the People's National Party in this act, for he is suggesting that no legal act seeking to legitimate anyone would exempt them from being a part of the rat race. This list is in two parts; the first refers to legal status – 'lawful, bastards and jackets (the children of a cuckolded relationship). The second list represents the names given to some of the toughest and most uncouth gunmen in the ghetto at the time. Marley is arguing that these names are better reserved for the political thugs who sit in parliament and who collaborate with international forces to exploit the poor. He is thus turning the tables on the system. The gorgon was as cold-hearted a badman as there could be. The term also connoted rank – a clear status of authority. But it was also clear that this was a malevolent figure. The guinea-gog is a similar figure to the gorgon. The reference probably harks back to some of the negative connotations given to things African.

After these introductions, Marley continues in this veiled way to sing coded words about the politics of the society. It is quite possible that the reference to the cat being away is to the kind of unrest that took place in Jamaica during the absence of the prime minister. The pattern should be familiar to anyone who has lived in a developing country where coups are the norm. Most coups tend to take place when the ruling leader is away. The place then becomes ripe for instability as the order of command has been somehow compromised. But Marley is not bashful about suggesting that the CIA is directly involved in creating instability in the country. In many ways, the articulation of this view was seen by some as incendiary and partisan. The reason is fairly simple. The Manley regime had been complaining for a while that the JLP, the opposition, was cosying up to the US and encouraging them to participate in a campaign to create enough social and political instability in the country to undermine Manley's leadership. The CIA, already displeased with Manley's embrace of democratic socialism and his close ties with Fidel Castro, was only too willing to oblige. While we now have evidence to prove that the rumours of such covert work were true, at the time these suggestions were seen as largely conjecture and it was difficult to discover exactly what was happening. Marley had no qualms about expressing his views, though. By boldly disassociating Rastas from the work of the CIA, Marley was making clear that his loyalty was to Jamaica. At the same time, he was putting in check any rumours (say-say) that he was somehow being co-opted by covert groups in the US to take sides in the political battles.

But, if he seems to be favouring one party over another, the lyrics that follow suggest that he may have been sending this song out as warning to those in power too.

He echoes an old proverb that he used in 'Simmer Down', 'chicken merry, me she / hawk deh near'. The answer to the apocalyptic sense of disaster and destruction is unity, 'collective security for surety' – an assonance- and alliteration-rich phrase that captures the value of peace and unity. Marley also suggests, as he does in so many songs of that period, that an understanding of history is, indeed, a means towards redemption. The proverb from the Book of Proverbs, that 'in the abundance of water / The fool is thirsty' points to Marley's conviction that access to the knowledge of the past and its relevance to the present is there for the taking. But he remains struck by the fact that people continue to ignore the signs. The song ends with Marley making clear that the race he is referring to is an abhorrent one that is quite different from the more benign human, dog and horse races. The rat race is a deadly by-product of the Babylon system. In the midst of it, the Rastafarian seeks refuge in unity and in an extrication of himself from those who bolster the system.

In 'Night Shift' a song that he had earlier recorded in a very James Brown-inspired number called 'It's Alright' during the Wail N' Soul years, Marley tells as personal a story as he can about his time in self-imposed exile in Delaware. In 1969 he spent several months there, trying to make some money to support his growing family and fund his music career but he certainly did not enjoy his time in the States. His jobs included working on a Chrysler assembly line and some part-time work as a forklift operator in a city warehouse. Marley stayed with his mother during those months and spent a good deal of his spare time writing songs that he would later return to Jamaica to record. His sense of being far from home is captured in 'Night Shift', but time has allowed him a little ironic distance. The affirmation of faith in the opening lines is one that will carry all the way through the song. He sees himself as a blessed one – as someone who has been chosen. This quality is something that would stay with Marley throughout his life. He sees himself as the 'lucky one' because his mother managed to see him survive all kinds of dangers. For Marley, the tie between mother and child is sacred and any breach of that pact represents a tragic dismantling of the natural order of things. His time in Delaware represented a reconnection with his mother and so, while the memory is of slaving on the 'night-shift', there is a suggestion of something positive in the references to his mother.

Marley is not bitter about the work. His work ethic was legendary, and he believed fully in the kind of work that was directed at some useful goal. In his other 'work' song, simply entitled 'Work', he champions the need for 'black people' to work. Hence his chant in 'Night Shift' is a boast – a statement made by a man who wants to remind people that he has come through much to arrive where he is.

As if intent on ensuring that his album is full of the kind of history that he thinks people need in order to have the resources to cope with the challenges of these 'end times', Marley offers a song that is largely an extended quotation of a speech delivered by Haile Selassie to the United Nations. What is clear in this speech is that Selassie was a pan-Africanist who saw the movement towards independence in the rest of Africa as a necessary part of the movement towards freedom in Ethiopia. Rastafarians embraced Selassie because of the clarity of many of his speeches. These speeches were rich with a sense of dignity and authority. Selassie's wealth and his position as a monarch all added to the mystique that surrounded him and the reverence that Rastas had for him. 'War' is credited to Alan 'Skill' Cole and Carlton Barrett but it is clear that this track was one that was shaped by Marley and his, by this time, remarkable creative team of musicians.

Selassie's speech was in support of the various struggles going on in Africa and, as Stephen Davis argues, the song thrust the Wailers into international matters in a way that had not happened before. Marley was speaking as a pan-Africanist whose embrace of the political struggle in Africa would grow more and more during the last five years of his life, culminating in the album *Survival*. 'War' is best seen as an example of the kinds of ideas that helped Marley form his political and ideological conception of the world. Because the song is a direct quotation from Jah himself, Marley does not include his usual scriptural articulation of faith and hope. Instead, he treats the words as prophecy. Given his greater openness about his faith, exemplified in the inclusion of the scriptural quotation on the jacket notes of the album – a reference to Joseph, the biblical figure who Marley was associated with when the elders of the Twelve Tribes of Israel bestowed the name on him during his ritual entry into the Tribes – 'War' allows Marley to at once express his faith in Jah and also to articulate a militant philosophy. Yet, unlike the more combative stance of *Natty Dread*, the songs on *Rastaman Vibration*, especially 'War', were 'reasonings'; philosophical discourses on the nature of the world and the need for knowledge and understanding.

Marley takes advantage of the rhythmic structure of Selassie's speech to create a mantra that is striking in its use of repetition and in the way the logic of its accumulation of arguments culminates in the elevated climax. In concert during that period, Marley would include the wars in Kingston – the wars in Rema, the wars in Jungle, the wars in Tivoli – in this chant, implying that these wars emerged out of the Babylon system that operated the kind of rat race that led to the destruction of the poor. The song, of course, ends with Selassie's own optimism – a moral belief that at some point good will triumph over evil. Marley's songwriting always wrestled with the relative truth of this statement. During his most depressed periods, the periods when he was fearful for his life or when he was bothered by the deaths of those he cared about, the poverty of those who lived with him or the duplicity of those who ingratiated themselves to him, he would question this paradigm – wondering openly if things would work out positively in this battle. In his more optimistic moments, any fatalism would be replaced by an aggressive dismissal of Babylon and its systems of repression. Marley is at his most hopeful and assured at the end of 'War'. He declares with the weight of prophecy that he knows that the poor will triumph in the battle between good and evil. In this song, however, Marley signals his movement from political interest in Jamaican politics to a sophisticated system of belief and political awareness that extended to the rest of the world. His vision has become global and he now finds value in the political importance of Haile Selassie – his pan Africanism and his targetted attack on apartheid and other systems of oppression. In *Rastaman Vibration* Marley takes on the world as his thematic concern and establishes himself as a voice of international relevance. Mozambique, South Africa and Angola are, apart from Ethiopia, some of the first countries outside of Jamaica that he mentions by name.

It is, at the end of it all, the defining note of *Rastaman Vibration*. Despite the terrible circumstances that Jamaicans faced in 1976, the message of hope in Selassie's speech arrives as a theme of optimism for Marley. Marley, however, produced songs that would warn his people to be wary of the political system. If Marley hinted at being disillusioned with the politics of Jamaica in earlier albums, in this one he settles everything once and for all. In later albums it is not even an issue. He assumes an internationalist perspective and, more importantly, he positions himself comfortably at a distance from the system of political intrigue – the rat race. His Rastafarian faith dominates, and becomes the prism through which he interprets the world he lives in.

Marley's growth as a songwriter was soon to be dramatically spurred on by a series of circumstances that would drive him to a level of lyrical introspection that he had not experienced for many years. Consequently, *Natty Dread* and *Rastaman Vibration* would stand out as a particularly defining period in his music. A period that would establish his international reputation as an artist speaking on the world stage about difficult political issues. This reputation would place enormous pressures on Marley, creating a tension in his work between his public responsibility and his personal needs, and led him to produce work of extraordinary complexity and depth in the last few years of his life.

3 Exodus And Kaya
Running Away: Songs Of Love, Crisis And Exile

'You getting a three in one music. You getting a happy rhythm with a sad sound with a good vibration... it's roots music.'
– Bob Marley, 1975

EXODUS (MAY 1977)
Natural Mystic / So Much Things To Say / Guiltiness / The Heathen / Exodus/ Jamming / Waiting In Vain / Turn Your Lights Down Low / Three Little Birds / One Love-People Get Ready

KAYA (MARCH 1978)
Easy Skanking / Kaya / Sun Is Shining / Is This Love? / Satisfy My Soul / She's Gone / Misty Morning / Crisis / Running Away / Time Will Tell

On Saturday 4 December 1976, Marley had finally managed a few hours of sleep. But once awake, he realised that he would have to decide whether he was going to perform at the Smile Jamaica concert in National Heroes Park in Jamaica. He could not forget the night before – after all, his wounds were fresh – a home-made bullet had grazed his chest bone just above his heart, and had cut into his right bicep. But he was alive. Down in Kingston, Don Taylor, his manager, was still wrestling for his life. Marley would tell interviewers that he had dreamt of the assassination attempt a night before it happened, but nothing could have prepared him for the tough decision he had to make. He was getting a lot of pressure from Michael Manley's representative, Anthony Spaulding, who continued to reassure Marley that it would be safe and that he had to do the concert. Rita Marley and many of Marley's close friends were pleading with him to call it off. Things were chaotic. Down in Kingston the police were searching for the scattered Wailers. Most were in hiding. The would-be assassins had not been found and it was not certain whether they would strike again. No one could say confidently why this attempt on Marley's life had been carried out. Jamaica was in terrible chaos. Michael Manley had announced, in the midst of a State of Emergency, that the elections would take place two weeks after the Smile Jamaica concert. Manley knew what he was doing. There was little chance that anyone would mistake the Marley concert as a tacit or even de facto endorsement of the PNP. Marley was angry at the thought, but he had already committed to the show and he decided he would do it anyway. Now, with the members of the Manley government around him – the security service guarding the plantation estate mansion, Strawberry Hills, that was now the hiding place for Marley, it was pointless to even try to argue that this was not an event that was going to be used by the PNP to gain more votes.

Marley's thoughts during those few hours before he finally decided to join a small crew of the Wailers band on stage in the heart of Kingston, in front of a crowd of almost 50,000 Jamaicans, were likely jumbled, confused and full of fear and anger. The heart of these emotions would stay with Marley for the five years that he had left to live. In those years, virtually every major recording session would generate yet another song about those traumatic days. Marley's greatest emotion was probably one of disbelief. If Marley was angry it was because he could not believe that anyone would have had the temerity to attempt to kill him. But what he could not believe was that any Jamaican would have allowed himself to be bribed into agreeing to go to the home of Bob Marley and attempt to kill him and those close to him.

Marley would go on to do the show. Rita Marley would follow him down the hill in her dressing gown and her hospital robes. She would stand on stage and perform the 90 minutes of electrifying reggae that marked that show. But the next day, Marley secretly boarded a private jet with Neville Garrick, leaving the island he loved so much for what would turn out to be a year of exile. During that year, Marley would explain to reporters that, yes, he was angry and yes, for a while he desired revenge. But eventually that anger was tempered by a realisation that vengeance was a futile thing to harbour. He would explain that he needed to stay away because there was no point in aggravating a bad situation. He would explain that he did not want to put his friends and family at risk. But during the first few months of 1977, while the rootsy Jamaican trio Culture sang about the apocalyptic happenings that were bound to come to Jamaica 'when the two sevens clash', Marley would write more than 30 songs. He would record 20 of them – these songs, offered from a place of exile in a studio in London, would be arranged into two albums, the anthemic *Exodus* and the controversial *Kaya*. A number of the remaining songs would later appear on the three final Island-produced Marley albums. All five of these albums, therefore, emerged out of the same complex emotional space.

It is not hard to imagine what Marley was going through at the time. On the one hand he was clearly in love. During a brief period just after the shooting, Marley stayed in Nassau, in the Bahamas, and was joined by Cindy Breakspeare who had recently been crowned Miss World in London. They escaped to a resort area called Paradise Island and, for a few weeks, lived the bucolic life of lovers. Breakspeare was not Marley's only lover, but the combination of circumstances, the pressure of the near-death experience, his disillusionment with Jamaica and Jamaican politics and his feeling of alienation in the UK, made him seek refuge in songs that he felt would be comforting. He returned to love songs with a vengeance. On *Kaya* and *Exodus* Marley wrote more love songs than appeared on all his other Island records combined. Many of the songs were clearly about Breakspeare, yet all of them were complex songs that did not function on formulaic lines. Marley was heavily criticized for turning to the love song during this time. He defended himself in many interviews. His most compelling reasoning amounted to this: he was the ruler of his own life. He knew his people, he knew his world and he knew that the songs he produced and released spoke to people and gave them a sense of what he was thinking. He felt it was important to cool down the rhetoric, to help people to see the beauty of life and take them away from ideas of war and strife. He was doing it to protect his friends, to protect those he cared about. What he did not say was that he was also doing it to protect himself. Marley came to the recording sessions in a state of emotional and psychological flux. He needed to affirm his faith in Jah, and he needed to remind himself of what he called the 'beauties'.

It was Chris Blackwell who decided how to divide the tracks into two albums. Blackwell arranged *Exodus* very carefully. He placed the militant songs and the songs that dealt directly with the memory of the assassination attempt along with Marley's spiritual answer to that experience on side one. On side two, Blackwell placed several key love songs and the songs that offered a strong sense of hope. The album ended with the anthem, 'One Love/People Get Ready'. If ever there was a song of optimism, it was this one. *Kaya*'s arrangements worked themselves out for Blackwell. It would seem as if he wanted to create a narrative massage – a letter back to Jamaica in *Kaya*. The album is full of mysterious songs, sardonic love songs, complex philosophical reasoning and some of the most self-reflexive and emotionally vulnerable songs Marley had ever released. The effect of these two albums on Marley's career is remarkable. He received a great deal of criticism for them in Jamaica, but they established him as a truly international voice. At the same time, the albums gave us an insight into Marley that we had not seen in a long time, if ever. Not since 'Hurting Inside' had he released a song as harrowing as 'Running Away' was. Most importantly, as a songwriter, Marley had arrived at a level of maturity and assurance.

The Jamaica that he left behind was a one that fed the complex emotions Marley was experiencing. Even while in the UK, Marley continued to listen to what was being played on the radio back in Jamaica. Reggae musicians, the new nomads of Jamaican life, were constantly travelling to the UK to record, to perform, to do business and to get away from the hot violence of Kingston. They would meet Marley, talk, jam, and try and help him live Jamaica in England. They would also give him news of Jamaica.

In the late 1970s, there was a strange sense of urgency in the air – a kind of pressured reality that encouraged prophecy. Kingston was a city of extremes. The sense of spiritual tension was palpable: what with the emergence of the new Christian Charismatic movement with its large meetings in New Kingston and the flaming of a middle-class praising in tongues; the arrival of evangelists from America with their star singers – black and hip – preaching a funky uncompromising gospel. It felt as if the world could be ending. The Rastas were saying that the world could end. The Jehovah's Witnesses were saying that the world was getting ready to end and Culture were declaring that catastrophe would fall when 'the two sevens clash'. We could be forgiven for believing in the very sense of apocalypse. Selassie was dead and Marley and the Wailers, with the help of Lee 'Scratch' Perry, had come together to assert that 'Jah Live' in a lyric so full of a touching affirmation of hope and faith not unlike the articulation of faith that Peter spoke of in the Book of Acts during the heady days of the Pentecost.

Yet we all had the odd suspicion that this was a watershed moment. We wanted to believe it too, as we drove on buses through the dusty hot city, the walls marked in green or red paint with the language of political turmoil: 'CIAGA' 'Deliverance is now', 'Socialism is the best', 'PNP Rule', 'JLP rule' and so on. We would read the daily tally of deaths to gunmen in the *Star* evening paper, trying to determine how far away from us the victims lived and then finding solace in the idea that we were a few miles away. After all, in the economy of Third World survival, rationalization of fear is one of the most important gifts to have.

None of us could look outside of the island for solace. I did not understand some of the nuances of world politics, but I knew that Cuba and the US were having words about places like Angola and Nicaragua. I knew that the Middle East was becoming a dangerous place and that Lebanon was no longer just a biblical word, but a place where ghastly things were happening to people. I knew that the US was experiencing an economic downturn and that there was a serious problem with oil. I also knew that there were hostages taken, and that there were terrorist killings, kidnappings and hijackings taking place around the world. I knew that America wanted Jamaica to agree to take on the austerity measures of the International Monetary Fund (IMF), and I also knew that Michael Manley was defiantly nationalizing certain industries in Jamaica and truly angering many foreign companies by demanding certain tariffs for the removal of bauxite.

As a teenager in Kingston I thought a great deal about dying. I worried that I would die and go to hell. On Sundays, I would be encouraged to leave the home of my apostate family of lapsed Catholics and avowed atheist Marxists to drive with our next-door neighbours (whose father had recently found religion) the 24 kilometres across the plains of St Andrew and St Catherine, to a large white sturdy church in Spanish Town where, each Sunday evening, a preacher reminded us of our pending doom. And every week he had a message about some hapless individual who had heard the gospel preached in the church the week before and had failed to repent, and how that person had fallen dead during the week. 'Don't let it be you,' the sweating preacher would say, and I would sit and fret about death. I would reach deep into me to try and find a way through the fear of the tongues, the loud handclapping and tambourine shaking, the chaos of religious fervour, wondering if this time was going to be my time for death. I never went up, not because of bravado or lack of faith, but because I was afraid to go to the front to face the possibility of falling into a stupor or screaming out loud in deep passionate revelation. I also feared that I could not discard my terribly penchant for drawing naked fat women having sex with slightly plump teenage boys. I was a filthy sinner and I could die at any minute. And as we drove to Kingston, stopping off to check the produce at our neighbour's property in the hills of Spanish Town, I would wonder how I was going to die or how the world was going to end. It felt like the world was going to end. And in all of this, sinner that I was, I knew that my greatest fear of death was prompted by the anxiety that I would die before I ever had sex. That would have been the most tragic consequence of an early death or the coming of the end times.

Cuba was our friend and consequently America was not happy. We knew that the CIA was in Jamaica and so it felt as if the end of the world might be near. It felt as if the world could end because people were running away from the end of the world – running away to America, to Miami – running away from the economic hardship, running away from becoming communists, running away from the austerity and those of us who stayed understood that what we were doing was either genuinely noble, because we were idealists, or necessarily noble, because we had no choice and we wanted to at least feel superior to those who were running. There is nothing to suggest a sense of doom like the flight of your neighbours.

Reggae music was deeply involved in this issue – Pluto Shervington was declaring loyalty and allegiance with his song, 'I Man Born Ya', a few months before he himself left the island for Miami on one of the five daily flights that he vowed he would never take. Leroy Smart was pleading with the youth to stop the fighting with his 'Badness Nuh Pay' – 'From the prison to the morgue to the cemetery / That's how I know bad man end up you see / Going around making disturbancies / Going around giving natty dread bad name...' And the songs announced doom: 'Ammaggedon Time' (Willie William), 'War', 'Jogging' (Freddie MacGregor), 'People Preparing for Armaggeddon'), 'Igzibier' (Peter Tosh), 'River Jordan' (Sugar Minott) and 'Hot Like a Melting Pot' (Dennis Brown). Rastas too seemed intent on leaving the country – Freddy Mackay would sing that he wanted to go home away from Rome. ('Rome is for the Romans / And Rome is not for me / Take me back to the land / Where I can get my liberty'), and Bunny Wailer, Judy Mowatt and Third World would reprise the old Wailers cover 'Dreamland', often described as one of the most evocative and brilliantly executed songs about the promised land of Africa. The Mighty Diamonds were prophesying the end of all things in 'Right Time' when some will 'bawl fe murder' and some 'A go run till dem, tumble down'. It was impossible not to at least be aware of the general feeling that it was all going to come to a head quite soon.

In 1978 we were aware that an election was a couple of years away, and we could already feel the disquiet of the population preparing for war. There were calamitous events – the burning of the Eventide Home that saw the death of so many indigent old people and babies. In Green Bay there was a massacre of people who were being described as guerillas by the joint police and armed forces. By early 1979 Joseph Magan, a leading politician who was running for office, was murdered. Now the victims were no longer merely the street thugs and the enforcers, but also people who ought to have been well protected. The Minister of Security, Dudley Thompson, appeared on television and, in a slow, deliberate tone of sheer aggression, leaned into the camera and declared that he was going to lead the forces to deal with the criminals in a simple and clear way, 'We will shoot them down like dogs in the street'.

So, when we read the newspapers and saw the photograph of Bob Marley sitting on a chair in his blood-stained shirt, with his arm lifted to show where the bullet had entered at his elbow, and when we read the caption that someone had tried to kill him, we knew that the end had to be at hand. Marley made a triumphant entry at the Smile Jamaica concert – he danced and pranced around, bared his chest and dared the gunmen to kill Jah's anointed. If he was going to die then he wanted to die on stage. He was not going to bullied. But he was. His secret flight to Bermuda a few days later, in the dead of night, convinced us that if Marley had taken flight at last, like everyone else, then it was clear that the end was now near.

The election of 1980 proved an end for almost 1,000 souls. But before that, Marley would write a letter home to Jamaica, trying, somehow, to bring some hope to a tough situation. He was in exile for the first time. He was away from home because he had to be, not because he wanted to be. Marley loved being in Jamaica, loved the vegetation, loved escaping to the hills to reason with nature, loved looking at the mountains from his very green Hope Road compound, loved playing football with his breddren from the ghetto, loved being the custos in residence holding court while people from Trench Town and Jones Town and all over the ghetto came to listen to music, sip some herb or just chat, so they could have a story to tell when they went back home. Marley loved to play dominoes, loved to hear the sound of people talking as he worked in the studio. He loved the heat, the steady persistent heat of Kingston. Yet he had to be away from all of this while his island moved towards the most dangerous time in its history. His children were in Jamaica, his life was in Jamaica and he was away trying to make sense of the trauma of his own departure from there.

It is out of this complex world of chaos that Marley would write the songs that appeared on the *Kaya* and *Exodus* albums. They emerged out of trauma and uncertainty. Marley left Jamaica at a time when his international fame was growing significantly. It was a good time, both because of his increasing fame and because of the excitement of his personal life. He was now inextricably linked with Cindy Breakspeare, with whom he was having a child. Rita Marley had decided to move out of the house in Hope Road because, she said, the environment was not a good one for the children. Part of it was the constant coming and going of strangers and hangers-on, the perpetual activity all day and all night, the ganja smoking at all times; but most of it was the fact that this was where Marley would entertain his women – particularly Cindy. According to Neville Garrick, Marley was in love with Cindy and would write love songs to her, singing to her as he sat out on her porch, his music wafting through the lattice work. Marley was embroiled in the kind of complex of relationships and friendships and family arrangements that was not entirely unusual in Jamaica; so for him, these were periods of drama and emotional tension.

Anyone who loves Marley's music is likely to have an album or two that he or she regards as the most important work by Marley. Often, that choice is quite personal and probably has little to do with the actual quality of the material. Like most of us who have grown up in a world in which music icons have been our companions, I have had a strong sense of connection with *Kaya* and *Exodus*. This may have a great deal to do with how I came to hear these albums. I first heard them when I was in my late teens: my older brother brought them home and played them to me – track after track. When he left for work I would sneak into his room and continue to play them. I heard them in a way that I had never heard Marley before because, for the first time, he was very much a lofty presence in my imagination. I heard them after I knew that someone had tried to kill him and that he had defied the killers and gone on stage and performed to thousands of Jamaicans, stripping his torso bare to show the wounds he had suffered, and then crouching into the position of Ivan taking snap shots in *The Harder They Come*, pointing his two guns at the crowd and laughing. This Marley was a different Marley from the one I used to know. This Marley was an international superstar, and I was staggered by the fact that he was a Jamaican who had created art of the highest order. This time I was reading the jacket notes of the albums. I was studying the lyrics. I was haunted by the fact that these lyrics were moments of sublime poetry, rich with metaphor, thick with allusions, elevated by biblical references and fired by passion and energy. I was studying Marley like I was studying the poetry of Gerard Manley Hopkins in school, and Marley was putting the old Oxford don to shame. It was these two albums that made clear to me that I was a product of reggae, in as much as I was a product of the politics of Michael Manley and the exploits of Clive Lloyd and that triumphant West Indian cricket team.

I have, since those days, gradually built up a narrative of Marley's state at the time of the production of these two albums and I return to it every time I hear them and each time I listen to a song that was recorded during that same period – a recasting of the old Wailers classic, 'Keep On Moving' that was done with Lee 'Scratch' Perry in London during a break from rehearsals for the *Exodus/Kaya* recordings. Marley sings a message home to his children, naming Ziggy and the family friend Ole Tartar and others and promising them, with a touch of deep nostalgia, that on his return they will have a 'big stage show at Ward' (Ward Theater is the largest theatre in Kingston). The genius who composed the songs on *Exodus* and *Kaya* was an exile, far from home. He, the Tuff Gong, the man known for his toughness and his ability to defy all enemies, could hear the rumours that he was running away. He was in a cold country, far from his family, missing the warmth and chaos of Kingston, missing a world that shaped his art and his person. He was a man working through the complexities of love, and the terrible realisation that betrayal was possible.

These two albums are wonderful companion sets that explore the many remarkable voices of Marley. One is a public album and the other a more personal and private album, but both share the theme of exile – they emerge out of the same psychic and emotional space.

Someone had tried to kill him – someone had shot at him, wounded him, wounded his wife, wounded his manager, wounded his friend – someone had invaded the sanctity of his home popping bullets through the night. The world was in turmoil. He heard rumours of the killings going on in his country everyday. He heard stories about the hardships that people were going through. He knew that his island was a football being kicked around by the two 'superpowers' and his people were caught up in the intrigues of politics and power. Yet he was away, in exile, far from it all and he was both happy to be away and saddened by the fact. Happy may be too strong a word, but Marley was seeking refuge and peace of mind, and he knew he could not have that in Jamaica. When asked why he was staying away, he explained that while he could go back to Jamaica, he knew that he would be putting those close to him at risk. He had to stay away. But he was sad because, despite Marley's dream of repatriation to Africa, he always would say that he loved Jamaica. 'Smile Jamaica' the song was not just a publicity stunt – he meant everything in that song: 'Then I came 'pon one who said / Hey Dread, smile Natty Dread / Smile, you're in Jamaica now.' So he was safe, but he was away because his country could no longer be trusted to protect him.

Despite this, I can only imagine that everyday he stepped into the studio in England, the land of the very colonial forces that he sang out against in many of his songs; the land, where, ironically, he had fled to for refuge, every day that he walked off the cold streets and stepped into the dark studio with the gleaming instruments, the familiar paraphernalia of his craft; every time he went behind the glass partition to sing into a microphone, he must have been transported to his home. Outside was an alien world but here, in the belly of his art, he was in Jamaica.

Marley always spoke and sang of the cold of the North as a kind of prison, a kind of place of exile, a place where he waged war with the knowledge that he would be able to return home where it was warm and comfortable.

As reggae music, tightly confident, assertive, lyrical and distinctly his, began to seep through the speakers, he felt transported to his world. *Exodus* and *Kaya* were the messages of an artist to his homeland.

These two albums represent Marley's most sincere expression of the meaning of being a figure of world repute who has to face the reality of his humanity – the simple reality of his own frailty. This is why these two albums manage to articulate so brilliantly the genius world view of Marley. There is a quality of honesty and vulnerability in these albums that is very revealing.

Written in a time of crisis, these albums have a remarkable capacity to communicate the heart of this artist in a most telling way. In these two albums Marley is at once a pained lover, a beleaguered revolutionary, an incendiary prophet, a reflective philosopher, a playful father and a mystic man – a monk seeking refuge in the deep recesses of his spirituality.

Exodus was named album of the 20th century by *Time* magazine during the turn of the century reflections that consumed the minds of the media on the eve of 2000. I was surprised by the assessment, not because I did not agree with it, but because I did not expect an American-based, Western publication to single out the work of a man from a small island in the Caribbean who played a style of music that emerged from the distinctive limits of Kingston, Jamaica, and to elevate it to the status of 'best'.

But it was clear that the editors of that magazine understood some important things about Marley's work. In their citation they described the universal appeal of the work in terms that are relevant to the shape and thrust of this book: 'Every song is a classic, from the message of love to the anthem of revolution... but more than that, the album is a political and cultural nexus, drawing inspiration from the Third World and then giving voice to it the world over.' In Harlem, some months ago, I heard Christopher John Farley, a senior editor at *Time* magazine and a Jamaican who had a hand in the choosing of *Exodus* as the album of the century, talking about the selection process. He said it took months of discussion, months of listening to the music, months of drawing people's attention to one of the most abiding truths about *Exodus*, which is that this was the album in which Marley's vision was able to be understood as at once parochial and deeply personal and, at the same time, a larger symbolic articulation about exile, love, struggle and the condition of human beings in the late 20th century. Marley was speaking to and for too many people from all over the world for his importance to be ignored. The other editors were convinced. They agreed with New York Times critic John Rockwell, who in a review after a Madison Square Gardens concert on 17 June 1977 articulated brilliantly the meaning of Marley's achievement at this stage of his career: 'Ultimately, the reason for both the unparochial impact of Marley's Rastafarianism and the success of his concert was his fusion of music with politics and mysticism. Mr Marley's images of exodus, resistance and paradise on earth aren't just Jamaican or even confined to undeveloped parts of the world; they can speak to everyone through the power of his music as a modern day Utopian vision.' Rockwell was, however, only partly right. Marley's vision offered hope and often seemed to promise a unity in the world, but that was just a superficial reading of Marley and the complexity of his vision. For every instance of hope and assurance, Marley reminded us of the tough truths of the world. *Kaya* and *Exodus* brought these two things together.

In *Exodus*, we find all the notes and tones that have shaped Marley's oeuvre collected together in one place. In many ways *Exodus* represents Marley at the height of his career. His political sensibility is honed and unapologetic, his commitment to the love song is secure and his faith in Rastafari has become most assured – an assurance shaped by the spirit that gave voice to the single 'Jah Live'. Musically, the Wailers had become a unit so well oiled by years of successful touring that they came to the recording with a good grasp of what makes a Marley tune work. Yet there is nothing monochrome about the album. It is varied. It moans, smiles, laughs, growls, howls, laments and anthems. At the same time, it whispers, gossips, flirts and giggles. Marley wears his status as reggae king without pretension. He is simply doing what he wants to do.

While *Exodus* was celebrated when it appeared, *Kaya* faced much criticism. It was felt that Marley had somehow become soft, that he had abandoned his political edge and given way to love songs and whimsical reflections on weed. This criticism, in the light of any closer encounter with the range and daring of *Kaya*, proves unfounded.

Placed beside *Exodus*, *Kaya* is a wonderfully lyrical work that stretched the range of reggae music in remarkable ways. At the same time, it offered Marley listeners an insight into his psyche during that troubled time – testament to his commitment to the notion that art can heal and transform.

Each song on these two albums represents an emblematic moment in Marley's work. Each track is rich with complexities and offers wonderful insights into the ideas that have come together to shape Marley's work.

But what is most striking about *Kaya* is the wonderfully complex range of moods that shape it. There is something in the album that speaks of an artist trying to find beauty in the memory of home. There is the quest for laughter, the relishing of memories of 'yaad' (yard), the playful sense of landscape and some of the touchstones of his security. At the same time, in *Kaya*, Marley offers a very reflective side of himself that faces the twisted contradictions of his life.

In songs like 'She's Gone' and 'Misty Morning' he gives us love songs that expose his own pain. He even takes old tunes that he once did with Lee 'Scratch' Perry and recasts them here with more lyrics and an increased complication of the ironies of the tune – a good example is what happens to 'Sun Is Shining'. These are not easy generic pop laments but a sophisticated, revealing, recounting of the man's struggle with love and what it means. I can't sing 'She's Gone' without the deep stomach pain of fear that I still have of losing my woman. It reaches into very vulnerable places. *Kaya* turned inward and this may have disturbed people, but what emerged was something beautiful and deeply hopeful, even in the face of pain.

What draws me to these two albums, then, apart from the confidence and maturity of the writing, apart from the beautiful poetic range that he demonstrates in theme, mood and style, is the very idea of exile and how exile shapes the way an artist faces the world.

Beyond that, though, *Exodus* and *Kaya* are ultimately quintessentially black narratives. Black because they understand the state of perpetual exile that has come to shape the mindset of the New World black over the last several hundred years.

Exodus opens with 'Natural Mystic' a song that gains its mysterious edge both from the way the music snakes up on us and from the lyrical insistence that what is happening around us is something deeply mystic. It was not a new song when Marley recorded it for *Exodus*. A horn-enriched version with a slightly different melodic line and a quite different bass line had been recorded in the very early 1970s. But in the 1977 version, Marley does not appear to be prophesying an apocalypse of violence as he does in the early version. Here, while the lyrics point to the end of all things the mysticism seems like a positive place. Marley would have been convinced that the world he was living in had changed drastically. The assassination attempt could have been a possible source of this song – his survival a part of a larger warning of some of the signs of the last days. But Marley is speaking of things beyond that. The song, after all, was written before anyone had tried to shoot him. Marley, however, is opening the album on a note of meditation and musing. There is nothing of the clear-minded preaching that we witnessed on *Rastaman Vibration* here.

Marley was seeking answers for everyone, and this included himself. The only answer he had was that something strange was happening and that same strangeness was related to the workings of Selassie. Anyone seeking absolute clarity in the song will be disappointed. Marley tries to suggest that we must listen beyond our reasoning. It is a warning that we ought to heed especially when we come to listen to a complex philosophical lyric like 'Misty Morning'.

This lyric announces the mysticism blowing around Marley. It has an elusive quality; a truth that only those who listen carefully will hear. Hearing, in this instance, represents access to the deeper truths of the universe – truths that, while available and fairly obvious to the initiated, remain elusive to the unfaithful. To listen, then, is part of the biblical calling to 'be doers and not just hearers of the word'. The trumpet sound announces the end of the world – an end that will bring with it suffering for many and death for even more.

Marley looks into the world and sees that there are inexplicable things. Filled with the millenarian philosophies of Rastafarianism, and also caught in a world that seemed determined to announce signs of the end, Marley cannot be blamed for seeing in the suffering of those around him evidence of the coming of a new age. This is Marley's reality. By admitting that he does not know why these things must happen, Marley is introducing a complexity to his lyrics that he had not offered to his listeners before.

In the next verse, Marley admits that he has no clear answers. The world has changed and everything that he could rely on is no longer dependable. He asks his listeners to face reality because it is the only way to cope with the uncertainty. Marley admits that he has tried to find answers without success. The only thing he can promise is that he will not lie.

In previous albums Marley would look to the past for models of what is to come and explanations for what was happening in the present. The songs about the relationship between slavery and the hardships of contemporary life offered a logical way to understand the universe that was comforting. In this logic the cyclical order of history made sense and the retribution of Jah made sense too. Those were the ideas of the 'retired slaveman' of 'African Herbsman' – a voice slightly different from the prophet of 'Natural Mystic'. Now, Marley sees the inadequacy of trying to 'live through the past'. When he says 'don't tell no lie', he is also saying 'I won't tell a lie' – meaning that he is being as honest as he can be here. And his honest answer is that he has no answers.

Perhaps, though, the most compelling idea in this song is one that Marley does not give much attention to. It is the phrase 'natural mystic'. The phrase, in its own way, represents what I have now come to call the essence of the reggae aesthetic, or at least how it was explored by Marley. The distinctive feature of Marley's mysticism was the manner in which it sought to root itself in an earthly reality. Marley's notion of paradise was as far removed from the clichéd image of heaven as a place filled with angels sipping milk and honey as one could get. For Marley, the sepia tones of the Ethiopian landscape evoked heaven. For him, the mysteries of existence lived among us and found voice not in flight but in reality. Marley's religious sensibility was earthbound and eschewed the notion of seeking some kind of restorative grace after life was over. But the mystic was important to life. The mystic was that which could not be explained easily by man, and the mystic was largely locked in the natural order of the universe. This aesthetic made it possible for Marley to speak of religion and sexuality in the same breath without hinting at a contradiction. The sensuality of reggae music – its bass line, its need to meet the needs of the community that sought the pleasure of sensual dance and mystic sublimation in the music – made it a music that was built to engage in the seemingly contradictory impulses of the term 'natural mystic'. *Exodus* and *Kaya* constitute complete examples of this 'natural mysticism'. Their free dance between Earth-centred songs of anger and revenge, songs of deep faith, songs about sexual love and songs about communal love represents the notion of 'natural mysticism'.

When Marley's voice, full of a world-weary wisdom, opens the tune, you know that he is enacting something remarkable – that he is speaking into darkness with the conviction of a man who intends to bring hope. It is easy to understand that this song is meant for the Jamaican landscape, the Jamaican spiritual space full of uncanny airs – a mysticism that makes it possible for people to remain spiritually rooted while struggling through a debauched and uncertain world.

As we listen to it we are discovering the mysticism that roots Marley's world. Marley's vision of a natural mystic is the philosophical anchor to his view of the world – the wonderful confluence of spiritual sublimation and *rootical* grounding.

As if engaging in an extended reasoning session with his audience, the first songs of *Exodus* have a slow meditative quality that reveal Marley in a reflective mood. He positions himself in the middle of these songs and offers them up with a self-consciousness about the business of trying to understand the world through song. Marley grew into the realisation that his songs were the way that he worked out his thoughts and found a way to articulate them clearly.

In interviews Marley was too busy trying to anticipate how the things he would say might be interpreted or reported. He would often guide his responses around the vibe he was getting from an interviewer. Many of his comments were filled with irony, and many were strained attempts to make clear things that he knew he could explain best in songs. This was because Marley worked long and hard on his songs – testing phrases, testing lines, altering things.

When he first recorded 'Chant Down Babylon' on a demo, to be returned to later, the song was called 'Bu'n Down Babylon'. Eventually he would change the word to 'chant' because he arrived at the position that he wanted to allow his song to have layered possibilities. He also did not want to be the one to encourage acts of violence in Jamaica. That kind of thought and consideration came from careful work on his songs. In 'So Much Things To Say' Marley is confessing what was clearly true for him in the months after the assassination attempt. He wanted to talk about it and he wanted to talk about it from his heart. He knew that the best way to talk about it was through his songwriting.

But while the song's title does suggest that it is Marley who has so much to say, we quickly realise that Marley is imagining a people looking at him and jeering him, taunting him, teasing him and asking him why he is running. They have so much to say now. Now that they have managed to cause him to leave Jamaica, now that they have forced him to assess his relationship with the island, they would have much to say. He calls the things they are saying rumours. And he is talking about the many rumours that were floating around about why Marley was shot. Those who claimed that he had brought it on through some botched horserace gambling scam, those who claimed that people were upset with Marley's relationship with Cindy Breakspeare, those who claimed that Marley had become too rich and, therefore, too soft and was now paying the price for it – they had much to say. Marley responds to these accusations by reminding himself and his audience that what has happened is a betrayal of someone that is bent on doing good things. He is making it clear that he sees his situation as one not unlike that which faced many other figures. Rather than spell out that he sees himself as a type of these figures, Marley simply offers the memory that all these things happened to greater people.

Marley tries to understand the events going on around him by first confronting the human part of his emotions. He sees himself as a victim, but he understands his status as a victim, not in a hopeless and useless way, but in a productive one. He finds solace in the idea that many others had suffered the betrayal of those close to them or those one looked to for support. He names three figures who are almost emblematic figures for Marley; revolutionary figures and role models that he declares he will never forget.

He first names Jesus Christ, whose crucifixion Marley sees as a betrayal by those who could not appreciate the things he had to say. Christ was, for Marley, a prophet who spoke profound truths. But Christ was also a revolutionary and political figure – a tragic victim of the hypocrisies of his time. His betrayal was part of the mythos that shaped Marley's view of the world and of himself.

Marcus Garvey ushered in the modern Rastafarian movement despite having been betrayed by the Jamaican people when he returned from the US after being convicted of mail fraud. Garvey had the opportunity to run for city council in Kingston and his prospects looked good. But a concerted effort was made by an élite group of landed Jamaicans to prevent him from doing so. They were aided by an able barrister at the time, Norman Manley (Michael Manley's father), who felt that Garvey would have been a dangerous figure. Legend has it that Garvey was betrayed when at least one of his supporters accepted the bribes from moneyed opposition to make an accusation that would land Garvey in prison. Garvey never recovered from this and left Jamaica.

Paul Bogle belonged to a completely different era. A member of the Native Baptist Church in the 1860s, he led a rebellion against the British colonial government in protest of the unfair way that labourers were being treated. Bogle was betrayed by the Maroons who had signed a treaty with the British – a treaty in which they committed themselves to assist the crown in quelling any insurrection that took place among the poor blacks. The Maroons were the ones who captured Bogle and took him to the British authorities. He was promptly tried and executed.

All three figures were men of struggle and Marley identified with them. By doing so, he was facing his own mortality. He had lived to fight another day, but he had to contemplate the implications of his brush with death. He had resolved the question of who he was and where he stood in the struggle. He had already resolved that he was a 'real revolutionary', but he would ask his listeners to make up their own minds about themselves, simply because the hardships he faced and the troubles going on in Jamaica were not isolated to that place and to those people: 'When the rain falls it don't fall on one man's house,' he intones, quoting from the Psalms.

Marley then goes on to explain what the basis of his life is. The song has a sombre quality to it that gains dignity because it emerges as a confession of commitment that comes in the face of real danger. Marley then offers a clear-cut dare to those who have so much to say. His lyrics come tumbling out in the verse in a rush of words that undulate around a breathless melodic line. The real line break in the first phrase is, in fact, on the word 'places'. The in the second extended line, he lengthens the syllable in 'while' in order to cover more ground and to vary, beautifully, the line's pacing. He declares that his battle is not against flesh or blood, but is in fact a spiritual one. His enemies will 'fight him down', but he will remain unmoved and give God praises. The phrase 'stand firm' is a Rasta-appropriated phrase from the Epistles of Paul who admonitions the new Christians to stand firm in their commitment to Christ. The phrase was then co-opted by the Jamaica Labour Party during their campaign for power in 1976, who offered it as a counter slogan to the PNP's 'have then under manners'. Marley reclaims the phrase for the Rastas in this song, restoring it to its more spiritual application. The call is for Rastas to stay faithful to Jah and his teachings in the face of the attacks of the enemy who are the propogators of the 'laws of men'. Marley is justified by faith.

To make this point he uses the pronoun 'I and I' again, intentionally asserting that what he is saying here is not based on an elevated sense of self, but based on the teachings of Rasta that all Rastas adhere to. He is laying out the manifesto of Rastafarians. In this he quotes Paul, who warns that the battle is not against flesh and blood. He also encourages his people not to succumb to the attacks of the enemy but to 'stand firm' – again quoting Paul the apostle. By using the Book of Corinthians, from which Marley draws on Paul's rejection of the wisdom and the laws of man, we understand how fully Marley has embraced the New Testament teaching of Paul and how he applies it to his role as a teacher. Paul's own words are filled with faith and combativeness:

> I care very little if I am judged by you or by any human court; indeed, I do not even judge myself. My conscience is clear, but that does not make me innocent. It is the Lord who judges me… he will bring to light what is hidden in the darkness and will expose the motives of men's hearts. (1 Cor. 4:3–4)

Marley will return to this theme more intensely in *Survival* and *Uprising*, singing in 'Forever Loving Jah' that 'what has been hidden from the wise and the prudent / Will reveal to the babe and the suckling'. The entire verse of 'So Much Things To Say' is so rooted in the allusions to Paul's letters of defiance and fierce faith in God and the things of God, that one can sense in Marley his identification with the beleaguered world that the early church figures such as Paul faced. They relied on their commitment to the work of Christ to sustain them. Paul would admonish his friends to stand firm in what he had taught them. He would also write extensively about 'justification by faith' – a teaching that would find its greatest expression in the Book of Hebrews, which some argued was written at least in part by Paul. The Hebrew writer understood the laws of men to be those laws of the Old Testament. Marley extends that to include the laws of Babylon – the laws of the land that he understood himself to be separate from. This was not a statement of rebellion against the laws, but it was a statement that he would not seek justification and protection from the temporal authorities because he understood that he would not receive justice from them. He would have to rely only on Jah. Marley then allows a certain sardonic wit to creep into the song. He takes us through several bars of 'la las', which are simulating the chatting of the rumour mongers and those who have so much to say. He then declares that they are 'lalaing all the while'. The song trails off with Marley turning this jeer into a direct insult – he accuses them of ignorance – they don't what they are doing. Yet he is also alluding to Christ's statement as he hung on the cross. Marley would only allow that kind of line to creep into the tail end of the song – it is a coded statement that grows out of his sense that the betrayal he experienced was one that was driven by the dangerous combination of poverty and power.

Marley's use of Christian typology and his open allusions to Christ and to Paul in these songs represents a relaxing of what was a rather strict anti-church sentiment that permeated more orthodox Rasta teaching. Marley's confidence in Rastafarianism was now strong enough to allow him a theological openness to the co-option of Christ and his teachings to Rasta cosmology. Rastas do not see Christ as a Messianic figure as Christians do, but in many Rasta teachings, including those of the Twelve Tribes of Israel, Christ is accepted as a true prophet of Jah; an important spiritual figure whose role and character has been corrupted by Western racist thought. Marley's references to Christ in 'So Much Things To Say' constitutes a show of doctrinal confidence and authority and could reflect Marley's interest in the teachings of the Ethiopian Orthodox Church.

Stephen Davis tells a delicious anecdote about Marley in his fast-paced but detailed biography of Marley. He describes a scene in which Marley is looking at a video taping of the Peace Concert of 1979. At the moment when he has Manley and Seaga on stage and he is blessing them, Marley was said to have muttered: 'guiltiness, rest on their conscience'. Davis recounts that in another moment Marley jokingly said that he should have killed the two leaders when he had them so close to him. The context of these two statements is important. By the time Marley saw the video it was clear that the peace initiative had crumbled. The men who had initiated it had died quite bloody deaths in the streets of Kingston. The months leading up to the 1980 election would see almost 1,000 people killed – an increase of some 700 over the same period before the last election. Marley blamed Manley and Seaga. There is little doubt about this. He spoke the words as a curse hoping that the weight of their conscience would consume them. It is the same sentiment that shaped the song in the first place. Marley was not sure, at least during those early months after the shooting, who the culprits behind it were. As he sought to take away the hunger for vengeance from his system, he turned to the promise of retribution by God. 'Guiltiness' is a scathing attack, a prophetic moment of censure and essentially a curse. Followed hotly by 'The Heathen', Marley's anger is seething here. He makes it clear that he sees the true culprits as people ('big fish') who are manipulating the smaller people ('small fish'). He is giving shape to a way of viewing Babylon that would be most clearly articulated in *Survival*. Marley would name them 'downpressors' in this song. This was not his coinage. This was a classic Rasta coinage. An oppressor would have to be a positive figure since he would be associated with that which was 'upful'. To ensure that there was no ambiguity in meaning, Rastas referred to oppressors as 'down' pressors. Peter Tosh would write a tough indictment of this figure in his signature tune 'Downpressorman'.

Marley's word choice is always carefully done in these honed songs. His use of the word 'materialize' in the phrase 'to materialize their every wish', is loaded with the implications of materialism and worldly concerns. The heart of the downpressor is to turn everything into material that can be consumed. It is this quality of cheapening the most holy of things –

the human spirit – that Marley is railing against. In the face of this, what he prophecies is that they will suffer. The Marley who sends out these curses here seems convinced that the righteous retribution will take place. He is far more reliant on the vengeance of Jah in *Exodus* than he was in earlier albums like *Catch A Fire* and *Burnin'* in which he, the revolutionary, was willing to assist Jah in carrying out these acts of retribution. Music now becomes his only weapon. In an interview in 1977 in Paris, Marley would say after a long discourse about the way that guns were being used in Jamaica to destroy the poor and after extricating himself from the use of guns: 'Well, yeah. The music is the biggest gun, because it save. It nuh kill, right? The other gun lick off ya head!' He was echoing his old mantra: 'One good thing about music / When it hits you feel no pain' from 'Trench Town Rock'. These chants, when thrown at Babylon, were becoming, increasingly, Marley's weapons of choice. The fate of the downpressors is clear – they will eat the 'bread of sorrows' and experience the sheer hopelessness of their 'sad tomorrows'. And yet, as he sought to speak of the protection of Jah and the promise of his justice, Marley understood that he needed to explain in some way, to his listeners, and especially, it would seem, to himself, why he was in exile – why he, the 'real revolutionary', was staying away from the battle and abandoning the battlefield.

'The Heathen' is another of the angry attacks at those who may have conspired in the shooting, but it, like all of Marley's work of that period, is establishing a way of coping with the system of Babylon that would become central to the Marley philosophy. 'The Heathen' is a song built for performance on stage. The punching militant, lock-step bass line is martial in its purposefulness. There are no frills here, no bridges, just the relentless circle of the bass line with the occasional phrasing shifts to create the dip and swing of the song. The song begins with a stark drum and bass interspersed with a moaning blues/rock guitar line that seems to be speaking back at Marley. The I-Threes begin to chant slowly 'Heathen back dey 'on the wall' – a statement of hope that will turn into a statement of truth by the time Marley has finished the song. In this singular moment, the 'we/them' arrangement is established. All who seek to do ill to the righteous are the heathens. The heathens are those who do not know the truth or who will not accept the truth. By the time the chant has become a hypnotic mantra, the main speaker has been ushered in.

On stage, Marley walks out of the dark and steps into the beam of light over the mic. He raises his open right palm out to the audience as if pronouncing a benediction. His voice then calls his audience to attention. Here, it seems, is Henry V standing before the rag-tag English army on St Crispin's Day; here is Toussaint rallying the Haitian warriors to face the French in the battle for freedom; here is Joshua rallying the children of Israel to bolster their courage and do battle for their Lord. But here is Marley also speaking to himself, assuring himself that he remains in the race, that he remains committed to the struggle and that he will be back again. *Exodus* was an album of resilience – an album that sought to remind people that they had so much to say, and that Marley was still engaged. When we listen to his voice calling to all fallen fighters and ordering them to rise to face battle again, the force of Marley's skill at using song for powerful oratory is made abundantly clear.

Marley lays it all out on the table. He has run away, but his point is that it is a strategic departure. Marley is also arguing for wisdom in the actions of men. His artistry was inextricably linked with his sense of purpose as a speaker for those who could not speak. He was expected to comment on affairs of the world and he was almost always expected to be an authority on what was happening in Jamaica. In 'The Heathen' he tells the fallen warriors to assume battle position again. The pragmatism of the speech is bold. Marley is quoting the old clichés of soldiers who have understood the offensive potential of a strategic retreat. But it is also clear that in keeping with the spirit of 'Guiltiness', Marley is now reliant on the retribution of Jah – the strange karmic justice that he found in the words of Job: 'Even as I have seen; they that plow iniquity and sow wickedness, reap the same' (Job 4:8) – words of a man who had suffered greatly. Paul would tell the Galatians the same thing in his attempt to assure that God would avenge those who seek to lead people astray and do harm to his people: 'Be not deceived, God is not mocked, for whatsoever a man soweth, that shall he also reap'. When Marley says that he knows that talk is cheap, he is admitting that the things he is saying may seem like excuses – vain talk and the language of someone who is trying to rationalize his fear or trying to bolster his face. He admits that 'talk is cheap', and that saying it is not enough. Instead he offers another way of understanding the suffering that he and others are going through – the suffering that words seem incapable of easing. He draws on an old Wailers mantra, which in turn came from the fiery gospel-driven song of the Pentecostal movement that was adapted as the campaign song for Michael Manley in 1972:

> Press along Joshua, press along
> In God's own name
> Press along Joshua press along
> In God's own name
> For persecution we must bear
> Trials and crosses in our way
> For the hotter the battle the sweeter the victory!

Marley finds hope in the very New Testament promise that as things get worse, as the signs show even more suffering, there is a promise, a guarantee, even, that these are signs that the last days are here and that a grand victory awaits all those who persevere.

The chant, then, that the 'heathens' have their backs against the wall is a statement of faith, a statement that can only make sense in light of belief in the unseen, but assured, narrative of the end times. For all intents and purposes, the heathen does not appear to be suffering. On one level of reality, the heathen has triumphed. Marley knows this – he knows that he has fled, he knows that they are saying things about him that he can do nothing about, he knows that he has been living with fear for his life, but that is the knowledge of the world. The deeper knowledge is the knowledge that grows out of his battle, not against 'flesh and blood', but against 'spiritual wickedness in high and low places' – and from that perspective, the battle is won: 'But the hotter the battle / A the sweeter Jah victory.' Marley, as we come to see in our look at the album *Uprising*, was not always able to sustain that faith in the divine war that had already been won. In 'The Heathens', his sense of assurance is at is height.

Anyone listening to the album *Exodus* for the first time would have to have been stunned by the way in which song after song on that first side represented some of the boldness and most remarkable statements about Rastafarianism and about the struggle against the system of Babylon that Marley would write. After the contagious and hypnotic sound of 'The Heathen', which fades away with a wailing guitar, 'Exodus' appears, with its four beats to the bar drum beat. This was the marching sound of the new Rockers music that had been developed by the bullying drum and bass team of Sly and Robbie – a team that would, in the 1980s and early 1990s, become one of the most sought after drum and bass combos in the music business worldwide. 'Exodus' is Marley's statement of faith in Rastafarianism. It is a song about exile, but it is Marley's most important song of repatriation. It is a sermon with a clear motive. He is asking the world to examine their own hearts and to determine whether or not they are pleased with their lives. He knows they will say no, and he knows that the answer to this problem is the clearest statement of faith for the Rastafarian: Exodus.

Rastafarians regarded the repatriation to Ethiopia as a tenet of their faith. It served as the one source of hope in their existence. This desire, this hope, even this doctrinal truth, was what truly distinguished Rastafarianism from any other millenarian belief system that was rooted in Judaeo-Christian ideas. For years the Rasta had been petitioning the Jamaican government to send them back to Africa to fulfil the mandate given to them by Marcus Garvey. For years many had made that journey back to Africa. Some had settled in parts of Africa while others had found a place in Ethiopia. There are still Rasta communes in Ethiopia at this time. But the desire for repatriation was most acute in the 1960s and 1970s. During those two decades the conditions for most Jamaican Rastas were so bad that Africa seemed a fitting paradise from the abuse and deprivation that many suffered. What they sought was not material improvement but a chance to belong to a world that was their own – a place of their ancestors. Garvey's dream of a powerful and united Africa was central to this thinking and Rastas, including Bob Marley, wanted to return to Africa. Yet it is this desire that received the greatest amount of ridicule among middle-class Jamaicans who had been convinced by the colonial brainwashing that Africa was a backward place and that the further away Jamaicans could be from Africa and the memory of Africa the better. Rastas were seen as eccentrics and lazy people who did not want to work but just wanted a free ride to a place they did not really understand. For the Rasta, the Exodus out of Babylon was elemental to the faith. It is this that allowed them to connect with the ethos of Judaism. The idea of a physical space, a promised land, was the key to the philosophy of Rastafarianism and allowed it to connect with a deeply political understanding of the world. It is no wonder that the song 'Exodus' would gain a significant amount of popularity among Jewish people. The song drew on the language of the struggle of the children of Israel in the Old Testament and in the centuries after that period. A myth of home was basic to the Rasta ideal and it is one that fed the song 'Exodus'.

'Exodus' assumes something very important: that the journey is underway and that these times are the times of exodus. In other words, exodus is not a time yet to come. For Marley, exodus was now underway, and so his point of reference was always the Book of Exodus – the period of journeying for 40 years through the wilderness. This position helped the Rasta to appreciate and accept that the sufferings, the tribulations, the battles, the moments of doubts, the crisis of leadership, the emergence of a people who would seek to stay in Egypt – a whole class of people – all of these things had meaning in light of the typology of the journey of the children of Israel. Michael Manley had failed to arrange for the Rastas to be returned to Africa as many had felt he would. So the journey was still going on. In 'Exodus' Marley says 'We know where we are going / ... We leaving Babylon'. Exodus is something they are 'in'. It is not something that is to come. I emphasize this point because it is important to appreciate that Marley's sense of hope was not based on a myth of return in the afterlife, but a genuine sense that a return was necessary for blacks. Here the 'natural' and the 'mystic' would merge in a single song about a singular tenet of faith. It is this that makes the song so compelling and so important.

The driving force of 'Exodus' is intentional. Marley is bullying, he is prodding, he is cajoling, he is the task master commanding the people to 'move'. He says this again and again. It is the same role of cheerleader that he assumes in 'Jamming'. In 'Exodus' the metaphor is once again music and the jam is the music that will carry the people to the promised land. Marley's mood is assured and confident. He is combative in his attack on the lyrics – he stands at the top of his game and speaks with an argumentative energy that reminds us of some of his more animated interviews in which a sardonic self-assurance underlies the words that he speaks. 'Exodus' is, to put it mildly, a song of immense energy, bravado and confrontation. Marley explodes with statements and counterstatements, questions, commands and sly bits of humour. Each aside, each interjection, creates an immediacy and improvisational quality in the performance, and yet the song is a carefully crafted piece of rhetoric.

The interjected questions are rich with Marley's combative tone. He throws them out in a manner that makes his questions seem rhetorical. These are things that are obvious and he is about to lay them out clearly. The energy is caught also in the loud laugh that emanates after he observes that people will fight you because you have expressed faith in Rastafari. The laugh is derisive – it points to the absurdity of the actions of the evil ones. For Marley the issues are drawn in black and white, 'if you're not wrong... / everything is all right' – that is, everything will be fine and everything is correct. Then he declares that this new generation of people are the ones who will march through Babylon in this time of the 'great tribulation'. After the first rising chorus, Marley focuses his fire on those who have not seen the light. The truest sign of their state is that their sense of history is shot. The message is the same as the one he offers in 'Natty Dread'; but here he teaches by example.

He asks a most profound question, a question that when answered will drive the listeners towards his way of thinking. When he calls the listeners to open their eyes and examine their own hearts, he is calling them to assess their present realities and, in so doing, to determine if they are satisfied with the current state of their lives. The question is rhetorical. The answer will be a resounding 'no'. The question is evangelistic – it presumes that when faced with the truth, people will know of the emptiness in their lives. It is the emptiness that Habbakuk, the Old Testament minor prophet, identifies in the Children of Israel in his appeal to them to turn from their evil. Marley then reiterates that, while the unfaithful may be unsatisfied, the faithful know where they are going and know what they are leaving behind. They have truth and this is the compelling example that he offers to his hearers.

The sheer force of the song is caught in Marley's performance, which was clearly a driven and energetic moment. In this album, for the first time, he would use the voices of male backing singers to add a certain militancy to the mix – a mannish voice. He busied himself coaxing the band to stay with him – he would count in the chorus, ensuring that the sweet dip between the horn line and the chorus was arrived at in good time. From there he begins to appeal for someone who can be the one to lead the people to the promised land.

Marley's appeal for a Moses is a loaded one. As a song for the Jamaican people in general, it reflects a feeling that those who had come to be leaders of the country had somehow failed the people. Marley was looking for someone like Garvey to come and rally his people to make the march to the promised land. It is telling that Marley would never presume to be the Moses. He saw himself as a singer, a psalmist who would offer hope to those who were involved with the struggle, but he too was looking out for another Moses. The cry is such a heartfelt and profound appeal that it would have resonated with struggling people all over the world who understood that the crisis of a society was marked by the crisis of leadership. The 'Red Sea' is the symbolic waterway that divides those in exile from their promised land. It is this same sea that would become transposed into the 'many rivers' of Jimmy Cliff's song and the rivers of escape and renewal that appear all over the blues and the negro spirituals. The Red Sea is the barrier separating the former slave from Africa. In all African diasporic cultures, baptism represents both a physical and a psychic journey through the waters to a place of redemption and hope. Marley continues this tradition in 'Exodus', in the process, connecting this song to all peoples of the African diaspora.

Finally, in a moment of unusual quiet in the song, Marley offers a benediction. It is a statement of complete faith and it is a mantra that promises the liberation of all the suffering. He makes it clear that salvation will come from Jah. Another 'brother Moses' will not bring the change, but the change will come from Jah whose authority is unassailable.

Marley is quoting the prophet Isaiah, a prophet who began as a reluctant emissary, a man acutely aware that his lips were unclean. Yet it is Isaiah who supplies Christ with the language with which to proclaim his divinity. It is Isaiah's prophecy that undergirds the language surrounding the work of Haile Selassie for the Rastafarians. Here are Isaiah's words in the King James rendering:

> The Spirit of GOD is upon me; because the LORD hath anointed me to preach good tidings unto the meek; he hath sent me to bind up the brokenhearted, to proclaim liberty to the captives, and the opening of the prison to them that are bound; To proclaim the acceptable year of the LORD, and the day of the vengeance of our God; to comfort all that mourn. (Isaiah 61:1–2)

Marley manages to achieve the cadence and force of Isaiah's words in tightly rhymed lines, rhyming 'downpression' with 'oppression' and 'equality' with 'free'. The gloomy, heavy words are eclipsed by the bright words of freedom. The symmetry is impeccable here. Marley's craft is sublime in these instances of stunning poetry. Jah does not 'rule with equality' or rule 'equally' but he rules equality, meaning that he controls equality and his very person reflects equality. In this way he can wipe aside both 'downpression' and 'transgression' – the former he breaks because of the force of his truth and the latter he wipes away by the power of his forgiveness. All the language of redemption and the triumph of good over evil that permeates the Bible is compressed into this extremely eloquent benediction.

After the power of this song, the party kicks into full gear with 'Jamming'. The energy of 'Jamming' recalls the celebration of the children of Israel upon crossing the Red Sea. Miriam dances, sings and the whole congregation jams along the banks of the river. They can probably see the bodies of the Egyptians as they hurtle down the river. The palpable evidence of the justice of God is manifest in this moment. 'Jamming' arrives, then, from a place of victory. If 'Jamming' is full of the seduction of a dub song that would demand that the dancers lock tightly and rub-a-dub all night, this must not be seen as a contradiction, a mixture of the profane and the spiritual. It must be seen instead as part of the natural mysticism that *Exodus* seeks to explore. 'Jamming' is laced with a bluesy guitar by Junior Marvin, newcomer to the Wailers, a Jamaican-born but US-raised blues guitarist whose lines spoke a language on the four beats to the bar drumming of Carly Barrett and the round bass line of Family Man. Lyrically, 'Jamming' is a call to the world to join in this party. But it is also a starkly serious statement about the way that Marley viewed his music and what he sought to accomplish with it. There is also in 'Jamming' something of a love song. It is a love song that can turn the word 'jamming' into a deeply sexual thing. But Marley is comfortable with letting these two things work together, for Marley saw in the business of love – even sexual love – something that was healing and transformative. 'Jamming' is therefore a song full of much of Marley's own thinking at the time. He was thinking about the assassination attempt, thinking of his love for Cindy (one assumes) and thinking also of his love for the people. He was, at the same time, calling his people to the same kind of warrior stance that he had in 'Exodus' and 'The Heathen'. Finally, 'Jamming' is a statement about why he generates music in the first place. In verse after verse, Marley sends a message – first about his own view of the music he makes. Marley announces that his music is not controlled by rules or vows, but that he can do it anyway he chooses and can be guided by any tastes, styles or persuasions in music. This freedom was important to Marley. He was aware, however, that such liberty came with a price tag. He declares himself to be a 'living sacrifice' by alluding to Paul's admonition to the early Christians to 'present their bodies as a living sacrifice holy and acceptable to God'. Marley is announcing that what he does as an artist is a sacred and priestly activity that is, in its purest manifestation, a selfless suppression of the ego for the sake of the mission.

Yet even as he speaks about the absence of rules that can destroy the jam – the musical jam, that is – there is also the suggesting that he is speaking about the expression of love between himself and his woman. There is a price to be paid for both activities and Marley was acutely aware of his need to pay both. He is able to assure his woman as well as those who would jam musically with him that he would not give them up – that he will be there until the 'jam is through'.

In the next verse, Marley alludes to the assassination and establishes his sense of pride and confidence. Marley has already said that he will not trust a politician and that he would never take a bribe. He repeats this here. He half-boasts that bullets cannot stop 'them' – that is those who like him are devoted to the jam. He also argues that they will not be behoven to anyone, especially politicians who trade favours for money. Marley will not be 'bought or sold'. In the phrase he reminds us that the system of patronage is akin to the trade in humans that slavery was. But the struggle is a daily one. A price is paid for holiness and faithfulness; a price is also paid for the quest for unity. In the end Marley articulates his core value: money cannot buy life.

The final line of the verse is a direct reference to those who he was convinced had been bribed to try and kill him. He is compassionate to them. They are, after all, his people and he sees in their betrayal a sign of what can go wrong with the poor. In this song Marley reminds us that he is producing music that emerges out of Jamaica and nowhere else. He had to face many questions about both his exile and the nature of his music, which were posed by reporters who sometimes suggested that he was going international and forgetting his roots. Marley's response is to declare in 'Jamming' that 'we jamming right straight from yaad'. 'Yaad' is, of course, 'yard' which is a Jamaicanism for 'home'; and, for expatriate Jamaicans, 'yaad' has come to be an affectionate word for Jamaica, Jamaican culture, Jamaican ways of viewing the world and basically everything else Jamaican too.

In the third verse, Marley moves back and forth between the playful sensuality and the political manifesto about his art. The 'jam' becomes synonymous with reggae music and the making of it. He declares that 'we jammin'' and that he wants to jam 'with you'. At the heart of his art then is the quest for true love, which he says now exists. It is a statement of hope that must be understood as a point of healing for Marley himself. In many ways, 'Jamming' is the bridging song that takes us into the love songs found on side two of the LP. When he appeals to the audience to jam by his side, he is writing about love – the love between an artist and his audience, which he has cast as the love between himself and a woman. At the same time, he is trying to convince his audience that he must continue to speak the truth even if it means that that very audience will not be satisfied. There is a sense in which Marley is asserting his need to live his own life and to articulate his vision in the way that he himself understands it. At the heart of this is his faith in Jah, which he affirms in what is one of the classic Marley statements of trust in the ascendancy of Jah. He declares that Jah sits in Mount Zion (Ethiopia) and from there he 'rules creation'.

The first side of *Exodus* would have satisfied the Marley roots audience. Marley had not sped up the music in any way, and the dread drum and bass of many of the combative tracks was quintessential roots reggae. Many of the bass lines would become classic lines in the Jamaican dancehall scene. Yet there are hints that Marley is not about to enter a battle. The hints would have been confirmed if the listener turned the LP over and locked the needle into the groove of 'Waiting In Vain', easily one of Marley's most successful and deeply felt love songs. In a promotional version, Marley would introduce the song on the B-side by asking warriors and traitors 'to be still, for Jah live', then he named the song with his voice full of laughter – indeed, the introduction ends with a big laugh from Marley.

This is a straightforward love song in which Marley pleads with his lover, telling her that he does not want to wait in vain for her love. For those who have suggested that Marley, in this love song, was working on a song that would have an international appeal, there seems to be some truth to this. But it would be wrong to think that this was a new development for Marley. Marley had written soul love songs steadily throughout his career. When he worked for Johnny Nash as a songwriter, he mastered the soul song and gave Nash the kind of lyrics that he felt would reach the North American audience. 'Waiting In Vain's use of language that clearly belonged to a temperate climate – 'summer is here... / Winter is here' – may have locked Marley into the position of someone writing not for a Jamaican audience but for a Western one. 'Waiting In Vain' arrived at a time when Dennis Brown, Jacob Miller and Gregory Isaacs were shaking the charts in Jamaica with love songs that were deeply rooted in the language and metaphors of Jamaican society in the way that Marley's early work had done. Despite this,

'Waiting In Vain' took Marley back to his time as a suitor convinced of the power of song to win his lover. This was the Marley of 'Bend Down Low', 'Mellow Mood' and 'Comma Comma'. This was the Marley who would sing 'It Hurts To Be Alone' and 'Lonesome Feeling'. This was a side of Marley that had not emerged in a while, and for many of Marley's older fans the songs on *Exodus* were a welcome development. But the Marley singing these songs differed in one important way. He was now a man, and not an uncertain teenager. He was a man with fame and a man who understood that women liked him and that they would respond to his charm.

There is a quality of confidence in these songs that removes some of the vulnerability that made the earlier songs so moving – so full of tears. Most women listening to the Marley of 'Waiting In Vain' would have wondered why he was pleading with this woman since it would have clear to them that he could have had any woman he wanted. This was, of course, the challenge of writing a genuine love song of rejection as a superstar and woman's man. Marley achieves this by laying out the details of his need and by writing a credible story of how shy he has been and the extent to which he is not sure that this woman will respond to his advances. He also achieves this by making it clear that it is his heart that is involved with this seduction and not his body. In 'Turn Your Lights Down Low' he turns on the charm, pulling together a song of seduction that was surely intended to be seen as a follow up to the pleading of 'Waiting In Vain'. Most striking in these songs is the centrality of faith and the position of Jah in them. Marley sees the manifestation of love in the dynamic relationship between Jah and his people. By the time Marley wrote these songs, his 'affairs' with women were becoming, for him, a kind of mission. He would admit that he felt that he was doing good by bringing them into an understanding of themselves. As arrogant as this thought was, there is a real sense in which Marley saw his relationships with women as part of his sense of his commitment to the people he cared about. Stephen Davis's extended quotation of a talk he had with Diane Dobson, Marley's attorney for many years and one of his closest confidantes, reveals the complicated nature of Marley's understanding of his relationships with women:

One time at Hope Road, Diane Dobson made a remark to Bob about the girls with whom he was dallying, and Bob rebuked her for it. 'I think it was actually a kind of warning,' Diane says. 'Like if I ever saw him with another woman, a sister who might be a glamour girl or a model type, in other words not a Rasta woman but a sporting child, a party girl, I wasn't to make any remarks. It was like in the Bible where they were complaining that Jesus was eating with the publicans, and Jesus said, 'He that is well is not in need of a physician'. With regard to these women, Bob said that I was to have the attitude that there but for the grace of God go I. Because if it was not for the influence of him [Bob], who knows which way I might have gone. Bob used to say, 'Diane, if she seh she love me, and you seh you love me, then you must love her too'.

– Bob Marley: Conquering Lion Of Reggae)

In song after song of this period Marley would reveal the accuracy of these observations.

In as much as it makes sense that we 'read' *Exodus* and *Kaya* as two separate recordings, there is a case for reading the love songs in them as a single body of work that traces the progression of a love affair in the way that the Song of Songs by Solomon traces the ups and downs of his relationship. 'Waiting In Vain', 'Turn Your Lights Down Low', 'She's Gone', 'Is This Love?', 'Sun Is Shining', 'Satisfy My Soul' and the strange 'Misty Morning' form a cycle of love songs that Marley may have intended to have been read together. Some of these songs were not new, but were reprised and reconstructed to fit the mood he was exploring. Taken as a study of the romantic as seen by Marley, they form a dramatic and touching look at the art of the love song. They can also be read as a narrative poem, filled with the complexities of a man riding through a range of emotions. Marley's gift in these songs was to the Caribbean that had not yet produced a poet who would embark on as accomplished a suite of sensual verse as this proved to be. Marley's love songs would alter the perception of the reggae singer of the 1970s as solely a warrior.

And yet there is a clear way in which, given the model of the Song of Songs, we can see in Marley the willingness to have these songs read both as an Earth-centred expression of love between a man and a woman, and as a metaphorical anthem of love between a man and his art or his god. The reason is simple: these songs always return to the praise of Jah as the recurring theme, the defining voice – the shaping sensibility.

A useful way to enter into the emotional range of these songs would be to impose an order on them that, even if Marley had not intended, offers us a way to see that these love songs were as much interested in the narrative of the dynamic of male/female love – the banter and battle of that dynamic – as he was in finding the best language to express an emotion. Marley's love songs on these albums share one basic characteristic – they are all miniature stories with a male lover at the centre and a female as the object of the emotional exchange. The male is at times assured, confident, filled with joy and confidence, and at other times angry, slyly vengeful, distressed, distant, ironic and desperate. As we chart a narrative by stringing these songs together, we begin to see the shifting emotional range. The journey is from the tentative discovery of love – the back narrative of how it began – ('Waiting In Vain') through a series of songs of seduction in which there is a promise of reward ('Turn Your Lights Down Low' and 'Sun Is Shining') to a period of calm, borne out of acceptance and the consummation of love ('Satisfy My Soul). The narrative continues with the hint of disquiet and uncertainty ('Is This Love?'), which is then complicated by the dramatic climax of the loss of love or, at least, the loss of the object of love ('She's Gone') – this is a moment of profound reflection that shows a complexity in Marley that is most significant. Finally, the suite ends with a mystical attempt to rationalize the hurt of that loss and a strange, but haunting quality of regret and loss that is shaped by a sense of landscape and atmosphere ('Misty Morning').

In these songs Marley is deeply aware of the world around him and the landscape is almost always rural, almost always filled with a sense of light and a sense of the fecund world of the natural environment. Here, more than in any other genre of song by Marley, we find nature to be a central figure – a figure that empathizes with the lover and somehow becomes a part of the telling. Marley's woman is elusive, and he is never sure he will be able to keep her attention. He hunts her down, hoping to win her, but he is always aware of his weaknesses. There are moments when his ability to empathize with his woman is transformative and a revelation. It is when Marley seems to suggest that the progression of love is never a pleasant one, but it is often painful and forces us to accept the contradictions of our desires. That Marley put these songs together around the same time speaks of his own immersion in the rich array of emotions that consumed him even as he struggled with his political questions. The desire for love, for the expression of love and for the comfort of a woman was most acute for Marley at this time and this may explain the depth of feeling that emerged in these songs.

'Waiting In Vain' is a classic pleading song, but the suitor is not begging blindly and stupidly. The lover understands that he is a 'big man' now (meaning an adult with some experience), and he is no longer going to wait for this woman. It is as close to an ultimatum as he dares but he is not ready to say that he will walk away. If he seems to oscillate between frustration that borders on anger and a need to assure her that he will do anything to have her, it is because he is uncertain, he is torn between his dignity as a 'big man' and his hunger for her love. Marley understood that this is just the kind of position that a woman fantasizes about. She, at least in this instance, has control. As with most popular art, the attendant narratives of pop rumour help feed the way we approach the song. Marley's friends would all say that Marley wrote the song for Cindy Breakspeare. Breakspeare herself made the same claim. The story is that Marley worked on the song on Breakspeare's porch as he tried to woo her. She was a reluctant lover.

Marley begins with the story of the first meeting. The male sees the female and is drawn by his eyes and then his heart. The term 'follow-through' is a term used by Jamaican men to encourage each other – it is a sporting term; in any sport, the follow through is the way to ensure the task is properly completed as far as technique goes. Marley plays on the ghetto youth image – the idea of a man out of his social league trying to win a woman who should not want him. He is 'way down on [her] line' but he will accept anything. He has accepted his lot and all he asks is that she treats him right – that she does not raise his hopes unnecessarily. Yet this show of uncertainty is counter-balanced by a boast that will grow as the song develops. Here the suitor demands respect and shows that he is truly waiting for her to 'come'. The pun on the word is intentional. It is a sly statement that belies the seeming desperation of the first few lines. Marley then enters the realm of hyperbole and the clichéd love lyric of 'climbing the highest mountain and fording the widest river', There is still something endearing about his persistence even in these lines. He is willing to use the language of the pop love song if that is what it is going to take to win the woman. He will wait through winter and summer (and presumably autumn and spring) for his woman. The lines clearly allude to the Carol King song 'You've Got A Friend', with its slightly sappy cataloguing of seasons.

In the second verse, Marley assumes a mock tone of negotiation. He is pressing his case with greater earnestness. He tells her how long he has been waiting and then, employing the language of the business transaction, he asks if she thinks it is 'feasible' for him to keep trying. The pathos of the request is part of its charm. He has given up the idea of asking her to accept him and has decided to settle for permission to keep pressing her, to keep pleading his case. The image of a man knocking a door is a turn around for Marley. In other songs of the early days, he would taunt the woman with the old blues standard line, 'you keep on knocking / But you can't come in,' ('Bend Down Low') a line based on Christ's 'below I stand at the door knocking'. Marley is now on the other side of the door. He is knocking now. Marley then pours on the intensity of his need with lines that show the man's vulnerability and ability to grasp the fact that love is painful, and that it ultimately brings him to the point of tears – the classic recourse of the male in the most intense of soul songs of the 1960s and 1970s.

The singer admits that life is hard ('lots of grief') and that his chances of being hurt are significant. He is suggesting that while he knows that he will face grief and pain by waiting for her, he is willing to do so. The Wailer begins to weep as Marley's voice enters a wailing plea as he declares that he has tears in his eyes as he waits for his turn. At no point does the narrator give up the wait or give up the quest for the woman's attention.

He persists, and so when he returns to the chorus, he renders it as if this is his last chance. Soon the cry by its repetition becomes almost playful and ironic. It is, of course in the fading and apparently ad-libbed lines of the song that Marley's underlying confidence begins to show. Before this he has made it clear that she is the one in control and that he is the one who has feelings. In his mind she does not have any feelings, and if he she does he will not presume to say. But in the final lines, he starts to offer a reason for her reticence. He tells her that she is actually running from his love. This suggestion about her fear is a slight nudge at her vulnerability. She is not rejecting him because she does not like him. She is holding back because she is afraid of what could happen to her emotionally if she allowed him in. It is a moment of sheer Marley charm and the very assured space of sexual confidence.

It is on this note that he begins the full frontal seduction of 'Turn Your Lights Down Low'. The persona is now quite confident – at least he is more confident than he was in the earlier song. He takes charge of the seduction and instructs the woman to prepare for her lover. The lines echo the elaborate words of sexual preparation that we hear from the lovers in Song of Songs. Marley's care for detail is important here. The line, 'pull your window curtains' is a wonderful Jamaicanism. Yet the most striking thing about these first few lines is the way Marley undermines the cliché of the moon with the word 'Jah'. But associating the glowing moon with Jah, Marley now makes it clear that for him, this is a love sanctioned by his faith. Marley is making spiritual the sexual act that he is about to carry out. The narrative is one of rekindled love. The song speaks of a love that may not quite have worked out in the past but is now finding voice.

Instead of the male lover being the one who has been waiting, in this instance, it appears that she has been waiting. As part of a large narrative, Marley seems to be playing with the power play that is central to the romantic stories that he tells. The 'message' he has been carrying for this girl all this time is that he wants to give her some love. In the Song of Songs, the author plays with a similar pattern of delayed love. The male lover comes and knocks on the door of his beloved. She does not respond. She complains that she does not want to dirty her feet since she has already bathed. But she is being difficult – she wants him to really hunger for her. Soon she no longer hears the knocking. She panics and runs to the door to find that her lover has gone. She then runs through the town pleading with everyone she runs into to help her find her lover. In a reversal of roles, Marley's male is aware that he has failed to persist enough, he is aware that he 'was never on time', but now he wants to 'get through' to her, this time 'on time'. This play with time and with the teasing game of lovers is fully explored here by Marley.

The seduction is caught in images that suggest sexual play. The undressing of the windows is a delicate image that suggests the disrobing of the woman. The image also points to the lover's willingness to let the world witness their love. It is an act of commitment that he does not want to hide behind the curtain to make love to her, but he wants to expose their love to the world, but most importantly to Jah, whose moon-glow will be a blessing on the consummation. Caught in the sensual interplay, Marley's entire language assumes a tactile quality – it is aware of the way sounds suggest emotions and feelings. Where the words are not enough, Marley lets gutturals, stuttering and the repetition of words simulate the sexual dynamic.

By the second verse, the weight of the direct offer of love, of 'good, good loving', which quickly takes it from an emotional place to a deeply sexual place, leads the male to raise the emotional force of his request some more. Now, Marley is pleading with the same intensity and disarming force of will that Marvin Gaye made into an art form in the classic song, 'Let's Get It On'.

In this verse, what was 'Jah moon' in the first verse has become 'my love'. However, his love is physical – it comes 'tumbling' in as a man would; as a man so in love that he is anxious and clumsy for it. But, for Marley, they are one and the same. Then Marley turns to the old standard line of a man trying to get a woman to sleep with him – he declares, 'oooh, I love ya!'. But Marley grants the line a thorough sincerity rooted in the hunger that he manages to evoke in the song. It is, though, the generosity of his need that is the clincher. The male is at once predictable and yet, because of the peculiar back narrative, the hint that he is actually trying to make up for some indiscretion or for having failed to act in the past, we are led to see the dynamic as still somewhat uncertain. Most importantly, as with Marvin Gaye's song, we are not sure if Marley wins her – we are not sure whether she eventually succumbs. That lack of closure is part of what makes the song rhetorically fresh each time.

While these are the only two love songs on *Exodus*, I am arguing that there is enough organic connection between the love songs on *Exodus* and those on *Kaya* to allow for a fascinating reading. 'Is This Love?' is the first love song to appear on *Kaya*. It begins a sequence of songs that appears to follow the narrative sequence that I have worked out. Perhaps Chris Blackwell is to be credited for this ordering of the songs – an art of the record album that is rarely written about in reggae works. If, indeed, the lover in 'Turn Your Lights Down Low' has managed to win the attention of his woman, 'Is This Love?' is a fleeting moment in which he is almost bewildered by the intensity of emotion that he is feeling. Yet Marley is making use of a very clever rhetorical strategy. It is rooted in the New Testament tradition that love is action, and the folk and street tradition that 'talk is cheap'. The more common saying is that 'actions speak louder than words'. But Marley presents his love as a question. He is almost asking her that if all of these feelings are true, how can she doubt that what he is feeling is love.

What I enjoy about the placement of this song in the sequence created is that it finally seeks to deconstruct and then reconstruct the meaning of the 'I love you' of 'Turn Your Lights Down Low', which is an expression that emerged in the heights of sexual need. Now there seems to be reflection and the poet is wondering about the meaning and nature of love itself. More importantly, however, the hyperbole and the sometimes clichéd inclinations of the earlier expressions are replaced by a more Earth-centred and Jamaican sensibility.

The song begins directly enough. The lover expresses what he desires to do to the woman who is his suitor. He has won her and now he is trying to explain exactly why he pursued her. He is also trying to be candid, and to abandon everything to love. He wants to treat her properly and love her all day and all night. He wants a domesticated relationship with her. They will share a home, a bed and shelter; they will eat together the food provided by Jah. Then he muses whether what he is feeling is love.

Like most of the songs on *Kaya*, this song is full of bright sounds and is buoyed by an energetic kick drum that stumps through the jam with a sense of lightness. Marley, however, presents his love in terms that are humble. First he wants to love her constantly. But he also wants to love with what little he has – the humble nature of his world, 'a roof', is summed up in the wonderful image in the line, 'the shelter of my single bed'. For Marley this humble setting, this place that does not a belong to a man of wealth or a man who values wealth, is the space of a true love. He offers an austere love, a love that is pure. Its purity is made more pronounced when he introduces Jah once again. This time it is Jah who will provide the bread, the sustenance for the lovers. For Marley, a woman's willingness to accept such a simple life amounts to a sign that she is not a creature of Babylon. But Marley understands that what he is doing is constructing an argument. It is better to ask if what he is feeling is love, than to state it is love. By doing so he seems less calculated. He appears to be overwhelmed by these inexplicable emotions and yet he is willing to reveal his deepest feelings.

He is not concealing anything here – he is revealing everything that he is feeling. The singer is assuring the lover that he is not playing a game. In this song, Marley effortlessly gifts Jamaican love narratives with a song that is completely rooted in the unadorned world of the humble Jamaican poor. He grants dignity to that passion without somehow romanticizing it. There are echoes here of the manner in which 'No Woman, No Cry' achieves an intimacy of emotional connection without ever mentioning the word 'love'. Here, love is at the core and the ins and outs of romantic love are explored fully.

If there seems to be a full immersion of the lover into a relationship in 'Is This Love?', the songs that follow it begin to complicate this relationship. 'Sun Is Shining' is a strange song on the list because it could easily be viewed as a not being a love song. It functions well in that parallel universe of Marley's relationship with home and his attempt to comment on what it meant to be away. At the same time, it can be read as an anthem for the grace of God. In a rising bridge he sings with full 'churchical' force: 'we lift our heads and give Jah praises'. If 'Turn Your Lights Down Low' is uncertain and full of a certain desperation, 'Sun Is

Shining' has a breezier confidence, one that allows the lover to enter into ironic hyperbole. Like many of the songs on *Kaya*, this song is marked by Marley's desire to see the world in a positive light. There is an intense determination to talk about the things of beauty, the weather, the way light works, the taste of ganja and its effects and so on. In the first suite of songs on this album it is as if Marley is trying to exorcise all of the despair and anger that may have haunted him for a while after the shooting. 'Sun Is Shining' is an old song, which he recorded with Lee 'Scratch' Perry during their years together in the early Upsetter days. In that early recording, the same impressionistic qualities were present and the non-linear progression of the lyric was also quite intact. In this version, Marley reorganizes the lyrics and tries to create a greater progression of ideas, granting the piece the storyline of a relationship. Reading it as a love song, one must regard it as an acknowledgement of the sheer good feelings that emerge when things are going well. There is a giddy happiness in the song that is contagious. Yet it is not without a sense of Marley trying to work through his own darker feelings. Despite what many have said about the 'brightness' of the music on *Kaya*, the truth is that the record is a clean expression of the dread sound of reggae. Family Man's bass lines are stark and the one drop dominates all the way through. In a killer break in 'Sun Is Shining' the Wailers enter a dub moment that is haunting. Marley counterpoints his hunger for dancing feet and sunshine with the stark foreboding broodiness of the music. This mixture of moods is clear in the vocal styling and the musical sounds themselves (the sweet bluesy guitar lines that dance in and out of every song are made disturbingly sardonic by the biting muted pluck of the lead guitar following the bass line in a style reminiscent of the best work by Ernest Ranglin in the late 1960s). What Marley was offering was change – new ways of seeing the world and of seeing Marley himself. His Jamaican audience was not quite ready for this at the time, but such a thing had happened before. The songs are now appreciated for their complex stretching of the reggae form, not towards something rock-like, but to something more basic – the earliest sounds of elemental drum and bass.

It is a counting song in which he counts the days of the week. Each day we see him moving from one level of assurance to another. Most important is that he is bringing himself to that place. He tells himself what to feel. This is a self conscious effort to capture the sweetness of dancing feet in a world that has not always been sunny. In this sense, in the sense that he sees himself as a rescuer of those in need, it is a love song. One imagines a superhero flying in. It is a whimsical image that Marley relishes. Yet he is always clear that the source of his pleasure and lighter mood is found in nature – in the sunlight. Marley pulled out songs that he had written in Jamaica at a time when he was enjoying the brilliant and unrelenting light of the Jamaican landscape, a time when everything seemed much simpler. These songs had emerged from the very experimental world of Lee 'Scratch' Perry's imagination – a place of playfulness, wit, surrealism and weirdness, but also a place of the most honest of emotions. 'Satisfy My Soul', 'Kaya' and 'Sun Is Shining' all emerged from the vaults as slivers of sunlight for Marley. In the darker world of wintry England, far from home and far from the people he loved, a world marked by the gloomy uncertainty of a decidedly complicated life, these songs must have been a rich tonic.

In the number chant that grows into a call/response dialogue between himself and the I-Threes, Marley is clearly pushing himself to be joyful. It is almost as if he is making a note to himself to tell himself that, as he says, 'a new day is rising'. Then he commands himself to get up, to 'get on the rise' to face the dawning new day. The song reads like a valiant world of exhortation to the depressed, ordering them to get up and face the beauty of the day.

Even as Marley appears to be singing to his lover, he is also, quite clearly, singing this song to himself. Seen as a peculiar dialogue between the artist and himself, the song reveals some powerful ideas that complicate its meaning.

As a love song, the lines point to the persistence of the lover. He appears and declares that he is here. It is comic and it is also endearing. But Marley seems to be suggesting more than that. In some ways the message is to Jamaica. He is counting the days like a prisoner, trying to make each day have some meaning. The mundane weight of days passing suggests something less than appealing but, on each day, he grows in his desire to beat the darkness. He speaks to himself, reminding himself that 'a new day is rising', and that 'a new day is dawning'. By Saturday it is clear that he wants the world to know that he has survived, that he remains filled with hope. It is at this point that he segues into the most stunning moment in the song due to the poetic power of the image he uses. The rainbow is granted marvellous properties in this moment.

Marley's evocation of landscape in this, and many other songs, reveals a man trying to reconstruct his world without succumbing to nostalgia. But these are songs of exile. They are, invariably, love songs about home. The rainbow image is a remarkable one that begins with the image of the morning gathering the rainbow. The image invokes a biblical image of God reaching his arms around Jerusalem as a mother gathers her children. But the rainbow has more specific connotations – the rainbow is the image of hope, the image of a covenant with God. Marley sees in the rainbow the language of commitment and covenant and at once declares himself to be a rainbow, a personification of this covenant with his people, with his woman and with his country. But this is a covenant of beauty, a covenant of art. The lover as a rainbow is a figure of many moods, many emotions and many ways of viewing the world, but it is also the figure of the lover as an object of beauty and as an object that promises riches.

From that point on, a tenderness enters the song and, as Marley sings, 'sun is shining, weather is sweet', the word 'sweet' becomes fully Jamaican. Sweet in Jamaican parlance is not quaint, not lovely in that proper way. Sweet is rude, sweet is the sensation of a tickle turning into open laughter. In Jamaican when someone has been entertained, when someone has been made to laugh, the person would say of the thing 'it sweet me you see?' Men stand in the street and whisper to passing women, 'hey sweetness,' totally convinced that what they are offering is the most beautiful compliment.

The sweetness, then, of the weather, is thick with sensuality, full of sexuality. And yet none of this is contradicted by the prayer that bridges the song. The singer has nothing else to do but to give thanks for the sweetness and for the resurrection that has been enacted in the song. Like the psalmist he lifts his head up to the hills where Jah dwells and from where his help will come.

As a romantic moment, this is one that transcends the specifics of a love affair because it expands our sense of the meaning of love song to include the range of relationships that are affected when we are faced with an emotional entity such as falling in love.

The love song 'Satisfy My Soul' was first recorded as 'Don't Rock My Boat'. In both the lover is trying to help his woman know that she satisfies him. The later version, however, seems more earnest, more intent on demonstrating love, and the extent to which that is expressed is the extent to which we begin to sense that something is not quite assured here. In the earlier version, the singer seems far more blase about the possibility of his woman walking away: 'and any time you should walk away for me, yeah / You know, I'll need your sympathy'. In the later version, there is a more intense sense of desperation, even though the lines never make it into the song. By granting more space to given lines, and by repeating lines that suggest the lover is not sure that his woman believes him, we begin to see how Marley has decided to increase the drama of this new 'telling' of the song. By the end of the song, we understand why the song begins as it does with that ominous request that the woman not 'rock his boat'.

The lover can see that something is wrong. The status quo of the single bed and the shining sun is somehow being shaken. He quickly offers that he likes it like this – he likes it just the way things are. And in that plea there is a sexual undertone: 'so keep it stiff'. It is a feature of the song that is downplayed more in the later version than in earlier versions of the song. In one more improvised, immediate version titled 'I Like It like This', Marley almost simulates the sexual act – his pleading amounting to a series of instructions to his lover to keep him at the heights of pleasure.

The sexual dimension is less overt in the *Kaya* version, but it is there nonetheless. He appeals to what she knows of him, she should know, he says, 'by now' that he likes things as they are. The singer then goes on to catalogue what he likes about the relationship. It is a wonderful image of two people finding pleasure in their togetherness. The title that Marley chooses over the old one is telling. The old title, 'Rock My Boat', points to what the singer most dreads, and draws too much attention to the negative. The new title assumes a tone of supplication – it captures the pleading that will end the song. He wants her to stay with him because she satisfies him. But she does not simply satisfy his body – that would be too easy and crass – she satisfies his very soul.

The singer then starts to put pressure on the lover to stay – he begins to blame her for changing his life, for making him a man who now needs her and depends on her. He explains that he is now dependent on her love because she has given him something and he has reacted. The humour in these lines is best seen when the song is seen in the larger narrative of love songs done by Marley. Even in this sequence that we are looking at, we can see that the lover, who previously pursued and begged a woman who appeared unwilling to acquiesce and take him on, now, having managed to persuade her to give in, having cajoled, pleaded, begged and seduced, is now blaming her for her action, which he reminds her 'produces a reaction'. He goes on, 'oh can't you see what you've done for me?' And what she has done is to make him 'happy inside all of the time'. She could have done worse.

In 'She's Gone' Marley enters his most familiar space. Almost all his earlier love songs – at least the strongest material produced by Lee 'Scratch' Perry – is striking in its repeated theme of a man being jilted by a lover. When Perry first met Marley, he was struck by Marley's emotional intensity. In the book *People Funny Boy* Perry describes the experience:

When I look 'pon Bob, is like somebody send him. From inside, I didn't want to do it [record with Marley] definitely, 'cause I didn't need no help from Bob or nobody. I did have a upsetting vibration and it was good enough for me, but Bob hear it and want to join it. I said, 'Ok then', but when I look I see that someone really sent him because he need help somewhere. I say, 'Let me hear the songs that you have to sing.' He sings this, 'My cup is overflowing, I don't know what to do.' I said to myself, as a producer listening to an artist's inspiration, this is a true confession, it's the truth! His cup run over and don't know what to do, so he need help. I didn't say that to him, but I think about it. I listen; I didn't want to take him on, because I didn't need no help and I didn't want to use any singers, 'cause them was behaving so stink and so rude and I didn't want to get involved, just wanted instrumentals. But then, I looked and I hear somebody's inside dark, and I want to hear what the person say, so I tell him to let me hear what song him have to sing and him say his cup is overflowing and he don't know what to do.

The song they would record together, 'My Cup' is a powerful lament by a man whose woman has left him. The raw sentiment within it attracted Perry. It was the darkness at the heart of the honesty in his confession – Perry would regard this as an insight into Marley that went beyond the narrative of his lost love. It was, after all, a song, a piece of art giving shape to an emotion. Perry liked the art, the way it revealed Marley's vulnerability. It was a quality that would make Perry take the Marley (then homeless) into his home and into his life. Marley would produce songs of longing and loss with Perry for the years they were together. To Perry, the teenage pop quality of Marley's earlier songs seemed light in comparison to the open wounds of emotions that Marley wrote with Perry. The verses that emerged are Marley classics, and they gave him an emotional range that he could return to when he began to put together the more mature material. 'She's Gone' must then be heard in light of songs like 'How Many Times', 'Stand Alone' and 'Chances Are' – all songs of loss and longing. In 'How Many Times' he makes use of the narrative of memory to fill his lover with shame for what she has done to him. It is a tactic he would use later in 'Satisfy My Soul' where he blames her for making him love her.

The drama of the song is stunning – the image of woman stepping into light, a light that suggests love, but a light that is fleeting as the love he will experience with her. He has not given up. He is using the stories of their first encounter to win her. In 'Waiting In Vain' and 'Turn Your Lights Down Low' he uses the same tactic of memory. Marley, in love song after love song, is always waiting to do something with the woman he wants – in 'Stir it Up' it has been 'a long, long time' since he had her on his mind. In 'Stand Alone' the loss sends Marley into poetic sublimation which is sharpened by the somewhat caustic edge of bitterness in the lines: 'there you are crying again / But your loveliness won't cover your shame' and the tough regret of 'How could I be so wrong / To think that we could get along? / Days I've wasted with you / If I count they'll be a million or two.' But the song itself becomes a sweet thing – what he calls 'rhapsodies that taunt' and 'memories that haunt'. Marley is standing alone in 'She's Gone' and he is as strong in the articulation of pain as in his earlier songs. What he shows in his more mature phase is an ability to empathize with the woman, to balance his regret with a realisation that she is the victim and that he may have deserved her departure. He is now a father, a man with responsibilities and his woman leaves him having made clear why she is going. Marley begins the song with a deadpan truth: 'My woman is gone'. He repeats it, this time feeding it with a slight desperation. The I-Threes echo him, but they seem to be a choric tease, the same teasing voices that doo-wopped and cooed in ''How Many Times'. The Wailers, bolstered then by the addition of Rita and her female singing friends, seem to mock when they finish Marley's sentences in the song. It is a comic drama. The women seem to be laughing at him and Marley hams up his sense of loss. This is earnest stuff.

In 'She's Gone' we get something of that quality. The I-Threes whisper, tease and reprimand in the choric commentary. The story Marley tells in this song gives us a stark look at the implications of his life and the circumstances around him that would have driven a woman away. As a reflection of Marley's own story, the song could be referring to several people, including Rita Marley and Cindy Breakspeare. But such biographical veracity is just a fanciful bit of gossip. The song's complete story of a love lost to the hardships of a man's life is a narrative in itself that is thick with the emotions that Marley struggled with as he considered the impact of his troubled life on those who loved him. Marley's use of detail here is striking – the note hanging on the door, the image of the jail and the way that even nature, once an accomplice to his seductions, seems now to be conspiring against him. Marley clearly lays out what he understands to be the reason for her departure. He has not done this quite so well in any other song. And in doing this, there is a resignation that is born out of maturity and not a little despair. Yet even as he seems to accept that she is leaving because 'she felt like a prisoner who needs to be free', and because he seems to have failed to give her attention because he has been distracted by 'the pressures' around him, he is also admitting that he cannot blame her for leaving since others have done the same having failed to cope with the challenges of loving a person in his position. He agrees that her life should 'never be another jail'. And at the end of it he acknowledges that he may have missed the signs and he should have known that her heart's desires were not being met. The clarity of his empathy is significant. Marley is not pleading for her to come back. He is weeping that she has gone.

When Marley talks to the mocking bird asking if it has heard anything, he is reaching for nature to sympathize and not mock him. The voices of the I-Threes taunt him like censuring mocking birds. The singer seems to have been taken aback for the first time by this rejection. These are words he has never heard before.

If the singer seems to have accepted the situation in the first verse, he does hint at a touch of suppressed disappointment at the woman in the second verse. First he says she 'couldn't take it' and then he adds that 'she couldn't make it'. On one level this seems like a statement of empathy but, on another level, it seems like a suggestion of her failure, her inability to stand up to the struggle. Then, in true Marley fashion, he turns up the emotional temperature and the wailing man who stands alone and who has been abandoned turns to his children begging them not to worry about him if he cries as it is because his woman has left him.

The song's strength lies in the shifting emotions and the clearly difficult attempt by the singer to be 'big about it all', to be 'mature about it'. It is a different posture than the ones that Marley employed in his younger days. Then he never stopped pleading directly for the woman to return to him, either by begging her outright or by reminding her of why she loved him in the first place. Here there are no sweet memories to invoke, and there is no plea for the return of a woman. The most telling line is in the realisation that a woman who feels like a prisoner is a woman who must leave – she must be allowed to leave.

This constructed sequence ends with the most complex and surrealistic of the songs on *Kaya* and perhaps in Marley's entire work. It is not that 'Misty Morning' is bizarre or outlandish, it is just that it seems to be rooted in a series of riddle-like allusions that are never grounded for the listener.

We are never quite sure what, or who, he is talking about. It defies narrative and we can't be blamed for looking for narrative in Marley's love songs. He has given us reliable narratives throughout his career as a writer of love songs. However, Marley's political and philosophical songs have experimented with imagism and mysticism – qualities that, ultimately, we have to associate with a song like 'Misty Morning'. Marley knows that the song is one whose accessibility is fleeting – he calls it 'Misty Morning' because he is writing behind a mist of language, leaping metaphors, truncated ideas and riddles and because he is trying to offer 'mysteries' he 'just can't express'. Of course, part of our struggle with the song comes from a desire to give it a genre. Is it a love song or is it a philosophical rant about the unreliability of people? It is both. Marley says it is a song about philosophies, but he also helps us by reminding us that he is dealing both with frivolous matters ('light like a feather') and weighty matters ('heavy as lead'). Understanding who or what the 'you' is, is elemental to how we will read the song. On the surface the you refers to the sun, and as we have seen in 'Sun Is Shining', 'Easy Skanking' and 'Kaya', Marley is hungry for those things that allow him to take flight, to glow, to rise above the toughness of his life. In 'Misty Morning' the sun is obscured, and it seems to be taunting him, teasing him and hiding from him.

In the series of songs about love and lost love, the sun has become a symbol of happiness and a symbol of the pleasures that come from love. By the time we arrive at 'Misty Morning' after 'She's Gone' we realise that the sunshine has gone. Like his woman who has gone, Marley imagines, somewhat bitterly that he knows she/it is 'out there somewhere having fun.'

Marley introduces one fundamental conundrum in the song. He identifies it as the one mystery he 'just can't express'. It is a question 'Why you give your more to receive your less?' He wonders, then, why it is that despite giving so much, the best of us receive less in return. The question is in the tone and style of David asking God why the wicked seem to get rich and to prosper, while he, a man named after God's own heart suffers so much. Marley, like David, has no useful answers – all he has is warning that he borrows from his good friend Jacob Miller who used the saying 'don't jump in the water if you can't swim' in a popular song in Jamaica at the time Marley was writing the songs for *Kaya* and *Exodus*. The message is that the business of giving, the business of being an artist, the business of being a lover, requires that we know beforehand that the returns are not pretty. These are contradictory truths – but they are at the heart of the philosophical mysteries of life.

In the chorus, Marley speaks to a 'you' that may be the sun, may be a lover or may even be the unnamed deity. The latter is the least likely, because Marley never missed an opportunity to speak clearly of Jah when that was who he was referring to. What is more likely is that Marley is speaking to his lover. His lover often collapses into his family and his audience, so the figure that he sees in the 'you' is the same figure as the elusive sun. Marley is pleading for some order and for something that will lead to a more pleasant life. He wants the sun to 'straighten out' his today, his tomorrow and his entire life. He wants to move from lingering despair to something brighter.

The song's meaning lies in the way that it fits into the fabric of ideas and emotions that Marley has constructed around the *Kaya/Exodus* recordings. The love narrative that we have followed ends with a hope for some solace that is as spiritual as it is emotional. In the context of Marley's art, these songs are moving examples of a man who had come to accept that his art would express the depth of human emotion and that his own emotions would be material for these expressions. If we appreciate that these songs emerged at the height of his own emotional crisis, we can then understand why they are such significant works.

There is another category of song produced on the the two albums that is worth some attention here. 'Three Little Birds' and 'One Love', which end *Exodus*, are songs of hope and joy. They share much with the two opening songs on *Kaya*, 'Easy Skanking' and 'Kaya'. The underlying theme of these four songs is the intense need to find hope and brightness. Marley reaches for these things in art, in the escape through ganja, in the natural world around him and in his memories.

'Three Little Birds', for instance, is a whimsical and playful ditty that some have called childlike. Its grace, though, lies in the repetition that becomes like a mantra. Marley knows that each line must be simple, direct and adequate to sustain repetition. There is an idealism here that is a jewel in Marley's imagination. The mantra of repetition and the affirmation of this haiku-like moment suggests something of hope and possibility. And yet it is an idealism that seems to be at odds with his own condition – his own place in the world and the narrative of his life to this point. He was healing from wounds, and yet he was dreaming of hope in the midst of all of this. Here Marley is showing that hope is a struggle, it is not derived from delusion or some myth of the happy-go-lucky island soul – he had lost that notion long ago. But he was still a smiler, he was a good-natured soul, he was an optimist and these things shine through the song, which I have always imagined to be a letter home.

As a man of roots and spirituality Marley offers this image of the birds as a prophecy – a vision that he passes on to those he loves: 'Everything little thing's gonna be all right' – a promise he made to his woman in 'No Woman, No Cry' a promise, then that he had made to all Jamaicans who would weep at the full organ sounds opening that song. He repeats the promise in 'Three Little Birds', when he assures us that the message came in the form of three magical birds – the figures of the Trinity, the figures that appeared to Christ's disciples when they saw him transcendent.

'One Love / People Get Ready' is an old standard that the Wailers had re-released many times in all musical forms imaginable. The song, an adaptation of Curtis Mayfield's 'People Get Ready' is an anthem of love and faith. Here Marley manages to create a simple lyric that merges wonderfully some old blues ideas, a revolutionary ethic and a moral hopefulness that is rooted in Judaeo-Christian traditions – and eventually Rastafarian traditions. The words 'One Love' are a wonderful coinage – a true Rasta coinage like 'I and I' that captures the meanings of community, individual love and a range of other loves.

If Marley's lyric seems blindly optimistic in the chorus, it proves to have grown out of a reflection of pain in the verses. 'One Love' is quite simply a catchy anthem that seems to present an optimistic vision of the world. Its appeal has more to do with the chorus than with the very evangelistic verses. Some people prefer not to know exactly what Marley is saying. They fear that somehow they will be excluded once they understand the lyrics. But the verse is important to Marley here. It is a verse of faith rooted in the belief that those who have done him wrong will have to face their judge in the time to come. He wonders if the selfish 'hopeless sinner' will end up in hell or in some other place. But he does not know the answer. He only asks. Then he offers a verse of millenarian prophecy and a rallying cry for war. The Christian 'holy battle' of the earlier version has by now changed into the end times Rasta doctrine of Armageddon. And yet Marley does not allow himself to succumb to the language of pure war. Instead he reaches towards love. This is a message of empathy, concern and hope. The chorus has the same kind of optimism that is sounded in The Beatles' 'All You Need Is Love', but Marley's sense of responsibility does not allow him to ignore what he sees as the judgment that will befall those who do not embrace this love.

While Marley remains weighed down by the pressures around him in 'One Love', in 'Easy Skanking', which opens *Kaya*, he decides to take flight – to escape. The two ganja songs are indulgent, but they are also healing moments for Marley. This is a space that he creates for himself and will not allow anyone to take it away from him. For Marley, the smoking of ganja will bring peace to the world. He is completely convinced of this. His anthem celebrates this belief. If this was merely an anthem to marijuana, it would be a good song, anyway. But this is more than that. It is the splendid and well thought through introduction to this album, which is about flight, about an artist's desire to withdraw and seek some understanding of himself, and about an artist's desire to eke out some pleasure in the midst of encroaching despondency. It is the story of an artist who seeks to find pleasure in the small things. The song is edged by its irony – 'Excuse me while I light my spliff' is his humble request to the listener.

The spliff is at once a source of pleasure and flippant flight, as it is a prompter of deep philosophical thought. Marley allows himself to go against everything he has said in previous songs about the need to face reality, to know history, to be fully aware. Here he says that he wants to drift from reality, and to do so he is relying on music ('this riff') – this new kind of music. Then his command is the same 'take it easy' – it is a Jamaicanism, a phrase full of the need that only Jamaicans would understand, to slow things down and to distance oneself from the hectic and violent energy that is Kingston's spirit. Marley then offers a Peter Tosh-like advertisement for ganja – one of his first in a long time: 'Herb for my wine, / Honey for my strong drink.'

Marley follows 'Easy Skanking' with 'Kaya'. The appeal is the same as in 'Easy Skanking' but Marley seems more determined to shake himself up. Marley will cajole himself in this way throughout the album – reviewing his feelings, thinking about his ideas about life and his future and psyching himself out of despair. 'Kaya' is a classic song that celebrates the idea that lovely things are also the subject for poets and for revolutionaries. Marley returned to a less troubled time to retrieve this song from the vaults – the years before the shooting, the complex woman problems, the money problems and the cancer. 'Kaya' is about searching out the lovelier things in life. Marley's work on *Kaya* is full of such moments – a poet trying to capture what is touching and beautiful about his world.

'Kaya' is a metaphor for sublimation. It is the value of art to buffer us from the hardships of life. But the theme is of flight. The poet is running away. The rain represents the annoyances of life – the storm, the flood. The high-flying singer wants to get above it all. This is not simply a wish, it is an earnest call, 'Get up and turn I loose...'

The final songs on these two albums are those that show the limitations of this attempt to run away. 'Crisis', 'Running Away' and 'Time Will Tell' are, I have to admit, three of my favourite Marley songs. I regard them as the last word by Marley on the mood of that time away from home, the mood that would be altered dramatically by his trip to Africa, from which he would return with a sense of political clarity and purpose – a time when he would write songs of power and weight – songs that presented him as a man totally given to his task of prophesying truth. If *Uprising* is a dark and brooding album, it is so because he was struggling with his mission and with the stark truth that the world is a cruel place. The dark lines of *Kaya* come from a different place, they come from a deep questioning of himself – from a place of doubt, and from a place of personal crisis. He sings his way out of it. It is this that makes Marley consistently redemptive.

'Crisis' emerges then as Marley's confrontation with the problems being faced by Jamaicans at the time he put the album together. Jamaica had just been through a bloody election and the guns on the streets that had been injected into the city to complicate the political warfare now belonged to a set of youths who had no ready income. The politicians who had won had naturally forgotten those who helped them win, and those who had lost were incapable of helping the youth. No longer employed, the youths used their guns to rob and rape. The crime rate in Jamaican would soar precipitously after each election – 1977 saw an extremely significant rise in crime. Marley saw most things now through the hindsight of his own crisis. Having concluded that what had happened was driven by political opportunism, his lyrics kept pointing to the way in which the world was now being run by people who could buy out the desperate. The old truths of the world that once gave solace were being constantly undermined. Selassie's 'We are confident in the victory of good over evil' was being sorely tested and Marley was singing about it. He was puzzled by the unfairness of the world that allows some people to experience no sunshine in their lives. And the love that is supposed to find its way to everyone is being undermined by those who want to make 'matters worse' for others. This is the nature of the crisis.

The hopes of people, and their faith in the reliable order of the universe, were clearly being tested. In many ways Marley is even questioning the the power of love to transform – the power that he sang about in 'One Love'. The pattern of hope was one of acceptance that eventually good things come out of crisis. The reality, according to Marley, is that too many people are busying themselves shattering the dreams of those who dream. Marley finds one way to cope with this and it is a means that he would return to with more and more regularity as he grew older and faced greater challenges in his life: give Jah thanks.

The elusive sunshine that Marley searches for in 'Misty Morning' continues to flee and yet, in the face of the dark, Marley commands his listeners and himself to give thanks and praise.

There are two fundamental observations that emerge from this song. The first is a simple truism that good things don't always come to the good and that there is a peculiar economy in this world that does not always gel with our sense of order. Marley does not make this observation with bitterness or irony, he simply describes what he has seen and proceeds from there. 'Why do bad things happen?' he seems to be asking. Yet he does not have an answer.

The second is Marley's growing quarrel with fatalism. He always returns to what people say, and what they often say is that things are the way they are because they have to be that way. And yet, what he observes is the wicked working hard to break the hope of the righteous. As he describes this situation, we half expect to hear Marley call us to get up and stand up and fight. Instead he offers worship and devotion. Marley sends this truth to the politicians who say much but do little for those who suffer – instead they kill and destroy. The picture is gloomy, but Marley commands us that no matter what the circumstance, we must give praise. Here is Marley without answers, again. It is a rare thing for him to be filled with this absence of simple solutions. So, like the psalmist, he turns to praise. It is all that makes sense.

If the absence of easy answers in 'Crisis' allows us an insight into Marley's humanity, his naked honesty and self-questioning in 'Running Away' represents what I regard as one of the most significant moments in Marley's artistic journey. The last lines spoken over the fading beat of 'Running Away' are the most telling aspect of the song. There is a sense in which the song begins like a sermon to others, but we quickly realise that Marley is being ironic. He is singing to himself. The dialogue between audience and artist is most pronounced in this song. Marley is the prophet who has something to say to the community as well as the prophet who is facing his own vulnerability, his fear and his need to clarify his relationship with his position. He seems to accuse someone that they must have done wrong. It is the only way to explain their exile, their homelessness.

At first we are quite certain that Marley is asking this of the person who he is accusing of running away. But the moment he begins to talk – intentionally changing the mode of discourse from song to speech to help us understand that all these voices that we have heard before have been mocking voices of self doubt and uncertainty that echoed the accusatory voices he is hearing from the world around him. He states that he is in fact not running away. Rather, he argues, he has simply moved away from the confusion of a divided and uncertain home to the proverbial 'roof top' where things are calmer. It is an act of pragmatic wisdom, a strategic withdrawal not unlike the one he mentions in 'The Heathens'. His withdrawal, though, is selfish – he has to protect his life. It is a decision that he is at pains to show to be not only reasonable but the right one, the proper one for him to make. But he knows that his actions have elicited censure, gossip and criticism from those who insist that he is, indeed, running away and being a coward. All this is said in a soft, pleading voice that eschews melody and song and turns to direct and plain speech. The speech turns out to be a trick, a kind of revelation that turns the song on its head. The subjects in the song have changed by the time we get to this speech.

The brilliance of this song lies in the irony; in the clever trick of the lyric. Marley begins with the typical posture of the prophet/preacher declaring statements about an unidentified 'you'. The 'you' has done so much: he/she is running away, doing wrong things, is lost and incapable of finding his/her path home and is confused. The 'you' is fickle and seems to be a ripe target for Marley's censure.

The suggestion is that he is addressing someone else, offering, in true Marley fashion, certain salient truths about living, about humanity and the foibles of the human character. Then he introduces what (in the context of what has come before) appears to be a rather mysterious and puzzling statement. It is a proverbial statement that seems to be an aside, an incongruity within the clearer preaching that has proceeded it. It is a proverb, which, when paraphrased, means that while everyone is convinced of the unique and superior horror of their pain, the truth is that the comparison of pains is a futile thing because whatever pain one person feels is sufficient pain for them. Marley proposes that we cannot look at someone else's pain as a means to determine whether our pain is a superior pain. The person who feels it, knows it.

What becomes slowly clear to us is that Marley's musings amount to a sophisticated dialogue with himself. On the one hand, he is using the voice of those who are accusing him of not being loyal to Jamaica, and in another voice, he attempts to respond to them. The 'trick' lies in the use of the accusative second person singular voice, which is naturally ambiguous because of the pattern of speech that allows the speaker to use that voice as a distancing mechanism in first person speech. During the period of *Kaya*, when Marley was in exile after the attempt on his life, the street talk was that Marley was abandoning the ways of Rasta and becoming far too deeply inscribed in the Babylon system of the rock and roll world. The accusation was that Marley was leaving his roots, his identity and himself behind. Much of this flowed out of speculations about his lifestyle – using American musicians in his band, his BMW, his apparent affluence – which, for a street thug of the 1960s and early 1970s, and a 'grounds' roots man of the mid-1970s, suggested a betrayal of his core principles and values.

It did not help that Marley was enjoying a relationship with Cindy Breakspeare, a light-skinned society woman – the kind that did not fit the profile of his Africanist Rastafarian sensibility. Marley's song, 'Running Away' is a defence of his credentials as a prophet, as a man, as a Rastaman and as a Jamaican. Thus his statements shift from voice to voice, creating a dialogue that would look something like this:

People: Yuh running and yuh running...etc...
Marley: But yuh can't run...etc...
People: Yuh must have done
       Something wrong...etc...

In his defence Marley argues that he can not run from himself, from his identity. He throws up the 'su-su' (gossip) of the street in a subtle but clear act of confrontation: 'This is what you say, but here is the truth – I know what you are saying about me....' Then, as the song begins to fade away, the heart of the song is spoken. The 'message', which is perhaps one of Marley's most overtly personal articulations, is contained in typical reggae fashion, at the end of the song – as if it is an out-take, a ramble that could be easily cut out from the body of the song – a kind of articulation that only appears because the microphone is, unbeknown to the singer, still 'hot'. But the verse form, the use of rhyme and the rhetorical gesture indicate that this is a key element of the song. Here he makes it clear that the accusations amount to an attack on his integrity.

He explains, alluding to the violence and turmoil that marked his life at the time, that he is really in exile as an act of escape – as a way of getting away from the threats on his life. He then addresses the full brunt of the accusation contained in the song by stating, 'But it's not true / I'm not running...' At this point it becomes clear that the refrain, sweetly harmonized by the I-Three, is bitterly ironic and is in essence a taunting cry. Suddenly, the extremely dry and pained quality of Marley's singing begins to make sense. As a prophet, as a voice with a responsibility to the community, he must address the assumption that he is selling out, that he is abandoning the battlefield at a time when many are dying and there is a great deal of upheaval in the nation.

Now we understand that when he says 'who feels it knows it' he is telling those who are whispering about him to try to live his life for a minute. He is telling them that they cannot tell him how to feel or how to handle the pressures he is facing. He is, in essence, saying that these events have affected him and have forced him to leave Jamaica and walk away from a world that he calls his home. *Kaya* and *Exodus* are the evidence of his assertion that 'you can't run away from yourself'. Marley is relying on his audience to remember the ways in which he has always identified with his people, the way in which the Rasta notion of 'I and I' collapsed any divide between himself and his people. In song after song, Marley would begin with his narrative and then quickly transform it into a narrative of the people – the 'we'. If they remember this, then they will understand, he seems to be saying, that if he cannot run away from himself, then it means that he cannot run away from his people, from the country that made him. It is, therefore, a very affirming song, one that finds a way towards hope. But it is also a painful song.

If Marley manages to mute the hint of self-pity that is suggested by his mood in 'Running Away' through the use of irony and the trick of the voice, in 'Time Will Tell' Marley wears his suffering on his sleeve. He places himself as the sacrificed lamb – the crucified Christ figure. The song is one of cold revenge. It is a curse and a warning that is slow and prayerful. In style, it is closest to 'Rastaman Chant' with the steady Rasta drumming forming the mantra-like quality to the song. Over it, there is the light and ironic interplay of guitar lines that have the sound of a slow take on West African guitar picking. Marley's voice is filled with terrible seriousness here. There is no hint of the I-Threes in this song. The voices are all male, which increases the sense that this is a warrior *groun'ation*. His enemies are clearly delineated. Marley reserves the use of the term 'baldhead' for only those he regards as the scum of the earth. In this song his indignation, though never vocally strident, is nevertheless quite intense.

The 'dread' is at once Selassie, all Rastafarian brethren and Marley himself. Selassie's deity has been questioned by many and their fate is sealed. But Marley is speaking a larger truth – that they will not be able to crucify the dread without facing the retribution of Jah. Like so many of the evildoers in Marley's songs, the ones in this song are oblivious to what they are going to face. Marley's voice is distant – almost as if he is trying to mute the dangerous words he is speaking. Marley tells his listeners to 'back up' those who have conspired to set up the righteous. 'Backing up' in this instance is not a term of support but a term referring to the threat that will force the evil doers to 'back up', to step back.

Marley reminds us that he does not blame those who were bribed to shoot him for what happened; but he blames those who 'set them up' – those who bought them out. They are set up, he argues, because they will die as a result of their mistake. He feels pity for them, but reserves his anger for those who orchestrated the assassination attempt. It is part of Marley's philosophy to take on the 'boss' and not the 'deputy'. He seeks to arrive at the heart of evil and to target it with his words.

Marley then appears to enter into a trance-like state and his words become indecipherable. The liner notes with the printed lyrics do not account for three lines. It seems as if Marley is speaking another language or is somehow doing a kind of scat – the kind of gap filler that he might have intended as a space to be filled in by lyrics later on. All this is speculation, but the next decipherable lines are a prayer to his people who he refers to as his children. These are not the same children as in 'She's Gone' – these are the children for who Marley sees himself as a father/prophet. He tells them to weep no more. As if those words in unknown tongues constituted a moment of vision, Marley emerges with that above words, which suggest that he has seen things in the future. In his vision he has seen Jah settle the score against his enemies, and he has also seen a sycamore tree that symbolizes freedom. Marley has entered a revelatory place that he treats as sacred. It is a place of worship and prayer, a circle where one senses Marley found restoration.

As the final song of the *Exodus/Kaya* sequence, 'Time Will Tell' reveals that Marley has made a journey of some significance. He has come to a place of total dependence on the power of the almighty to resolve the troubles he has encountered in this life. Marley, however, seems more alone than ever before. There appears to be a movement for Marley's life from a place of community and collaboration to a place of isolation. Yet the isolation is not something that is imposed on him, but a movement towards the completion of his artistic vision. For all intents and purposes, 'Redemption Song' represented Marley's last statement to his audience while he was alive. It is a story that he tells alone. A man with his guitar speaking about his own journey which then takes him to a place of communal strength. But he is alone. That quality of standing alone is something that haunted all of Marley's work, but for a while there was a feeling that he found strength in the collaborations that he had with original Wailers team of Bunny and Peter, and throughout his life he would collaborate, finding teams with whom to work. But, as most of his friends have said in interviews, Marley became increasingly distant as the pressure of his life and the circumstances of his art began to increase. He became more and more distrustful of those around him and he would eventually surround himself with only those people he had relied on from the beginning.

In an interview with Dermot Hussey in 1975, Marley spoke candidly about the split with the Wailers and about his mistrust of so many around him. According to Hussey, he seemed angry and disturbed by the things people were saying about him. The program was aired, and then Marley asked Hussey to destroy the tape. What remains is Hussey's memory of the conversation, a recollection he shared with Stephen Davis. The most striking thing Marley said when he was asked about the sources of his inspiration was that he got inspiration from three sources: Selassie, his mother and his enemies. In another interview in 1973, Neville Willoughby asked Marley about the themes of pain and weeping in his songs, and

Marley told Willoughby that he started his life crying: 'Started out crying. Started out crying, y'now. And then music becomes a part (of my life) because me grateful to Jah.'

The moment he speaks of is the moment in which an artist finds himself alone in the world and filled with inexplicable emotions that can only come out in tears. Marley would then find music and words to give voice to the deeply personal sensation. Marley would call music a delicate thing and would always say that music has to come from within the artist's sense of self. He resisted categorization because he wanted to make it clear that his music came out of an artist's core – a place of deep isolation and yet a place that would have to eventually grapple with the realities of the world.

Marley would tell the story of his art in what remains one of his most beautiful songs. The quest for music is a quest for happiness, a quest that came out of loss and a sense that something was taken away from him. The song is ostensibly about love, but 'Hurting Inside' is really about the artist's own journey towards hope.

In 1977, Marley probably understood this song more than at any other point in his life and the songs he wrote during that time expressed the desire to bring happiness into his life. He chose to do so through art. And he managed to produce a rich gift of song in the process.

Marley would never really leave the themes that he dealt with so intimately during the *Exodus/Kaya* period. While he did not return to the love songs of that period, he would continue to write songs about the shooting and about his reaction to it. These were not simple songs rehearsing the events. Marley was a far better writer than that. Instead, he turned the incident into a mythic narrative, a moment in his personal history and his imaginative history that would serve as a touchstone for his ideas after that. The shooting unsettled much for him, but it also confirmed for him his faith in Jah and his commitment to his mission as a singer. The Marley that emerged from this period was decidedly more spiritually centred and, at the same time, far more international in his perspective about the prophetic developments in the world. Marley's final writing period was marked by a tremendous amount of pressure and would end with the weighty fact of his illness. His songwriting would remain as emotionally charged as ever, but for the first time one could sense doubt in Marley – doubt and a sense of despair. Yet it is during this latter period of his life that Marley would write some of his most affirming and moving songs of faith. These contradictory impulses made sense within an artist who seemed to be carrying the weight of the world on his shoulders.

4 Survival, Uprising And Confrontation
Redemption Songs

'Babylon is everywhere. You have wrong and you have right.
Wrong is what we call Babylon. I could have been born in England.
I could have been born in America. It make no difference where
me born because Babylon is everywhere.'

– Bob Marley, 1975

SURVIVAL (OCTOBER 1979)
So Much Trouble In The World / Zimbabwe / Top Rankin' / Babylon
System / Survival / Africa Unite / One Drop / Ride Natty Ride / Ambush
In The Night / Wake Up And Live

UPRISING (JUNE 1980)
Coming In From The Cold / Real Situation / Bad Card / We And Dem /
Work / Zion Train / Pimper's Paradise / Could You Be Loved / Forever
Loving Jah / Redemption Song

CONFRONTATION (MAY 1983)
Chant Down Babylon / Buffalo Soldier / Jump Niyahbinghi / Mix Up,
Mix Up / Give Thanks And Praises / Blackman Redemption / Trench
Town / Stiff Necked Fools / I Know / Rastaman Live Up

By 1979, Marley had returned to Jamaica. His exile was over. But in
reality it was not finished because he was touring. In fact, the last three
years of Marley's life were spent on the road. He toured the world, he
filled stadiums and he had his eyes set on the triumph of America. The
assassination attempt, though, had changed something in Marley. There

is a peculiar way in which the songs that appear on *Survival* and *Uprising* seem to have a haunting quality in the light of his death. But, according to Marley's friends, he did not have any idea that he was facing death. Neville Garrick was with Marley when he had the treatment on his toe in 1979. Marley was not able to walk on the toe for a while in order to allow the surgical scars to heal. In their minds – at least according to Garrick – the cancer had been dealt with. The toe had been treated and they were getting on with life. But others would say that Marley was never without pain. They would say that the toe never really healed, and that Marley, during the last three years of his life, always suffered pain when performing. What is known is that Marley was kept on cancer medication after the surgery and he would remain on that medication for the rest of his life. Marley may not have known how ill he really was, but was constantly aware of his own mortality and of this diabolic illness that seemed to have taken a hold of him.

When the cancer was finally 'discovered' in 1980 after he collapsed in Central Park while jogging, it had metastasized in his lungs and his brain. He had two fairly large malignant brain tumours. The initial diagnosis was that he would be dead within six weeks at the most. He lived for almost a year. But what is clear is that the man who toured Europe and the US in 1979 was a sick man. Marley was tired. He complained of fatigue and he complained about the pressures of being on the road, of having to keep a great deal of things together. Marley was now running a massive operation, and he was being called upon to maintain his role as the financial support for over 300 people in Jamaica while, at the same time, maintaining a band, keeping up a rigorous touring schedule and continuing to record and produce album after album. He was also still managing several romantic affairs and trying to handle the politics of being a man with many children by several different women. The strain did not lead Marley to maudlin songs. It led him to Jah – to his father, to his faith and to the sharing of that faith.

Marley would have understood that his problems were minor compared to the problems that were facing Jamaicans during those years after the shooting. Two years of some of the worst violence and mayhem that Jamaica would ever see began in 1979. Things were hard in Jamaica.

The economy was in shambles and the US was now quite decided about putting pressure on Jamaica to punish her for her associations with Fidel Castro in Cuba. But that was not all. The US was also punishing Jamaica for daring to establish heavy tariffs and taxes for the extraction of bauxite where, in the past, multi-national companies had had free rein to extract at a massive profit. Manley had said some troubling things at international conferences – things that showed a clear case of arrogance, self-assurance and a peculiar attitude that suggested that Jamaicans were willing to go it alone no matter what the big powers like America decided to do.

At home, the JLP was garnering its strength to make much of the upcoming elections in 1980. The classic mode of Jamaican political violence was in full swing, and all the features of CIA-driven unrest and instability in the society were at work. People were being killed. There were rumours that an invasion by Cuba was imminent. There was a proliferation of guns and the authorities were suggesting that the source for these guns was suspect – some other force, it was argued, was supplying the guns to these Jamaican gunmen. The battle for the Jamaican people was in full swing. Tensions surrounded the dramatic and charismatic nationalism of Michael Manley who, for the past ten years, had managed to get the Jamaicans who stayed to accept the idea that sacrifice would pay off in the long run, and that independence meant 'turning your hand mek fashion' and 'self-reliance' – all catchphrases and slogans of the PNP. Such slogans can be unpicked in this way – there are severe food shortages, serious import restrictions and you can't get the goods from America that you have become used to. But the desire for those things is a sin, rooted in colonial values and anti-nationalist desires. The true Jamaican will forego those things and look to local produce, local food and crafts and all kinds of other locally developed products, so that the country can grow. Improvise, rely on local raw material. This is how Jamaica will survive the onslaught of the imperialist American forces.

The counter argument from the JLP was remarkably simple – vote in the JLP and you will be able to get American shoes, American apples and cornflakes. You gave the austerity a try and it did not work. You want the good things in life, you want to have 'money jingling in your pockets', so vote for the JLP and America will be happy and will prove to be a more reliable benefactor than Cuba or the Soviet Union could ever be. Given the choice between a Ford and a Lada, which would you pick? As blatant and materialistic as this appeal appeared, it was compelling in a country where people were beginning to feel as if they had given the socialist idea a chance and had somehow been betrayed by the corruption and ineptitude of those leading the socialist cause. This was a backlash. Things African had been the order of the day during the Manley period, but that had clearly fallen apart. Selassie was dead and Ethiopia was suffering a terrible famine. If the myth of Rasta was gaining some foothold in the early 1970s, by 1979 it had lost currency and appeal.

In 1979 the killings started, the scandals began and the spy stories grabbed headlines. There were betrayals, there were intrigues and the country was nationalizing everything. Jamaicans began fleeing the country and telling stories of their departure as if they were telling the story of *Cry Freedom*. Their stories included dramatic late-night rides deep into the rural parts to catch a clandestine flight out to Miami. Those who had stayed to weather the storm were now going, and those of us who stayed, either because we had to or because we believed in the dream, spent much of our time maligning these sell-outs who could afford to settle in Canada and the US. We suspected them of being filthy rich. Now it was all proving to be true.

The poor, of course, were suffering. There were long lines for bread, flour and other goods that were in short supply. I remember my mother getting word from a neighbour that the supermarket had managed to get some flour and that if we hurried to the Chinese-owned store on Red Hills Road, we could get some of it before it ran out. I remember running out to try and get in line. That was what we did. It was all quite normal for a 16-year-old. But things were quite rough. Manley was promising better once he was given a chance. People were wondering if they could take any more.

Bob Marley returned to Jamaica to try and broker peace between the warring factions of the JLP and the PNP. He had been lured away from England to come and do this Peace concert. Here he was, faced with another potentially volatile concert that was been spearheaded by some of the most notorious gunmen in Jamaica. These men came to Marley to say that they were tired of the war, that they understood the absurdity of it and the sheer madness of all the deaths that were going on. They wanted Marley to come back to Jamaica and headline a concert that would remind the nation of exactly what its motto was: 'Out of many, one people'.

Marley was no longer just a star singer in Jamaica. He was a symbol. He was a prophet. In an interview Marley remarked that his trip to Ethiopia gave him the kind of grounding that allowed him to write 'Zimbabwe'. He said it made him feel like a prophet or something like that. He said this with a sense of amazement and an unwillingness to presume to be a prophet. Yet he knew that the songs he was writing at this point were driven by his desire to speak to the people, to address his people as a teacher, as a shepherd, as someone who now found himself in something of an odd position of authority and leadership. The weight of this responsibility was clear to him.

Survival is the first Marley album without a single love song on it. Some argue that after baring his soul on *Kaya* and *Exodus*, and after the criticism he received for it from Jamaicans and from many in the music community and the recording studios in Jamaica, Marley decided to remind people that he was not getting soft, that he remained as political as ever. It did not matter if what was being said was a misread of what he had done in *Kaya* and *Exodus* – the point is that Marley arrived with *Survival* with a clear sense of mission and a powerfully political agenda. In *Kaya*, he was grappling with his role as an artist in Jamaica. He was grappling with his doubts and with a serious sense of disappointment over the assassination attempt. *Kaya* was a deeply philosophical album, very much a lyrical searching into self to try and find meaning. *Kaya* was also an effort to evoke hope, pleasure and distraction. But *Kaya*'s thoughtfulness and direct confrontation of fears and personal concerns is what could be called the watershed moment in his writing. Now that the deck was cleared, we were faced with the new Marley. Every song on *Survival* was written specifically for that album. In all the previous albums, Marley would drag a previously recorded song out of the vaults, dust it off and recast it in a new Wailers mode. But *Survival* was full of songs that were written while Marley was travelling. 'Zimbabwe', for example, was written while he was in Ethiopia. He marvelled at the power of the song and credited it to being in Ethiopia – in Africa. It is clear from interviews that Marley saw *Survival* as a new moment for him with his songwriting. Going to Africa was a renewing experience – a time that would give him renewed energy to press ahead.

In *Survival* and *Uprising*, Marley's sense of the world has expanded. He begins to extend his commentary on Babylon as a world force that is clearly shaping the lives of the poor. But even as he addresses the world, he is constantly pitting that large and intimidating world against the small man. For Marley, the fundamental sin of Babylon is hubris. The very sin that led to the destruction of the Tower of Babel – the sin of inordinate power and a desire to consolidate this power into worldwide control is the way Rastafarians have defined the Western world. In this world, major world powers have somehow conspired with the Pope to create a world order that, in its size and homogeneity, is bent on squeezing to death the poor and the helpless. Marley's feeling of the apocalypse was so intense at this time that it makes sense that he saw the world of nuclear proliferation, superpower races, the economic stranglehold that a few countries had on the rest of the world and the powerful cultural influence of Hollywood and the American entertainment machinery as mammoth forces that could intimidate and then leave the small human being feeling totally overwhelmed. Marley was not the only one experiencing this sense of alienation. It was clearly a theme that was emerging in the lyrics of other artists around the world. But Marley's vision has never been one of hopelessness. The very act of interpreting these events in the world as part of the larger plan of the universe, a plan laid out by scripture and by the prophecy of Selassie, places the Rastafarian at the centre of a movement of redemption. Above all, through this interpretive device, Marley was taking control of the situation and placing the Rastaman at the centre of hope and redemption. The script has been written: Babylon will fall. But the telling of the fall of Babylon is the cataloguing of the sins of Babylon:

Like Jah say, the West must perish. It's Devil's country all right.
Devils are real people and capitalism and penalism (are a) type of

devilism and Draculazing. It's Devil controlling, Devil running part of the earth while God is in Africa waiting for we to agree that there's devil running this. (June 1975)

The philosophy that underlies these songs, and that stands out more than in any other of Marley's albums, is the notion that an understanding of the nature of Babylon is central to an understanding of the truth of Rastafarianism. In song after song, Marley offers a portrait of Babylon that ultimately becomes a portrait of survival. It is impossible to speak of survival without laying out the forces that will work to prevent such survival. In these songs, Marley seems committed to the task of exploring all the nuances of Babylonian activity. In 'Ride Natty Ride', the Rastaman is a lone quixotic figure facing all the machinations of Babylon. There is a remarkable sense of importance that Marley endows the Rastaman with – and even as he condemns the hubris of Babylon, he manages to grant the Rastaman a central position in the discourse of all cosmic forces at work in the world. Babylon, he argues, is committed to one task and one task only: to fight against the Rastaman. The radical nature of this assertion is part of what distinguishes Marley as an artist. For him it was not absurd to see the Rastaman as the source of all righteousness in the world, and that by destroying the Rastaman, Babylon was in fact carrying out the ultimate act of power and control. This would be arrogance if it was not steeped in such humble sincerity and an intense sense of mission. Yet, there is a way in which this construction of the Rastaman as the figure of what is good and right in the world actually led to the opening up of the ideas of Rastafarianism to the rest of the world. For those who loved his music and understood their affiliation to be against Babylon, they accepted the logic that those who spoke against Babylon and acted against Babylon were, by dint of their choice, Rastas at heart. So for Marley, the Rasta is both the chosen and the elect, as well as the representative of the people, the poor, the downtrodden. The Rasta stands as a symbol in which all who think righteously and fairly can be contained. Therefore that which could have been read as a parochial sense of self-importance could be understood as an expression of a universal quest for the souls of all the good people of the world.

Yet there is a sense in which Marley's decision to address the issues of politics and oppression at large – that is, in the language that avoids the details of Jamaican political life in the manner that he covered, for example, in *Natty Dread* and *Rastaman Vibration* – may have been prompted by his own awareness of the danger of speaking into the deeply volatile world of Jamaican politics. In interview after interview, Marley indicated that he was reluctant to talk about Jamaican politics. By 1980, during the height of the autumn elections, Marley had been away touring for almost a year. He had no regrets about being away from Jamaica. The elections were enough to justify his absence. There is something deeply human about Marley's view of the hardships in Jamaica. Marley wanted to be away from it and he wanted to avoid its dangers:

> It's worse (in Jamaica) than it ever used to be in the sense of political pressure. A lot of people dying every day. Some of dem I know. People no see where dem things are lading and that dem have an alternative – Rasta. Dem cause so much fight against Rasta because Rasta is the only redemption to fight. But this pressure, is not Rasta fight. We're not fighting a revolution down there. Two people fight, it's madness. Double wrong. People in Jamaica, dem have guns. Where people get guns? Government give people the guns. Right now it explode mon. Something bad have to happen. One of dem (cause of troubles) American and the other Russian. (August 1980)

In *Survival*, Marley does confront local themes and problems, but his vision is still rooted in a sense of the world that is wider than ever. He manages to take the detail of the particular to articulate a world vision.

'So Much Trouble In The World' is a perfect signal to the world that Marley's palette has expanded to include world affairs in ways that were not as apparent in earlier albums. What he manages to do is apply the very same principles that operated in his attack on the political systems that created islands like Jamaica to the larger world. There is something critical about this act for, in doing this, Marley positions the Rastafarian, and by extension the Jamaican, in the middle of world affairs. The song opens with hope. God is alive, he is the still point of security in a turning world, and this is the answer to the assertion: 'So much trouble in the world'. Mornings are symbols of hope for Marley. The number of 'morning' songs in Marley's repertoire is quite remarkable. His embrace of morning as a moment of possibility is rooted in the Psalms – it is a Davidian trope. In 'Sun Is Shining' he waxes poetic: 'When the morning gathers the rainbow / Want you to know, I'm a rainbow, too'; in 'Three Little Birds' morning is a place of meditation: 'Rise up this morning, / Smile with the shining sun..'; in 'Misty Morning' the morning mist is toying with the singer in the way a woman would and in 'Burnin' And Lootin'' the morning is a place of danger – in the ghetto, the arrival of men in uniforms of brutality shatters what should be a time of peace and calm. In many interviews, Marley would talk about the morning as a moment of new hope. Part of his physical regimen was to wake up in the mornings and play football and run. Apart from the discipline involved, Marley regarded early morning as a time of renewal: 'Mek you run in the morningtime. When you run you clear out your head. The world wake up round you.'

The song, then, begins with hope. The authority of hope lies in the presence of God/Jah in the sunlight, in the ritual arrival of day and for the songwriter, this arrival is a blessing on the eyes. In this new day, 'anything can happen'. It is at this point that he begins to talk about the sins of Babylon. The 'we/them' praxis is enacted in direct terms. The 'we' are those associated with nature, with the cycles of the universe that involve a connectedness with the divinity of Jah in controlling the ends of those who live in the world. In contrast, the material world of machinery and industry constitutes the world of 'them' – the Babylonian world. The symbols of Babylon reappear in Marley's songs. First there is the space ship, which is the incarnation of their grand 'ego trip'. This ship will allow Babylon to expand its range, but it is clear that this act of indulgence is done at the expense of the poor: 'no care for you, no care for me'.

Marley then addresses the system in a sardonic tone. The arrogance of Babylon is reflected in its constant assertion that it has solved the problems of the world. But, for Marley, the teachings of Babylon are the forcing of the 'devil's illusions' on the minds of the oppressed and the

Rastaman. The statement is full of the prophetic language of the Bible. While the 'heathen raves', the apocalyptic wrath of Jah is about to land upon them. For Marley this ability of the world to miss the truth is one that he finds himself expressing again and again. His music is about trying to help people to see the truth that he sees. He speaks of the way in which people misunderstand his music and fail to see that what he is saying has relevance to their lives. But in the order of the universe the pattern of the underdog rising up will reenact itself again and again. The rejected will become the 'head cornerstone'. This is the constant reassurance that guides the actions of the Rastaman.

Marley then address the 'we' in the equation. He now assumes the mantle of the preacher and he exhorts the people to stand up and continue the struggle. The talking of the 'street' people is as central to Marley's work as anything else that he focuses on. For Marley the music is the way for people to talk and the fact that the people – the poor or the silent – can talk now is an important and revolutionary moment. They talk through music and music is the vehicle with which he faces the silence of centuries.

Marley's call for action in many of these songs, however, will clearly be the substance of exhortation and not of specific radical action. Marley never wanted to be accused of inciting violent action and he often seemed to have a fatalistic position on the matter. For him, if violence is going to happen as a means of bringing about revolutionary change then it must happen. He never positioned himself as a leader of violent action. He always tried to suggest that he was busy trying to find his own means of resistance. Resistance was by singing. He acknowledged that others found other means of resistance. But for him, music was his source of resistance. At the same time, however, he was clear that while he did not like violence he, as an individual, would have to defend himself if faced with violence. In another interview, Marley suggested that while he did not like war, if he decided to go and live in Africa, and war became necessary, he would have to fight, albeit reluctantly.

Marley's political discourse was rooted, then, not in the push for violent physical action, but in the movement towards liberation through a liberation of the mind that's come through the music. This is how one can trace Marley's maturation. Some have, of course, read it as a softening of his position. The rude boy of the 1960s seemed quite ready to defend himself and to act in a violent way as clearly and unequivocally as when he sang about it. The radical revolutionary of the 1970s seemed to have a taste for the kind of political solutions that were being discussed by people in Jamaica at the time, and it seems fair to say that Marley, although avoiding any direct association with any political party in Jamaica, was at least in some dialogue with those who were speaking about revolutionary action that involved some physical struggle. By the time of his last few albums, Marley would seem to have found the language of metaphor and the more mystical sense of the place of revolutionary action.

It is arguable that the Marley who wrote the songs on his last three or four albums was a man acutely aware of his power and the way in which leaders can lead people to their death. He was disillusioned by the lack of spiritual integrity in the calls made by these leaders. He increasingly sought a political agenda that was rooted in the transformation of self through understanding and awareness. What was happening, then, was that Marley was facing the limitations of revolution and revolutionary action. The gradual shift was very much a pattern that seemed to follow the journey of most liberal and radical movements in the world at the time. The 1970s had taken a toll not only on Jamaica, but on Jamaicans like Bob Marley.

Thus Marley would inject the radical action into struggles that he felt were quite clear cut. And the most clear-cut struggle he could identify at the time was the struggle of blacks for liberation in Africa. The song 'Zimbabwe' was one that Marley felt he could render with the fullest commitment to armed struggle. It was far enough away from him to allow him to offer a clear political position. Marley himself would see this song as a watershed moment. In September 1980, an interviewer suggested that he returned from Africa, after the Zimbabwe independence celebration where Marley performed, as 'a changed man'. Marley's response is remarkable in its unabashed enthusiasm and for the clarity with which he spoke of the relationship between that journey to Africa and the development of his writing:

You can say that again. But I really get the re-charge from Ethiopia because that song 'Zimbabwe' was written in a land called Shashamani (in Ethiopia). So you can say it's a full re-charge that, and when the song came out, it just happen. So you can imagine if it was in Ethiopia where you wrote all your songs, then nearly every song you write could happen then maybe somebody would say 'Boy, he is a prophet'.

'Zimbabwe' opens with a declaration. The song is structured as a deposition. Marley offers a statement of what he regards as truth. He proposes a way to understand the world and this proposition is locked into, ironically, the best of the humanist ideas that have come to shape much of the thinking of Western societies, including, particularly, the US. Marley presents his 'bill of rights' – that everyone has the same right to determine his or her destiny. It was a sticking point for Marley, who was constantly at pains to explain that, above everything else, to be free to do what he wanted to do was the most important gift and right that he cherished and fought for. He explains that the statement is a judgement that is applicable, without partiality, to everyone. The judgement, however, is also a reference to the 'end times', the period in which God will judge 'the living and the dead'. The Armageddon war is being waged in this 'little struggle' and the fighters work arm in arm and *with* arms to bring about the freedom of the oppressed.

Here we see Marley's mastery of rhyme and assonance at work. The very phrasing of the song allows him to generate lines that seem to carry with the naturalness of ordinary speech, while the use of rhyme emerges when the song is heard. It is the phrasing, really, that allows us to enjoy the 'his/is' and the 'arms/can' rhymes – the latter being the more subtle of the two. But the use of repetition and the echoing of phrases combine to create a lyric full of the unity of sounds that we expect in the best formal poetry. Indeed, the wonderful play on words in the line 'arm in arm with arms' shows Marley's pleasure in the way words can sound and create multiple meanings. He moves from the idea of unity, a kind of passive sense of oneness among people, to the violence of arms. There seems to be a contradiction in Marley's call for action. It is a call for peace and unity and yet it is a call for action. The understatement of the use of 'lickle' to refer to the decade-long war of independence fought by Mugabe and his freedom fighters is a moment of *braggadocio* and toughness. It is the bad man looking at the most insurmountable obstacle and declaring it nothing. Marley is suggesting that once there is unity of 'arm in arm', then the trouble will seem 'lickle' (little).

The enemy of this struggle, is, of course, Babylon, and, as in most of the songs on this album, Marley helps us to understand the *modus operandi* of Babylon. He makes use of the language of newspapers and news reporting to construct the argument against the system of Babylon. 'Divide and rule' is the classical device of those invested in winning power in the colonial world. Marley understands that part of the struggle in Southern Africa has been exacerbated by the fact that other African forces had been co-opted by the colonial forces – the Rhodesian government – to fight the freedom fighters. This act of division is central to Marley's agenda in this song. Unity is critical to Marley and it is unity of struggle that he sees as the liberating force against the regime.

In the second verse, we see that, for Marley, the enemies to the struggle are often internal, causing internal divisions. When those are resolved, the struggle itself seems small. Marley then invokes an old song to help us to understand that, while his vision has become global, he remains committed to the basic struggle for the rights of the oppressed. In 'Talkin' Blues' he asks, 'Who is gonna stay at home / When the freedom fighters are fighting?' For Marley, internal struggle and strife is the sin that brings down the Africans. He does not want a contrary people. He expands on this problem in the next verse in which he makes clear that internal struggle is not entirely an accident of circumstance but a crucial part of the weaponry of Babylon. Once he has made clear the source of weakness, Marley then turns to another central tenet of his own thinking. It is that, at the end of the day, the act of unity, the act of struggle and the movement towards victory is driven by the heart of the individual. He makes it clear that change is not a mass act, but the act of each individual taking a stance. 'In every man's chest / There beats a heart.' At which point he returns to the most critical question: who is the true revolutionary? For Marley there are those who are part of the struggle and those who are working against it.

Zimbabwe allowed him to speak of this question of commitment because the struggle there was one rooted in questions of loyalty and clarity of vision. The final phrases of the verse make clear Marley's reading of the situation. It is true that one of the great challenges of the struggle for independence in Zimbabwe was the manner in which the Rhodesian government effectively employed mercenaries who came from South Africa, Israel, Europe and the US to try to defeat the forces of liberation. Marley articulates the dilemma of the struggle and he offers this as a message to those involved, those who are still dying for the sake of this liberation. For Marley there is no ambivalence as to what should happen in Africa, and this armed struggle for liberation in Rhodesia would have been as critical to him as was the South African struggle that he sang about in 'War'.

But here he is catching the struggle at a point when things had come to a head in that war. It was clear to many that Mugabe would be successful and the sounds from Rhodesia suggested that the ruling racist government was coming to terms with this news. The only chance of failure lay in the success of Mugabe in either negotiating with other leaders of the struggle or finding a way to assert his authority over them. Marley's statement that by writing the song when he did and while he was in Africa is both a beautiful demonstration of his pleasure in a song successfully rendered and his gradual recognition of the function of his music in the affairs of the world. Marley's statement is slightly tongue-in-cheek and is, at best, a self-deprecating understanding that sometimes his work had some import. What is undeniable, however, is that his sense of mission was most intense during the last few years of his life, with his recordings at that time reflecting his newfound seriousness.

In 'Top Rankin'', Marley draws on the language of the Kingston street to continue to ask the question 'who is the real revolutionary?' It is a striking song when we consider that the top ranking in Jamaican parlance usually refers to the top man in the ghetto – the gang leader, the ranking leader who has a great deal of authority over those around him. In a quite different song released in Jamaica during that time, Althea and Donna, two middle-class girls with aspirations to be popular female DJs, described themselves as 'uptown top rankings'. They were not declaring their readiness to lead criminal lives in the uptown area, but they were making use of the term to suggest that they were at the top of their DJ-ing game. The term, then, was in common use in Jamaica during the late 1970s and early 1980s, and the most notorious top rankings were at the very least close acquaintances of Bob Marley. Two of them had approached Marley in England in 1979 to return to Jamaica to perform in the Peace Concert in an attempt to end the political and gang warfare that was claiming the lives of so many poor Jamaicans during the tensions leading up to the 1980 elections. Claudie Massop, a JLP ranking gunman and Bucky Marshall, a PNP ranking gunman, were enemies. They had fought many battles against each other. But while in prison during the period of martial law that reigned in Jamaica in 1978, they found common ground in Bob Marley's music and determined that if they could convince Marley to return to do a peace concert it could lead to an end of the internal warfare going on in the country. They were convinced that peace was necessary. Marley agreed to meet with Massop and PNP gunman Tony Welch in London to discuss the plan and plans for the concert went ahead. Eventually, both Massop (in 1979) and Marshall (in 1980) would die very violent deaths in Jamaica. The peace did not last for long and the 1980 elections would be remembered for almost 1,000 deaths in the months leading up to the voting day.

Marley, in 'Top Rankin'', is clearly talking to those who have worn the label of leader and top ranking. In very much the same manner that he seemed to turn on his political friends in the mid-1970s by writing probing songs that made it clear that he did not want to be seen as a follower or supporter of any particular party of political leader in songs like 'Revolution', Marley's approach to 'Top Rankin'' suggests that he was seriously questioning the commitment to peace of those who had called for peace in the first place. But Marley is subtle in his admonition. Or, rather, he is deft about rendering his criticism in the form of a question. He cannot sit in judgment of them, but he is seriously challenging the nature of their support for the right things.

The key to the clever dualism of this song is the word 'skanking'. Marley understands that the word means several things in Jamaican language. On the one hand, skanking means dancing. The person who is skanking is dancing and dancing, quite specifically, to reggae. The reggae skank is the reggae dance – a walking dance that has come to be the most basic of dance moves in Jamaica for nearly 40 years. But there is an alternative meaning of the word skank that is more negative. It was often associated with stealing or some kind of duplicitous act of deception. So when Marley asks the Top Rankin', 'are you skanking?' he is at once asking the individual if he is part of the revolution, part of the grand and noble dance to freedom or if he is, in some ways, robbing those who have trusted him or somehow deceiving them.

The 'we/them' motif, unabashedly at the core of many of Marley's songs of this period, opens the song. The 'they' is quite clearly Babylon, and for Marley there is little problem with not having to name Babylon. Babylon is defined by her actions, her complicity in the destruction of the black man. Consequently, Marley has no problem allowing such an open-ended generalization to stand. It is the same generalization that allows him to construct a community of like-minded individuals – a community that will be both his audience and the people he is deeply concerned about.. The agenda of Babylon, of 'they', is laid out in clear terms. First Bablyon does not want to see those interested in the fight for equality, those who are poor and victims of oppression and those who are the faithful, the Rastas, unite. They prefer to see them 'fussing and fighting'. Marley expands on the sentiment in the next lines – 'they' don't want these people to 'live together', but prefer to encourage the 'internal struggle' of people killing each other. Babylon's diabolical agenda is quite clear to Marley.

Given this agenda, Marley is then able to ask a three option question in the chorus. The question is whether the top ranking is skanking to the beat of Babylon and Babylon's agenda; whether he is skanking to the beat of those who are seeking to battle Babylon or, finally, whether he is in fact playing a two-faced game and somehow working against the righteous. The question is a critical one because the very tactic used by Babylon – that is to create disunity in the same way that Marley suggests that they do in 'Zimbabwe' – is what is at stake here. The lyric, when placed in the context of Jamaica in 1979–80, is a direct and forceful statement of truth. Marley is watching all those who are dying because they believe that they are doing so in support of their leader. But what

Marley is arguing is a larger conspiracy that thrives on the divisions that are caused in the society.

In the late 1970s the air was thick with conspiracies and rumours of the most complex intrigues that were aimed at making the island ungovernable. A very cynical approach to power was being employed by both political parties and their supporting patrons in the Cold War-defined world. The accusations were wonderfully elaborate and came with the ring of conviction and the smell of authenticity in each instance. I remember gradually coming to the conclusion that the Jamaican saying, 'what don' go so, nearly go soh', was really a cynical view that suggested that any rumour that has any useful currency must be based at least in part on some truth. So one morning, the JLP would announce that a group of guerillas dressed in suspiciously Cuban-looking military fatigues were witnessed making an amphibious landing on the isolated south coast of the island. Then the PNP will announce that they had seized weapons that had arrived in Jamaica with a clear return address to the CIA. The stories would continue, and spies would be ejected from the country and other spies would be accused and they would disappear. The intrigue would grow into mythic proportions and we all began to imagine that we were all being bugged and that someone was working hard to find out what our political affiliations were. In the meantime, the police were killing gunmen with impunity and the Minister of Security, an ex-RAF fighter and legendary road warrior, was putting in his memorable television appearance, threatening to shoot criminals down like dogs in the streets.

Were the promise not so sinister and completely sincere, there would have been a Churchillian quality to his boldness and his use of metaphor. The police did manage to shoot people down like dogs in the street. And we would read the newspapers each day and play a wonderful national sport of keeping count of the killings. A weekend with eight or more killings was a full one and sadly a common one in Jamaica at the time. The intensity of the divisions in the country over political affiliation would sometimes descend into the bizarre and tragic. Schoolgirls dressed in school tunics that just happened to be green – the colour of the JLP – would be killed because they had on the wrong clothes. So we all learned to wear neutral colours in the months leading up to the election. We knew that anything could spark an act of violence. Reds, oranges and greens were not a good idea. My sisters went to school in their green tunics but knew not to linger on the streets late at night. I remember feeling a peculiar sense of relief at the fact that my school colours were blue at the time. At times the issues would spill over into some of the most innocent of past times. Football matches between schools were slowly becoming dangerous, especially when the teams that were doing battle on the field belonged to warring areas. The threat of explosive violence was in the air. If the 1970s seemed like the period leading to the end times of the apocalypse, then 1980 was the culmination of everything.

Marley stayed away from Jamaica. He was on tour and so he probably could not have been on the island anyway, but it is clear that he was taking his own advice – advice from the Book of Proverbs that he had quoted as an explanation for his absence during his first self-imposed exile: 'It is better to live on the housetop than to live in a house full of confusion.' But he would write about this confusion, and it is telling that he sought to address, not the politicians who, as part of the Babylonian world, were beyond help, but those who were supposed to be leading the people from the trenches. Marley had heard that the peace effort had crumbled and the very same men who he had held hands with at the One Love Peace concert had effectively abandoned their project and returned to violent warfare. At that concert, Marley had achieved something that most of us thought could never happen. Writers today have often dismissed the act of bringing the two leaders of the political parties in Jamaica together on stage as a stunt that would eventually have no lasting effect. Anyone, however, who lived in Jamaica at the time, would have understood that the animosity that reigned between Edward Seaga and Michael Manley was so intense that we all imagined that, given the chance, they would start hitting each other if forced to share the same space. Like the men and women who were the die-hard supporters and frontline fighters of these two men, many of us who did not appreciate the nature of power in Jamaica and the almost Machiavellian compact that these political leaders had with each other, regarded a coming together of either of these men as not only impossible, but a potential betrayal of their loyal followers. This is how thorough the narrative of warfare and hatred had been, and we understood that these men, like all their followers, were filled with abject distaste for each other, and we were sure that this vitriol was consistent throughout the leadership in both parties. It would have startled me had I known then that many of these warring politicians still got together for cocktail parties and chuckled about the various stages of their political campaign, just as schoolboys would discuss a cricket game. It was all cricket, really, and all good sport. Marley had a sense of this terrible truth and, in many ways, his act of forcing the two politicians on stage was rooted in his awareness that image was more important to both men than a question of integrity. He knew that if one man was to take the stage, the other would have to follow suit or be accused of being a war-monger and the true instigator of all the violence.

So they had both gone up on stage. Seaga stood awkwardly, not sure whether to smile or look serious. Beside Marley he looked rhythmless and stereotypically white. A reggae concert where both him and Manley had been raked over the coals in no uncertain terms by Peter Tosh not long before Marley took the stage was clearly somewhere that neither man wanted to be. Manley, the man of the people, arrived later. He wore his khaki shirt and, standing beside Marley, his handsome, tall bearing seemed crude and out of sync with the people of the country. Seaga and Manley were two men with incredible charisma and power when they were on stage railing against the evils of the opposing party. They were powerful men in their own rights but, at a reggae concert filled with very black, dreadlocked men and women who clearly belonged to the working class and who had effectively sung about the evils of Babylon system, both men looked quite small, and quite out of place.

There is something that has always struck me about the image of these two men forming an arc of friendship over the shorter and impossibly energetic Marley who could not keep still, who kept leaping around the stage, causing the band members to stare with something like bemused awe. It always felt to me like a parent of some social standing arriving at a party put on my his teenage children – the parent trying to look cool, but realising that nothing in his sense of language, of rhythm and of the world could make him cool in that place. We were stunned by what

Marley managed to do, and some of us had the idea that perhaps this was going to be the start of something new, something hopeful and an end to the violence. Marley may actually have believed this himself. He could not be blamed for thinking that perhaps something would change. But not long after the incident, it became clear that the peace project would not last. The killing started up again. The stakes were too high and the politicians were quite clear about what they were doing. In the quiet place of conspiracy and patronage, they managed to maintain their power and to reassure their followers that the war would go on and on to the end.

So it makes sense that Marley would now have to ask the men, who had played such a pivotal part in making that concert actually come about, whether they were skanking with the politicians or with the people, with the poor. The questions he asks in the chorus are therefore direct and loaded. The key question is, to paraphrase, 'how did you mean what you said, now?' Marley wants to know what has changed and whether what was said in the past remains the same. He wants to know how the Top Rankin' has managed to secure his position as a ranking person – as a man in the area with respect and authority. In these questions, Marley is preparing the listener for the new model of leadership, for a leadership that is rooted in hope. He moves into the spiritual and the prophetic because he has clearly lost faith in any political solution.

In the first verse, in Marley's eschatology, the demise of Babylon is almost synonymous with the prophecies of hope that are assurances to the elect. Of course, Marley has learned this way of thinking from the Book of Revelations in which John both prophecies the destruction of Babylon while promising the hope of a new earth for the believers. For Marley, the bloodline of the Rastaman is one that has been passed down from generation to generation and one that ultimately reaches back to the prophecies of an ancient time. The reference to John is an old one for Marley and the Wailers. Indeed it is part of a Rastafarian construction that owes much to the Pentecostal and Baptist songs that fed the spiritual iconography of the Wailers and other reggae artists of the 1960s. On an extremely successful DJ version of the Wailers 'Hypocrites' rhythm, the chanter declares, 'John saw them coming / And the wicked dem running...'

it is the same John, but this time his truth is double-edged. On one hand it speaks of the end of all things – the demise of Babylon – and on the other it speaks of the unity of the brethren, a unity about which Marley, in these last albums, would write a series of graceful lyrics of deepest desire. Here the morning motif recurs and in this place of new possibilities, Marley sees the unity of the brethren. Marley sings tenderly and hopefully of the brotherly and sisterly love that he feels. He feels it in the morning – a time of day for Marley that is full of the promise of new beginnings. In identifying the song as a 'morning song', Marley somehow foregrounds its writerliness. In other words, he is more than hinting that the song was *written* in the morning. The song then becomes a morning prayer of devotion that reminds us of the Psalm of David in which he sings:

'Oh Lord in the morning will I direct
my prayer unto Thee and will look up.'

The odd thing about the refrain, 'Top Rankin' are you skankin'?' is the way it becomes a call to dance to those who are listening to the tune. There is, with Marley, a strange way in which the uplifting possibilities of a choric line can sometimes reach its audience in a counter-rational way. It is something like what would have happened to some listeners when they heard 'Born In The USA' by Springstein. With Marley, in this instance, however, there is a something to the idea that we are all the top rankings and this is achieved once the ode to brotherly and sisterly love is sung. At this time the call is to a dance, a dance of unity and love. So the final query moves from the disappointing political leaders to the people themselves. It is part of Marley's ability to construct a populist anthem of hope even as he articulates a moment of terrible sadness in Jamaica's history.

There is no such ambivalence or dualism in 'Babylon System'. Here Marley writes a song in the spirit and style of songs like 'Redemption Song', 'Ride Natty' and 'Rat Race'. These are powerful attacks on Babylon, which are tempered by a call to action and hope for the elect – the Rastaman. In 'Babylon System' Marley's songwriting is consummate. He is packing a great deal into a format that does not lend itself to verbosity. But the secret to Marley's success here is the easy conversational tone. The lyrics grow slowly as a thoughtful consideration of reality. Marley is making an argument. Like all the first lines of this album, Marley is positing a case that he will go on to defend with evidence and then make a very direct call to arms. It is important to Marley to make clear what he wants people to rebel against and why he wants them to rebel. In this instance, he is calling for rebellion against a system and that system has a long enough track record of wrongs to make rebellion not only necessary, but inevitable. Marley speaks to 'them' again and he is speaking for 'we'. The greatest tool of the Babylon system, the colonial system and the imperialist system is to try and force the people of the world to conform to their ideas and views. Central to the work of Babylon is to demean the 'we' in the equation, it is to suggest that without the Babylonian way of thinking, the people would be worthless, and would have nothing. The song lays out exactly what Babylon is saying to the people and then Marley defies Babylon by offering the truth. He uses the language of deception to undermine the work of Babylon. Babylon speaks in terms that are seemingly positive and hopeful. Babylon talks about 'equal opportunity' but the truth is that Babylon never grants true equal opportunity because it keeps denying equality by suggesting that it is superior to the poor, to the downtrodden, to us. No one presses wine in Jamaica, and slaves certainly did not press wine. They pressed sugar cane, but they did so with the machinery of the estate. Marley, however, decides to use this metaphor because he is most interested in the biblical connection and also in the image of the drunkenness and debauchery of Babylon that wine production evokes. It is against all that this represents that Marley asks the people to rebel. The opening lines arrive as a kind of introductory statement and with a melody that is not repeated anywhere else in the song.

The song begins with decided defiance. Marley, speaking on behalf of his people, announces that they refuse to conform to the image of themselves that has been constructed by Babylon. In Babylon's eyes, the people are created to serve the quest for wealth of the system. Marley announces that his people have their own self-identity; they are, he says, what they are and 'that's the way it's going to be', in spite of the brain worship of education that gives the false promise of 'equal opportunity' and offers false talk of freedom. Marley is sceptical about the machinations of Babylon.

In this song, we can see that Marley has avoided the basic order of verse / chorus and has instead created a series of asymmetrical verses that do not follow the same melodic line. Indeed, the song is a series of different melodic shifts even though he is still working with a basic three/four chord pattern. The consistent and unifying element is the chorus which joins the many Marley rallying cries on this album that are seeking to move people to action: 'Ride Natty Ride', 'Africa Unite' and 'Wake Up And Live'. Here, the imperative is backed by an accumulative argument. The logic is dreadfully simple; we have slaved on behalf of Babylon much too long, a slavery captured in the metaphor of the winepress. Rebellion is the only answer. Marley and the I-Three shout 'Rebel!' It is a call to arms.

Marley then begins to establish quite clearly the sins of Babylon. They are worth listing here because in many ways they constitute the core arguments that Marley would repeatedly direct against the Babylonian system, confirming his own reaction to these in the manner in which he has approached his life.

The bloodiest language is used to describe the way the system of Babylon destroys those who are struggling to live. Marley paints the picture of a vampire figure – an image that was, in the 1970s and early 1980s, very much part of the popular discourse, in part because of Hollywood movies, and also because of the myths and urban legends that travelled through Kingston about a real-life vampire who was allegedly going around the city, breaking into the homes of women and sucking their blood. Marley's intention is not comic. The demonized Babylon is cast as a voracious creature. But it is also a massive apparatus epitomized for Marley in the way that it trains its people to become the kinds of leaders who will steal and destroy in the most 'civil' of ways. Marley's accusations about Babylon also include the church that, in Rasta teachings, represents one of the central forces in the work of Babylon. For many Rastas, the Catholic Church is the very heart of the Babylon system. Indeed, the first illustration done by Neville Garrick for the cover art for Marley's posthumous album, *Confrontation*, clearly depicted

Marley as St George, piercing the heart of the dragon that wore the Pope's mitre. In deference to Marley's Catholic fans, the image was altered. But in Rasta teaching the idea is central. Marley would not talk a great deal about the church in his songs. There are two most memorable moments when he does. In 'Talkin' Blues' he confesses that he feels like 'bombing a church' on realising that 'the preacher is lying'. And here he associates the formation of churches with the expansion of Babylon's deception. These are not stark indictments but, coupled with the incendiary doctrinal declaration in 'Get Up Stand Up', we are left with a strong sense that the vast deception of the poor by the authorities, in many cases the colonial authorities, is what Marley is attacking quite directly.

The segue into the cry for truth is one of the most powerful musical moments for me in the songs of Marley. He will repeat that line eight times, each time with a melodic shift that strengthens the appeal. This imperative is a painful cry for truth, a call for some honesty in the system. For Marley, the great sin of Babylon is its capacity to deceive. 'Tell the children the truth,' he says, again and again, until he is joined in flawless harmony and wailing force by the I-Threes. We hear the culmination of a man's growing sense of anger, frustration and abiding indignation at the deception of the poor. In song after song, he is trying to tell what he sees to be the truth, he is embarked on an intense campaign of making the truth plain and clear. He is teaching in these albums because he wants his audience to learn, and he is doing so because he is convinced that Babylon is lying to the children. Marley's children, are, by this point, not merely the little ones that he would write about in his song for his own children, 'Children playing in the streets / On broken bottles and rubbish heaps', but his children, his people. Marley stands as a father figure. He is only 34 and yet he feels like a shepherd, like someone who, once given voice, needs to address his listeners as a father would. The final bars of the song are marked by Marley's signature scats in which he often offers some of the weightiest ideas in a song. In this song, he manages to lay out clearly that the need to rebel is forged from years of abuse. His voice achieves that high-pitched quality in a sinuous melody that undulates around the syntax of the line. He declares that the condition of being slaves on the winepress has been the lot of blacks from the day they left the shores of Africa, the land of the forefathers. The song, in that moment, situates itself most clearly as a song of exile, a diasporal song about the Middle Passage. Marley's cleverness with lyrics, his constant playing with words, is nicely seen here. The image of oppression is caught in the vision of people trampling on grapes to make wine for the oppressor. But for Marley, while they are trampling, they are in fact trampling on themselves. This play on language, this capacity to find the irony in language, is part of what Marley contributes to a tradition of extensive language play in Rastafarian tradition. What is most moving about that last phrasing is the evenness of the lines and the way Marley rolls them off comfortably in the melody, improvising around the chorus. It is a study in the art of phrasing, of call and response and the gospel art of extemporizing in song. Marley's skill here is remarkable.

The album *Survival* was to have been called *Black Survival*. For some reason, this was changed. One can imagine all the reasons that were given at that meeting, but it is pointless speculating. It is easier and perhaps more useful to talk about the implications of such a title. The album and the title song are quite clearly about black survival and, in many ways, Marley's songs are very specific about their relationship to blackness and to Africa. This song continues the conversation that he has been having with Babylon throughout the album. He begins with a simple question, and the question is in response to something that has been said to him. The most telling thing about the opening of the song is that it suggests dialogue – it suggests that someone has been trying to convince Marley of something and he is not accepting it. He is challenging it because he sees the deception in what is being said. The conversation, of course, is with someone that Marley has to talk to a lot. There is a quality of familiarity here that is disarming. The question flows out with casual ease; deceptively simple lines because there are formal elements that help it to retain its poetic efficiency. The 'care/there/everywhere' rhymes hold the lines together even as the syntax flows with naturalness. He wants to understand the callousness of the enemy – of Babylon or those who have been co-opted by Babylon by the fact of their complacency – that has allowed them to sit around idly while the people are suffering all around them. It is a tough, blunt question.

In Marley's vision of the world, the basic politics are simple. There are those who have and those who do not. But Marley understands that there are greater nuances to this situation. Marley defines those who have in the language that they are likely to use. Through a series of dualisms, Marley plays on the American government's power committee 'The Ways and Means Committee' to draw a connection between those who have everything and those who have nothing but 'hopes and dreams'. The dichotomy continues in those who have the elements of the rationalism, 'facts and claims' and 'plots and schemes' while the poor – the survivors – are marked by their conscience and their unwillingness to be driven by the materialism and greed that Babylon people have. Finally, in the third set of dualisms, the lines are no longer quite clear. It would seem that those who prefer not to be fixated on the outward appearance (those who keep the best inside), are those who will not 'wait for long' and will seek change. Those who 'put the best outside' are those whose hearts are weak and who are incapable of withstanding the lure of Babylon.

Even as Marley is exploring these dualities as evidence of the war between Babylon and the survivors, he tells the story of biblical figures of survival and, in doing so, suggests that resistance to the system of Babylon is indeed within the same spirit as the efforts of Daniel and his friends Shadrach, Michach and Abednego to defy the hubris of King Nebuchadnezzar by praying to their God despite the laws ordering that they shouldn't. The fire does not destroy them, and they become, for Rastafarians, symbols of resistance in an oppressive environment. In this swirl of prophetic language, it makes sense that Marley alludes to the Book of Daniel (one of the key prophetic works of the Bible and one that is constantly quoted by Rastafarians), even as it announces that these are in fact the end times. 'Preaching and talking is done' because 'the father's time has come'. The complete lack of humanity of Babylon is captured in the description of the age that faces humanity. Marley's complaint is not with technology, but it is clearly with the misuse of modern technological advancements, with the way that they pervert the world into something that dehumanizes and destroys the spirit of human kindness.

For Marley there is a way in which language seems to deceive by turning what is obviously a positive idea into something abjectly evil. He is intent on deconstructing the language of the world in a act of truth telling. Energy, for instance, is a good thing, but when married to 'nuclear' it becomes, for Marley, an oxymoron. He corrects this. Where the advent of high technology would seem to benefit humanity, Marley argues that it is actually the source of dehumanization. Then he turns the prevailing language about security into a harsh indictment of the nuclear arms race and all that it entails. There is a sense in which these developments are undermining any sense of security that the world might have. In a later song, he will have to plead with the world to 'have no fear for atomic energy / 'Cause none of them can stop the time.' In all of this, of course, Marley is asking the listener to make a decision. He asks, 'which way will we choose?' The song demonstrates that Marley sees the potential for good in everyone, but also understands that the lure of Babylon is intense enough to drag people away from the righteous path. But the apocalypse is earnestly announced. For Marley the end of things is at hand. He preaches, 'We better hurry, oh hurry, oh hurry / 'Cause we got no time to lose'.

That Marley understands himself to be a prophet is made clear in yet another of his ever-important brief improvised commentaries at the end of the song. After the clear assurance and confidence of the song in which he outlines the nature of Babylon and the choice facing the listener, he suddenly personalizes his role as a truth teller and he does it with a hint of doubt. It is spoken as the song fades away, and it is a striking confession because it seems to have no logical link with the voice that has spoken the song. It arrives as a postscript, an expression of vulnerability that, in many ways, distinguishes Marley from so many of his contemporaries. In this cavaet he makes two terse and ironic observations. The first is the biblical assertion that a good man is never honoured or respected at home, or a prophet, as Christ said, is never honoured in his home country. The second is even more sardonic: he argues that nothing changes; but, more than that, that he does not see this as strange but indeed understands it to be the order of things. That he admits that he is not shocked by the fact that nothing has changed and that nothing will change seems like an expression of pessimism and fatalism. That, coupled with his lament, about 'a good man', is a coded postscript for the Jamaican people. It also helps to understand that Marley, during his lifetime, was never seen as a prophetic voice by Jamaica. This may be quite difficult for us to appreciate now that he is clearly quite close to being named an official national hero. But, at the time when Marley was writing this song, he felt that his ideas would not always be well received in Jamaica and by Jamaicans. Marley is virtually giving an explanation for his desire to travel, to tour the world. He is also making it clear that he knew and felt the pain of the fact that he gained far more respect and admiration from foreign media and his fans abroad than he did in Jamaica. Marley, however, is less concerned about being seen as a star than he is about the fact that his message will not be heard at home. He is, of course, quoting the biblical prophets and Christ himself who had the hardest time of all being accepted in Nazareth where he was born and raised. Yet, despite the seeming despair in these last lines, Marley remains convinced of the importance of survival, of defying the odds and trying to find some change. Instead of eclipsing the hope in the song, those expressions of vulnerability and doubt bolster the resolve of the song to confront such doubt and project a spirit of hope and possibility.

The shift from 'Survival' to 'Africa Unite' is a tight one on the *Survival* album. In fact, the record was mixed in such a way that there was little space between the songs. The effect is of an album of statements flowing one into the other to make a larger statement. The famous opening lines of 'Africa Unite' express the very hope that seems to be in slight doubt at the end of 'Survival'. This is a song of exodus, a song of repatriation. The assertions are articulations of faith and, at the same time, point to the condition of the black survivor. Rastas held to the view that moving forward, constantly 'trodding' through creation and never looking back, was to be the condition of the black person. For Marley, the song is also a genuine expression of his desire to go to Africa. Marley would talk about repatriation a great deal during the latter part of his life. His visit to Ethiopia led him to offer very realistic ideas about what moving to Africa would entail. Marley never seemed to hold to the view that Ethiopia would be easy. Indeed, in some of his interviews he made it clear that he did not want to go to Ethiopia as a tourist, but he wanted to go there as someone who would contribute to the needs of that society. He wanted to retire there. He saw in Ethiopia the promise of a rural life, a life lived close to the earth, a life of subsistence farming and communing with nature. Marley had always maintained that at heart he was a farmer and that farming was in his blood. In 'Africa Unite' Marley renders the vision offered by Marcus Garvey and taken up by pan-Africanists in the latter part of the 20th century. The vision is for a unified Africa, a place where a biblical existence can be enacted. In songs like this, Marley was constructing a myth of Africa through songs of devotion and hope. In many ways, then, he was recasting the myth of the promised land that shapes and directs much of the Book of Psalms, in a language that spoke directly to the black man. Africa, the new promised land for the 20th century, required a language and a sense of time and place that would refresh the ideas of hope and redemption. Marley's songs, therefore, represented a very important post-colonial and post-imperial act. Here was Marley rewriting the narratives of a society that to many seemed borrowed, into the language and ethos of Jamaica and the black person. What was done by the Haitians with Vodoun was being carried out here in perhaps even more radical ways. Where David would identify 'the wicked' as a collective force of evil and wrong-doing, Marley would position Babylon in that place. David's psalms tended, quite often, to speak directly to God, where Marley offers psalms of prophecy and preaching. But there are those songs that are clearly shaped by the psalmic devotion of David: 'Guide and protect I and I oh, Jah-Jah / Through all these stages,' in 'Give Thanks And Praises'.

At the heart of these songs, however, is Marley's self-consciousness about music as a force that transforms and that serves as a metaphor for the journey towards redemption. Marley is a singer and he calls people through song. Their reaction is to dance. But dancing for him, as we see in 'Top Rankin'' is both an act of pleasure and an indication of commitment to a struggle. The dance is an act of resistance and an act of defiance. Reggae music is sacred music for Marley. Its political power is without question, but he will just as gladly give praise to reggae as he will to Jah. They are one and the same. There is much in his veneration of the music and the form of the music that echoes the way that blues artists would talk about the blues. In 'One Drop' Marley announces something that we have always known about his music, at least as it was produced in the last ten years. The bedrock sound behind the music was always the drum and bass. And the drummer who gave Marley his signature sound was Carlton Barrett. Carly mastered the one drop and found ways to improvise on this most basic of the reggae rhythms. The song 'One Drop' works, like most of Marley's tunes, on several levels. It is telling that this song was released as a single in Jamaica and that it was such a success on the charts. It is, in many ways, a song that functions in the way songs worked for the Wailers in the 1960s. It is a song that says that despite all the new rhythms that are emerging – particularly the rapid, bully-riding sound of rockers that eschewed the three-beat for the one beat, but managed to use syncopation and a very active high hat and snare pattern to ensure that the off-kilter bop of reggae was still working. Sly Dunbar and Robbie Shakespeare were pulverizing the charts with this new rhythm and almost every artist who worked with them was riding on this new sound. Marley would have heard Black Uhuru's fresh and aggressive sound, as well as the same rhythm section giving new life to artists like Dennis Brown and the old Wailer, Peter Tosh. Marley was simply reminding his competitors that the good old 'one drop' was still the killer sound. The very words 'one drop', while effectively describing the technical feature of the music (a single stress on each measure), also have a street connotation of violence. There is the suggestion that a one-drop person is able to dispose of an enemy with a single blow. The song is a dare – a celebration, by the high-riding Wailers, of their musical signature and a boast and dare to all comers that they are still the champions of reggae. This would have been enough for many artists, but Marley learned in the old days that any street dare that was to have lasting currency in the dancehall had to be layered with meanings that extended beyond the obvious. Even as Marley is singing about this particular musical style, he is also writing a praise song to Jah and setting down the rhythm section for the revolution.

In this song, Marley lays out again the value he places on music in great detail. This is a metaphor, yes, but it is clearly more than a metaphor.

The music is literally a transformative force and there is much in what Marley says here that helps us to understand what the ritual of reggae music and all its musical signatures means to those who feed at its trough whenever they can. The 'it' that we must feel in the one drop is the heart of resistance and the heart of hope in the face of oppression. But there is the business of feeling a rhythm that musicians talk about a great deal. The feel of swing, the feel of the blues, the feel of son music are all examples of this often inexplicable entity. If we allow ourselves to feel the 'one drop' we will have time to talk, to reason and to bridge the gaps that separate us. In the first chorus, Marley points to one of the great gaps – the generation gap. In the second chorus he explains how the music will solve the problem. The Rastaman will fill the gap and become the conduit of peace between divided people. More importantly, however, the Rastaman will serve as the one who bridges the gaps of history by ensuring that those in the present do not forget the details of history. Reggae serves this role and, for Marley, it is a sacred role. To feel the one drop we have to stop and listen to it, feel it and then find something of its transformative power.

When Marley announces the drumbeat, Carly Barrett snaps sharp and tight on the snare. It is the signal of the reggae song that ushers in the heartbeat sound of bass and drum. It is the rhythm that beats within even as it beats without. For Marley reggae offers a pulse that works within the mind and soul to do one thing: resist 'against the system' and against, 'isms and skisms'. The latter are features of the political order in society. The 'ism' had by then become a Rastafarian term for wickedness, cruelty, trickery and acts of unfairness. The 'skisms' of course, refer to the divisions caused by the Babylon system. Marley would return to this 'ism-skism' phrase in his rendering of 'Get Up Stand Up' on the live *Babylon By Bus* version.

The pleasure of music, therefore, is not an end in itself, but a way to struggle. Given this introduction, we ought not to be surprised at what comes next: a further cataloguing of Babylon. This time he lays the responsibility of starvation and war on the hands of 'them': Babylon. Yet he is clear that, in the face of this oppression, the survivors will have to keep on fighting. The prophecy is quite clear. These are end times.

Buoyed by the chant of suffering as the male and female backing singers chant 'dread, dread, dread', Marley helps us to see what his biblical sources are. First the Lamentations of Jeremiah, offered when the children were in exile and in search of the hope for their promised land. Then he suggests that instead of lamenting and falling into despair in the face of the hardships outlined here, we look to the path of prophecy for redemption. Quite quickly, this music celebration becomes a championing of the teachings of Rastafarianism. Marley makes sacred this music that would have been drawing people out to dance on the floor at the sound of the bass line. This is a highly danceable tune and it is a song about music. Yet, quite rapidly, Marley has transformed the dancehall into what Robert Lee, a St Lucian poet, calls 'a holy place' (in 'Attoinette's Boogie').

In the second pass on the verse and chorus, Marley allows himself some space to adlib over the backing singers. His short, explosive phrases are loaded with implications and it is important to pay attention to them as they point to an attitude that is shaping the song. Here the singer is aggressively tossing barbs at the enemy, and he does it as a DJ would have done it in the dancehall of the 1960s. He argues that the 'teaching of His Majesty,' will be given with or will be like a 'stick-up'. This is thug language. It continues with the sharp commentary in 'yuh lucky' (which is of course ironic), and the questions, 'a wha mek dem a gwaan soh?' and 'a wha frighten dem?' – which are two decidedly Jamaican statements of *braggadocio*. The question is not literally asking what is causing fear in 'them', but in street parlance there is an understanding that absurd, aggressive or foolish behaviour by an opponent is driven by fear and not by true bravery. Of course this is how the tough protagonist sees it and this is how he will taunt the opponent. It, in fact, becomes a way of calling the enemy a 'punk', a coward.

What is noteworthy about this stretch of performance is the way in which Marley resorts to a heavy Jamaican language in offering his challenge to Babylon. It is a pattern that we see in Marley a great deal. In 'Ride Natty Ride' he shifts smoothly along the language continuum in a manner that could actually confuse listeners that are not Jamaica. 'Dready' is the archetypal Rastaman and his story is the one that Marley tells in this song. In a series of rhymes, Marley makes clear that he sees the journey of the Rastaman as one that is being undermined by the system of Babylon. Here the Rastaman sits at the centre of the struggle for righteousness. This is Marley's world view. It is the world view of a member of a small beleaguered group that finds complex ways to understand the world through his very specific vision. Of course, the effect is one of inordinate self-importance in the larger scheme of the world. But Marley manages to avoid being a crazed cultist largely because the enemy is so generic and so clearly a figure of evil to all poor people and all those who have suffered oppression. It is in this way that Marley's listeners would be able to empathize with 'Dready', and actually identify with him. The song is a slow affirmation of faith. The chorus takes on the language of the cowboy movie and applies it to the journey of the Rastafarian, thus giving him a heroic status. Like all the great cowboy heroes of Western films, Natty Dread rides forward to face his enemy. But his journey is not a physical journey into war, but a journey into the mysterious world of supernatural warfare. The phrase 'mystics of tomorrow' is an instant of metaphysical consideration that echoes much of Marley's tone in his *Kaya* phase.

From here, Marley shifts to the basic Jamaican dialect that can be dense for the non-Jamaican listener. In many transcriptions of the song on various websites, painstaking efforts by many Marley fans have generated quite valiant but wrong readings. Marley states here that everything that is happening in the world, and especially in Jamaica, is 'to fight against the Rastaman'. To achieve this, 'they' build Babel façades of 'confusion' that celebrate what Marley calls 'the Devil's illusion'. The allusion to Babel Tower reminds us of the hubris of Babylon's agenda and also reminds us that this agenda will be confounded by Jah. This hope is, for Marley, everything in these songs. Faith in Rasta, a faith that was refused and abused, will assume the status of 'head cornerstone'; and the 'games' of Babylon's oppression will wilt away when the fire of rebellion and righteous anger begins to burn 'everything'. The resource available to the Rastaman is the weapon of the apocalypse. It is fire. Fire burns everything. The song echoes the old spiritual 'God showed Noah a rainbow sign / No more water / Fire next time'. The reference to Noah is fairly extensive in the remainder of Marley's sequence. First there is the reference to the birds which are the only creatures that will be able to escape and take flight. In this line he is also referring back to a rather famous ska tune that the Wailers performed in the 1960s: 'If I had the wings of a dove / I will fly, fly away / Fly away and be at rest.' The landscape in the heart of the apocalypse is one that demands a clear set of rules of behaviour.

The seemingly puzzling statement of faith: 'brothers you should know and not believe' is another Rastafarian concern for the accuracy of language. For the Rastafarian 'belief' is a sign of doubt, a sign of uncertainty. The Christian notion of belief is, for the Rasta, clear evidence of their failure to hold to a secure faith. For the Rastafarian, knowledge is a greater assurance that belief. The knowledge is of the end times. Here Marley alludes again to Noah's prophecy and to the negro spiritual. He moves from the idea that the flood will not be the new sign of judgment, but fire that will withstand all the efforts by Babylon to cool things. Beyond this moment, Marley takes us to the world of the apocalypse. The events of the last days are retold in the last sequence after the band has wailed 'fire' with a chilling intensity. As the world of apocalypse becomes clear, we begin to realise that the riding Natty may not, in fact be a cowboy, but a righteous force of the apocalypse. The image of Christ in the Book of Revelations is one of a man riding a white stallion to battle against the Whore of Babylon. Marley associates the Rastaman who is riding triumphantly through the seared landscape of the apocalypse with this Christ figure. The Rastaman stands as a figure of judgment in these last days and assumes the role of the elect as spelled out by the John in Revelations. This is just one of the many references to the apocalypse that we see in these last three albums by Marley.

Marley paints a picture of the apocalypse – the fire is out of control, there is panic in all the cities as people – the wicked, really – are crying about the loss of their gold. Everywhere around them fires are burning and creating the kind of harrowing holocaust that signals the demise of Babylon.

From the position of the oppressed, there is a great deal of glee in the demise of the wicked and the wealthy. The image of Babylon, needless to say, is sharply stereotyped. Babylon is only concerned for his wealth and he will be concerned not for his soul, even at this time of the end, but for his gold. Of course Marley reminds us and Babylon that the destruction of the soul will be part of the judgment. In the second micro verse, he draws another picture of destruction and decay. This time, the setting is the beach, and the generic 'leader' emerges. Marley's 'leaders' tend to be the politicians who he sees as the ones bent on leading the Rastafarian astray and destroying the life of the people. At this last moment, the leader, whose power in the temporal world was his capacity to give charismatic and convincing speeches, is made to seem completely absurd. The Rastafarian has an answer for him. He tells the leader that it is too late. It is the cry of the elect to the wicked. The language is deeply evangelical and not very far from the language of Pentecostal preachers. Marley also relishes the turned tables of these last days. Power has shifted and the dreadlock tells Babylon to confront his own sin and his own damnation: 'fire is burning, man pull your own weight'. The final image in the song is that of the mounted Rastaman who is triumphant as he rides through all kinds of circumstances. It is a moment of assurance and power. One imagines him bestriding the burning cityscapes, triumphant and fully heroic. He rides through the storm and the calm.

The I-Threes form a gathering of the elect spurring on the Rastafarian with the Jamaican charge of encouragement 'go deh', which literally translates to 'go there' as in 'oh, you go there, girl' that is found in African-American parlance.

All the songs on this album maintain the basic format established in 'Ride Natty Ride', where Marley assumes the position of the generic dread and proceeds to preach to and for that dread. The message is clear: Babylon is working against the lives of the dreads and they must continue to struggle in the face of this opposition. There is a mission to be completed, one that will culminate in the last days when the end of all things will be determined. But there is one song in the sequence that seems to belong to an earlier period. 'Ambush In The Night' may have been written during Marley's exile in England when he put together the *Exodus/Kaya* albums. The themes come from that period and the mode of offering a narrative – a personal narrative – at the centre of the song harks back to that period and even the period before that. But what places this album comfortably in *Survival* is that it is the one song that speaks most directly to the question of survival for Marley. While Marley shared ideas about faith and hope in the songs that precede this one, he finally offers a narrative from his life as a kind of testimony to support what he has been saying. Moving, then from that lyric to 'Wake Up And Live' is a movement from testifying to praise and lively worship.

We need not repeat the circumstances that Marley is likely to be referring to in 'Ambush In The Night'. What is telling here, however, is the way in which the details about the situation seem to be more forthcoming than they were. In 'Guiltiness' and 'The Heathen' – two of the most direct statements about the shooting on the *Exodus/Kaya* albums – Marley resorts to scripture and a more metaphorical attack on the experience. It is as if he is reluctant to recall the story in detail. But by the release of *Survival*, a number of things had already happened. Based on the accounts by Marley's manager, and even Marley in interviews, it is apparent that those who had attempted to kill him had, by then, been caught and executed in the ghetto. Some accounts indicate that Marley was present for these executions. Regardless of whether he was or not, it is probably fair to say that Marley had now seen justice (at least as he saw it) done, and he could speak of the demise of Babylon and those, like these men, who accepted Babylon's money to do Babylon's work. In 'Ambush In The Night' he is able to take his story, tell it and then use it as a larger metaphor about the end of all things. The story he tells is fascinating because it appears to lay out exactly how Marley interpreted the shooting. It is as if the dreadlocks man of 'Ride Natty Ride' is back on the beach, speaking judgment on the leaders and the other figures of Babylon who are now facing the truth of their ways in the final hour. Marley positions the dread (himself) as the truth speaker in this place.

As a statement about the assassination attempt, 'Ambush In The Night' holds to the view that this is the work of Babylon who has managed to bribe and coerce those who could have been brothers to carry out the act of murder. It is Babylon, defined by the ubiquitous 'dem' that stands as the first accused. Their effort is, as has been quite clearly laid out in other songs on the album, to seek power. But the ominous warning lies in the matter of 'the hour'. Babylon is notorious for not knowing the hour and for assuming that everything is as it has been. Marley sees his rescue by Jah as a clear sign that he has a mission to accomplish. Nothing that Babylon attempts will succeed at bringing down the messenger.

Other songs in these albums may have an international audience in mind, but the Babylonian methods of this song are decidedly Jamaican. The objects with which they bribe are the currency of hardship-strapped 1970s Jamaica. The order is interesting: 'guns, spare-parts and money'. The guns were given as incentives to those who wanted to rob others to make a living. But they were also given to ensure loyalty. The spare-parts were offered as bribes because part of the austere economy of Jamaica was the inability of anyone to get spare-parts to fix cars or any other kind of machinery. The typical cry from auto mechanics, plumbers, appliance technicians and engineers was that they just did not have the parts and so they could not fix whatever you were asking them to fix. There was a black market on auto spare-parts in Jamaica at that time. This was a potent bribe. The other strategies reveal Marley's complete distrust of politicians and politics. There is something decidedly cynical in the attitude of Babylon people who boldly declare that they are the sole givers of knowledge and that it is because they hold all knowledge that they can 'reach' the poor man. It is a deeply insulting statement, but one that Marley understood all too well. The very project he was embarked on was one that walked directly in the face of this kind of thinking. Ignorance was the assumed condition of the poor, and they were seen as incapable of thought and incapable of independent thinking. Not only does Babylon miseducate the poor, but it boldly flaunts the power that such miseducation gives him over the poor. The strategy of ensuring that hunger is the perpetual condition of the poor is part of the cynicism of Babylon. Here, Marley points to a pattern of creating dependence in the poor that would lead to a system of patronage which would then ensure that the poor could be controlled by Babylon. In a matter of a few lines, Marley lays out the corrupt system of political rule that was operating with impunity in Jamaica in the years leading up to the 1980 elections. The greatest insult for Marley was, of course, the manner in which the poor was co-opted into becoming a betrayer of the brotherhood of sufferers. It is in this manner that Marley is able to explain the actions of those who came to kill him.

As is clear from the things that people closest to Marley said of his mood at that time, Marley was both shocked and dismayed at the men who tried to kill him. He did not know them, but he knew that they were poor and he knew that someone had paid them to do it. He was shocked because before then he had felt that no one in Jamaica, no poor ghetto youth, would allow himself to be bribed into taking a shot at Bob Marley. He had a faith in these people that grew out of his sense that they would see beyond the strategies of Babylon and not be bought out. Of course, Marley was also angry because he perceived himself as a tough man, as a man with a great deal of power, and his confidence about his security grew out of a knowledge that he was known on the streets as a man well connected to the ghetto and in many ways protected by it. Something had fallen away. It made sense that he would start to doubt his ability to trust anyone. He would have expected to have had more than just a dream of this disaster. He would have expected the ghetto grapevine to inform him of what was to come. It did not. Babylon had effectively used its strategy to bring these men into the dark, tree-filled Hope Road compound to shoot at Bob Marley and to hit him, his manager Don Taylor, Rita Marley and several others. It was a bold gesture. So, when Marley sings the chorus of the song, anyone who knows anything of his recent history would know that he is talking about this moment. Yet, Marley would not be Marley if he did not seek in this a metaphor for the battle between Babylon and the chosen, in the affirmation that he has been 'protected by His Majesty'.

The simple structure of this song, which moves from verse to chorus to verse and then ends with a chorus, allows Marley to establish a rhetorical strategy that helps him propose an argument and then counter that argument with the truth. Babylon's ideas about the dread are wrong, he argues. Indeed, their ignorance is complete when he makes it clear that he sees the elect as standing outside of the strategies of repression and coercion. The heart of the song speaks to this truth – not merely its meaning, but its very existence and its purpose, which is to teach a counter truth to the one being propagated by Babylon. Where before the argument was that the people are ignorant and therefore malleable and easily exploited, Marley, having established that His Majesty Jah Rastafari is on the side of the people, presents the truth. The truth is that what the people know is not, as Babylon might think, what was taught to them by Babylon's systems. Consequently, Marley argues, the people are not ignorant and this makes them untouchable. Their knowledge, he goes on to argue, comes from the Power of the Most High, which allows them to constantly resurface and survive.

One is reminded of the image of Marley prancing on stage sporting a wound on his arm, defiantly singing at a concert that it appears the gunmen had planned to force an end to. For Marley, the theme of survival will become his mantra of thanksgiving for the rest of his career. He rejoices in his survival and he composes psalms to celebrate this. There is in this something of David's tendency to sing praise to God for his rescue from the attacks of his enemies. What Marley sought to do was to take his own survival and treat it as a rallying cry for his people.

In the second chorus, and towards the end of the song, Marley is more explicit about who the true enemy is. He declares that the ambush was 'planned by society'. The line is important not because it reveals the extent of Marley's paranoia – but because it does not. The word 'society' has a more specific meaning in Jamaican language than it does in standard English. 'Society' refers specifically to the uppercrust of Jamaican society. A 'society dread' for instance, would have been a middle- to upperclass Rastafarian. Something of an oxymoron for many. But when Marley states that the ambush was 'planned by society' he is clearly stating that those who really tried to kill him were not the poor, but the wealthy, the power mongers who were intent on keeping down the poor. In this way 'Ambush In The Night' thrives on the dynamic relationship between personal history and the expression of faith in song.

The journey that the song takes us through may not be as harrowingly open-ended as the songs of self-doubt (or questioning) and vulnerability in the *Exodus/Kaya* albums, but we are witnessing the progression of a man through the crisis of trauma into something embracing the capacity to find hope after the hardship. The personal narrative helps the listener to find a currency that gives validity to his preaching. It is, then, almost as if he now feels, at the end of the album, that he has earned the right to preach wholeheartedly. The final song on the album is the 'preachiest'.

'Wake Up And Live' is a song of imperatives. Yet if the song is 'preachy' it is not so in the common way of self-righteousness that we associate with 'preachiness'. There is an authority of the sermon that guards the work and the willingness to experiment with metaphor and proverb allows Marley to speak with the kind of authority that seems so age-worn and timeless. By peppering his song with allusions to the tried and proven preachers of history, Marley lends an air of authority to his voice in order to bring off a song so thick with commandments. But he also tempers the preachiness by seasoning his commands with exhortation and encouragement. This is sermonizing at the highest level.

Marley is preaching as forcefully in this song as in any of his other compositions. His message, in this song, however, is directly to the sufferah. He ignores Babylon who has been defeated in song after song on the rest of the album. Here he manages to combine Western proverbs with proverbial sayings that borrow from the language and ethos of Jamaican folk society. By using the imagery of folk proverbs that has been honed over centuries, Marley positions himself as a part of the larger tradition of folk intelligence that is a central feature of Jamaican art and popular culture. He begins with a metaphorical observation – life is a journey with many signposts on the road. They can be confusing. He advocates the value of a simpler life, the uncomplicated path through the inevitable ruts. It is a Rasta assumption that complications are part of the vain imaginings of proud mankind. The straight path is laid out in three bits of advice. First, he warns that hate should be avoided along with 'mischief and jealousy'. Second he commands that the faithful not be ignorant nor should they embrace a suppression of thought. 'Reasoning' is a tenet of Rasta belief. All Rastas must reason with one another. Rasta is not counterrational, but indeed values the exploration of thought. Finally he asks the people to apply their ability to dream dreams and see visions to the realities of life. The phrase seems contradictory, but Marley is arguing that visions are useless unless they are applied to the realities of life. This rapid-fire succession of admonitions in the first verse quickly establish that the simpler life of humility and goodness is far better than the much more complex life of mischief and pride. Yet Marley is adamant that the teachings of Rastafarianism are not rooted in myth and fanciful notions but in what he terms 'reality'. Other songs by the Wailers also emphasize the need for a 'reality'-based sense of spiritual assurance over a belief system that is predicated on the hope of a salvation that occurs sometime in the future.

From here, Marley's tone becomes even more celebratory. The naming of the Rasta people as 'mighty' is an allusion to Marcus Garvey, who repeatedly referred to blacks as the mighty race. Marley here combines the celebration of the dignity and power of the black people with a series of affirmations that remain firmly rooted in the imperatives of the song. First he commands the people to rise and do the work that needs to be done. He bolsters them with the promise that their mission is one sanctioned by prophecy. These are, for Marley, the true Israelites. By quoting the promise of God to Abraham that his people will be more numerous than the sand on the seashore, Marley positions the song as a part of the Judaic tradition. These are the black Jews – the true children of Israel. In the second verse, Marley turns to a couplet of Jamaican proverbs that are not obviously connected to each other. He combines them by turning them into a perfectly structured rhyming couplet. It is in these moments that we see the resourcefulness of Marley's songwriting, and the manner in which he brings together a series of literary traditions to create something that is distinctively his own. The phrase 'one-one cocoa full a basket' is a Jamaican proverb that gives value to the patient act of saving, of doing things in small increments, one step at a time. Marley is reminding his people that the labour may seem tedious and may not seem to be leading anywhere quickly. But it is accumulative, he is saying: one step at a time. The value of this approach is explained in the second proverb in which he asks what use it would be for anyone to live with quick results, fast riches that will have no lasting value and that, it is implied, will pressage death.

The agrarian proverb argues that the patience of slow and systematic labour will eventually pay off. This attitude is antithetical to the Babylonian manner of greed that demands immediate gratification. The second proverb helps to qualify the first. The greed and impatience of

Babylon is futile and utterly vain. In this Marley alludes to the proverbial truths of King Solomon who declares the labours of the rich to acquire wealth a complete vanity. The reason is simple: death will come quickly and all that is accumulated will have been lost. Marley rejects this materialism and offers a view of the world that is based on enjoying the pleasures of the moment with patience and grace.

Survival is an album that is marked by a consistent message and a tone that is captured in the imperatives of 'Wake Up And Live'. These imperatives are only possible because Marley has established a relationship with his audience that is quite clear. He is a teacher and a teller of truths. This position allows him to say the things he does. More tellingly, Marley does a thorough job of establishing the fundamental character of Babylon. It is critical to the album that Babylon be understood as the enemy of the people. The Marley that emerges in this album, and the albums that follow, is someone who has moved on from the reflexivity of *Kaya*. But what he manages to achieve in this album is the assurance of a leader – a mature artist whose commitment to speaking the truth of Jah will not be compromised in any way. While some have argued that Marley's turning away from the love song in this album represented an over-compensation for the criticism he had received for the number of love songs on *Kaya*, it may be wiser to argue that a certain earnestness of spiritual purpose had set in for Marley during his exile, while he was thinking about Africa and his own legacy. There are no intimations of mortality in any of Marley's songs, but one does feel in the overt devotion to mission that marks this album, a sense of urgency and complete seriousness about teaching the people. The year in which such teaching was not only possible but inevitable was 1980. Other artists were doing the same thing. Aware that the socialist experiment of the 1970s was now clearly a failure and, even worse, that the decade had revealed the corruption and frailty of the leaders who had promised so much to Jamaicans, Marley determined that the old political manner of temporal revolution would have to be transformed into a spiritual revolution. The songs failed to stir up the same radical action that earlier songs did, but Marley purposely turned more to the symbolic and the metaphoric in these songs, using the layering of language to create revolutionary songs that saw the truest form of resistance in the belief in Rastafarianism. If Marley's listeners felt increasingly distanced from these songs because of their strong Rasta identification and black themes, he relied on the completely generic characterization of Babylon to allow them to at least identify with Marley against this enemy.

Where *Survival* seemed intent on exploring an international political landscape, and also seemed committed to offering as candid a picture of Babylon as Marley could muster, *Uprising* pulled him back to Jamaica and back to its internal affairs. The very first song on the album establishes this idea of return, and then, song after song, culminating in the remarkable narrative of the Middle Passage in 'Redemption Song', Marley looks at the Jamaica that he sees evolving around him. The post-election Jamaica of 1980 became, quite quickly, a place very distinct from the pre-1980 Jamaica. Part of the changes were actual and perhaps superficial. But these superficial changes were deeply symbolic. The Jamaica Labour Party, led by Edward Seaga, immediately changed the fashion of formal occasions so that the Cuba-inspired bush-jacket (a costume that won favour because of its pragmatic appropriateness to the heat of Jamaica), was replaced by the Western coat and tie. What was represented in this act was a peculiar kind of nostalgia for the pre-1970s Jamaica when the socialist values had not set in. The odd thing is that the cultural values associated with the pre-1970s Jamaica were those that gave privilege to the élite and brown-skinned cultural values of Jamaican society. The JLP had effectively presented the case that the world was far better when Jamaica was in a very comfortable relationship with America, when the music was the ska music of Byron Lee and the Dragonaires and when people dressed like the rest of the Western world – in suit and tie. The changes of the 1970s were seen as changes that allowed the values of the street, the values of the poor and the black world to dominate and somehow pervert the true spirit of Jamaica. It is not likely that many had these views because of a diabolical or evil intent. The truth is that many of the politicians coming into power with the JLP were last in office in the 1960s and so all the trimmings of that period were seen as symbolic of all that was lost in the near communist 1970s. But there was some clear evidence that many felt that Michael Manley had taken the Black Power thing a little too far during his time in power and felt that the return of the JLP constituted an open door for the return of the brown man.

Many Jamaicans who had fled the island in the 1970s for Miami and Canada found themselves looking at the possibility of returning. It just so happened that most of these people were middle-class, brown Jamaicans whose flight from Jamaica was tied to an often whispered feeling that a new kind of racism had taken hold of Jamaicans. The rise of reggae music, with its emphasis on roots and the politics of Rastafarianism, was seen as part of that new trend that was going to be redressed in the new era. Institutions like the Institute of Jamaica had reorganized their emphasis to focus greatly on the African presence in Jamaica, and the Miss Jamaica Beauty contest had been a flash point for discussions about race and beauty. By the late 1970s, one of the first truly black women was named Miss Jamaica. If no one actually declared in public that the new era would presage the resurrection of 'brown' Jamaican values, it was an unspoken truth that was clearly being spoken by many.

The promise of the new era was that things were going to get better quickly, and that this would be tied in with the economy. Edward Seaga was celebrated as an economic genius who would help to salvage the botched job that had been done by the all-too adventurous PNP economists. Supermarkets were soon stocking cornflakes and American apples, commodities that had disappeared because of the austerity measures of the 1970s and the doctrine that argued that Jamaicans were better off getting used to their own local produce and products rather than relying on foreign tastes. Jamaicans chose otherwise. They had opted for the apples, and for other imported goods. Seaga's victory was cemented when Ronald Reagan invited him to the White House as one of the first international figures to visit the new Reagan administration. Jamaica was becoming part of the Caribbean Basin and the Caribbean Basin Initiative. Cuba had lost that battle and so, therefore, had the USSR. The Ladas that had arrived in Jamaica in the 1970s as cheap automobiles, quickly seemed like an ideological anachronism. The same was true of the new schools that had been built with Cuban workers and Cuban money.

The morning after the election results had been announced, the streets looked like the aftermath of a carnival. The strewn palms of JLP victory covered parts of the sidewalk and the posters of both parties were already becoming tattered and worn – their messages would soon follow. It was over and it seemed clear that all the killing had been for nothing. Those of us who were able to wake on the morning after the results were announced had the feeling of being survivors and, even at that time, we all had a sense of having being through something that we would remember for a long time to come. And there was relief, and this relief would find expression in the way the society's artists responded. Within a year, the theatre was no longer producing work that seemed intent on articulating some political statement or laying out the details of the world of hardships. Instead, the plays that began to gain currency and fame were the roots plays – the plays of escape into debauchery, a great deal of sexual innuendo and narrative lines that were about infidelity, sexual scandal and sexual play. This was the arrival of the 'boops' era, and soon DJ after DJ was generating a new version of these songs about men who were being cuckolded by their women. If the 1970s were the era of roots music that was 'conscious' and intent on speaking to the political realities of Jamaica and on exploring Rastafarianism, the 1980s would become the DJ era and the music would shift towards a celebration of the dancehall, of the party and of the sexual. The music would seem to return to the dancehall energy of the mid-1960s, when consciousness was second to the party. These comparisons are being drawn tentatively – they are simply being employed to try to metaphorize what was clearly a change in the mood of the country, and the change was fundamentally one driven by pragmatism. The powerful message of self-reliance was now being termed a bit of idealism that would pit a small island like Jamaica against an impossible enemy like America. This was clearly a quixotic equation and the new thinking was that it was a foolish proposition. It was seen as impractical and cynical mumbling that it was time to start talking to the people with money to see what one could get from those talks became the order of the society and the order of the day. Where tourism was being pursued with a little too much pride in national independence and a little too much disdain for the exploitative tourists during the 1970s, the 1980s became a period in which the mantra was that the tourist came first and the tourist was always right.

As if on cue, Jamaica began to see more and more evangelists from America arriving to win the souls of those who had been abused by the socialist threat. They arrived on this island, which still held the world record for churches per square mile, to win souls. The vision of many of these evangelists was impossible to distinguish from the policies of the American Basin Initiative, but it was really pointless drawing attention to these ironies because the society had tired of the knee-jerk cry of 'imperialist exploiter' at any hint of Americanism because the society was aware that it was too worn out, too broken to even begin to argue with the new order of things.

The Jamaica that Marley would meet when he returned from touring was an island that was hopeful about the future, but one that would also have been quite sheepish and embarrassed by the message of the election results. The message was that a whole decade had been wasted. Those who had embraced the spirit of that decade were now embarrassed by the fact that they may have given up – that they may have been wrong and had to face it. There were those who saw the change as the beginning of the end of privilege for the poor. The 1970s had brought in free education, and the freeness mentality had somehow become a part of the culture of that decade. This mentality was constantly being berated by the wealthy and the middle class, who felt that it was in fact making poor people lazy and giving them a sense of entitlement. But the poor, it would seem, were aware that the political change would mean that many of these privileges would be taken away. There were those who knew that with the change of government, almost ten years of living without the benefit of patronage would be over. So while some were happy many were sad and forsaken.

The songs on *Uprising* were written before the elections of 1980, but while Marley was working on the album in early 1980 in London, the political violence was already raging in Jamaica in anticipation of the elections. The record was released into the new Jamaica and there is a strong sense in which the themes and ideas were speaking directly to the new condition of Jamaican society. Marley's own mood during the period of recording both *Survival* and *Uprising* was decidedly complex. He had spent time trying to recover from the injury to his toe and the cancer associated with it. Marley knew he had cancer and, while Neville Garrick says that they all felt that the treatment had gone well and that Marley, by late 1977, was completed healed, Marley was on cancer medication well into 1980. He was also dealing with tensions in his management. In 1979 he had fired Don Taylor after the latter had made a mess of a tour of Gabon by the Wailers and after he was also found to be allegedly robbing Marley. Marley returned to the UK in early 1980 to record the songs that would appear on the *Uprising* album, but he was a depressed man, a man trying to work through a great deal of pressures in his personal and business life. Marley was spending very little time in Jamaica. Much of that time away was spent on tour, but it would be fair to say that Bob would never be quite as comfortable in Jamaica as he had been prior to the shooting. The fact that in each successive album after the assassination attempt he would write about the shooting and the aftermath of it was evidence enough that it remained a deep preoccupation and concern of his.

Uprising at least understood quite clearly that the solution to the problems of the world would not come through the actions of politicians. Marley would mix elements of his own personal narrative and mood with a strong desire to celebrate the hope of Selassie in the songs that appeared on *Uprising*.

'Coming In From The Cold' could be seen as a statement by Marley about his constant desire to return home to the warmth of Jamaica after the cold lands where he was touring for most of his town. This is possible, but the line is clearly packed with symbolic meaning. The cold is clearly a place of oppression and alienation. There is safety in the place where the man is entering. It is shelter that sits at the heart of this song. But there is also an allusion to a fairly popular spy thriller – a film that featured a cold-war spy returning from the cold of his espionage activities. The hero of the film is a figure that would have had some currency and popularity in Jamaica. Marley, quite likely, did not expect too intense an association with the film, but the phrase would seem to have been one of those that he co-opted for his own purposes. The most striking thing about the song, however, is not the title. Marley appears to be talking to someone directly. After seeing the manner in which he uses the second person singular in a song like 'Running Away' it is easy to see in this song an attempt at Marley to put in song his own encouragement of himself in the face of the troubles that he has been confronted with. Of course, one must also imagine that he is speaking to a generic audience. The personalizing of the lyric is what gives it its greatest power and impact.

There is an insistence in the address of the song – the repetition of the phrase 'It's you'. Marley seems to be trying hard to get the attention of his imagined listener who he says looks 'sad and forsaken'. Of course the obvious target of the song is the Jamaican poor, who may have been despondent about the absence of change in their lives despite the promise of better made by politicians. More than that, the song would have been written in the same spirit as was 'Smile Jamaica', which Marley insisted was a message of hope and exhortation for a people that he knew were suffering. His answer to them is that a way will always be made even if things look bad for the moment. He then challenges them not to let the system, the force responsible for the sorrow, destroy their hope, lead them to compromise their values or lead them to war against each other.

The weight of the system in the society is such that it can lead men to kill each other. Marley has sung about this problem again and again and at much greater length on the *Survival* album. Here he manages to make the appeal more tender. It is, in many ways, a curious play on a personal moment of self-encouragement and a moment of gentle encouragement to the listener. In the second pass on this verse, Marley asks if 'you' will allow the 'system to get on top your head'. The chant in response is 'no, dread, no'. Then Marley applies a proverb that seeks to summarize why there needs to be a fearlessness in those he is addressing: 'the biggest man you ever did see was just a baby'. 'Coming In From The

Cold' is not a very complex song, but its easy groove and wonderfully rendered bass line gives the ideas in the song a hopeful quality that helps us to enjoy the promise of the lyrics.

'Real Situation', however, is far more complex a song and one that tries to speak to the realities of the world. It is also one of the most pessimistic of Marley's songs. Where we wait desperately for the signature Marley movement from a prophetic statement of doom to an expression of hope, Marley gives us nothing. He sees the world and he is depressed by what he sees. The hope is a dubious one – it rests in the prophecies of the end times. Total destruction is the solution he offers. The end of all things. Marley, it is said, was not aware of how sick he was, but it is clear that he understood that he was weak, easily tired and not feeling himself. There is a definite sense of despair in these songs that Marley does not try to mask. The call to look at reality is elemental to the Marley message and, in order to bring understanding, Marley tries to describe what the real situation is: 'nations war against nations'. He follows this with a series of questions for which he has no answers. Again, this is an unusual moment for Marley.

The 'them' that occurred throughout *Survival* were always stopped in their tracks. They showed power, they showed their force but, somehow, the forces of prophecy and the forces of Rasta seemed always to triumph against them in the end. But here, Marley despairs that no one can stop them now. The prophecy that emerges from this series of observations is a particularly ominous one 'well it seem like total destruction is the only solution'.

In 'Bad Card' there is some fight, but there is enough here to suggest that Marley is speaking directly to Don Taylor who betrayed him. If this is true, it, in a funny way, confirms that Marley was in a less than hopeful mood during the writing of the songs for *Uprising*. The song is combative, but in the smaller and deeply temporal sense that marked his rude bwai days. It is a tough guy's song – a rude bwai song that tellingly, does not rely on the judgment of Jah to bring order to a situation as we would have seen in so many of Marley's earlier anthems of damnation on Babylon. The 'we/them' construct is still at work in these songs, but the 'them' is not the global force of Babylon. The 'them' sometimes seems petty and entirely parochial. But there is more here. The 'dem' is not in a position of defeat. Marley says that he has no answers.

In 'We and Dem' he admits, 'me nuh know how me an' dem a go work it out.' Marley tries to rally some hope in prophecy in the song. Someone must pay, he warns, for the blood of the innocent that has been shed in all the battles raging in Jamaica and the world everyday. They have to pay simply because the Bible says that they will. Of course, the statement 'me nuh know how... etc' must also be read in the context of the rude bwai posture. It must, in other words, be also read as a statement of toughness. This is the cool threat of a man looking at another man and saying, 'I am sorry, but I can't help you here, I am just going to have to kill you.' The sense of resignation to the fact that the differences are so intense and the pressure to carry out justice so weighty, combine to make the statement an ominous one. Yet, Marley is clearly not in control. Even if his is a threat, it is a threat of what is to come... it is not a statement of assurance that some justice will be meted out. It is the language of a battle that is going on the ground. And when he turns to the Bible, he arrives at the same conclusion that he is left with at the end of 'Real Situation'. Marley's vision is a bleak one. In these last days the very purposes of man – the task of occupying the earth and being a good steward of that which has been given to him by Jah – have become corrupted. Man has lost his way and has arrived at a fallen state of faithlessness. It is too late for anything to be done, says Marley. He ends the verse with the harrowing image of man's destruction of the earth because of his greed. In the face of all this, Marley is left in a decidedly uncharacteristic state: he does not know, he had no answer. The important thing here is that he admits it. He shows us his struggle with hopelessness.

While the connection to the rude bwai era of singing about issues that are close to the ground, close to the street is apparent here, there is a quality of hopelessness in these songs that are a far cry from the *braggadocio* of the rude bwai songs. Here, Marley seems world-weary, convinced of the void in the human soul that he keeps seeing around him. In the face of the cannibalism of the faithless, Marley has no answers.

If this is not enough, Marley then adds 'Work' to the list of songs of world-weariness. As tragically sad as these songs may seem to be, they constitute the truest expression of Marley's art that there is. For, in entering this kind of self-revealing anguish in song, Marley would elevate his music from mere superficial anthems of faith to a more complex and, I would argue, honest grappling with the issues of faith and the meaning of life. With very few exceptions, reggae songs simply did not go there. While the rock song was familiar with instances of self-revelation in song, what Marley undertook was an attempt to bring this quality to bear on issues of world politics and religious faith. Perhaps the most effective model of this kind of art in the popular song would have to be Marvin Gaye's album 'What's Going On', which is loaded with those kind of troubling questions and self-doubt. But Marley would have listened to the songs of Bob Dylan and Paul Simon and he would have appreciated that his own art was predicated on an honesty of voice, an ability to bring that honesty to bear on his songwriting. *Uprising* is a decidedly truthful album.

In 'Work' he carries his own fatigue for touring day in and day out to the song. Marley was a hard-working singer and, for the last three years of his life, the Wailers were one of the hardest-touring bands in the business. And yet there is a reaching for some explanation of why he works as hard as he does in this song. It is to work for Jah. He manages to play on the idea of work as both a statement about the way that a positive solution can come out of effort, and just a simple statement about the grind of daily touring and performing. While the album seems to begin with abject despair, it gradually attempts to move out of it. This movement begins with 'Work', which is a statement that, with effort, something positive can emerge. Of course, the problem with this notion of despair is that 'Work' is musically a very upbeat song. The use of the counting system is infectious and Marley enjoys the dialogue with his backing singers in this song. The interesting thing about such songs is that Marley does not only use the I-Threes for his backing singers. He sometimes makes use of all the male voices in the band, which creates a rather masculine energy to the songs. Thus 'Work' has the pared-down feel of a work song. This is not accidental. Marley is using the slave and prison song to suggest that the world is a place of desperate drudgery for the black man. At the same time, however, Marley understands that the capacity to make art out of this drudgery is part of what has allowed the suffering people of the world – especially the black people – to not only survive, but thrive. As the male voices chant 'work', Marley encourages 'Five days to go'. In the rising appeal of the opening lines, the entire Wailers contingent is fully convincing in the declaration 'We can make it work' The I-Threes drag out that word 'we' until it becomes something of a ululation – a communal shout that stirs faith in the audience. It is easy, then, to see how what begins as a description of hardship and labour can be turned into an imperative to unity and the discipline of work. If the Sisyphean suggestion of the line, 'working for a next day', seems somewhat fatalistic and deeply existential, this is a reflection of Marley's condition at the time: there seems to be a cyclical futility to this work that he is doing. But this futility is undercut by the very artistry of the song – the capacity to turn this wry observation into a call to arms, a call to make the labour worthwhile.

The complexity of sentiment that we see in 'Work' continues in 'Pimper's Paradise' but, in the latter, Marley's focus appears to be more intimate, more locked into what seems to be a personal narrative. In 'Pimper's Paradise' Marley departs, at least partially, from the larger themes of 'we and them' and returns to a quality of personal detail that we last saw in *Kaya*. But, as with all of Marley's compositions, the larger cosmology of the struggle between Babylon and the Rastafarian still informs the ideas in the song. The most seductive reading of this song, is of course of it being a commentary on Marley's failing relationship with Cindy Breakspeare. It is not clear whether this was the subject of the song, and it is very possible that Marley wrote the song about one of his other 'model' girlfriends, of which there were several. Regardless of the true subject, what is clear is that Marley is telling the story of a relationship that has crumbled because of the materialism of the woman. Yet, even as we read the song as a narrative of a personal relationship falling apart, we cannot miss the larger metaphor of the song as it applies to Jamaica as an island growing increasingly reliant on the larger pimping super-powers for its survival. Such a reading is in keeping with the organizing cosmology that shapes Marley's writing at so many levels. Nonetheless, the song almost demands a close reading of its vicious attack on this woman. More importantly, it also begs a reading of the seemingly adlibbed lines that end the tune as they reveal Marley's own confessional tendency once more, right at the end of the song. His use of pronouns is very careful in this song and it is worth following their use throughout.

The song's condemnation of the woman is gradual. It begins rather innocuously, but slowly the elements of her sinfulness become apparent. Her desire to party and to have a good time is, in itself, not a bad thing. But the first indication of her failing is in the fact that she indulges in cocaine. Gradually we see a woman who is at best false and, at worst, slightly unhinged: 'She'll be laughing when there ain't no joke'. The chorus rests on a clever turn of phrase. The 'pimper' is the pimp, of course, and she constitutes a paradise for the pimp. It is a rather unsubtle way of calling her a whore. The use of the past tense in the chorus may be significant. At the very least it suggests that the persona who is singing has ended any dealings with this woman. Whatever was there belongs to the past. It will set up the sense of betrayal that emerges later in the song. Marley also complicates the character of the woman by suggesting that she is not simply a woman intent on material gain, but one who is driven by something more profoundly psychological. 'Every need got an ego to feed.' It is a proverbial phrase whose origins I have not been able to trace, but the compactness of that statement allows it to apply both to the woman – someone who is driven by the desire for attention and fame; and the persona himself who has allowed his ego needs to drag him into a relationship with this creature.

The second verse offers even more details – this time, quite specific. The woman is a model perhaps, but she may also be simply the type who enjoys the fashions of the day. Her vanity continues in the fact that she is deeply engrossed in the 'scramble' – the 'rat race', which she manages to handle with passion. Marley then returns to the image of the hard drugs, but this time transforms it into a narrative of hubris – a kind of Icarus image. In New Testament parlance, her effort to fly high is a preamble for the tragic fall. Everything about this woman is false. Her bluesing without the blues represents yet another of her deceptions. The business of pretending to live with the blues while she has not even started to understand them suggests a woman who is attempting to co-opt the lifestyle and the attendant toughness of the poor. However, she is not able to experience it fully. The blues, Marley appreciates, are, above all, truth and honesty – they are real. This woman epitomizes the very opposite of this.

Marley then leads us into the final chorus, which is loaded with his carefully interjected qualifiers. They extend the narrative and, more importantly, they help us to appreciate the censure that is involved in the song. Like so many of the songs on this album, there is no triumphant judgment on the evil that some of the figures in these songs represent. Apart from accusing her of being a whore, Marley appears to just accept her presence as one of the realities of life. What he also does, though, in the final chorus, is to suggest that the persona is somehow a victim of the woman's actions. Yet, we are also quite sure that a hint of empathy creeps into the song, and soon he seems to be offering warnings to the woman. These warnings suddenly colour the entire song, which, in the face of the seemingly adlibbed lines, becomes a song of gentle admonition and reproof.

The challenge here is to decipher all the pronouns that fill the last phrases of the song. First there is the victim who could be both this woman and those who are used by this woman. Marley is sorry for the victim. One wonders if he, too, sees himself as a victim. He then introduces the 'they/them' construct. Because the suggestion is that 'they' (whoever they are) are going to bow, going to be defeated, one is tempted to see them as the generic Babylon. But he may also be talking about the victims. And, furthermore, he may now have transformed the single woman into a collective of women. It is their heads that will bow. Each of these are possibilities. It is not absolutely necessary to determine which applies because, in a sense, they all do. When Marley begins to speak to 'you', introducing the third pronoun and subject shift, we know that the entire conundrum is compounded. Yet the content of the lines points to the idea that Marley is somehow softening his condemnation and trying to encourage this woman. Here, then, his quarrel is with the selling of the self – the prostituting of self that points to a failure of integrity. It is these lines, along with the use of the word 'paradise', that has made many of us view this song as a larger metaphor for his reading of Jamaica and his fear that Jamaica may be heading down a path of prostitution. After all, the IMF deals had been made during the time when Marley would have written the song. I must confess, though, that, had the song been written in 1981, it would have been so perfectly prescient and very well timed. Marley may have seen the decay coming, and he may have heard the politicians who were lambasting the PNP and all its nationalistic calls for self-reliance, and this may have been Marley's warning. That is the nobler reading. The more likely reading is that Marley was taking on a woman – a generic kind of woman, or a specific woman, and the poetics of that attack allowed the song to resonate beyond the specifics.

The last time Marley had taken on a woman in such a frontal attack was the song 'Adam And Eve', which the Wailers covered in the 1960s. The final line of the song was, 'woman is the root of all evil'. Riding sweetly seductive gospel/ska rhythm, this song comes across as a cold articulation of Marley's sometimes troubling view of women. Marley would never render women in that manner in a song again until 'Pimper's Paradise'. The latter is not as harsh as the former, which offers a proposition about all women that Marley does not attempt to do in 'Pimper's Paradise'. This is a specific kind of woman. Of course, it is all ironic because Marley's own moral compass when it came to the management of women was, even to his own admission, a problem. He would say in interviews that his own weakness was women. Marley saw the multiple affairs that he had as a weakness – a kind of vice. For him, as for many Rastafarians, and frankly many men in general, the double standard of expecting complete purity and loyalty from a woman while feeling free to move from woman to woman constituted a kind of entitlement that was rarely critiqued or challenged. Apart from the noble mothers and reluctant lovers that peopled Marley songs, this woman and the woman who leaves him in 'She's Gone' represent the two most assertive female figures in his oeuvre. There is, of course, a suggestion that the woman in 'Waiting In Vain' is a tough, assertive figure who is likely to keep him waiting. Marley pleads, begs, cajoles and whines for her attention. Yet the song is, at its core, a song of consummate seduction. The desperation is not as thorough as it seems to have been in earlier love songs. Nonetheless, the interesting thing is that the woman in

'Pimper's Paradise' appears to be the one who challenges the male and for it she gets verbally attacked. Marley's gentle embrace of her in the end, and his wise warnings, can sometimes seem oddly pathological. And this is the strange grace of the song, the way that it reflects Marley moving back and forth in his attitude to the woman.

What has not changed is the fact that the world of *Uprising* is a fallen world. The sinners are thriving and the righteous seem helpless to do anything about it. These are certainly disturbing times for Marley. He is baring his soul and what we are seeing is a man who appears to be struggling with a universe that is not conforming to the order that Rastafari represents. It would be a stretch to say that Marley was experiencing a crisis of faith. The more accurate observation would be to say that Marley was becoming increasingly distressed by what he saw as the propensity of evil in the world, and seemed incapable of simply applying the prophecies of his faith to them. He offered us a bleak vision of the world – a stark Jeremiah without the final redemptive chapters – in 'Could You Be Loved' the song becomes a striking study in the unchecked stream of consciousness of an artist trying to speak words of encouragement without shying away from the tough ironies of life. Every phrase is loaded with dualisms and contradictions. The question is 'Could you be loved?' It is a peculiar question because it throws the onus on the person who is receiving love and forces us to consider whether it is enough to simply love. After all, if we love and the person that we are attempting to love cannot receive love, then what do we have? This would be a cynical question coming from someone else. For Marley it constitutes the kind of mystery that he feels must be solved for love to prevail. Yet the most obvious thing that can be said about this song is that it seems to strain the notion of a unified theme and focus. Marley is venting – somehow trying to pack a number ideas into a single song. The chorus is what must pull this song together. At the end of each exploration of the vicissitudes of life, Marley takes us back to the all-healing power of love and its capacity to change everything. This then allows him to return to the chorus, which asks 'Could you be loved?' The question, then becomes a dare, a kind of challenge to the listener to respond to the struggles of life and the deceptions of Babylon with love. It is in keeping with the tone of the album that rather than order us to love in the chorus, he asks us if we are can be loved.

Babylon returns in full force in this track in the figure of 'them'. In one of his last concerts, Marley can be heard appealing to his audience as his distrust of Babylon is thorough. As in many of his songs, he points to the the education system that seems bent on controlling the mind of the righteous and, in so doing, maintaining the oppression of the poor. The Western education system is an object of mistrust for the Rastafarian because it is this system that has worked hard at eliminating the African from the annals of civilization. So when Marley states 'we've got a mind of our own / So go to hell if what you're thinking is not right', while there is a quality of petulance (mind of our own), something larger is being stated here. It is the same statement that shapes the lines, 'well what we know is not what they tell us / And we're not ignorant,...' in 'Ambush In The Night' and the lines 'building church and university / deceiving the people continually' in 'Babylon System'. The mind that is being referred to here embraces a view of history, a view of the future, a view of the politics of society, a view of morality, a view of God and an entirely distinct cosmology. The world view of the 'we' is at constant variance with the world view of 'them'. But the most crucial feature of this way of thinking is the presence of love – its centrality in all that 'we' do. The expression of this faith in love in this song, hints, however, at a kind of hopeful prayer – an assertion that is also something of a question: 'Love would never leave us alone'. This love is a force of goodness, a force that will bring light to darkness. Marley is quoting the New Testament and the Book of Proverbs: the things that are done in darkness will be revealed in the light. It is a theme that he has explored in other songs, but here the need for faith in this saying – the maxim of the believers – is especially poignant. It is this earnest energy that allows Marley to sound openly angry in one moment 'Go to hell if what you thinking is not right' and urgently forceful in his exhortation 'love your brotherman!' The position of the 'you' is a curious one in this song. In many ways, the 'you' here is similar to the wayward woman in 'Pimper's Paradise'. Marley is speaking to those who should know better but appear to have gone astray or are, at least, moving dangerously close to a moral lapse. When he quotes from 'Judge Not' he actually helps us to understand that in many ways the song belongs to that pure combative mode that guided his writing during those early days. The melody here is different – far less soothing and playful. The I-Threes sing this in unison, their attack on the words staccato and edged with aggression.

In these seemingly parenthetical asides, Marley offers us reasons why love may be difficult for some of us. The tendency to judge others and to assume ourselves better than others is an inordinate sin that grows out of the influence of Babylon. Thus, when Marley sings the second verse and asks us to avoid being changed by Babylon, we are now aware that he regards his listeners as co-combatants in a war against Babylon. And in this battle, the Rastafarian maxim of vitality and fitness is essential for survival. This appeal to fitness is clearly close to Marley's heart. He exercised daily for as long as he could. Rastafarians saw the proper care of the body as elemental to the faith.

A true sign of Babylonian-inspired debauchery was unfitness. In the late 1970s and early 1980s a number of reggae artists, most notably Freddie MacGregor and Black Uhuru would sing about fitness. In the former, fitness is requisite for survival in the end times. The popular soccer gear of the day is named in what would today be called a truly bizarre case of product placement in song: 'Oh yes dem wearing de Puma / Oh yes dem wearing Adidas...' Black Uhuru would spit out in their Sly-and-Robbie-inspired bullying tones 'fit yuh haffe fit yuh haffe fit-fit-fit...' Marley joins them when he declares 'Only, only, only the fittest of the fittest shall survive / Stay alive...' Yet the idea of fitness is not merely a matter of physical fitness. There is more than the suggestion of being 'fit' in the sense of being the appropriate person, being the chosen. What defines this idea of fitness, however, is the ghetto-driven notion that the world is a cold place in which one will be destroyed if one is unable to struggle and fight back. It is a Darwinian world, and therefore shaped by the Darwinian concept of survival. In 'Concrete Jungle' Marley sang of one having to be the 'very best' in a place 'where the living is hardest'.

In the next parenthetical sequence, Marley seems again to be distracted by other issues. He quotes Peter Tosh this time. Of course, the proverb is not Tosh's, but it is one that Tosh would use famously in his caustic love song 'What You Gonna Do'. Two proverbs emerge. In one he states that a person will not miss the water until they no longer have a viable source of water; a well. The second is a pessimistic view of humanity: no matter what you give to people (men), they will never be satisfied.

Again the I-Threes sing in unison. That he gives these elliptical passages to them allows us to see the passages as slight shifts in focus – a kind of miniature lesson about the nature of love. In this instance, love is something that we shouldn't take for granted, something that we will eventually miss and regret losing. The second lesson seems like a contradiction. On one hand, the first lyric advocates that one be watchful of love and not take it for granted. Yet the second seems to suggest that even when we do love, it will not be enough because the object of love, if he is a certain kind of man, will never be satisfied with the love that we give. Suffice it to say that these contradictory impulses manage to complicate the question, 'Could you be loved and be loved?' If the 'you' is the same in the proverbial lessons, then the question is whether we (meaning, the you) belong to the group to which the 'man' belongs, or whether we will find a way to be loved and be satisfied with the love. Marley then embarks on one of the liveliest sequences of the album when he literally sounds like he is leaping, moving, turning and rocking as he pleads with his listener to say something. The phrase begins as a vocal cue for the backing singers. Marley learned the art of making vocal cues part of the narrative and meaning of the song from artists like James Brown, whose funk improvisations in this regard represent some of the most fascinating examples of contemporary call and response performance. Marley takes it up and then makes the call for voice a mantra, a kind of plea for an answer to the question 'Could you be loved?' He repeats the phrase 'say something' until the I-Threes call back 'say something' and together they complete the phrase at least 16 times before the music fades out. The only answer to this question, then, becomes one of Marley's reliable answers: music. Music is the answer to the questions that confrontations with Babylon bring. In this song as in so many of Marley songs, he turns to music and sees music as the salvation. There is no difference between the call 'reggae, reggae' and 'rockers, rockers' and his declaration on 'Trench Town' 'we free the people with music...'.

It is his only answer. It is not the kind of assured answer that we get from Marley, but it is an answer that makes sense in the face of the funk and jump of the song. It is love that guides and shapes this song, making it a powerful expression of hope by means of its energy and optimistic tone. The disconnection between the lyrical open-endedness and the musical grace and assurance is entirely consistent with Marley's art. It comes from an understanding of the nature of being an artist in a popular business. But it is also more than that. Reggae is a musical form that is built on finding voice for the hardships and troubles of the tough life that people live – reggae, then, is a music that is rooted in reality and in the articulation of reality. Yet, as with most music of the African diaspora, reggae is a music of escape, it is a music that allows the community to escape from the hardships of life and to enter the subliminal space of spiritual and psychic transportation – an escape into the pleasures of the sexual and the physical act of moving, dancing, sweating, jumping, laughing and finding joy despite the pain. These are contradictory impulses, but they are the bedrock of the music to which reggae is inextricably connected. These songs can make us weep and laugh at the same time. The best of Marley's songs will do that. 'Could You Be Loved', for example, was a dance hit in the UK in 1980 peaking at number five.

After these songs of conflicting ideas, Marley ends the album with two tracks that are arguably some of the best songs of his career. In both songs, he manages to pull together the strands of his work that seem to have the greatest meaning for him and composes lyrics that speak from as personal a place as possible. In these songs, he achieves the magical act of transforming something with a sleight of hand, turning the intimate details of his personal journey into a communal narrative that assumes mammoth proportions. They are simply fine examples of his songwriting and have a haunting sense of the tragic developments that are to come.

Given the range of emotion and the shift from pure assurance that we have seen in *Uprising*, 'Forever Loving Jah' is an expression of faith that should be understood as a direct response to the sombre notes of some of the songs on the album. Marley returns to his feeling of having been betrayed by those who sought to kill him, and yet, he also seems to be carrying in him a range of disappointments with the larger world around him. To this he offers the promise of judgment and retribution. In this song, Marley muses about the righteous authority of Jah and seeks to assure his people – those he speaks to as a shepherd would to his flock ('children mark my word') that the order of Jah has been restored. The song is a welcome moment of hope after the sometimes bleak and open-ended encounters with evil that we see in earlier songs. In verse after verse, Marley creates lyrics that transform the evil constructs of the world into something positive. The very structure of each verse reflects the movement from despair to hope. A proposition is made and then a counter statement is offered as a path for the righteous to take. The song, while cast in the voice of a preacher, achieves an intimacy that comes from the sense of vulnerability that Marley evokes in each verse. His choice of language, his use of proverbs and his transformation of proverbial constructs into personal articulation are all elements of Marley's technique at its height. This is as close to a hymn, an expression of faith, as is possible for a pop song.

Marley begins by locating the song in Jamaica, in the streets. The street is so important to Marley's work. His songs take us along streets, down roads, through the avenues of the ghetto, along paths in the hills – his landscape is almost always outdoors. The world is a world where people are constantly walking, 'trodding through Babylon'. The 'them' are those who will speak evil of the righteous 'us'. Marley is positioned as a part of 'we', and there is a sense in which he is speaking about his own experience and the manner in which others have been speaking ill of him. Of course, after the assassination attempt, many gave Marley a hard time for leaving Jamaica. After he released *Kaya*, there were yet more cries that he had sold out. When he bought a BMW (because he said the name stood for Bob Marley and the Wailers), 'they' continued to accuse him of losing his edge. When he agreed to do the Peace concert, many felt he was again pandering to politicians. Marley, in many interviews, would indicate that he could see that many were speaking ill of him, questioning his motives and his actions. In 'Running Away' he confronts this dilemma by making it clear that it has bothered him, that the things they have said have caused him pain. Marley carried a great deal. His decision to not amputate his toe was one such decision that he took on his own. Others worried about his choice. Marley understood fear when he wrote this song, and for him the way to cast away fear, to contend with the debilitating weight of being Bob Marley, was to focus outside of himself onto Haile Selassie, on Jah, his creator. This is the way to avoid the tears. Love. The love of Jah is a thorough one that Marley understands to be endless, to transcend the temporal. This is the central struggle of the song: that of the temporal versus the eternal.

The second verse is one of the most beautiful that Marley has written. He begins by invoking the old negro spiritual, 'Old Man River'. That song is a lament, the song of a man contending with the drudgery of life and seeking to find some way of facing the future. The river is a metaphor for the way that life keeps moving on – it is a metaphor of hope and yet also one of despair. Marley rejects the lamentation. He does not want to sing sad songs of hopelessness and self-pity, and so he asks that the river not cry for him. In this carefully wrought couplet, Marley replaces the despairing flow of the river with the stream of love that he carries. It is a transformative love that transcends the blues.

In rejecting the song 'Old Man River' he is also subtly turning away from the traditional ethos of the blues – that secular sense of the world as powerful and capable of consuming the living. Marley's declaration that he will never be blue grows out of this allusion to the negro spiritual. Jah love is offered as something distinctive from the ethos of the African-American world of blues and seemingly despairing spirituals. Marley's is not a criticism, but a reaction to at least two forms of black response to suffering. For him, the negro spiritual and the blues are not adequate responses. He wants to propose a third – the Rastafarian response, which is defiant. The defiance is caught in the almost improvised manner in which Marley rhymes stages with rages and changes. The stages are clear – they represent the Sisyphean progression towards futility, challenge after futile challenge that seeks to destroy the sufferer. The rages represent the anger that emerges because of these obstacles. These are the rages brought on by Babylon. And in all of this, Marley declares, 'we'll never be blue'. It is at once a prayer and an affirmation of faith. The path from there to the chorus is transcendent, a quality of grace that can only be appreciated when listened to carefully.

In the third of four cleanly drawn lessons, Marley quotes from the Book of Proverbs. He selects one of the many lessons about the fool and uses it to speak of faith. Marley has spoken of fools in other songs. The fools of Marley songs are biblical fools, those that as the psalmist declares, 'say in their heart there is no good'. In the single 'Jah Live' Marley would declare 'The fools says in their heart / Rasta your God is dead', and in *Exodus* he would sing of the stiff-necked fools who think they are cool. Marley's fools were those without faith, those who allowed their faithlessness to define their actions. Here the fool is one who relies purely on his own sense of what is right. In a true Rastafarian elision, 'understanding' is rightly cast as 'misunderstanding' – an immensely reasonable correction of the language. Marley then quotes again, this time quoting Jesus Christ who prophecies that only those who are like children will be capable of entering the kingdom and of finding oneness with God. For Marley, mankind's faults lie primarily in inordinate pride, but there is a time of reckoning when all truth will be revealed. The wise and the prudent are full of their own notions of their views of the world. Theirs is a false wisdom. And this idea is one that always amused Marley, who would talk about education as something that would have made him a damn fool. His status as a 'lickle man', as a person of no importance, who has been granted the capacity to offer truth to the world, is one that Marley found great solace in. He understood the irony of his music reaching out from the poverty-stricken world of the Jamaican ghetto to become a music of profound impact on the world. He understood it and saw it as part of the complex workings of Jah. It is the way of the world.

In the final verse, he draws upon the psalms and intones these lines in the language of Elizabethan English. Marley, like most Rastas, relished the weightiness and authority of the King James Bible and saw in it a power of poetry and statement that worked comfortably with the Jamaican language. He does not finish the first quotation. He begins it but allows us to finish. The tree that is planted by the rivers of waters in one reckoning, shall not be removed. The message is one of steadfastness and faithfulness. But there is also another tree, planted by the rivers of waters, that brings good fruit. There, as rotted as the tree is, its purpose of bringing fruit and giving life is elemental. For Marley the incomplete simile is referring to the righteous, to the Rastafarian. Yet even as he allows that unspoken implication to resonate, he introduces a parallel construct.

This is part of Marley's lyrical genius – his capacity to create overlapping lines of meaning that stay in constant dialogue with each other and somehow do not cancel each other out. The order of the tree that remains rooted by the river and the tree that bears fruit because it is close to the water (the water, of course, taking us back to the 'rolling streams of love') is completed by the fact that such things represent the order of God. 'Everything in life got its purpose.' Marley is, of course, quoting the Book of Ecclesiastes here in which Solomon lays out the order of the world – there is a time for everything under the sun. Ecclesiastes is a book of existentialist futility without the last cry for the hope in God. There is something of that quality in Marley, who has seen the wealth of the world, and who has seen everything that he would want to see, but remains convinced that it is all 'vanity, a chasing after the wind'. Marley's philosophy as expressed here is complete in its calmer acceptance of the divinity of Jah in the ordering of events. For Marley, the absolute ability to be able to trust that everything indeed has a purpose and a reason is the singular moment of hope in the face of all his despair.

What anyone will notice in this lyric is that Marley at no point demands action. There are no imperatives here. Marley is finding a place of comfort in allowing himself to simply trust. It may appear to be a softening, a passing away of the edge of radical action that much of Marley's early persona revealed. But there is something to be said here about the movement that has taken place in the philosopher's mind. He has aged, he has arrived at a place of wisdom that is profound and that allows him to reach for peace and comfort. Fighting, he is aware, is not going to resolve everything. *Uprising*, then, becomes a peculiar title for the album. There is not a single song on the album that has the word 'uprising' in it. Given Marley's track record, one would expect that *Uprising* would be a cry for rebellious action, for radical action. But Marley has played an important joke on his audience. The uprising that finally takes place is an uprising of spiritual assurance – a kind of lifting of one's faith that allows the Rasta to confront the world of hardship with grace and hope. It is this raising of a resistance through spiritual strengthening that defines the tone and shape of the final song on the album, 'Redemption Song'. The call is for the people to sing. This is, at the end of the day, Marley's truest call for resistance because it is the form of resistance that he carries out with the greatest consistency. It is the kind of resistance that he turns to again and again throughout his career. He is demanding that we achieve things that cannot be done by force of arms. They are internal transformations. They constitute a shift in the position of the heart. The song, then, comes to transform the soul, and it is at this level of spiritual change that Marley offers 'Redemption Song'. But Marley is not writing a song that stands outside of the harsh details of history, of time and place, of social relevance to the times. On the contrary, 'Redemption Song' begins with what has become the classic narrative of the African in the diaspora. The striking power of the song is the manner in which he takes us from there and compels us to see everything as resolved only through a spiritual act of song.

Many have rightly linked the song to Marley's increasing self-identification with the figure of Joseph from the Bible. Joseph was the one who was somehow chosen in spite of himself, but his position created jealousy among those closest to him – his brothers. They betrayed him and sold him to merchants who then took him to Egypt where he, after much hardship, slowly prospered and eventually became a wealthy ruler and a close confidant of the Pharoah. Joseph would eventually serve as a saviour for his people, the children of Israel, who suffered much during the years of drought that consumed the land. Eventually Joseph would forgive his brothers, and usher in the period of exile for the children of Israel in Egypt. It would be Moses who would eventually lead them out of Egypt to the promised land. Marley would have identified with the diasporic narrative of Joseph and his people but, more importantly, he would have understood himself to be one of the fortunate ones who could then use his success to help those less fortunate. Marley was passionate about this role and impatient with those who failed to see that this was central to his sense of self.

The power of the the song lies in the way that Marley layers this narrative of Joseph onto the epic narrative of slavery and capture that brought Africans to this new Egypt – this new Babylon. By marrying the word 'merchant' with the word 'ship' Marley immediately and efficiently evokes both narratives. The principle of typology, then, for Marley, began with the foundation of biblical truth, which would then give meaning to historical truth, which would in turn given meaning and relevance to personal truth.

'Redemption Song' is a tight fist of a song. Its efficiency is remarkable. The song achieves the simplicity of the best poems that have a lasting impact because of their memorable structure, their clear rhetoric voice and the way that they reveal the personality of the singer. Marley is writing from a very specific place – the place of the Jamaican who is becoming increasingly aware of the larger world and the unavoidable connection that exists between these two worlds. 'Redemption Song' outlines the history of blacks in the New World, and then proceeds to argue for a new kind of freedom – a freedom from the new oppressive systems. 'Redemption Song' is locked into the now standard Marley construct of 'we'and 'them'. The forces of Babylon have conspired to make the world of the Rastafarian a difficult one. The only path for hope is through the act of singing. In four minutes, Marley tells of a history that spans 400 years.

The branding of the forces of Babylon as pirates in the first verse is the signalling of the tone of the song. Marley makes it clearly that those who participated in the slave trade were in fact pirates and not mere merchants. For him the robbery of the slave, from Africa, from his people and from himself, is the most basic act of piracy that there is. The 'I' then becomes the collective Rastafarian 'I' representing, at once, Africa and Africans as well as the singer himself. Marley throws himself back in time. The abuses of the trade are not things of the past. They are things that shape the present. For Marley, the enslavement of Africans is not a distant fact of history, but a present fact – a reality that allows him to speak of the act as a present truth. Marley also makes it clear that the mercantile system that has effectively provided the West with the basis for all its current wealth and power is not a benign system. The merchant ship is tied directly to the bottomless pit that alludes to the hull of the slave ships where Africans were held as cargo, but also to the bottomless pit of slavery and the exile in Babylon that the Africans faced. The devouring horizon, its ability to consume African after African over so many centuries, is what Marley laments in these lines. But as quickly as Marley outlines the horrors of the middle passage, he also speaks of the transcendence out of the mire of the system through the 'hand of the Almighty'. Marley has sung about revolutionary heroes who fought for freedom, he has called his people to 'rebel' to 'get up / stand up', to 'chase the crazy baldheads out of town', to burn and loot all night, and to 'Jump Niyahbinghi', so he does understand the contribution that rebellion and resistance had to the struggle for freedom for the blacks. Yet he turns to an articulation of faith and the understanding that the battle is fundamentally a spiritual one in this song. It is in keeping with Marley's direction in the last few years of his life. He speaks of the support of Jah's hand in the struggle and then declares that the people will 'forward' in the new generation with a sense of victory.

Marley's use of form is nicely demonstrated here. The first verse ends with an introduction to the second verse both in terms of theme and focus. He will sing, in the second verse, about this generation. And in this generation there is still the spectre of slavery, but now slavery appears in a different form. Having established the discourse of slavery, Marley uses the language of enslavement to talk about the new challenges facing the African. Yet he manages to show that the message of freedom from the Babylonian system is a universal one, and not just only a struggle for Africans.

The new slavery from which he says we must emancipate ourselves is, of course, an enslavement of the mind, not the body. The emancipation proclamation of 1838 was entirely the freedom from the physical bonds of slavery, but a greater slavery, the slavery of colonialism and the slavery that is shaped by a view of the self that is demeaning and hopeless, is the slavery that entraps the current generations. Marley, in 'Concrete Jungle', speaks of the new phenomenon when he sings, 'no chains around my feet but I'm not free / I know I am bound here in captivity.' The new captivity is mental, it is psychic, but, for Marley, the movement out of this enslavement is driven by the self. This is a Rastafarian tenet of faith – a faith that is predicated on action and not a kind of fatalism that relies on God to change all things. Marley has to believe that the freeing of the mind is possible and for him the path towards a free mind is through singing songs of redemption.

Yet those who sing the songs and those who teach the people to sing are the ones who are constantly under attack and the ones who are turning into martyrs. Marley understood his position as a target, and many of the songs on this album are wry reminders of his vulnerability ('a good man is never honoured in his own country'). However, he, does not simply accuse Babylon of killing the 'prophets' of the good way and of the revolution, but he also implicates the people, his people, as well, for their complicity.

Marley confronts the notion of fatalism that has haunted this album. Is this just the way things will be? he seems to be asking. In earlier songs he declares that it is too late, that he has no idea how things are going to work out, and offers other hints of resignation to the idea that the world order has shifted and Babylon will hold sway. Those who say 'it's just a part of it' and that the killing of prophets is a mere fulfilment of the book are those, it seems, who have given up, and who have at least come to see the end times as very present. It would seem that if we simply accept the verse for what it is – that is, if the verse ends where it does, then we would have to see Marley as accepting that these things are happening because they must happen. But Marley takes us on to the chorus and the chorus points to an alternative view, responding to despair by calling on the people to help him sing songs that redeem, songs that bring salvation, songs that stand up in the face of despair and fatalism.

Marley almost always sang this song solo. He performed it alone during his last performance in Pittsburgh in 1980. The recording does not reveal that Marley had just learned that he was dying of a brain tumour. There is no evidence that the doctors had told him that he only had weeks to live. Marley had insisted that he would do that last show. We can hear the audience whistling and cheering, then over the crowd we hear Marley plucking tentatively the introductory lines of the song. He plays an open minor chord, and then raises his voice into a long wail of a scream: 'Yeeeeeaaaaahhh!' Then in a classic understatement that shows his own sense of humility, he introduces the song, 'this lickle song here is call 'Old Pirates', yuh know, 'Redemption Song'.' Then he begins to sing – his voice alone in the crowd, a voice full of the world-weary pressures of his life, and a voice that is aware he is trying to say something profound to the people around him. That he calls the song 'Old Pirates' first helps us to see the central dichotomy that shapes this song. This is a song of pirates and a song of redemption. The path is from the trauma of loss to the hope of redemption.

'Redemption Song' would confirm Marley's commitment to the task of teaching and leading his people out of a world marked by oppression and hopelessness into a place of survival. The cry is for his people to sing a song of freedom. Marley, in his own way, was making one of the most telling confessions of his art when he sang, 'all I ever had / Redemption songs'. It is all that Marley can lay claim to. The song is, for him, the basis of his revolutionary instinct and the full enactment of his quest for revolution. Marley always tried to find the hope of redemption in his songs and, as is clear in this example, he understood that to find redemption, the death of exploitation and destruction would have to exist. There is, then, a sense in which the pattern of the grand redemptive narrative is the fulfilment of prophecy, the fulfilment of the book.

Jamaicans have adopted this song as a fitting narrative of their own journey. Marley understood and celebrated the place of Africa, the Middle Passage and slavery in the shaping of the Jamaican psyche. If for years this history had been denied or looked upon with shame, Marley and the other reggae artists of the 1970s were committed to retelling the stories of survival, both as a warning to those who sought to perpetuate the oppressive pattern, and as an exhortation to those who represented the survival that the ancestors went through. They did it with songs such as '96 Degrees in the Shade' (Third World), 'Slavery Days' (Burning Spear), 'Border' (Gregory Isaacs) and 'Redemption Song', along with many other classic narratives of the history of these people. In doing this, Marley was leading a society towards the use of its own language and its own history to find and celebrate the beauty of this complex world. By putting flesh on a philosophy that challenged the imposed philosophies of colonialism and the system that followed, Marley gave Jamaicans a sense of their own unique ability to speak into the issues of the world through songs that would resonate with people from all over the globe. 'Redemption Song' is a fine lyric – a tidy and efficiently written song that would lead Derek Walcott, the Nobel Laureate, to speak of it as a work that he envied for its ability to say so much in such a short space. These emblematic moments of poetic sublimation are all part of the legacy of Bob Marley.

Confrontation appeared two years after Marley's death. It is tempting to think that Marley requested the songs that should go on the album before his death. He certainly had the time to do so in the year between the news of his cancer and his death. It is also tempting to see the album as his last will and testament – his final statement from the grave. But there is no clear evidence to suggest that this was the case. The composition of the album, however, suggests that many of the songs were written during the last few years of his life. Some were tracks that had been recorded as singles and as pieces to appear in future albums. Marley tended to do this. 'Buffalo Soldier' for instance, was written and recorded in the US in 1978. But anyone following the progression of Marley's writing can tell that the album belongs to the period of *Survival* and *Uprising* in theme and style. Some of the songs on this album are quite easily stunning examples of Marley writing at the height of his skills. Philosophical, Marley is the prophet and shepherd here. He is teaching. His cry for battle is rooted in a spiritual devotion and there is a maturity of voice that is consistent with the work on the previous two albums. We can hear in Marley's voice an intensity that is never strident, but is, instead, filled with a grave honesty – a sincerity that lends many of these songs a tremendous power. The subjects in these songs are remarkably consistent with the basic themes of Marley's work. There are no love songs in this album either. The key categories, however, are the warrior songs such as 'Chant Down Babylon', 'Jump Niyahbinghi', 'Buffalo Soldier' and 'Rastaman Live Up'. They are songs directed at Rastafarians for the most part, and are quite clearly speaking to that community with an unabashed frankness. Only in 'Buffalo Soldier' does Marley seem to be reaching out to a wider audience. 'Rastaman Live Up' is a call for Rastas to stand by their faith and their beliefs. Then there are the most powerful devotional and psalmic praise songs like 'Give Thanks And Praises' and 'I Know', in which Marley bares his spiritual soul in what are essentially beautiful hymns. I regard the songwriting in 'Give Thanks And Praises' to be of the highest order. Marley does not slow down in the song, and he eases into a series of melodic turns around the most consummate of lyric writing. His songs of social commentary that remain tied to the betrayal he never stopped feeling about the assassination attempt can be found in 'Stiff Necked Fools' and 'Mix Up, Mix Up'. Then there is the confessional intimacy of 'Trench Town', in which Marley reminds us that he knows where he is coming from and he knows that what he is doing is making music as a revolutionary act. In this album, song after song reminds us that music is the salvation.

Listening to, and studying, the songs on *Confrontation* is really a process of discovering something of Marley's writing process. This was not an album of songs that were written at the same time. Much of the material had already been recorded and released as singles years before, and much of it had not seen the light of day. The orchestration, the instrumental work and many of the basic rhythm tracks were added long after Marley had died. Yet the stories behind many of these songs, and the information that we can unearth about the times of composition for many of these songs, help us to understand something of Marley's changing state of mind during the last few years of his life. It would be safe to say that *Uprising* was Marley's last statement to us as listeners. But *Confrontation* presents us with a few final comments by Marley that were intended to come out at some point. The Wailers team that put the album together was still heavily under the influence of Marley and understood his mood and his style thoroughly at that point. The music we get is powerful and decidedly Marley's work. Most importantly, however, this album contains songs that constitute some of Marley's really important work.

'Chant Down Babylon' belongs to the confrontational songs that Marley recorded at various stages of his career. The pattern is the same.

This song was conceived and developed in late 1979 during the *Survival* tour and just before the Wailers made their way to Gabon to perform. The Wailers, and Marley especially, were still riding the high of their trip to Zimbabwe and the excitement of his earlier trip to Ethiopia, where Marley wrote a number of songs that truly excited him. He built 'Chant Down Babylon' around a jam session on the tour bus with keyboardist Earl 'Wire' Lindo who played a percussive beat to Marley's guitar work. During the preparations for the Gabon tour, Marley worked with Carly Barrett in the studio to put down the rhythm and vocal work for 'Chant Down Babylon.' Marley, no doubt, intended to return to this song later. This version builds on the work that had been done earlier. But it is clear that the energy and optimism that was there in the Wailers' camp carried over into the song. Gabon, of course, was a disaster, and when the Wailers returned, Marley was decidedly morose, angry and disappointed at having been betrayed by his manager. Understanding the timing of the song helps us to appreciate, then, how it contrasts with many of the songs that would appear in *Uprising*. 'Chant Down Babylon' firmly belongs to the *Survival* period and his central aim is to add another nail to the coffin of Babylon.

He describes Babylon, argues for the weakness of Babylon in the face of the prophecies of her demise and then proceeds to push the people to fight Babylon and destroy her. Unlike the songs on *Uprising*, however, Marley is buoyant in his confidence that Babylon can be destroyed. He resorts to the language of the street declaring them 'sof'' – meaning they have no ability to resist and that they belong to those who are weak of heart and mind. There is a rallying energy to the song, and one that bubbles with the drive of a ring-leader gathering a mob to battle Babylon. The idea of chanting Babylon 'one more time' suggests that this is something that they have done before. There is almost a hint of Marley asking them to join him in the chanting down of Babylon one more time. Marley is always careful to show that he is calling, not for a physical destruction of Babylon, but for an act of prophesying against Babylon through music. But he is playful about it in the same way that he toys with the idea of burning down Babylon in 'Burnin' And Lootin''. There he masterfully transforms the incendiary lyrics that suggest revolutionary action, into a song about a mental battle: 'Burning all illusion tonight / Burning all pollution tonight'. Here he moves from 'come we go burn down' to 'come we go chant down'. They are one and the same if we agree with Marley that music is 'the key'. The destruction of Babylon is given to us in a vision.

Their 'dreams and aspirations' will all fall away and so will their wicked intentions. Here Marley reminds us that Babylon is not merely a threat to the Rastafarian or to the black person, but to the whole of the human race. The stereotyping of Babylon is thorough. For Marley, Babylon is not a a complex figure full of contradictions, Babylon is evil.

It is in the second round of the chorus that Marley makes clear that this is a song about taking out Babylon with music. This then becomes Marley's warrior anthem. For him music is the powerful force that will take out Babylon.

He speaks directly to music, trying in the process to co-opt it for the struggle. It is the only time Marley does this. He then creates this fascinating monologue in which he asks who music is to speak to, and then answers the question, 'Please talk to me'. He then asks music to carry the Rastafarian's voice to the world. It is Marley's cry to his muse, his cry to the source of his life and the source of his sense of purpose. He is praying for the ability to speak this music to the world.

There is the same optimism and energy in 'Jump Niyahbinghi', which is yet another attack on the system of Babylon. But Marley is a mood of celebration here, and there is a clear sense that he is optimistic about the struggle against Babylon. This is not the Marley weighed down with despair in *Uprising*. In this song, he is writing about the power of music. It is a celebration of music and Marley opens his heart to the audience to reveal what he truly enjoys about music. The party quality of the song is unquestionable and the rhythm of the song calls for the dancers to leap and jump in keeping with the spirit of Niyahbinghi. This is a song about Rastafarian survival through dance and through the act of chanting. It is also a celebration of the Rasta values – the use of the herb and the sense that a coming together to smoke, to dance and to chant down Babylon is a force for pleasure as well as for survival. If Marley is struggling for meaning and for hope in *Uprising*, here he is fully charged to create a party. Marley foregoes the conventional structure of verse and chorus and creates a lyric that keeps unfolding. The opening verse, which is repeated in virtually the same way with a few improvised variations, is a good example of the way Marley can create a relaxed tone that suggests a man talking to people he is familiar with. The audience is not full of strangers.

Carried by the worshipful shouts of the I-Three chanting 'Hallelujah', the singer comes onto the stage, and smiles at the rolling wave of bodies as they find the distinct hiccup of the reggae rhythm and begin to move in unison. Marley knows that there is nothing as powerful and affirming as the sight of a large audience finding the snaky feel of a reggae bass line and moving to its pulse together, as one. So he smiles at them and tells the audience that he is pleased. Then in a series of beautifully constructed phrases he begins to outline the nature of music and dance as a form of revolutionary action. It is action that must come from deep within. The dance that he, in an earlier song, commanded us all to do after forgetting the burdens of our troubles, is the same dance that he is celebrating here. Marley's ability to paint a scene is wonderfully demonstrated here. We hear in him a love for the hope of unity in the vision of people moving together to the rhythm in a dance or at a concert. But the dance is not external – it is not superficial, but, rather, it is a dance that comes from within; from the soul. The quality of togetherness is not uniform and militanistic, but individualistic – everyone is doing their own thing because they are doing it from their soul. The only requirement is that they do their best. The phrase 'dancing from within' brilliantly captures the spirit that Marley is reaching for in his art. It embraces what he thinks about the salvation of reggae music. The music is a soul thing and the response is also a soul thing. One cannot mistake here Marley's happiness – it is a far cry from the sombre tones of *Uprising*.

Then Marley personalizes the telling. He openly recalls and makes it clear that he is remembering. The sermon is intimate and the example that he turns to is plainly laid out. The story of the children of Israel marching around the walls of Jericho is one that has been the basis of many songs that children have sung again and again. It is a Sunday school lesson, the lesson of the people marching until the miracle of collapse takes place. It is not the first time that Marley has invoked that image. It is an image that is very important to him because, to all intents and purposes, the collapse of the walls of Jericho is prompted by music. It is when the trumpet sounds and when the stomping Israelites have circled the wall with their chanting and shouting that these walls fall.

The genius of this segue into the biblical scripture is the way in which Marley speaks of the story as if he was actually present there at the time too and, not only him, but also the people who are gathered. In one simple phrase, Marley transforms a passage of the Bible into a part of the narrative of his people: He speaks of the 'days in Jericho' as if he is speaking of the days in Trench Town. He does this effortlessly. Those who trampled down Jericho's walls are Marley and the audience. Time collapses and the power of that historical moment in time somehow reaches the present moment, turning the occasion of the song into a mythic one. Then he calls the audience to join him: 'Sing your song yah!' And one can imagine an audience leaping on the spot like Masai warriors as the song explodes in the chorus. This is a joyous moment, and yet there is a threatening undercurrent that would be lost on an audience that is not aware of the cult of Niyahbinghi and the history of that cult's relationship with Rastafarianism. It is a Marley moment. He is actually invoking far greater forces of resistance to Babylon than he appears to be doing. The Niyahbinghi sect of Rastafarianism drew its inspiration from Kenyan warriors who formed a secret society committed to battle the British white colonial force until death. Their central vow was to kill the white man. The term 'niyahbinghi' is directly associated with that vow. For Marley, of course, the wholesale murder of whites is not part of his call, but there is a sense in which he has transferred the force of this code to Babylon. That Babylon is often represented by the white man makes the song a decidedly radical one. The chorus and the entire song is drawing on the very thing that the Rastas committed to Niyahbinghi were noted for. Theirs was a dance that involved spinning, seemingly out of control hopping and leaping and the ritual flashing of the locks. Many have observed that Marley's own movements on stage replicated many of the Niyahbinghi movements. Marley is on stage enacting a spiritual act of worship and resistance. It is all connected.

Associated with the ritual of dancing is the ritual of the smoking of marijuana that, for Marley, constituted one of the ways to take on Babylon. The suru board is the rough burlap-covered board on which the ganja would be rubbed to remove seeds and other impurities. The ritual of cleaning the weed and making it ready for smoking is central to the act of rebellion. There is something of a taunting of the authorities in this statement. Yet the most telling statement in the chorus is the declaration that we can do what we want because 'we ain't got nothing to lose'. The force of that lies in a devil-may-care attitude that seems to underlie the song. It is not quite a statement of hopelessness, but a statement of faith, an assurance that there will be no loss with Jah on their side and, furthermore, those who are starting at the bottom can only go up.

Marley's energy here is contagious, and the song has the feel of a communal stomp, a collective howl that is reinforced by the constant wail of the I-Threes as they sing 'hallelujah', and by Marley goading and prodding the listener to sing a little louder and to jump.

The same energy drives 'Buffalo Soldier', a song that I must confess always puzzled me, and further puzzled me the more that I learned about the original Buffalo Soldiers. The song was a massive hit and has remained one of the most popular of Marley's songs in North America. The song is often credited to a collaboration between American producer Sporty and Marley. Marley recorded it during the *Kaya* tour in 1979 and it was released as a single. It is an important song because of what Marley is attempting to do here. He includes the African-American history into his song in a way that he has not done before in any direct way. Of course, Marley has always been in dialogue with the African-American musical tradition, but here he appropriates a narrative of some of the original rebels of African-American history and uses the story to construct a powerful statement about blacks in the Americas. Marley begins the song with the most important statement of all: 'Buffalo Soldier, Dreadlock Rasta'. His point is that they are one and the same. This is the basis of the song. This is the justification. They are one and the same because they share the same instinct for radical action. They share the same passion for being different, being outside the main stream. And, they are also locks-wearing people together. Marley is therefore telling a story that connects the histories of the Caribbean with the histories of the African American.

The story of the Buffalo Soldiers of the 19th century does not gel as comfortably with Marley's telling. The four cavalry and infantry regiments made up of African-American men who had done time in the Civil War are the subject of this song. But the story of this group of soldiers is quite complex. Their patriotism was unquestioned as they became a part of the process of defeating and subjugating the Native American population in America. It seems unlikely that Marley, a strong advocate of resistance against the system of Babylon, which would have been represented in acts like the destruction of native peoples, would see in the Buffalo Soldiers a model of Rasta resistance. But Marley's song draws on those things that appealed to him about the Buffalo Soldiers – their heroism, their capacity to do battle, their significance as figures of change in American history and the fact that all of this had been hidden from the world for so many years. Marley's telling, then, is not a mere retelling of history but the presentation of a proposition that celebrates the mystery and power of the African diaspora. The myth-making instinct that shaped the Rastafarian movement is the same one that operates here. Marley, then, is creating what I would like to call a meta-history that reaches, not for the details of history, but for a way of seeing this history and applying it to the present. I had no idea of the extent of Marley's popularity until I watched a crowd of revellers in a huge hall in Fredericton, New Brunswick in 1987, leaping in the air and screaming the chorus of 'Buffalo Soldier'. It was clear to me that they did not know what the rest of the song was saying, but they understood instinctively that the call was for them to leap and jump and chant and celebrate. 'Buffalo Soldier' had been a hit in the US and the UK and continues to be one of Marley's best-known songs. Given the themes of this song, this should not be the case. 'Buffalo Soldier', like many of the songs on *Confrontation*, is a clear statement about blackness and about the African diaspora.

Marley, however, is doing a great deal more in the song. His construction of a pan-America story of the black man in this hemisphere speaks to his desire to reach and gain a foothold in the African-American market. This was not an economic proposition but a desire by Marley to have his message reach this area of the world and his people in these areas. It is with that aim in mind that we can really understand the spirit of Buffalo Soldier, which makes an effort to show that there is a strong link between Rastafarians and African Americans. By declaring that the 'Buffalo Soldier' is a dreadlock Rasta, Marley is reminding us that the spirit of Rasta is a spirit of resistance and anti-Babylon struggle above anything else. Marley introduces his proposition as a personal one. He helps us to see him reasoning this out and coming to the conclusion that there is a connection between the Rastafarian and the Buffalo Soldier. The tone is conversational and there is a quiet sense of revelation that grows out of this reasoning. This truth is a knowledge of history that is important to Marley. He is fully aware that he is embarking on a stretch of reasoning. He is making an important argument that is bent on showing the connections between people of the African diaspora. He analyzes what he calls the 'stench' of conventional history telling and he finds sense in the proposition that the Dreadlocks Rasta is a descendant of the Buffalo Soldier. The logic is simple: they were both victims of slavery – taken from the same source and brought to the Americas. More than that, the Buffalo Soldiers are a romantic archetype – Western cowboys made famous by American films who were, unlike how they were portrayed in these films, black. At last a model of American romantic heroism that is defined by the black identity! It is important to Marley, however, because it is a long hidden truth of history.

Marley then goes on to associate himself with the Buffalo Soldier, declaring, 'I'm just a Buffalo Soldier…'. He selects one of the heroes of African-American history and identifies himself with this figure. The truth is that the Buffalo Soldiers were unsung heroes in America. Many blacks had no idea that there was a black military presence that fought in the Civil War. Few would know that at least 33,000 African Americans died on the union side in the Civil War and that, after the war, these soldiers, all regarded as a suspect group of humans by many of their white counterparts, formed two cavalry units that played a critical role for almost 30 years in the winning of the Western frontier for the American government. Their battles took them as far west as Mexico and deep into the heart of Texas. Many were called upon to do battle in the Dakotas and throughout the emerging frontier. They battled major Native American resistance groups, gangs of outlaws with such famous names as Billy the Kid, Poncho Villa, Geronimo and many other major figures of the unruly West. The fought in conjunction with Custer and Sherman and developed a reputation for effective skills as warriors and horsemen. On the eve of the 20th century, the units were disbanded. Many were collapsed into the rough riders who fought in wars in San Juan and Cuba. Indeed, the famous battle of San Juan Hill that involved Teddy Roosevelt was won largely because of the efforts of these black soldiers. Roosevelt was less than gracious in his acknowledgement of their role in saving him and his battle, but eventually the truth of their role was to be made known. The key element of the story that would have moved Marley was the fact that this grand story of heroism and dignity had been suppressed by Babylon for so long. So when he confronts his listeners who were clearly asking who these Buffalo Soldiers were, Marley is addressing this pattern of suppressing or distorting the history of Africans in the Americas. What Marley had learned clearly made a lot of sense to him.

In Marley's telling, the journey of the Buffalo Soldier is from victory in America to a kind of exile into the 'heart of the Caribbean'. Marley is constructing a lineage of warriorhood that he sees as his own. The Rastafarian attraction to the cavalry warriors is related to their fascination and celebration of the horseback riding soldiers that were led by Haile Selassie into war against the Italian army. The cover of *Confrontation* shows a stylized version of Bob Marley, armed with a lance, riding a white steed towards a massive dragon. The lance has pierced the breast of the dragon. This warrior image is an echo of the images of battle and warfare that we hear in the first three songs of the album. In each of the songs there is a battle cry, whether it is 'woy-yo-yo' of 'Buffalo Soldier', 'chant down, chant down, chant down Babylon' of 'Chant Down Babylon or 'jump, jump, jump Niyahbinghi'. The affirmation of victory is quite different from the edgy cynicism that marks much of the *Uprising* album. Of course, *Confrontation* is not an album put together by Marley. Hence there are songs that seem to be more suited to various moments in Marley's career.

'Mix Up, Mix Up' is a startling lyric because of the stream of consciousness that guides is meandering considerations. If there is a cynical quality in any of Marley's songs it is most strikingly revealed in this song. Marley is speaking to his imagined nay sayers who have appeared as fitting objects of his anger and reflection in songs like 'Running Away'. What is notable about this subject – this 'you' – is that there are moments when it is hard to distinguish the 'you' from an internal advocate that seems to creep up in Marley in many of his deeply reflective songs. I would not be surprised if 'Mix Up, Mix Up' was recorded during the *Uprising* sessions. The themes that emerge here seem to have a direct connection with the source of his anger and frustration during the months when he was putting together the *Uprising* tracks in England. 'Mix Up, Mix Up' was apparently culled together from a two-track recording by Marley that was found by Rita Marley in her archives. The original cut was a 25 minute ramble by Marley singing alone with an acoustic guitar. This recording revealed exactly how Marley composed his songs. Very often, it seems, Marley would simply record himself working through a melody and a series of lyrics, making changes as he went along until he felt he had something useful down. He would then file the recording until he was ready to bring it together in a full composition. Neville Garrick and Family Man Barrett took the extended recording and began to select segments from it and put them down on a rhythm that would work. The effect is a song that still seems like a rant. Lyrically, Marley was still searching for the best rhymes and the best transitions from one idea to another. Despite its limitations, this recording teaches us a great deal about the way Marley's imagination functioned and how he worked on his songs. There is something raw about this song – something unrefined, with his ideas being held together by the chorus.

It is no surprise that this song is perhaps one of the longest lyrics written by Marley. It is possible that Marley wrote this song specifically for Don Taylor, his manager, who had been found out in the 'mix up, mix up' (the duplicitous misappropriation of funds) that led to a terrible beating at the hands of Marley. The problem had bothered Marley greatly, and it would appear that several of the songs on *Uprising* were directed at Taylor. 'Mix Up, Mix Up' unfolds as a series of riddles that reveal

Marley trying to work through what has happened. He makes use of metaphors, and then finds himself leaving those metaphors behind for different ones. It is likely that Marley would have worked longer at bringing the lyrics into a more cohesive form before releasing the song had he lived to do so, but this is not to suggest that the song is weaker for it. The truth is that we can see in this song a great deal of Marley's way of creating his lyrics through improvisation and through a process of testing an image against another set of images. As he does this, he does not try to make all the ends line up comfortably and easily. Instead he allows himself a few ellipsis that come across as massive shifts from idea to idea. There is a post-modern surrealism to the way the song unfolds, because it is so much a song about a writer trying to put his thoughts together. The first verse emerges as a justification for his conviction that the culprit is really the person that has been accused even despite the denials by the culprit: 'He who hide the wrong he did / Surely did the wrong thing still.'

Marley then reaches for a metaphor that grows out of his experience. The studio becomes, for him, a place where he comes to understand the world and where he finds wisdom. The metaphor of recording is an interesting one here, because he uses it to suggest that the person who has lied is simply trying to put together another lie, another version. Marley says that he does not want another such version. The version, of course, is a term that was used in the Jamaican studios for various takes on a given track. The version was often the stripped-down recording of a given song that was used in the dancehall or used as the basis for DJs to chant their lyrics. The studio becomes a place where people experience 'the good and bad'. It is the 'studio of time and experience'. When Marley cries out that he wants a 'session' and not just 'another version', he is distinguishing between a recording moment that is fresh and one that is a mere repetition of material that has been done before. The deception is associated with the false art of those version sessions where real art does not take place. With the studio as a place of meaning and truth, a holy place, if you will, anything that threatens to destroy the truth of that environment is seen as an abomination, a terrible force: 'they're so much stumbling blocks right in-a our way'. The travesty is greed, which has become the daily interruption of the true vocation of the artist – to make music.

In the verse that follows, Marley then directly addresses the object of what can only be described as his intense anger. There is a boastful assertion of his power that emerges in this verse. It is a curious boast because it somehow privileges his sense of entitlement and a sense that he was called to be in a position of power. At first the statement that he was born in the country would seem to be a statement about his humble beginnings and the wisdom that comes from such an environment. But he is pointing to the fact that he was born on top of the hill. The suggestion here is that he was born in a position of power. The house on the hill was often the house that overlooked the land. The 'busha', or leading figure in the community, usually had a home on the hill. It was strategic for the slave holders to build their homes on the hill so that they could have a good vantage point in the event of a rebellion. Marley then says that he was born on the hill and he will remain on the hill – that nothing that this figure can do will unseat him from his position of power. The extent of the evil done is something that Marley lays out in lines full of a spontaneous anger and aggression. In all of this, the battle remains between the people of Jah and the evil of Babylon. He offers a proverb that is essentially a riddle. It unfolds into rather profound couplets.

Marley is arguing that to the fool, the deaf person, or the person who appears to be deaf, is actually a wise person. The deaf is wise simply because he is not hearing the lies of the fool. And by not hearing the lies that the fool tells, the deaf will manage to avoid the deception. The second part of the couplet extends this idea by suggesting that the wise person is able to either 'size up' (that is understand) or reduce the fool to his right diminutive size. Then Marley enters a mode that is quite callous and decidedly draconian. He wants to make sure that everything is cleared regardless of the consequences to those who will suffer as a result. The clearing of the wheels is a clearing of the business end of his career to ensure that progress is not stunted by anything done to undermine the smooth running of the wheels.

Marley then ends the song with a very odd moment of cynicism. He is the music man and he realises that it is music that the people want to hear and not this diatribe about all those who have cheated him and tried to do him wrong. So he assumes the voice of the listener when he asks, 'Hey? Mr Music, why don't you wanna play? / Don't you know today is a bright holiday?' Marley is clearly contrasting the desire for partying and lively music of the holiday with the clearly bitter words that he is singing in the song. To those who are 'waiting for the message that [he] bring[s]' and those who are 'listening to every word that [he'll] sing' he does not have joyous words to give. All he has to offer is the chant: 'too much mix up mix up'. One can't help but feel that when he then asks his audience if they will 'groove along now' he is being decidedly ironic.

I can't think of another Bob Marley song that is so filled with a level of anger and open irony that is never quite resolved. Of course the groove to this song is classically sweet and appealing and Marley, though sounding weary, appears to have a touch of laughter in his voice. It is this combination that helps us to understand even better the tone that drives this song. It is a song that does not have a turn for the better. Instead, Marley appears to be trying to justify his actions. If, indeed, I am correct in assuming that he is referring to Don Taylor and the two beatings that Taylor claims Marley gave him – a claim confirmed in court by Marley's closest friend, Alan 'Skill' Cole who said he held Taylor at gunpoint while Marley beat him) – then the song can be safely read as Marley rationalizing his actions without the slightest hint of regret or remorse at all.

'Give Thanks And Praises' is, therefore, the most unlikely of songs to follow 'Mix Up, Mix Up'. In the former, Marley is in a completely different mood and there is a striking contrast between his devotion and submission to the will of Jah in 'Give Thanks And Praises' and the self-assured willingness to take action himself that we see in 'Mix Up, Mix Up'. Of course, these are two traits that are both elemental to the Marley persona that emerges in his songs. 'Give Thanks And Praises', however, is as revealing a personal testament as anything Marley has written. Where a 1968 song 'Thank You Lord', which shares much of the devotional praise elements as 'I Know' and 'Give Thanks And Praises', would have the feel of a congregational worship service, and where the Wailers were still using 'Lord' instead of Jah, revealing the gradual movement towards full devotion to Rastafari, the songs on *Confrontation* are starkly personal. Marley stands alone as he sings. It is a defining moment in his work. Both 'I Know' and 'Give Thanks And Praises' present us with a Marley who is looking at the world as a tough and difficult place. We meet a man who has found that the path to his success and his hope is complete devotion to Jah. These two songs are testimonies of the faithfulness of Jah. But they are not vain testimonies filled with clichés of emotion and sentiment but are, instead, starkly honest confessions of vulnerability and metaphysical debates with the self about the relationship between the artist and his God. As doctrinal statements, these songs have much in common with the devotional poems of Herbert, Marvell and Donne, and the very carefully structured spiritual discourse of a poet like Gerard Manley Hopkins. For all of these artists, there is a set of beliefs that has come to shape their sense of the world, but each of them appreciates that arriving at faith in such a belief is not a given – that it takes a movement through doubt and uncertainty to arrive at devotion. Marley takes us through these moments towards faith in these songs. But, as with all devotional songs, this one emerges as a testimony, as a statement of faith after the fact. Therefore we are always aware throughout the chorus that there is a place of redemption at the core of the songs. As an expression of communal faith, this structure is not only necessary but is elemental. Furthermore, as with all devotional songs that are marked by the movement from suffering to redemption, Marley's songs are communal even while being deeply personal. His ability to balance these things is his clear genius.

The songs would have been composed at different times. 'I Know' was initially recorded during the *Rastaman Vibration* sessions. Marley had been playing with a funky rendering of some of his songs and this was one such experiment. The idea for the kind of straightforward funk backbeat riding an easy reggae style would eventually become realised in *Exodus*. But 'I Know' was shelved during the *Rastaman Vibration* sessions. The story is that while Marley was receiving treatment in Germany, fully aware that he was in very bad shape, he had the wherewithal to call, on an impulse, Family Man, and ask him to retrieve the track and release it in Jamaica as a extended mix single. Marley, no doubt, hoped to offer it as a message to the people of Jamaica who would have known of his illness. There is something quite haunting about this recording, particularly because Marley allowed us to interpret it in light of his illness. It is a statement of faith in the midst of terrible hardship and we can see how profound was Marley's sense of devotion to Jah.

'Give Thanks And Praises' appears to have been a later song and is normally seen as a response to the assassination attempt. Lyrically, however, Marley is exploring a great deal more than just that singular incident. The Marley that we have met throughout this book has been a man who has felt things deeply and carried the hurt of his history and his relationships on his shoulders – at least in his songs, which are as public as one can be. When Marley found himself sharing a small kitchen with Vincent Ford, his friend during the year or so after his mother had moved to the US and both Marley and Bunny Wailer had been evicted from the Trench Town home they had shared, there is no question that Marley appreciated the hardship of living in the ghetto. When he faced rejection and exploitation by the many producers he worked with, he would have felt even greater despair. When Marley's many efforts to 'make it' seemed to be thwarted by those who promised much then failed to live up to their promises, he would have felt a certain amount of despair. And when Marley watched the leaders of his country continue to create conditions that made the poor suffer and that led to the deaths of so many of his friends, Marley would sing about these things with a clear sense of pain. These tough circumstances are central to both songs. But they pale in the face of the illness that consumed his last few months – the sense of helplessness and the shattering of everything that he relied upon, his ability to make music, his ability to lead others by the force of his personality and by his work ethic, his ability to seduce and win the affections of women, his ability to play soccer – when all these where taken from him, and when all he was left with was his faith, Marley must have been confronting a terrible sense of despair. These two songs were not actually written during that period, but one can't help but associate the hope and faith found in them with his strong faith during those months.

Formally, 'Give Thanks And Praises' follows a rhetorically predictable pattern. It begins with the statement of faith that will become the chorus of the song. He is exhorting himself to give thanks to Jah, but he is also enacting this praise – that is the 'I' is implied in the line, 'Give thanks and praises'. But he is also calling his community to sing this song with him. Yet as soon as he enters the first verse, which turns out to be the only verse if we are to look at the song in conventional terms, we realise that this is a confessional song – a psalm that grows out of experience. Other musicians had written wonderful praise songs to Jah, most notably Peter Tosh's anthem 'Rastafari Is' and Third World's rendition of the much recorded, 'Satta A-Massa Gaana'. Yet in these the personal is held at bay. There is a communal strength to these songs. Marley's song has more in common with the deeply devotional songs by Culture, a group whose lead singer Joseph Hill made constant use of proverbs to frame his deeply evangelistic praise songs to Jah. Marley's lament of pain is compelling and deeply convincing. He begins a biblical basis for the praises that he is offering. That is he begins, not with the personal, but with the larger doctrinal rationale for his faith in Jah. The teachings about the origins of the black race that formed part of the racist rationale that shaped the principles of Christianity's complicity with slavery during the 19th century are invoked here. Marley's understanding of the Genesis scripture about the way that the world was divided after the flood is rooted in the traditional belief that the sons of Ham were in fact the African race.

While this same idea was thus interpreted by racist Europeans as a justification for the enslavement of blacks, Marley, in keeping with the teachings of Rastafari, offered this as proof of the divinity of Selassie, the elect status of Africans and the legitimacy of the prophecies that point to Selassie as the returned Messiah. Marley was always aware that this proposition was easily controversial and a stumbling block for those who did not believe. Marley assures the listeners that Jah will never deceive us and that the truth of prophecy will become manifest in due season.

When he commands us to remove the veil from our eyes, he alludes to Paul's metaphor about the way that we see the truths of prophecy. Paul proposed that we are looking through a veil darkly (or a dark veil) and that eventually the truth will be revealed. Paul himself was playing with an Old Testament notion of the veil that separated the Holy of

Holies where the host dwelled from the place where the believers could enter while they worshipped. When Christ died, the veil or curtain that separated the Holy of Holies from the rest of the temple is said, by scripture, to have torn 'asunder', symbolically, of course, demonstrating that the new dispensation of grace and access to the throne room was now at hand. Marley commands his listeners to take the veil from their eyes and to look at reality. This fixation on reality, on the here and now, is a critical feature of Rastafarianism, particularly the brand of Rasta that Marley espoused – one that was grounded in the everyday realities of life. Prophecy was not an ephemeral things hidden somewhere in the ether, but was, instead unfolding in the details of everyday life.

Anyone trying to follow the lines of this song would have likely, at some point, stumbled at the lines, 'Noah had three sons, Ham, Shem and Japhet / And in Ham is known to be the Prophet.' Marley manages to pack tightly into the line a rich narrative. Yet there is no sense of crowding when we listen to how he manages to make the melody embrace these lines. After the compaction of images and words in the first two lines, Marley then allows space for the moment of praise, and he does so by turning to a choric mode that is full of rich melodic sweetness. The declaration, repeated twice, is that the Prophet – namely Selassie – has arrived, and his arrival has eternal significance ('through all these ages' and 'through all these stages').

Then, without turning to a chorus, Marley's voice rises up again to offer the personal testimony that gives weight to the doctrinal teaching that he has just shared with the listener. The complex melodic line here is simply beautifully executed. They are lines full of emotional heights and reflective lows and then the comfort of the familiar. It is a personal confession of the healing power of Jah and his capacity to touch the deepest emotional needs of his children. Marley sings that when his soul was consumed by hurt at the deepest level and when he was desperately worried about being free, it was the guidance and protection of Jah that rescued him. Marley then quickly pulls us from the personal and expands the prayer to include 'I and I' – his people, who are the collective 'we'. But the beauty of the Rasta coinage 'I and I' is that Marley never has to lose the intimacy of his confession even as he reaches to include the larger community, for 'I and I' means both the 'I' of 'me' and 'us' of 'we', as we have seen. From there, Marley still does not return to the comfort of the chorus. There is a sense in which he is now building his case and the passion of his praise has gotten the better of him. His voice then rises into a literal wail with the ultimate declaration: 'Rastafari is his name!'. For the Rastafarian, this name is a sacred name and the speaking of the name is a holy moment. In concert, Marley would begin the evening, as would many other reggae artists, with a scripture that would end with the shout 'Jah' and the crowd would be expected to intone in response, 'Rastafari' as part of a communal act of benediction and worship. Then, just when we are sure that Marley is going to return to the chorus, he turns to a confessional chant that takes us to the heart of Marley's own considerations about his mortality. He asks two simple questions that turn out to be quite complex. The first is simple enough: 'If Jah didn't love I/.. Would I be around today?' Here he is celebrating the grace of Jah and his mercy in sparing Marley's life. The second is complex only because it introduces another Rastafarian tenet of faith that helps us understand something of Marley's own view of the world. He asks, 'If I didn't love I/... Would I be around today?' Is this a celebration of self-love? In a sense it is. The logic is that without a love of self the individual could have no sense of dignity and value. But the doctrine explored here is far more complex. Marley, like most Rastafarians, understood the scriptures, particularly the Book of Psalms and much of the New Testament, to be proposing the divinity of the individual believer. The idea of the 'I' is part of the mystery of the relationship between the individual and the divine. The name Selassie I is not normally spoken by Rastas as 'Selassie the first', but as Selassie-*I* – the letter assuming a mystical power that would make it one of the most magical vowels in Rasta speech. Thus, there is a sense in which the 'I' referred to in the second question is Selassie I himself but, more importantly, is Selassie as a presence in the 'I' of the individual too. But since we have seen that the 'I' is also a communal I, there is a suggestion of communal love in the lines too. That is, 'if I did love I and I' etc, but the bottom line is that without a love prompted by faith in Jah, survival would be impossible. Marley is not merely speaking, though, about the fact that he has survived the assassination attempt, but he is also speaking about his mission. With love and the message of Selassie's divinity as his mission in life, he is suggesting that it is the love that he believes in that is keeping him around at that point.

Out of this rich complex of ideas, Marley returns to the chorus. It has been a long time since he has offered that praise, but now we appreciate it more and we have the reason for praise. Just writing about the song is clearly inadequate. Listening to its full richness, the calming grace of the instrumentation and the worn voice of Marley invoking his faith with the most profound of tones is, quite simply, a spiritual moment.

'I Know' shares much of the confessional power of 'Give Thanks And Praises' but Marley is less intent on a biblical lesson here than he is in using the examples of everyday life – especially his own life – to give weight and credibility to what is for him an important truth. Where 'Give Thanks And Praises' is prayerful and often turns in on itself, 'I Know' is a monologue given to an audience. It is making an argument, pointing out that in the midst of the greatest hardship, there is one good piece of news, Jah will be waiting. Marley's love songs often explored the idea of waiting. Usually the singer is waiting for something to happen, for love to come down, for a tough lover to say yes. The unpredictability of these tenuous love hopes that we see in 'I'm Still Waiting,' 'Waiting In Vain' and 'Turn Your Lights Down' are shown to be fickle in the face of something more reliable – the love of Jah. What Marley does is to write a love song replacing the role of the lover with Jah. Thus when he turns to the hyperbole of the lover waiting through summer, winter, spring and autumn, Marley is employing the language of the Western pop song. These seasons mean very little to the Jamaican audience, but Marley's intentions are clear. He is painting Jah as the faithful lover who will wait patiently for the lover who may have gone astray, or the lover who has now come to see the need for his protection. Indeed, the opening stanza of the song could lead us to think that this is a love song. Marley's use of 'Natty' instead of 'Jah' in that stanza leads us to assume that the 'natty' is referring to himself, the Rastafarian lover.

What Marley does not do is offer a rosy picture of the world. The person he describes in the first stanza is faced with a great deal of pain and no small amount of despair. The person stops to think about his or her condition and concludes that he or she is a victim of the system. Instead of calling the 'you' to rise up and stomp the system, Marley gives hope. He offers assurances. For the person who finds himself struggling in a Sysiphean struggle, running in a race that seems virtually impossible to win, a moment of reflection will set things in order. It will become clear that the problem is not with the person who is struggling, but with the system that is set against the struggler. In the face of such a hopeless situation, there is only one answer. The system will let you down, but 'Natty' – Selassie – will not abandon the believer. In yet another piece marked by a fluid conversational syntax, but shaped around a consistent rhyme scheme, Marley describes in detail the nature of despair. First he alludes to the Pauline admonition to treat one's walk in the faith as a race. For Marley, the race has become quite difficult because the pace is too intense. The pressure is evident in the fact that the person he is describing is incapable of having fun because she/he keeps crying. The person is forced to wonder if she/he is 'a victim of the system'. The answer to the question is not far behind: the system is the culprit and it will constantly let down the believer. Having established in clear detail the symptoms of despair, Marley then assures the persona that Jah will be there to help.

By the time we come to the second verse, we are quite certain that this is a hymn to Jah. Marley then introduces the 'I' narrative to replace the 'you' narrative.

On the page the language seems self-consciously literary. The syntax of 'many a time I sit and wonder why' is as far from Jamaican patois as one can imagine. But Marley manages to combine the syntax of patois with the affected syntax of some of these lines to create a sound that is quite natural. On the recording none of this sounds affected, even if the cliché of the ship 'tossed and driven' does not represent the best of Marley's lyrics. But Marley does not rest for long in the clichéd image. Instead he creates something of a conceit from it. The poetic instinct at work here is quite accomplished. Using the ocean metaphor, Marley then offers an image of a unruly tide constituting change. The tide is an object of change and a symbol of the passing of time. In this instance though, this tide is flaming – there is a fire here that Marley fears. Therefore when he declares, 'Don't let the fury fall on me' the appeal is still rooted in the metaphor of the sea. The song's heart is what allows him to use the language that he does. The lines are self-conscious because they represent Marley admitting that he is contemplating the hardships of his life and that his song is about trying to work through these things. The conversational tone is achieved as Marley points out that his song is both a song for his soul and a song for his community. His word of encouragement to himself is the biblically derived 'take courage'. Given the circumstances that Marley was living with at the time, there is something quite powerful in the stunningly rendered imagery of the lines.

I have never quite understood the last refrain of the song – not fully, anyway. One imagines that there is a clear intent here, but even as I reach for meaning, I have the feeling I might be missing something. The idea of being 'lost' and then 'found' seems straightforward enough. The statement is part of the language of salvation and it would make sense that Marley is celebrating the fact that he was once lost and now he is found. The more puzzling phrase is 'speak I give', which he repeats a few times in this movement. The only way I have extracted some sense here is to simply ignore the word 'who' and then read the two verbs, speak and give as acts related to each other. Hence as he speaks he is giving and as he hears something spoken he gives it to the listener. There is a riddle here that could actually make sense. If indeed the theme of this movement is the revelation of truth – that is, that which is lost shall be found by the act of speaking and giving – then the lines have a coherence that is appealing.

'Blackman Redemption' is one of the few songs (the other notable one is 'Survival') in which Marley speaks directly of the black man as a subject. Of course it is implied in all his songs, but it is clear that Marley did not feel the need until later in his songwriting career to speak in the language of Black Power that guided his work in the mid- to late 1960s and the early 1970s. 'Blackman Redemption' is a return to the themes of songs like 'African Herbsman' and 'Black Progress' (a 1968 Perry production in which Marley chants – 'Black progress! / Got to get it / Black progress! / No matter what the cost / Black progress! / We've been down too long' while riding a James Brown-inspired rhythm). These were songs that drove the work of the Wailers when the clearly pro-Black Power advocate, Peter Tosh, was present in the group and when the spirit of the Black Power Movement had swept Jamaica. Marley's credentials as a Black Power advocate are not in question, but where Tosh would go on to write an anthem like 'Africans' ('No matter where you come from / As long as you're a black man / You're an African'), Marley would agree to alter the name of the *Survival* album from *Black Survival* to simply *Survival*.

In 'Blackman Redemption' Marley produces a song that is thoroughly public in that it is a chanting song that is geared for a collective singing. Almost all the way through, Marley is singing with his backing team. There are no stretches of solo singing here. It is a rousing anthem that captures the spirit of the three opening songs of the album – songs that are filled with optimism, a warrior's energy and a populist sensibility. The declarations are direct. He is prophesying that this is the time of the black man's redemption, and when he asks, 'can you stop it?' the answer returns, 'oh no!'. Marley then makes use of very current (at the time) language to challenge those who are worried about this cry for the redemption of the black man.

He employs the language of the youth of the time. To get 'bumpy' is to get disgruntled and nervous. The phrase 'cool runnings' was on the street at the time and Marley's song would make it even more popular. Like so many of the Jamaican phrases that connote a calmer approach to life, 'cool runnings' would becomes a term of greeting, a phrase of assurance and a symbol of peace. Finally, he then calls on the black man to 'spread out' as part of the redemptive process, which, no doubt, is the propagation of the black man around the world. This dispersal is derived from the promises that God made to Abraham about his seed – promises that Marley alludes to in his song 'Wake Up And Live' ('you're more than sand on the seashore / you're more than numbered'). In another movement, Marley connects the redemption of the black man with the arrival of Haile Selassie. After all, this is the point of the Rastafarian belief. Selassie is the Messiah who has come to fulfil the prophecy of Marcus Garvey, which is to redeem the lost children of Israel. But Marley makes it clear that while Selassie is the redeemer of the black man, his lineage is decidedly royal and biblically sound. He lays out the lineage of Haile Selassie in the middle of the song, and then continues to exhort those who may be panicked by this 'new' development, not to get 'jumpy' (scared) or to 'walk away'. Marley gently reminds his listeners that Selassie belongs to the house of David and comes from his lineage.

As a descendant of David, Selassie fulfils a necessary biblical requirement for the Messiah. Haile Selassie himself claimed this heritage for himself. The long history of Christianity and Judaism in Ethiopia made this kind of lineage as important to Ethiopian notions of monarchial authority as they were to the faith of the Rastafarians.

'Trench Town', which follows 'Blackman Redemption' on the album, is strikingly different in tone and style. 'Trench Town' shows Marley in a reflexive mood, contemplating the implications of his journey from the ghettoes of Trench Town to where he is now. It is a long journey. There is a quality of irony in the song, an irony borne out by the fact that Marley represents that 'good thing' that they said could never come out of Trench Town. Yet as reflexive as the song is, it is also a poignant lament about the persistence of poverty and hardship in the ghetto despite the years of promise and the years of so-called change in the society. Marley starts in the poet's place of quite contemplation. His is a pastoral setting. But here he is unable to enjoy the pastoral of 'Cane River'. He must, instead, return to the squalor of Trench Town and proceed to speak of the hardships that are still there. The song, though, finds its redemptive force in the very thing that Marley seems to return to whenever he is faced with the relentless truth of poverty and hardship. The lamentation about the poor is echoed fully by one other song on the album, 'Stiff Necked Fools' and, in both, is the song that is the path towards some hope. There is much in the thoughts of 'Trench Town' that remind us of Marley's philosophical questioning in 'Redemption Song'. Even if they were not written at around the same time, they share Marley's unwillingness to accept the idea that the poor are fated to remain poor and that the destruction of the poor is simply a part of it – a fulfilment of the book. Marley would prefer to sing his songs of freedom and free the people with music. As in many of the songs on this album, Marley assumes a rather conversational tone as he retells a narrative. This quality lends the song an intimacy that is only strengthened by the fact that we know that Marley is singing a tribute to Trench Town. But this should not be mistaken for a celebration of Trench Town as a wonderful place to live. That is not Marley's intention. For all his gratitude for the things that he learned in Trench Town, Bob Marley was never in danger of romanticizing the ghetto. He was more likely to romanticize the country but even then he saw the country as a place where people worked, where they saw the fruit of their labour and found dignity in the simplicity of that life. In the relative calm of the rural Cane River, Trench Town's stark conditions fill Marley with prophetic thoughts. His aim here is to suggest that despite the poverty of the ghetto, those who live there are people of dignity and people with a humanity that needs to be cherished and honoured.

Marley is at Cane River to purify himself. The cleansing of his dreads is a kind of re-baptism. The locks are a sacred feature of the Rastafarian and, as such, are treated with care and respect. At the same time, the cleansing of the locks becomes a metaphor for the removal of all impurities that may have gathered during the time down in the world. Marley is taking stock and trying to make sense of the things that have been seen. The fact of the 'oppression' that operates in Trench Town, comes, then, in a vision.

With the locks purification ceremony completed, Marley has ritually cleansed his mind and is now able to receive visions and revelations. It is not the oppressions that he sees. That is fairly obvious. The revelation comes 'through' the sea of oppression. It is thus a revelation that transcends the oppression and that arrives despite the oppression. His prayer is that he will not be a prisoner. This hope is especially telling as he sits in the relative openness of the hills. But Marley understands that there are many prisons beyond the physical prison of jail (which was always a real threat for Marley). The prison of the mind and the chains of spiritual enslavement are themes that we see again and again in Marley's songs.

In the second verse, Marley's disquiet is vividly captured in the weariness of his tone and in the manner in which the verse opens: 'Oh, my head'.

This metaphor of the head or the mind as a battleground for the dread is important. Despite the cleansing, the vision takes Marley back to a place of unease. The reasons are clearly laid out. The first is the desperate condition that operates for those who are trying to find something to eat. Hunger is, for Marley, one of the critical causes for the kind of behaviour that is destructive to the soul. In 'Ambush In The Night' he reminds us that it's when the quest for food becomes quite pressing that one begins to betray one's brother. In 'Them Belly Full' he declares, 'a hungry mob is an angry mob'. In 'Soh Jah Seh' he prophecies that 'not one of my sheep / Shall sit in the side walk and beg bread.' It is not a reality – it is a prayer, a hope. Marley understood hunger. He himself would experience the kind of hunger that would force him to depend on friends in the ghetto like Joe Higgs, Coxsone Dodd, Lee 'Scratch' Perry and his close friend Vincent Ford for a simple meal just to get through the day. Marley's devotion to music and his determination to make a success of his life through it is quite likely what kept him from turning to other desperate measures for a meal. So when he sings of those 'desolate places' to find bread, he is speaking of the things that many had to do to find a meal. Rita Marley talked about the fact that when they lived in the ghetto they often sought food in the dump grounds by the seashore. In the face of such unquestionable hardships, the fatalistic suggestion that it is just 'another page in history' sounds like the resignation of the line, 'we've got to fulfil the book' in 'Redemption Song'.

Marley's answer to this seeming hopelessness is to remind himself of what he does. His only recourse is music. The music is a music of faith and struggle. It is the way that Marley speaks despite those who say it is hard for him and the people of Trench Town to speak. According to Marley in this song, it is love that will bring about some change and some redemption. As in many of Marley's complaints about Babylon, there is here a promise of retribution to those who he sees as being responsible for the poverty and hardship of the ghetto. Babylon's intention is always to tell the poor that they cannot speak and that they do not have a voice. In many ways, Marley's art and the art of many reggae artists of his generation was to change the perception of the ignorance of the poor and so-called uneducated. These voices would emerge as their own individual voices, voices that no longer relied on some middle-class, educated speaker to speak on behalf of the poor person. The art of Marley would bring those who once spoke for the poor to learn from the poor. The music of Marley is the source of power and liberation, the power that will bring retribution and order to the universe.

So when Marley quotes them in their insulting question, 'can anything come out of Trench Town?' he is being ironic. Something good has come out of Trench Town. It is the music, it is Marley, it is this revolutionary art that will defy all those who dismiss Rastafarians and poor people.

'Stiff Necked Fools' is one of those Marley songs that relies heavily and almost exclusively on the use of scripture. While we have shown many instances where Marley used scripture and where Marley's songs were indeed fairly sophisticated exegesis of scripture, it would be helpful to trace the way in which he applied doctrine to song in this composition both because of what it tells us about the songwriting strengths of Marley, and because it allows us to appreciate more his understanding of his role as a prophet and teacher in his community.

Marley quotes proverbs, psalms and from the prophets in a song that belongs quite clearly to the *Exodus/Kaya* period. There is very little here that was not treated in a song like 'Heathen' for instance. But where 'Heathen' has a combative edge, 'Stiff Necked Fools' turns out to be a fairly complex discussion about his role as a teacher of the ignorant. By definition, the stiff-necked fool, is, of course, a person who hears truth and does not obey or heed the truth because his neck is so set in old ways that he is completely incapable of change. The 'stiff-necked' person is quite different from Babylon. In the Book of Exodus where the phrase first appears in the Old Testament, God is speaking to the children of Israel and reprimanding them for being a 'stiff-necked' people because they disobeyed God by building a golden calf to worship out of their frustration with God. God tells Moses that these people are a stiff-necked people who have angered him. He leaves them to suffer while he deals with his anger. God tells Moses that he will then build a nation out of them (Exodus 32:9).

What is most important is these people are not aware of how wayward they are. Marley presents them as a people who think they are cool when, in fact, they are fools. Their failure, of course, is vanity, a sin to which Solomon devotes at least two books. In Proverbs and Ecclesiastes, Solomon outlines the hopelessness and futility of vanity. Vanity constitutes the kind of hubris that leads man to perceive of the temporal as the central thing of worth in life. It is a function of pride and one that is dealt with by destruction. Marley quotes the Book of Romans when he accuses the stiff-necked fools of being 'mixed up with vain imagination'. Paul had offered the same censure against those who had seen the truth of God's existence in his creation and had somehow turned to their own way of thinking, forcing God to give them up to their sinful nature (Romans 1:21).

The stiff-necked fool that Marley describes is a lover of vanity and a hater of simplicity. This vanity is blinding and leads to wrong interpretations of scriptures. The answer to this act of vanity and the foolishness of vain imaginings, according to Marley, is to recognise the truth of God's power in nature. In a sense, Marley is offering the same answer that Paul presents in the Book of Romans. Marley is virtually paraphrasing the sentiment of the scripture in these lines. Paul's letter to the Romans states in the King James Version:

> For the invisible things of him from the creation of the world are clearly seen, being understood by the things that are made, even his eternal power and Godhead; so that they are without excuse; Because that when they knew God, they glorified him not as God, neither were thankful; but became vain in their imaginations, and their foolish heart was darkened. Professing themselves to be wise, they became fools. And changed the glory of the incorruptible God into an image made like to corruptible man, and to birds, and fourfooted beasts and creeping things. (Romans 1:20–22)

Paul is alluding to the actions of the children of Israel who turned to the worship of the golden calf when they began to doubt that God would rescue them from the desert. Marley recognizes the connection between the two scriptures and quotes them in a way that forces us to appreciate that he is speaking about the hubris of man to allow his imagination to dictate the nature of his relationship with the world and with God.

Marley renders the truth of this scripture, which argues that ignorance of the truth of God – his deity and authority as creator – is without excuse since he has revealed himself in the things created, by calling on the ignorant and the fools to allow the evidence of Jah's creation to erase their 'fantasy' and their 'vain imaginations'.

In the verses that follow, Marley quotes from the Book of Proverbs and, at the same time, constructs a series of teachings that give attention to the role of the teacher or, as in his case, the singer, in the larger community. He alters the lines of the proverbs as he works towards a truth about the struggle that the person who is seeking to teach those who are stubborn has. Solomon in the Book of Proverbs, states: 'The lips of the righteous feed many / but fools die for want of wisdom.' (Proverbs 10:15). Marley renders it as: 'The lips of the righteous teach many, / But fools die for want of wisdom.' The use of 'teach' instead of 'feed' may have been prompted by a particular translation (although I could find none that used this rendering), but it is easy to see why Marley would have preferred 'teach'. Apart from the logic inherent in the use of the word since the passage is about teaching, after all, it is clear that Marley sought to bring the proverb in line with the central message of his song. He follows this with another proverb from Solomon: 'The rich man's wealth is in his city; / The righteous' wealth is in his Holy Place'. The second part of this does not appear in this form in the Book of Proverbs, but the sentiment and the meaning are at the core of the Book of Proverbs and the Book of Ecclesiastes. Solomon teaches that 'The rich man's wealth is his strong city: the destruction of the poor is their poverty.' (Proverbs 10:21). Marley takes these verses and puts them together in a series of observations that allow him to explore the rich metaphor and imagery that the Bible uses.

In the 'we/them' praxis, the rich man finds his wealth in the city – a true symbol, for Marley, of Babylon. In 'Ride Natty' Marley's apocalypse takes place in the city where there is great panic. The city is the fortress where Babylon rules. In Jamaica, the power that rules the cities is the police, who are almost synonymous with city existence. The righteous, on the other hand, places his riches in heaven. This is an allusion to a letter from Paul to Timothy in the New Testament where he encourages

Timothy to exhort the rich in his congregation not to rely on their earthly riches but to gather a store of righteousness in heaven where things are eternal. Marley is also alluding to a psalm that celebrates the principle of finding riches in righteousness, which cannot be destroyed by time.

Having established this order of truth, Marley then begins to dialogue with the stiff-necked fools, trying to determine how he is going to react to their reluctance. In the books of Exodus and Romans, God's decision is to leave them alone to their vain imaginations. He punishes them by allowing the consequences of their vanity to carry out a punishment. In other words, God does not wrestle with them. But Moses pleads with God on behalf of the children of Israel and God eventually relents. Marley, as the prophet, faces the same dilemma. He makes it clear that he is not sure whether he wants to devote the time and energy to teach a people who will not listen. Marley is the reluctant prophet who seems to want to dust off his feet and move on. He forcefully explains what he does not want to do. He does not want to rule, fool or school the people. In other words he is reluctant to be their leader. Yet, despite saying that, he continues to speak to them, trying somehow to point them away from their ignorance.

Marley does not resolve the dilemma. He leaves the song in limbo and we are left to question whether he plans to continue to struggle with fools. Of course, the very presence of the song constitutes a contradiction because it is a teaching. It is an attempt to make right by offering wisdom. What we see here is that Marley made constant use of the Bible but never simply quoted scriptures without a clear interpretive bent. His reading of the Bible was always sophisticated and complex. That he did not resolve some of the dilemmas raised in these scriptures speaks to an honesty about how to apply scripture to his life and to his relationship with his community.

In this, as well as many songs, Marley found ways to make contemporary and relevant the archaic language of the King James Bible. He did this by capitalizing on the regal cadence of the Elizabethan language while making syntactic and lexical alteration to somehow localize the scriptures. One of the most telling examples of this act of 'creolization' comes in the final song of the album, 'Rastaman Live Up'. The song was co-written with Lee 'Scratch' Perry and was likely to have been composed during the late 1970s. The simplified verse/chorus structure reflects Perry's influence as he tended to prefer simple song structures – this allowed him to carry out his experimentations with sound and musical arrangement. Structurally, the song unfolds as a collaborative song might. The verses emerge one after the other with self-contained lessons – teachings shaped by biblical passages that, while pointing to the admonition to the Rasta to 'live up', are stand-alone ideas. The song contains a medley of references to the Bible, but these are allusions and brief retellings of the scriptures that are meant to encourage the believer about the faithfulness of Jah.

The song is a grand command to the Rastaman to 'live up'. There is much that is packed into the phrase 'live up'. In an earlier Marley song, 'Crisis', which was also influenced by Perry, Marley calls on Rastas to 'live it up, live it up' by giving 'Jah all the thanks and praises'. The phrase is, at one level, a shortened version of 'living upful', which is as close to an admonition to live a righteous life as there is. On another level, there is a double positive in the phrase 'live up' that elevates the challenge to live into something more proactive and total. There is also the suggestion of the phrase 'lively up', which points to something that is quite the opposite of the dead existence associated with Babylon. Living in an upful manner is a call to live in a way that is filled with the effort to do the right things. To 'live up' is to live a life committed to the teachings of Rastafari and to live without compromise. The song is saying all of these things and more. And Marley manages to say all this in a language that is distinctly his own. There is nothing as amusing and yet telling as the way in which he renders the Sunday school lesson catchphrase 'the jawbone of an ass' into the very Jamaican, 'donkey jawbone'. One is efficient and to the point – it manages to take away the mystery of myth from the narrative by bringing to it a stark realism. In doing this, Marley is pointing to the pragmatic and Earth-centred position of the Rasta doctrine.

The song begins with a clear addressing of the Rastaman. The various names are all important. The 'bongoman' refers to the Rastaman's connection with the drum; the 'congoman' refers to his connection with

Africa; and the 'binghi-man' is a reference to the Niyahbinghi cult of Rastafarianism. As the song continues 'Natty Dread' and 'Iyaman' (or 'Higher Man') are added to the list. The 'Iyaman' draws on the ubiquitous 'I' in Rasta discourse but in this instance it is transformed to the word 'high', which is rendered without the 'h' in Rasta and Jamaican speech. So the 'Iyaman' is both the 'I-man' and the 'Higher man'. The African connection is very important here as Marley, like most Rastas, understood that one of the curious insults directed at the Rastas was to associate them with the so called backwardness of Africa. The simple irony is that this was the kind of connection that Rastas wanted to draw attention to. Marley then echoes a statement that he used in 'Natty Dread' when he encouraged the 'children' to 'get their culture'. The need for culture is critical to the Rastafarian because the key weapon of Babylon is to take away the black man's culture and the black man's pride in that culture. The deprivation of a people of its culture is the act of the ubiquitous vulture that recurs in so many reggae songs. These predatory images are used repeatedly in Marley's songs to refer to Babylon. The growing of the dreadlocks and the preservation of culture are two acts of defiance against Babylon that the Rasta is encouraged to carry out in this song.

By positioning the Rasta as an underdog battling against the overwhelming forces of Babylon, Marley and Perry construct an epic narrative that is key to the attitude of the Rastafarian in a hostile world. To give emphasis to this struggle, Marley makes use of the story of David and Goliath as well as the story of Samson and the Philistines. The Babylonian enemy is the same in both examples, and the odds here do not appear to be in favour of either of these two men of God. David is a crucial figure in Rastafarian mythology. David is the root of the throne and it is through the lineage of David that Selassie emerges as the conquering Lion of the tribe of Judah. Samson is important because he represents the Nazarene code from which the teachings about growing the locks and not allowing a razor to cut those locks is at least in part derived. Samson's slaying of the Philistines with the most crude of implements and David's use of a slingshot to kill Goliath are both critical metaphors for Marley, for both men make use of the most unlikely implements to carry out the greatest miracles. Marley often saw his music as such a tool – a simple weapon that could transform the world.

In the third verse, the image of the Rastaman walking through 'creation' is one that echoes so many of Marley's lyrics about the Rasta as a figure who spends time owning the landscape by walking. The image of the Rastafarian was almost always associated with walking in the Kingston where I grew up. Rastas tended to walk great distances, either selling their wears (brooms and other crafts) or simply as they preached their faith to others. The Rastafarian was one who walked, and in walking enacted the ritual of journey – the nomadic journey of the son of man who has nowhere to lay his head. Marley alludes to the prophecies of Hosea who promised that in the last days, when the Spirit was poured out on the believers, 'young men would dream visions'. For Marley and Perry, these were the last days and the apocalyptic Armageddon was at hand.

In the final verse of the song the connection to the end times is maintained but the allusion is to an earlier scripture that actually is the basis of the concept of Babylon. The theory of Babylon begins with the Tower of Babel where mankind sought to create a world with a single language and a single way of viewing the word. God did not like the homogenization of his creation and so struck the people with the gift of multiple languages and thus prompted a scattering of people across nations. This miraculous act of confounding the Babel people with language is something that Marley and Perry relish greatly and so the confounding that takes place when people are unable to grasp Rasta talk is seen as not only appropriate but the preferred outcome. The song suggests that all attempts to try and collect the powers of the world under a single titular ruler will be confounded. Rasta teaching tended to share the same end-time view of the world with evangelical Christians. Rastas often cited the Pope as the head of a new regime. The Pope in some renderings was the anti-Christ. All of this was to be confounded in these times ('iwa'=hour), as it was in the past.

The song ends with a prophecy that points to a militancy in the Rastafarian' 'A-tell you, one man a-walkin'; / And a billion man a-sparkin'.' Like David and Goliath, contained in the relatively small numbers of Rastas is the force and strength of a million men. This cult of the underdog gave strength and authority to Rastas and shaped the way that Marley saw the world and also sought to face it.

Epilogue

Lillian Allen, the Canadian-based Jamaican dub poet, likes to speak of the 'University of Bob Marley'. What she means is that in his heart there is so much that can be studied and so much that can be learned about history, human emotion, politics and about the deep inner workings of the imagination. In many ways, I have always known the Marley of the political and religious statement – the Marley whose poetic was public and totally inscribed in the dynamics of social consciousness. The Marley, however, who touched me as an artist and as a man was the Marley who showed himself to be a wholly modern artist – a man who saw his art as a way to express experience and to try and bring order to the chaos of his life. This book has forced me to work through this more complex figure, whose art and life offer contradictory expressions that make for the most beautiful and meaningful of creations.

There is something inadequate about this book and that is how it ought to be. I have found myself realising that I could actually have devoted whole chapters to individual Marley songs, charting the range of allusions and the craft of his songwriting. Indeed I could have explored every one of the allusions contained in the songs – the allusions to the work of other artists, to Jamaican proverbs, to history and to the Bible. I could then have gone even further and shown how his art has influenced the work of other songwriters, poets, novelists, dancers and artists. Just text on 'Revolution' alone could have become a huge chapter in itself. This realisation is at once humbling and the source of pride and vindication. Pride and vindication because it confirms what I have always suspected – that there is a genius to the art of Marley.

There is much more to write about Marley, work that goes beyond the biographies to enter further into his imagination and art. The songs that he wrote between 1961 and 1973 offer a powerful story of the shaping of an artist's imagination and they fill me with that strange, stomach-flipping sensation of nostalgia – a memory of the gummy heat of Kingston, the terrible violence, the pungent smell of mango, the acrid scent of a city's exhaust, the socialist euphoria, the Holy Ghost's flaming sword in my heart, the sound of a woman's laughter and that adolescent fear that I will remain impossibly horny for the rest of my life. Marley sits at the centre of these moments with his ska, rock steady and early reggae music so full of its contradictions, fears and passions.

There is something validating about a book that ends with the hope of another book. What I feel is not fatigue, but an excitement to try and make a bid for my PhD at the University of Bob Marley.

Bibliography

Booker, Cedella, *Bob Marley: An Intimate Portrait By His Mother*, Viking: 1996.

Bradley, Lloyd, *Bass Culture: When Reggae Was King*, Viking: 2000.

Bradley, Lloyd, *Reggae on CD: The Essential Guide*, Kyle Cathie: 1996.

Bradley, Lloyd, *This is Reggae Music: The Story Of Jamaica's Music*, Grove: 2000.

Danticatt, Edwidge, *After the Dance*, Crown: 2002.

Davis, Stephen, *Bob Marley: Conquering Lion Of Reggae*, Plexus: 1983.

Dawes, Kwame, *Natural Mysticism: Towards A New Reggae Aesthetic*, Peepal Tree:1999.

Edmonds, Ennis. *Rastafari: From Outcasts to Culture Bearers*, OUP

(forthcoming)

Foehr, Stephen, *Waking Up In Jamaica*, Sanctuary Publishing: 2002.

Foster, Chuck, *Roots, Rock, Reggae: An Oral History Of Reggae Music Ska to Dancehall*, Billboard: 1999.

Haskins, James, *One Love, One Heart: A History Of Reggae*, Jump at the Sun: 2002.

Hausman, Gerald, *The Kebra Nagast: The Lost Bible Of Rastafarian Wisdom And Faith From Ethiopia And Jamaica*, St Martins:

1997.

Hawkes, Harry (transcriber), *Songs of Freedom: Complete Lyrics Of Bob Marley*, Omnibus: 2001.

Katz, David, *People Funny Boy: The Genius Of Lee 'Scratch' Perry*, Payback Press: 2000.

Macann, Ian, ed, *Bob Marley: In His Own Words*, Omnibus Press: 1997.

Morrow, Chris, *Stir It Up: Reggae Cover Art*, Thames and Hudson: 1999).

Prahlad, Anand, Sw, *Reggae Wisdom: Proverbs In Jamaican Music*, Jacakson: 2001.

Salewicz, Chris and Adrian Boot, *Reggae Explosion: The Story Of Jamaican Music*, Harry N Abrams: 2001.

Stolzoff, C. Norman, *Wake The Town And Tell The People: Dancehall Culture In Jamaica*, Duke University Press: 2000.

Index

Album titles are in italics; individual songs are in single quotes.

'Adam And Eve' 299
Africa: as Jamaican homeland 22, 25-7, 58, 60; links with Jamaica 109; Marley and 46, 79-80, 273; pan-Africanism 177, 179, 272-3, (see also Ethiopia)
'Africa Unite' 267, 272-3
African Herbsman 65
'African Herbsman' 196, 335
African-Americans, Marley and 161-2
'Africans' (Peter Tosh) 336
Afro-Christian sects 142
'All Day All Night' 60
'All You Need Is Love' (The Beatles) 234
Alphonso, Roland 32
Althea and Donna 258-9
'Ambush In The Night' 34, 279-83, 301, 339
American language, in Marley's songs 114

'Ammaggedon Time' (Willie Williams) 187
Anderson, Beverly 59, 109
Anderson, Esther 132-3

'Baby We've Got A Date' 63, 64
Babylon 76, 78, 141-2, 250-1, 257, 266, 278-9, 316; Trench Town as 143, 145
'Babylon System' 67, 265-8, 301
'Babylon You Throne Gone Down' (chant) 76
backing singers: I-Threes 136; male 209, 241, 295
'Bad Card' 293
'Badness Nuh Pay' (Leroy Smart) 187
Barrett, Aston 'Family Man' 113, 115, 211, 223, 324, 328
Barrett, Carlton 113, 178, 211, 274, 275, 316
'Battering Down Sentence' 92
Beatles, The 234

'Bend Down Low' 113, 218
'Better Must Come' (Delroy Wilson) 59
Bible: and Rastafarianism 78-9, 142-3; Marley's use of 29, 94-5, 137, 270, 301, 309, 341, 343; Apocrypha 24; Corinthians 90, 200; Daniel 270; Ecclesiastes 90, 308, 341; Exodus 207, 340, 343; Genesis 330; Hebrews 201; Isaiah 164-5, 210; King James version 90, 120, 307-8, 343; Lamentations of Jeremiah 276; Proverbs 176, 262, 301, 307, 341, 342; Psalms 23, 29-30, 90, 91, 165, 253, 265, 273, 307, 332; Revelations 78, 264, 278; Romans 341, 343; Song of Songs 216, 219
'Black Heart Man' (Bunny Wailer) 98

Black Power 171, 336
'Black Progress' 57
Black Survival (original
    title of *Survival*) 45,
    269
Black Uhuru 274, 302
'Blackman Redemption'
    45, 336-7
Blackwell, Chris 18, 47,
    60, 74, 160, 184, 221
blues 69, 148
'Bob Marley: Songs of
    Freedom' 33
Bogle, Paul 26, 67, 199
Booker, Cedella
    (Marley's mother) 28,
    30, 46, 51, 166
'Border' (Gregory Isaacs)
    313
'Brainwashing' 88-9
Breakspeare, Cindy 34,
    183, 189, 217, 229,
    296-7
Brooks, Cedric IM 109
Brown, Dennis 155-6,
    187, 213, 274
Brown, James 57, 113,
    303
brukkins 124
'Buffalo Soldier' 315,
    320-3
Burnin' 40, 41, 42, 75-
    100
'Burnin' And Lootin" 42,
    53-4, 75, 84-9, 115-
    16, 253, 316-17
Burning Spear 55, 56,
    155-6, 313
Burru men 93, 124
Byron Lee and the
    Dragonaires 287

carnival 130
Catch A Fire 40-78;
    album cover 40;

critical reception 75;
    songs eliminated by
    Blackwell 60
'Chances Are' 228
Channer, Colin 107-8
'Chant Down Babylon'
    55, 197, 314, 315-17,
    323
Christ (see Jesus Christ)
the church 30, 150, 267-
    8; American
    evangelists 290; Pope
    250, 346
CIA in Jamaica 175-6,
    247
Clapton, Eric 82-3
Cliff, Jimmy 42, 59, 86,
    209
Cogill, L 113
Cole, Alan 'Skill' 8-9,
    74, 132-3, 178, 327
'Coming In From The
    Cold' 291-3
'Concrete Jungle' 41-2,
    42, 43, 47-51, 54, 55-
    6, 302, 311
Confrontation 245, 267-
    8, 314-47; cover 323
Cook, Sam 100
'Could You Be Loved'
    300-4
Count Ossie 60, 77, 109
counting songs 144, 224,
    295
'Crazy Baldheads' 67,
    141, 169, 171-4
'Crisis' 235, 236-7, 344
'Cry To Me' 62, 165,
    166, 168
Culture 183, 330

dance 124-5, 126-7,
    130-1, 273
Danticatt, Edwidge 130
Davis, Stephen 35, 132-

3, 178, 202, 214, 242
Dekker, Desmond 42
Delaware, Marley in
    176-7
dinki mini 124
'Do It Twice' 63, 121
Dobson, Diane 35, 215
Dodd, Coxsone 18, 36,
    98, 156, 339
'Don't Rock My Boat'
    (original title of
    'Satisfy My Soul') 62-
    3, 226-7
'Downpressorman'
    (Peter Tosh) 202
'Dreamland' 187
drugs: and Marley 53-4,
    88, 129-30, (see also
    marijuana)
drumming 77, 109, (see
    also *Burru men*)
Drummond, Don 32
Dunbar, Sly 274
'Duppy Conqueror' 75,
    92-6
Dylan, Bob 82
Dynamic Sounds 91

'Easy Skanking' 232,
    234
Ethiopia 142, 206-7,
    272-3; as homeland
    22, 25-7, 58, 60;
    importance to
    Rastafarians 23-4;
    Marley in 249-50;
    repatriation to 58, 79,
    206-7, 272-3, (see
    also *Africa; Zion*)
Ethiopian Orthodox
    Church 201
Exodus 37, 62, 181-244,
    307; as album of the
    20th century 192-3
'Exodus' 206-10

Family Man (see *Barrett, Aston*)
Farley, Christopher John 192
Federal Records 91
'Fly Away Home' (chant) 76
fools 307
Ford, Vincent 'Tartar' 113, 329, 339
'Forever Loving Jah' 200, 304-8
'400 years' 68, 69
The Fugees 121

Gabon tour 291, 316
Garrick, Neville 45, 46, 182, 189, 246, 267-8, 291, 324
Garvey, Marcus 19, 26-7, 55, 67, 198, 206, 273
Gaye, Marvin 100, 220, 295
'Get Up, Stand Up' 42, 75, 79, 135, 268; (Babylon By Bus) 275
'Give Thanks And Praises' 315, 328-33
'Great Men' (Burning Spear) 55
Griffith, Marcia 62, 135
'Guava Jelly' 62
'Guiltiness' 34, 202-3, 280

Habbakuk 208
Haile Selassie (Rastafari) (see *Selassie, Haile*)
'Hallelujah Time' 96
'The Harder They Come' (Jimmy Cliff) 42
'Harlem' (Langston Hughes) 84
Havens, Richie 78, 96

'The Heathen' 202, 203-5, 238, 280
Henzel, Perry, *The Harder They Come* 42-3, 59, 85
Hibbert, Toots 171
Higgs, Joe 28, 32, 74, 339
'High Tide or Low Tide' 60
Hill, Joseph 330
'Hot Like A Melting Pot' (Dennis Brown) 187
'How Many' 63
'How Many Times' 228
Howell, Leonard 124
Hughes, Langston 84, 172
'Hurting Inside' 243
Hussey, Dermot 82, 242

'I and I' 137-8, 331-2
'I Know' 315, 327, 328, 333-6
'I Like It Like This' (version of 'Satisfy My Soul') 226
'I Man Born Ya' (Pluto Shervington) 187
'I Shot The Sheriff' 42, 67, 75, 80-4, 157, 171
I-Threes 135, 229, 302
'Igzibier' (Peter Tosh) 187
'I'll Fly Away' 79-80
'I'm Still Waiting' 62, 333
'Is This Love?' 48, 215, 216, 221-2
Isaacs, Gregory 63, 213, 313
Island Records 37, (see also *Blackwell, Chris*)
'It Hurts To Be Alone' 62

'It's Alright' 176-7

JAD Records 60, 112
'Jah Live' 21, 185, 193, 307
Jamaica: Africa as homeland 22, 25-7, 58, 60; in late 70s 184-7; links with Africa 109; Marley and 28, 141, 188, 252, 305; politics (see *politics, Jamaica*)
Jamaica Labour Party (JLP) 151-2, 175-6, 200, 247-8, 287
Jamaican dialect, Marley's use of 19, 83, 122-3, 127-8, 167, 277
'Jamming' 207-8, 210-12
Jesus Christ 198, 201, 272; and Selassie 21-2
JLP (see *Jamaica Labour Party*)
'Jogging' (Freddie MacGregor) 187, 302
John, Elton 82
'Johnny Too Bad' (Slickers) 42
'Johnny Was' 162-5
'Judge Not' 34, 166, 301-2
'Jump Niyahbinghi' 311, 314, 317-20, 323

Kaya 37, 41, 62, 130, 181-244, 249
'Kaya' 41, 224, 232
Kebra Negast 23, 24
'Keep On Moving' 190
King James Bible (see *Bible, King James version*)

King, Martin Luther Jr
19
'Kinky Reggae' 40, 41,
70, 72-4
Kong, Leslie 18, 156
Kumina (dance) 124

language (see *American
language; Jamaican
dialect*)
'Legalize It' (Tosh) 98
'Let's Get It On' (Marvin
Gaye) 100, 220
'Lick Samba' 63, 64
Liele, George 25
Light of Saba Band 109
Lindo, Earl 'Wire' 316
'Lively Up Yourself' 112-
13, 113-15, 161
Lomax brothers 77
'Lonesome Feeling' 62
love songs, Marley's 41,
46-7, 60-5, 116, 121,
183, 213-14, 215-17

MacGregor, Freddie 187,
302
Mackay, Freddie 187
Magan, Joseph 187
Malcolm, Omeriah
(Marley's grandfather)
28, 166
Malcolm X 19
Manley, Michael 58-9,
105, 108; campaign
song 205; Marley and
128, 132, 151-2, 174-
5, 202; meetings with
African leaders 109;
and Peace Concert
202, 263; reforms and
changes 127, 152,
172-3, 174-5, 247,
248, 287-8; and Smile
Jamaica concert 182

Manley, Norman 199
marijuana 129-30, 133,
234, 317, (see also
drugs)
Marley, Bob:
assassination attempt
34, 181-2, 194-5,
198, 212, 241, 243,
245-6, 280-2; illness
246, 329; influences
19, 29, 32, 57, 67-8;
interviews 19; as
Joseph figure 309;
mistrust of others
168; mysticism 195;
racial identity 45-6,
51; relationships with
women 214-15, 299;
songs credited to
others 113;
songwriting process
31-8, 156-7, 249-50,
315; sources of
inspiration 242-3;
timing of releases 38;
Trench Town and 43;
and violence 253;
women in songs 61,
122
Marley, Norval
(Marley's father) 51,
134
Marley, Rita 181, 182,
229, 324, 339; I-
Threes 135, 229;
'Johnny Was' 162; life
with Marley 28, 189,
339; on Marley 34,
45, 46, 53; Marley's
songs and 85, 324;
and Smile Jamaica
concert 181, 182;
songs written for 118
Marshall, Bucky 259
Marvin, Junior 211

Massop, Claudie 259
Mayal 124, 142
Mayfield, Curtis 233
'Mellow Mood' 63, 64,
113
Michael, Ras 77, 109
'Midnight Ravers' 40,
41, 70-2, 74
The Mighty Diamonds
156, 187
Miller, Jacob 213, 231
Minott, Sugar 187
'Misty Morning' 194,
195, 215, 216, 231,
253
'Mix Up, Mix Up' 315,
324-7
Morgan, Derrick 125
'morning' songs 253
Mowatt, Judy 135, 187
'Mr Brown' 41, 92-3
'Mr Chatterbox' 41
Mugabe, Robert 258
music: education
through 57;
importance to Marley
53-4, 55, 88, 203,
253-4, 273-4, 274-5,
303-4
'Music Lesson' 54
'My Cup' 228

Nash, Johnny 36, 157,
213
Natty Dread 102, 111-
55
'Natty Dread' 13, 87,
98, 109-10, 112, 137,
141, 143-6, 345
'Natural Mystic' 194,
196
'The Negro Speaks Of
Rivers' (Langston
Hughes) 172
Nettleford, Rex 58

'Nice Time' 62
'Night Nurse' (Gregory Isaacs) 63
'Night Shift' 176-7
'96 Degrees in the Shade' (Third World) 313
Niyahbinghi 124-5, 146, 317, 319, 344-5
'No More Trouble' 41, 69-70
'No Water' 63
'No Woman No Cry' 113, 115-22, 155, 222, 233

'Oh Freedom' 79
'Old Man River' (negro spiritual) 306
'One Drop' 274-6
'One Foundation' 97
One Love Peace concert 202, 248, 259, 263
'One Love/People Get Ready' 184, 232, 233-4

'Pass It On' 96
Patterson, Seeco 32
Paul, St 90, 200-1, 204, 330-1, 341
Peace Concert (see One Love Peace Concert)
Peart, H 113
'People Get Ready' (Curtis Mayfield) 233
People's National Party (PLP) (Jamaica) 59, 106, 108
People's National Party (PNP) (Jamaica) 175, 200, 247, 248
Perry, Lee 'Scratch', 'the Upsetter' 57, 156, 223, 339, 343-4; and African Herbsman 65;

collaborations with Marley 18, 36, 62-3, 112-13, 185, 190, 223, 335-6; and dominant record companies 91; imagination in songs 224; influence on Marley 29, 73-4; on Marley 46, 227-8; Marley and 94-5, 339; People Funny Boy 227
'Pimper's Paradise' 296-300, 301
Planno, Mortimer 57, 60, 77
PLP (see People's National Party)
Pocomania 124, 142
police 85, 132, 163-4
political songs, Marley's 41-2, 111-12, 151-2, 153, 158, 175, 249, 252
politics: colour politics 45; Jamaica 105-9, 127-9, 132, 169-70, 236, 246-9, 261, 287-91; Marley's 151-2, 153-4, 157-8, 202, 248-9, 252
'Positive Vibrations' 157-60
praise songs 329-30
prison 93-4
'Put It On' 75, 98, 170

Ranglin, Ernest 32, 223
'Rastafari Is' (Peter Tosh) 330
Rastafari (see Selassie, Haile)
Rastafarianism 20-5, 142-3; and Babylon

133, 250-1; 'belief' and 278; David figure in mythology 345; descriptors 145-6; fitness and 302; history 21-3; 'living up' 344; Marley and 27-8, 29, 59-60, 139, 170, 200; repatriation to Ethiopia 58, 79, 206-7, 272-3; values 317; worship 76-7
'Rastaman Chant' 75, 76, 77-8, 80, 240
'Rastaman Live Up' 315, 343-4
Rastaman Vibration 102, 155-79
'Rat Race' 169, 174-6, 265
'Real Situation' 293, 294
'Rebel Music' (3 O'Clock Road Block) 113, 131-7, 153
Redding, Otis 100
'Redemption Song' 48, 67, 242, 265, 287, 309-14, 337, 339
reggae 113, 146, 160, 187, 273, 275, 304; African-Americans and 162; and politics 106
repatriation to Ethiopia 58, 79, 206-7, 272-3
'Revolution' 113, 151-4
'Ride Natty Ride' 251, 265, 267, 276-9, 342
river, image of 86-7, 306
'River Jordan' (Sugar Minott) 187
'Road Block' (original name for 'Rebel Music') 131
'Rock It Baby (Baby We

Got A Date)' 41
'Rocking Steady' 64, 160
Rockwell, John 192-3
Rodney, Walter 19, 57
'Roots, Rock, Reggae'
160-2
'Running Away' 184,
235, 237-40, 305-6,
324

'Satisfy My Soul' 170,
215, 216, 224, 226-7,
228
'Satta A-Massa Gaana'
(Third World) 330
'Screw Face' 93, 167
Seaga, Edward 108, 202,
263, 287, 288
Selassie, Haile
(Rastafari) 78-9;
divinity 330; influence
on Marley 139, 170,
306; lineage 336-7,
345; as prophet 331;
and Rastafarianism
20; significance of
coronation 142-3;
speeches 177-9; visit
to Jamaica 58, 59
'Selassie Is The Chapel'
170
Shakespeare, Robbie 274
Shakespeare, William 23,
173
'Shanty Town'
(Desmond Dekker) 42
Sharpe, 'Daddy' Sam 26
Shervington, Pluto 187
'She's Gone' 194, 215,
216, 227-30, 229-30,
299
'Simmer Down' 70, 144,
176
Simms, Danny 36
The Skatelites 32, 60, 77

'Slave Driver' 41-2, 56-7,
65-8
slavery 51, 57, 66-7,
310-11
'Slavery Days' (Burning
Spear) 313
Slickers 42
Sly and Robbie 206
'Small Axe' 75, 89-91
Smart, Leroy 187
'Smile Jamaica' 191
Smile Jamaica concert
181, 188, 189
Smith, JAG 58
'So Jah Seh' 137-40, 339
'So Much Things To Say'
197-201
'So Much Trouble In The
World' 252-4
Sons of Negus 109
Spaulding, Anthony 181
Sporty 320
'Stand Alone' 62, 228
'Stepping Razor' (Peter
Tosh) 95
'Stiff Necked Fools' 315,
337, 340-3
'Stir It Up' 41, 60-1, 63-
5, 121, 228
'Stop That Train' 68-9
Studio One 91
'Sun Is Shining' 194,
215, 216, 223-5, 253
Survival 37, 45-6, 245,
246, 250, 269-87
'Survival' 269-72

Tacky 26
'Talkin' Blues' 115-16,
147-51, 257, 268
Taylor, Don 181, 291,
293, 324, 327
'Thank You Lord' 327
'Them Belly Full (But We
Hungry)' 113, 122-

31, 339
Third World 187, 313,
330
'This Train' 68
Thompson, Dudley 187-
8
'Three Little Birds' 232-
3, 253
'Three O'Clock Road
Block' (see 'Rebel
Music')
Time magazine 192
'Time Will Tell' 235,
240-2
Toots and the Maytals
59, 171
'Top Rankin' 259-65
Tosh, Peter 55, 202, 263,
274, 301-2; Burnin'
contributions 75, 97-
8; Catch A Fire
contributions 41, 67-
9; collaborations with
Marley 67-8, 100,
242; influence on
Wailers 336;
meanings behind
songs 88-9, 95, 187;
musical style 67;
praise songs 330;
radical views 97-8,
133, 263; as roots
artist 155; 'Small Axe'
and 91; and Trench
Town 43
'Touch Me' 62
'Trench Town' 52, 315,
337-9
Trench Town (Jamaica)
104-5, 119; as
Babylon 143, 145;
Marley and 43-4, 51-
2, 111, 119
'Trench Town Rock' 161
'Turn Your Lights Down

Low' 63, 214, 215, 216, 219-22, 228, 333
'twanging' 114

United States: and Jamaican politics 175-6, 247-8, 289-90; Marley and 162, 176-7
Uprising 235, 245, 246, 250, 252, 287-314, 324

Wail N' Souls label 112-13, 170
Wailer, Bunny 74, 187; *Burnin'* contributions 75, 96-7; *Catch A Fire* contributions 67-8; collaborations with Marley 67, 100, 242; individual voice 97-8; on Marley's songwriting 31-2; meanings behind

songs 92, 187; musical style 67; and Perry 29; as roots artist 155; on Trench Town 43
The Wailers 92, 106, 193, 295; break-up 97-8, 100, 242; Manley, support for 59, 205; Marley and 75-6, 315; Rastafarianism and 76
'Waiting In Vain' 214, 215, 216, 217-19, 228, 299, 333
'Wake Up And Live' 267, 280, 284-7, 336
Walcott, Derek 117
'Want More' 165-9
'War' 70, 177-9, 187, 258
'We And Dem' 293-4
'We Build This City' (Burning Spear) 55
Welch, Tony 259

'What You Gonna Do' 301-2
'What's Going On' (Marvin Gaye) 295
White, Garth 44
White, Timothy 113
'Who The Cap Fit' 48, 166, 167
William, Willie 187
Willoughby, Neville 242-3
Wilson, Delroy 59
'Wings Of A Dove' 79
'Work' 177, 294-6

'You Can't Blame the Youths' (Peter Tosh) 55, 88-9

'Zimbabwe' 249-50, 255-8
Zion 79, 94, (see also *Ethiopia*)

CPSIA information can be obtained
at www.ICGtesting.com
Printed in the USA
LVHW021614260521
688579LV00011B/631

9 780825 673528